TRANSCENDING BOUNDARIES

STUDIES IN CHILDREN'S LITERATURE AND CULTURE
VOLUME 13
GARLAND REFERENCE LIBRARY OF THE HUMANITIES
VOLUME 2152

CHILDREN'S LITERATURE AND CULTURE
JACK ZIPES, *Series Editor*

TRANSCENDING BOUNDARIES

WRITING FOR A DUAL AUDIENCE OF CHILDREN AND ADULTS

edited by

SANDRA L. BECKETT

GARLAND PUBLISHING, Inc.
A member of the Taylor & Francis Group
New York & London / 1999

Published in 1999 by
Garland Publishing, Inc.
A Member of the Taylor & Francis Group
19 Union Square West
New York, NY 10003

10   9   8   7   6   5   4   3   2   1

Library of Congress Cataloging-in-Publication Data
Transcending boundaries : writing for a dual audience of children and
    adults / edited by Sandra L. Beckett.
        p.   cm. — (Garland reference library of the humanities : v.
    2152. Children's literature and culture ; v. 13)
        Includes bibliographical references and index.
        ISBN 0-8153-3359-5
        1. Children's literature—History and criticism.   2. Children's
    literature—Authorship.   3. Children—Books and reading.   4. Authors
    and readers.   5. Books and reading.   6. Authorship.   7. Adulthood.
    I. Beckett, Sandra L., 1953–   .   II. Series: Garland reference
    library of the humanities ; vol. 2152.   III. Series: Garland
    reference library of the humanities. Children's literature and
    culture ; v. 13.
    ✓PN1009.A1T69   1999
        809'.89282—dc21   99-39096
                                                                            CIP

Printed on acid-free, 250-year-life paper
Manufactured in the United States of America

Contents

v

Series Editor's Foreword

Dedicated to furthering original research in children's literature and culture, the Children's Literature and Culture series includes monographs on individual authors and illustrators, historical examinations of different periods, literary analyses of genres, and comparative studies on literature and the mass media. The series is international in scope and is intended to encourage innovative research in children's literature with a focus on interdisciplinary methodology.

Children's literature and culture are understood in the broadest sense of the term children to encompass the period of childhood up through late adolescence. Owing to the fact that the notion of childhood has changed so much since the origination of children's literature, this Garland series is particularly concerned with transformations in children's culture and how they have affected the representation and socialization of children. While the emphasis of the series is on children's literature, all types of studies that deal with children's radio, film, television, and art are included in an endeavor to grasp the aesthetics and values of children's culture. Not only have there been momentous changes in children's culture in the last fifty years, but there have been radical shifts in the scholarship that deals with these changes. In this regard, the goal of the Children's Literature and Culture series is to enhance research in this field and, at the same time, point to new directions that bring together the best scholarly work throughout the world.

Jack Zipes

Introduction

Transcending Boundaries was born out of my growing fascination, over the past decade, with authors who write for both children and adults, a subject that has received surprisingly little critical attention until very recently. Although my own interest in dual-audience authors was kindled by French literature, the editing of *Reflections of Change: Children's Literature Since 1945*, the selected proceedings of the 1995 congress of the International Research Society for Children's Literature, called my attention to the fact that the "Shifting Boundaries Between Children's and Adult Literature"[1] constituted a significant international trend in contemporary literature. One of the most striking aspects of these shifting boundaries seemed quite simply to be the marked increase in the number of authors crossing them. In order to explore the topic further, I organized a workshop on "Border Crossings: Narratives for a Dual Audience of Children and Adults" for the International Society for the Study of European Ideas conference in 1998, which was held at Haifa University on the theme of "Twentieth-Century European Narratives: Tradition and Innovation." Six of the fourteen contributors to *Transcending Boundaries* participated in the workshop, and their essays are for the most part longer and substantially revised versions of the papers presented in Israel.

In spite of the growing interest in the crossover phenomenon in the 1990s, publications in this area are still relatively scarce and generally limited to a particular author or a very specific aspect of the problem. The essays in this volume approach the art of writing for a dual audience of children and adults from a wide variety of perspectives, aesthetic as well as sociocultural. The term "crosswriting child and adult," which has been widely adopted in recent years to refer to this phenomenon, seems to have been coined by U. C. Knoeflmacher. In any case, my own use of the term dates from my participation in his session "Crosswriting Child and Adult: Fictions with Dual Readerships, Authors with Double Audiences" at the 1993 Modern Language Association Convention.[2] The special issue of *Children's Literature* devoted to "Cross-Writing Child and Adult" (1997), which Knoepflmacher subsequently edited with Mitzi Myers, deals almost exclusively with English-language literature from the nineteenth or early twentieth centuries. Although earlier dual-audience classics, in particular Carroll's *Alice* books and Collodi's *Pinocchio*, find their way into the present volume in their role as precursors or prototypes, offering points of departure for an analysis of later works, *Transcending Boundaries* is devoted to twentieth-century literature, for the most part post-World War II and largely contemporary. Scholars from eight countries contributed to the volume, and, although the majority of the texts discussed are firmly rooted in the Western tradition, they nonetheless represent a very broad cultural and geographical area from Canada to the Caribbean, from the former Soviet Union to Australia, from Scandinavia to the Mediterranean. Multiple facets of the art of crosswriting child and adult are explored in the essays of *Transcending Boundaries*. The grouping of the essays reflects only one of a myriad of possible configurations and the subheadings are deliberately broad, evocative, and somewhat nebulous, in the hope that they will not serve as demarcations, but will open up new horizons and encourage readers to continue to cross borders, exploring the multifarious connections and contrasts, parallels and polarizations offered by alternative essay clusters.

The art of crosswriting child and adult obviously is not a new phenomenon. Since the boundaries between adult and children's fiction were first drawn in the mid-eighteenth century, authors have been crossing them in both directions. The texts of even earlier authors, such as Charles Perrault, Jean de La Fontaine, Fénélon, John Bunyan, and Jonathan Swift, have traditionally had a dual audience of children and adults. Crosswriting is a characteristic feature of the children's classics that constitute the core of the children's literature canon, as Bettina Kümmerling-Meibauer's ambitious international encyclopedia of children's classics clearly shows.[3] A number of essays in the present volume focus on dual-audience "children's" classics from several national literatures, including British, German, French, and Italian. The latter half of the twentieth century has been a particularly productive period for dual-audience texts, a trend that seems to be sharply on the rise in recent years.

Children's literature, like other aspects of children's culture and almost every other field of human endeavour, has undergone striking changes in the latter half of the twentieth century, changes that seem to be unfolding at an ever accelerating pace as we approach the end of the millennium. The shifting and the redrawing of the boundaries between children's and adult fiction has led some critics to argue that the borders are not just changing, but disappearing altogether, a sign, they believe, of the imminent death of children's literature. Dual-readership authors often are cited as evidence of the collapse of the borders. Other critics claim, on the contrary, that the boundaries are becoming more pronounced and are being drawn with even greater precision. What all critics seem to agree on, however, is the surge in border traffic in most Western countries. *Grensverkeer* (Border traffic) is the title of a recent study by Peter van den Hoven, who points to the increasing traffic that is taking place from both sides of the border in Dutch literature.[4] The contributors to *Transcending Boundaries* would certainly seem to corroborate the findings of Helma van Lierop-Debrauwer, that is, that this border traffic may be taking place in both directions, but that the phenomenon generally interests only children's literature scholars or those that have a foot in both the children's and the adult literary systems. If children's literature does sometimes succeed in briefly arresting the attention of scholars and critics of mainstream literature, it is largely attributable to well-known authors for adults who have crossed over.

The list of authors who have written for both children and adults is lengthy, diverse, and distinguished, and even includes the names of a few Nobel Prize winners. Many crosswriters start out writing for adults and, at some point, often rather late in their career, take up writing for children. A large number of these authors are content to leave only one or two books on children's bookshelves. Some writers cross over in the opposite direction, establishing themselves as children's authors and later turning their hand to writing for an adult audience, but this career path is less common. A few writers even begin writing for children as potential authors for adults, that is, with the intention of, as Patricia Wrightson puts it, "graduat[ing] to adult novels some day."[5] Another, rarer category of crosswriters consists of those David Galef qualifies as "polygraphic authors," whose diverse and varied oeuvre has always included texts for both audiences.[6] The extensive list of dual-audience authors is greatly reduced, however, when limited only to those whose works have made it into both the children's literature canon and the canon for adults. Helma van Lierop-Debrauwer's claim with regard to Dutch-language literature no doubt holds true for most Western literatures, that is, "the majority of authors are canonized in one, but not in the other literary system, or are marginalized in both systems." This situation, however, does seem to be changing and a growing number of authors not only manage to establish themselves in both literary systems, but also succeed in winning wide acclaim in both.

The largest group of crosswriters are, of course, the authors who address children and adults in separate works, and many of them continue, as John Stephens points out, to maintain a clear distinction between their two audiences. Adult narratives are sometimes used as raw material to create books for a young audience, as Julius Lester demonstrates brilliantly in *To Be a Slave*. Some authors rewrite works originally addressed to one audience for the other. The rewriting of adult texts for children is certainly the more common practice, but texts initially addressed to a young audience also have been rewritten for adults. In the case of Isabella Leitner's rewriting of her memoirs for children, the result is a very different text, showing how the Holocaust functions as a clear border between adult and children's works, increasing the gap between the two audiences. On the other hand, when Michel Tournier rewrote his bestselling adult novel for children, he claimed simply to have written an improved version for all ages.

Many authors now aspire to and engage in the form of crosswriting that consists of addressing the same texts to young and old alike. In fact, the cross-audienced phenomenon has become so widespread that a new word recently has been coined in some languages to refer to this literature for all ages, as for example the term "*allalderslitteratur*" in Norwegian (*allålderslitteratur* in Swedish). One also could point to the creation of ambitious series such as Ediciones Siruela's distinguished Las Tres Edades (The three ages) in Spain that, as the name clearly suggests, offers books intended for readers of all ages. Much of the contemporary children's fiction that comes under scrutiny in this volume attempts to speak to the child and the adult simultaneously and on equal terms in what Barbara Wall calls *dual address*, as opposed to more conventional single or double address.[7] Several authors, however, call attention to the increasing number of children's books that are so concerned with addressing the adult over the child's shoulder that they virtually ignore the child addressee.

A glance at the table of contents of *Transcending Boundaries* reveals the multifaceted nature of crossover literature and the variety of ways in which writers cross the borders to address a dual readership of children and adults. Many contemporary authors have drawn inspiration from fairy tales, folklore, and the oral tradition in order to appeal to an audience of all ages. In the work of some crosswriters there seems to be no tangible demarcation between their writing for children and their writing for adults. A few, the most striking example perhaps being the French author Michel Tournier, are true masters of the art of recycling their fiction for multiple readerships, and their versatile texts cross over the borders in both directions and back again with an ease that it is both prodigious and disconcerting. Sometimes, so many intratextual allusions connect an author's so-called adult and children's books that they constitute an interwoven oeuvre that cannot really be divided into two distinct corpuses. Some works are never recognized as dual-audience texts, but their ambivalent address results in them being categorized alternately as children's books and books for adults. Books published for one audience quite often are released later for the other in another context, either another time period or in another country and/or cultural setting. Novels published for adults in one country are sometimes marketed for a juvenile audience in another, or occasionally, the reverse. The international bestseller *Sofies verden* (*Sophie's World*), by Jostein Gaarder, is a prime example of the latter. It was published in Norway, and subsequently in most European countries, as a book for young adults, as the author intended it to be, but when it crossed the Atlantic, it was marketed in the United States as a novel for adults.

The role of the paratext can be crucial in determining the target audience of a text, and minor cosmetic changes have turned many works written for adults into children's books. Short stories for adults, in particular, have often undergone this transposition, but so too have poems, plays, excerpts from novels, and diverse other types of texts. It should be noted, however, that it is not always an adult text that is later published for children; the reverse phenomenon, albeit much less common, also occurs. Although the publisher is often responsible for crossovers of this nature, it also can be at the author's initiative. A book originally published for an audience other than the one for which it was written may thus be redirected to its intended readership. Maria Nikolajeva rightly points to the prejudices about young readers that govern the marketing of books that otherwise target both children and adults. The publishing history of crossover texts is often of vital importance in understanding how they successfully address a dual audience.

Perhaps more than any other genre, the picturebook has redrawn boundaries and expanded literary horizons in recent years. Contemporary picturebook makers continually are breaking new ground and challenging accepted forms and conventions. Although the picturebook traditionally has been seen as a children's genre, in the eyes of many contemporary authors and illustrators, it is a narrative form that can address any or all age groups. Like Jon Scieszka and Lane Smith's *The Stinky Cheese Man and Other Fairly Stupid Tales*, many picturebooks could proudly display the recommendation: "Ages: All." Innovative graphics and the creative, often complex dialogue between text and image provide multiple levels of meaning and invite readings on different levels by all ages. Carole Scott sees in picturebooks a unique opportunity for "a collaborative relationship" between children and adults, as they empower the two audiences more equally than other narrative forms. The reading experience offered by contemporary picturebooks varies greatly, however, and the dual-audience relationship can range from one of collaboration to one of confrontation or even exclusion, in which the child and the adult seem to be reading entirely different texts. In an essay that the author warns us *"n'est pas un essai"* (the borders seem to be coming down everywhere!), Rod McGillis nimbly examines the "all ages" phenomenon through the eyes of four well-known figures who all have some knowledge of writing for both children and adults, but who ignore completely the "playful wisdom" of the children who from time to time interrupt their heated debate. As the children come and go unheeded, Zohar Shavit's words echo in our ears: "What do adults really know about children's culture . . .?" Is the voice of the child reader being heard in the current debate about literature for all ages? Can crossover literature really appeal equally to adults and children?

Extraliterary circumstances can prompt authors to write "children's books" addressed to a dual audience of adults and children. What are in fact sophisticated, subversive texts sometimes are disguised as children's books to avoid censorship. In the sociopolitical context of the Soviet Union, the authors of what Larissa Tumanov calls "Aesopian children's literature," actually addressed a triple audience, because in addition to the child reader and the insightful adult reader, there also was the censor who was intended to read more like a child than an adult. A similar phenomenon occurred during slavery in the southern United States, where the stories of Brer Rabbit told by the Blacks for a dual audience of children and adults were to be seen by adult Whites as mere "children's" stories. Audience ambivalence in these cases is intentional and crucial.

In *Poetics of Children's Literature*, Zohar Shavit insisted on "the ambivalent status" of all children's texts,[8] and in this volume she further explores the "double attribution" of children's literature, which always has an adult addressee in addition to the child addressee, because children's books are written, published, evaluated, and distributed by adults. This ambivalence has been encouraged, she points out, by authors attempting to break free of the children's system with claims such as C. S. Lewis's oft-cited dictum: "I am almost inclined to set it up as a canon that a children's story which is enjoyed only by children is a bad children's story."[9] Although the status of children's literature has improved appreciably in recent decades, children's authors rarely enjoy the prestige of their counterparts in mainstream literature. Crossing over to adult literature or writing dual-audience texts undoubtedly constitutes for many an attempt to escape the inferior status of writers for children and the stigma of children's literature, and to climb upward on the literary ladder. Dual-audience authors whose children's books have gained them an international reputation and handsome profits often deny their position as a children's author, or the child addressee of their texts, or even that there is a distinction between children's and adult literature, determined, it would seem, not to allow themselves to be labeled as "children's authors." They have no doubt taken notes from predecessors who have more willingly embraced the label "children's author" and subsequently found themselves marginalized and excluded from the canon and literary histories.

Contemporary children's literature has become a field of innovation and experimentation, challenging the conventions, codes, and norms that traditionally governed the genre. Strongly influenced by the aesthetics of modernism and postmodernism, children's literature now reflects the dominant trends in adult literature and sometimes even initiates them. A wide range of previously taboo subjects and complex narrative strategies—including polyfocalization, composite genres, deviations from chronological, linear narrative, fragmentation and gaps, absence of closure, intertextuality, irony, parody, metafiction—trangress the traditional demarcations separating children's from adult literature. Some children's books seem to be no less sophisticated or demanding of their readers than those apparently written and marketed for adults. Furthermore, it is not unusual for dual-audience authors to be more innovative and provocative in their writing for children than in their adult texts. This "coming of age of children's literature"[10] seems to be encouraging more authors for adults to cross over. This, of course, in turn helps to further demarginalize and emancipate children's literature, in spite of the fact that many writers still feel obliged to justify such a move and to attempt to blur the borders between children's and adult fiction.[11] This blurring of the borders is taking place, however, from both sides. Whereas some authors maintain that "good" children's literature also must appeal to adults, with statements that echo C. S. Lewis's ("No book is really worth reading at the age of ten which is not equally (and often far more) worth reading at the age of fifty"[12]), others, like Michel Tournier, prefer to approach the border from the opposite direction, insisting that "good" adult literature must be accessible to children.

The essays in *Transcending Boundaries* all attest to the shifting borders between children's and adult literature as we approach the end of the twentieth century. But are the borders really disappearing? Is the gloomy prediction of the death of children's literature merely a manifestation of our *fin de siècle* or *fin de millénium* fears? A few authors point to the widening gap between children's and adult culture, which would suggest that the polarization between child and adult will become more pronounced and the demarcations between children's and adult literature more distinct. The majority of the essays clearly suggest, however, that crossover literature or "allalderslitteratur," to borrow the convenient Norwegian and Swedish term, is a major, widespread trend that appears to be sharply on the rise. An increasing number of authors seek to efface all borders with dual-audience texts and are only satisfied when a work appeals to both audiences, regardless of which one it happens to be marketed for. More and more books illustrate the limitations of audience age as a defining category and refuse to be confined by any such arbitrary boundary constraints. Scieszka's defiant "Ages: all" could well serve as a slogan for this new literature that denies and defies publishers' often very age-specific categories of readers. But publishers, too, have climbed on the bandwagon with the creation, in the 1990s, of series, like Siruela's Las Tres Edades, for readers of all ages, or in this particular case "from eight to eighty-eight," in the belief that "no clear boundaries exist between titles for children and adults."[13] Crossover literature confronts and contests what Paula Connolly terms "the hegemonic notions of the definition of 'children's' and 'adult' literature." The shift away from age as a defining category seems to be one of the markers of the post-postmodern age that is being ushered in with the new millennium. The best dual-audience picture books illustrate, as Carole Scott rightly observes, that "the child-adult reader distinction is not a schismatic division, but a continuum of understanding." It is in contemporary poetry that Lissa Paul, in her final, forward-looking essay, sees signs that knowledge and schooling are replacing age as determining characteristics in the movement that is supplanting postmodernism. Perhaps the twenty-first century will bring an age in which "child" and "adult" are no longer defining categories and crosswriting will no longer be seen as a transgressing or transcending of "borders."

NOTES

1. This is the title of part II of *Reflections of Change: Children's Literature Since 1945*, ed. Sandra L. Beckett, 33–56 (Westport, Conn.: Greenwood Press, 1997).

2. My first major article on the topic was published in Sweden in 1995. See Sandra L. Beckett, "From the Art of Rewriting to the Art of Crosswriting Child and Adult: The Secret of Michel Tournier's Dual Readership," in *Voices from Far Away: Current Trends in International Children's Literature Research* 24, ed. Maria Nikolajeva, 9–34 (Stockholm: Centrum för barnkulturforskning, 1995).

3. Bettina Kümmerling-Meibauer points out in her essay that seventy-six percent of the authors cited in her *Klassiker der Kinder- und Jugendliteratur: Ein internationales Lexikon* are, in some sense of the word, crosswriters (2 vols.) (Stuttgart: Metzler, 1999).

4. Peter van den Hoven, *Grenzverkeer* (The Hague: NBLC, 1994). Helma van Lierop-Debrauwer refers to Van den Hoven's work in her essay, where she translates an excerpt.

5. Quoted by John Rowe Townsend, *A Sense of Story* (London: Longman, 1971), 212.

6. David Galef, "Crossing Over: Authors Who Write Both Children's and Adults' Fiction," *Children's Literature Association Quarterly* 20, no. 1 (1995): 29.

7. Barbara Wall, *The Narrator's Voice: The Dilemma of Children's Fiction* (New York: St. Martin's Press, 1991), 9.

8. Zohar Shavit, *Poetics of Children's Literature* (Athens: The University of Georgia Press, 1986). Chapter 3 is titled "The Ambivalent Status of Texts."

9. Quoted in Sheila Egoff et al., *Only Connect* (New York: Oxford University Press, 1969), 210. See Zohar Shavit, *Poetics of Children's Literature* (Athens: University of Georgia Press, 1986), 41.

10. See Maria Nikolajeva, *Children's Literature Comes of Age: Toward a New Aesthetic* (New York and London: Garland, 1996).

11. A recent issue of *Literatuur zonder leeftijd*, a Dutch children's literature journal that regularly explores the boundaries between children's literature and

adult literature, suggests that the increase in dual readership authors is one of the signs of the recent emancipation of children's literature in Dutch. See issue 12, no. 47 (Fall/Winter 1998). Helma van Lierop-Debrauwer, who is on the editorial board of the journal, rightfully points out in her essay on Dutch literature that the same phenomenon can be witnessed in many Western literatures.

12. C. S. Lewis, "On Stories," in *Essays Presented to Charles Williams* (London: Oxford, 1947), 100. Quoted in Marilyn Apseloff, "Children's Books by Famous Writers for Adults," *Children's Literature* 2 (1973): 130.

13. Michi Strausfeld, "Las Tres Edades: de ocho a ochenta y ocho años." *CLIJ* 50 (May 1993): 44.

TRANSCENDING BOUNDARIES

PART I

Critics, Crosswriting, and the Canon

CHAPTER 1

Crossing the Border

Authors Do It, but Do Critics? The Reception of

Dual-Readership Authors in the Netherlands

HELMA VAN LIEROP-DEBRAUWER

INTRODUCTION

Ever since the emergence of a literature specifically meant for children in the second half of the eighteenth century, there have been authors who write for adults as well as for children (henceforth called dual-readership authors[1]). In the beginning, when children's literature was still developing into an independent literary market, there were many dual-readership authors. The reason these authors did not write exclusively for children, but combined it with writing for adults, was mainly financial: The target group of young readers was relatively small. It also undoubtedly had something to do with the low status of children's literature. A significant number of children's books were published anonymously.[2] Particularly for men with a high social status, it was considered inappropriate to write for children. The general view was that women were closer to children and therefore better suited for the task. When, in the course of the nineteenth century, the division between children's literature and adult literature became sharper and the demand for children's books increased, the financial argument declined and the number of dual-readership authors went down. The low status of children's literature, however, did not change.

In the past two decades, the number of dual-readership authors has again increased. This goes for the Dutch-speaking regions, as well as for other language areas.[3] In Dutch-speaking regions this increase is explained by the literary emancipation of children's literature in the 1980s and 1990s. In children's literature, attention now is paid to the literary form of the text, whereas, in the 1970s, people focused on the *engagé* content. As a consequence of this literary emancipation, the gap between writing for children and writing for adults where form has been stressed since the beginning of the twentieth century[4] has been diminishing.

Galef divides the group of dual-readership authors into three categories. According to him, the most frequent category is the group of authors of adult literature who, for some reason, begin writing for children during their career. An example of an author with such a career is Roald Dahl. The second category of authors develops a career in the opposite way: They start as authors for children, then decide to write for adults. Galef mentions Russell Hoban as a representative of this category. The third group of authors is described by Galef with the term "polygraphy," a designation that indicates that this group consists of authors who have always combined their writing for children with writing for adults.[5] A. A. Milne is one such writer.

Although there has been a substantial number of Dutch-speaking dual-readership authors since the second half of the eighteenth century, only a few have succeeded in being highly valued in both literary systems.[6] The majority of the authors are canonized in one, but not in the other literary system, or are marginalized in both systems. In the last fifteen years, however, many authors have established themselves in both literary systems.

The question is if, and in what respect, contemporary dual-readership authors influence the relation between children's literature and adult literature. In what way does their presence change the heretofore low status of children's literature when compared with adult literature? The answer to this question requires an analysis of the reception of these authors in recent literary studies and contemporary reviews in journals of both literary systems.

LITERARY STUDIES

The first thing that strikes one when searching in Dutch literary studies for an answer to the question just raised is that in children's literature studies done since the 1980s, there is structural attention to the literary emancipation of children's literature. These developments have led to discussion of whether or not the traditional borderline between children's and adult literature still exists. In this debate, dual-readership authors are mentioned several times as an illustration of the blurring of these borderlines:

> That in the past few years the traditional demarcation between children's literature and adult literature has been breached several times might best

be illustrated by the growing border traffic. From both directions, authors who want to augment their radius of action go on a scouting expe-
dition. . . . In any case, the number of authors of adult literature who have
published one or more children's books in the past few years, is striking.[7]

A majority of the authors mentioned by Van den Hoven (1994) are authors
from Galef's first category: authors of adult literature who at a certain moment made their debut in children's literature, for example, Mensje van
Keulen, Sjoerd Kuyper, Toon Tellegen, Nicolaas Matsier, and Willem van
Toorn.

For some people, especially academics, the developments in children's literature are a reason to argue that children's literature should
have a position equal to that of adult literature. A few scholars[8] are even
inclined to integrate children's literature into adult literature.

In the same period, literary critics within the adult literary system
have paid little structural attention to children's literature and the border
traffic between children's literature and adult literature. Occasionally,
there is some interest: A single journal devotes a special issue to children's literature[9] and, in some histories of literature, the authors do not
confine themselves to occasional notes on a single children's author, but
instead give an overview of recent developments in children's literature.[10] It must be said that the authors of these overviews either are working in the field of children's literature or working within both the
children's literary system and the adult literary system. In one of the essays, the growing number of dual-readership authors is explicitly related
to the literary renovation of children's literature: "This change of climate
appeals to authors who traditionally write for adults."[11]

Once again, this situation is not unique to the Dutch language area.
In the English language area, for example, the boundaries between children's literature and adult literature also are mainly explored by the children's literary system, whereas there is relatively little interest in the
border traffic within the adult literary system. A few literary compendia
have an entry on children's literature[12] and now and then a journal on
adult literature publishes a special issue on children's books.[13]

Literary Prizes

Since the end of the 1980s, Dutch children's literature has two important
literary prizes that are awarded annually: the Golden and Silver Slate
Pencil and the Libris Woutertje Pieterse Prize. This last prize is a result

of the literary innovations in children's literature. The prize was introduced in 1987 by the Woutertje Pieterse Foundation at the initiative of several well-known Dutch reviewers who wished to see the children's book as a full literary genre. For that reason, they wanted a prize for a book of Dutch origin for children or young adults with exceptional qualities with respect to language and content as well as image and graphic design.

An overview of the prizes awarded in the last ten years shows that debuts in children's literature of authors who had previously only written for adults, like Mensje van Keulen, Guus Middag and Toon Tellegen, are often awarded, in any case, more frequently than other debuts. Moreover, these authors also are awarded relatively often for their later books. Dual-readership author Toon Tellegen, for example, is the author who has most frequently won the Libris Woutertje Pieterse Prize.

Although the literary qualities of the prize-winning books have certainly been decisive, it is likely, on the basis of the previously mentioned pleas for affiliation with adult literature, that the need of the children's literary system to blur the boundaries between children's literature and adult literature and, subsequently, advance in status, has played a role. Awarding literary prizes to well-known authors of adult literature breeches traditional boundaries and helps to establish a positive image.

The reverse takes place in adult literature. The nomination of a children's book[14] for an important literary prize for adult literature in the Netherlands, the AKO Prize for Literature, induced several well-known critics to object against such an affiliation of children's literature with adult literature. A year later, the rules were changed to prevent that from happening again. An "adult" prize for a children's book is bad for the reputation of adult literature and more far-reaching than a special issue or attention in a history of literature, where children's literature is carefully distinguished from adult literature. A prize stands for explicitly awarded quality.

LITERARY REVIEWS

The weekly reviews in cultural supplements form, together with the literary studies and prizes, a good measure for developments in literature. Therefore, a logical question is whether or not the degree of attention paid to the border traffic and the role of dual-readership authors in literary studies is shared by reviewers in both literary systems. This question will be answered by means of a case study of the reception of the oeuvre of the Dutch author Mensje van Keulen by critics.

Mensje van Keulen had her debut in 1972 with *Bleekers Zomer* (Bleeker's summer) as an author for adults. Since then she has written twelve books for adults. Her last novel, *Olifanten op een web* (Elephants on a web), was published in 1997. Her debut as a children's author was in 1985 with the fantasy story *Tommie Station* (Tommy Station). Her most recent children's book, *Pas op voor Bez* (*Beware of Bez*), was published in 1996.

When comparing the reviews of Van Keulen's children's books with the reviews of her work for adults, one is immediately struck by the fact that there are fewer reviews of the latter (on the average, thirteen per children's book and sixteen per book for adults). Moreover, the reviews of her books for children are on the whole substantially shorter than the reviews of her adult books. The reviews of her children's literature debut average 314 words, whereas critics on the average devote 846 words to her debut in adult literature. Moreover, in reviews of her children's books, more lines are devoted to a reproduction of the content than in reviews of her adult books. The majority of the reviews of the children's books describe the content and end with a brief evaluation, most of the time without arguments. The reviews of Van Keulen's oeuvre seem to indicate that the conclusions of a research study on children's literature reviews that was undertaken in the 1980s still apply.[15] In this study, the researchers pointed to the poor quality of children's books reviews as a consequence of the above mentioned imbalance between description of content and argumentation.

Another important difference between the reviews of children's books and the critiques of adult books is that, in the former, the application possibilities of the books are often mentioned, as well as the appropriate age to read the book and the kind of children that will appreciate it. The increased attention paid to the literary aspects of children's literature in literary studies is almost absent in the newspaper critiques. The pedagogical approach to children's literature appears to be still firmly fixed in critical practice. The most likely explanation of this are the readers of these reviews. Critics of children's literature write their reviews primarily for the "common" buyer of children's books, that is, children's caregivers, who are mainly interested in which book is appropriate and interesting for the child that they are raising.

The target group also seems responsible for the superficial attention in the critiques to the question whether and, if so, to what extent dual-readership authors like Van Keulen change the relation between children's literature and adult literature. Because children's caregivers are not interested in the question of the status of children's literature, little attention is paid to the borderline traffic. When Van Keulen launched her career as a children's writer, critics limited themselves to the statement that she also had written for adults.

Critiques of Van Keulen's oeuvre for adults also do not pay much attention to the relationship between children's literature and adult literature. In fact, this subject was only raised in reviews of *De rode strik* (The red bow), because that book was written from a child's perspective. After her debut as a children's writer, there were a few critics who, in their reviews of her books for adults, mentioned that Van Keulen also wrote for children. This in itself is new, because authors who only write for children are normally never mentioned at all by critics of adult literature. When one takes a closer look at what is written about children's literature, then one can read between the lines that the critics impute to children's literature fewer literary qualities than to adult literature. It is generally when critics find fault with elements in Van Keulen's adult novels that they make references to (genres in) children's literature. Her adult novel *Overspel* (Adultery), for example, is criticized because of the excess of clichés. For one critic, these clichés call up associations with girl's books.

The adult literary critics and the children's literary reviewers agree with one another on one point in their evaluation of Van Keulen. In almost all the reviews, regardless of the audience the book is written for, her style is praised. Again and again, it is stated that Mensje van Keulen is an author who writes clearly and without frills and is able to evoke a certain atmosphere. In children's literature reviews, a good storyteller is almost inevitably praised. When, in addition, an author succeeds in fitting in with the child's imaginary world, then success is guaranteed. And critics are of the opinion that Van Keulen pays a lot of attention to the child's fantasy world.

Within the adult literary system, being a good storyteller is not enough for an author to get approval. That is the reason that a few of her books, in which qualities other than a good style are found to be absent, are not entirely appreciated.

The question whether or not the appreciation of Van Keulen in children's literature reviews is influenced by her status as an adult author cannot be answered on the basis of explicit statements. The number of reviews devoted to her debut with *Tommie Station* (28 notices), however, and the award of a Silver Slate Pencil are striking. Authors publishing their first children's book normally get less attention if they have not already published for adults. Furthermore, the large number of references to her adult books in the reviews of *Tommie Station* also point to a special interest in Mensje van Keulen due to the fact that she was already a well-known author of adult literature. This explicit attention to that part of her oeuvre has, however, disappeared in reviews of her later children's books.

For the critics of adult literature, the fact that Mensje van Keulen also has been writing for children since 1985 is of minor importance. The author does not gain status by doing so. On the contrary, it is, as said, mainly the negative aspects of her work that lead to remarks about children's literature.

CONCLUSION

Within the children's literary system, the literary emancipation of children's literature has led to a structural discussion of the borderlines between children's literature and adult literature. This discussion has, although in dribs and drabs, also pushed its way into the adult literary system. This interest in children's literature and the reason for it (the literary emancipation of children's literature) have obviously given a few authors of adult literature a legitimation to extend their radius of action. This seems at least a plausible explanation for the increase of dual-readership authors in the last fifteen years. Such a development, however, in a literary career is not self-evident; witness the fact that a majority of these authors feel compelled to justify this step. In their arguments, they emphatically try to blur the borders between children's literature and adult literature. A typical example is the answer given by Nicolaas Matsier, a well-known Dutch author, to the question why he began to write for children:

> Sometimes a poet decides to write prose, or vice versa. Sometimes somebody takes a new genre by storm—increase of territory. As far as I am concerned, I can only hope that even more authors will go in search of adventure now and then.[16]

Writing children's books is the same as choosing a genre other than the one in which one is used to writing.

The conscious blurring of borders seems to be motivated by the low status of children's literature. Denying the borders is an attempt to escape from this low status. A comparable phenomenon has been occurring for years within the children's system itself. Shavit shows how authors of children's books who are highly valued within the children's literature system try to increase their status by denying that they write for children.[17]

Dual-readership authors, for their part, are responsible for the fact that authoritative adult literature critics now and then pay attention to children's literature. When that interest becomes permanent, one can expect that it will positively influence the recognition of children's literature in literary studies. And that can only further raise the status of children's literature.

NOTES

1. Now and then a book that was originally published for adults is published as a children's book in another language area. It also occurs that a book is first published as a book for adults, whereas it is released as a children's book in another time period. Authors of these books are not categorized as dual-readership authors, because these processes are usually beyond the scope of the author.

2. Zohar Shavit, *Poetics of Children's Literature* (Athens, Ga., and London: The University of Georgia Press, 1986).

3. For the English-language area, see Marian Allsobrook, "Major Authors' Work for Children," in *International Companion Encyclopedia of Children's Literature*, ed. Peter Hunt and Sheila Ray, 691–709 (London: Routledge, 1996). For the German-speaking regions see Hans-Heino Ewers, "Grenzverwischungen und Grenzüberschreitungen," *Julit* 1 (1997): 4–19.

4. Meyer Howard Abrams, *The Mirror and the Lamp: Romantic Theory and the Critical Tradition*, 1953 (London: Oxford University Press, 1979).

5. David Galef, "Crossing Over: Authors Who Write Both Children's and Adults' Fiction," *Children's Literature Association Quarterly* 20, no. 1 (1995): 29–35.

6. For the English-language area, see also Galef, "Crossing Over": 29–35.

7. Peter van den Hoven, *Grensverkeer* (The Hague: NBLC, 1994): 13–14. The translation is mine.

8. See, for example, Harry Bekkering, "Oktober 1955: De Gouden Griffel wordt voor de eerste maal uitgereikt—De emancipatie van de kinder-en jeugdliteratuur" (October 1955: The Golden Slate Pencil Awarded for the First Time—The Emancipation of Children's Literature), in *Nederlandse literatuur, een geschiedenis* (Dutch literature, a history), ed. M. A. Schenkeveld-Van der Dussen et al. (Groningen: Martinus Nijhoff, 1993), 743–751.

9. See, for example, *Raster* (1991). *Raster* is a Dutch periodical on adult literature.

10. M. A. Schenkeveld-Van der Dussen et al., eds. *Nederlandse Literatuur, een geschiedenis* (Groningen: Martinus Nijhoff, 1993); Nicolaas Matsier et al.,

eds. *Het literaire klimaat, 1986–1992* (The literary climate, 1986–1992) (Amsterdam: De Bezige Bij, 1992).

11. Bregje Boonstra, "Er was eens een waseens" (Once upon a time there was a once-upon-a-time), in Nicolaas Matsier et al., eds. *Het literaire klimaat 1986–1992* (Amsterdam: De Bezig Bij, 1992), 141.

12. See, for example, James Ousby, ed., *The Cambridge Guide to Literature in English* (Cambridge: Cambridge University Press, 1993); Margaret Drabble, ed., *The Oxford Companion to English Literature* (Oxford: Oxford University Press, 1985); Christine Gillie, *Longman Companion to English Literature* (London: Longman, 1977).

13. For example, *Poetics Today* 1 (1992).

14. Anne Vegter, *Verse bekken! (Fresh faces!)* (Amsterdam: Querido, 1991).

15. Bea Ros and Margot Krikhaar, *Een Spannend Boek. Warm Aanbevolen! Een Onderzoek naar Twintig Jaar Jeugdliteraire Kritiek (1965–1984) (A Thrilling Book. Warmly recommended! A study of twenty years of childrens' literature reviews (1965–1984))* (doctoral thesis, Nijmegen University, 1986).

16. Nicolaas Matsier, "Een kind is voor literatuur in de wieg gelegd" (A child is born for literature), *Vrij Nederland*, Literary supplement (May 1996): 5.

17. Zohar Shavit, *Poetics of Children's Literature* (Athens, Ga., and London: The University of Georgia Press, 1986), 39–40.

REFERENCES

Abrams, Meyer Howard. *The Mirror and the Lamp: Romantic Theory and the Critical Tradition.* 1953. London: Oxford University Press, 1979.

Allsobrook, Marian. "Major Authors' Work for Children." In *International Companion Encyclopedia of Children's Literature*, ed. Peter Hunt and Sheila Ray, 691–709. London: Routledge, 1996.

Bekkering, Harry. "Oktober 1955. De Gouden Griffel voor de eerste maal uitgereikt—De emancipatie van de kinder-en jeugdliteratuur." (October 1955: The Golden Slate Pencil Awarded for the First Time—The Emancipation of Children's Literature). In *Nederlandse Literatuur een Geschiedenis* (Dutch literature, a history), ed. M. A. Schenkeveld-Van der Dussen et al., 743–751. Groningen: Martinus Nijhoff, 1993.

Boonstra, Bregje. "Er was eens een waseens"(Once upon a time there was a once-upon-a-time). In *Het Literaire Klimaat 1986–1992* (The Literary Climate, 1986–1992), ed. Nicolaas Matsier et al., 125–154. Amsterdam: De Bezige Bij, 1992.

Drabble, Margaret, ed. *The Oxford Companion to English Literature.* Oxford: Oxford University Press, 1985.

Ewers, Hans-Heino. "Grenzverwischungen und Grenzüberschreitungen," *Julit* 1 (1976): 4–19.

Galef, David. "Crossing Over: Authors Who Write Both Children's and Adults' Fiction." *Children's Literature Association Quarterly* 20, no. 1 (1995): 29–35.

Gillie, Christine, ed. *Longman Companion to English Literature*. London: Longman, 1977.

Hoven, Peter van den. *Grenzverkeer* (Border traffic). The Hague: NBLC, 1994.

Keulen, Mensje van. *Bleekers zomer*. Amsterdam: Thomas Rap, 1972.

———. *Overspel*. Amsterdam: De Arbeiderspers, 1982.

———. *Tommie Station*. Amsterdam: Querido, 1986.

———. *De rode strik*. Amsterdam: Atlas, 1994.

———. *Pas op voor Bez*. Amsterdam: Querido, 1996.

———. *Olifanten op een web*. Amsterdam: Atlas, 1997.

Matsier, Nicolaas et al., eds. *Het Literaire Klimaat 1986–1992* (The literary climate 1986–1992). Amsterdam: De Bezige Bij, 1992.

———. "Een kind is voor literatuur in de wieg gelegd." *Vrij Nederland*, Literary supplement (May 1996): 5.

Ousby, James, ed. *The Cambridge Guide to Literature in English*. Cambridge: Cambridge University Press, 1993.

Ros, Bea and Margot Krikhaar. *Een spannend boek. Warm aanbevolen! Een onderzoek naar twintig jaar jeugdliteraire kritiek (1965–1984). (A thrilling book. Warmly recommended! A study of twenty years of children's literature reviews (1965–1984))*. Doctoral thesis, Nijmegen University, 1986.

Schenkeveld-Van der Dussen, M. A. *Nederlandse Literatuur, een Geschiedenis* (Dutch literature, a history). Groningen: Martinus Nijhoff, 1993.

Shavit, Zohar. *Poetics of Children's Literature*. Athens, Ga., and London: University of Georgia Press, 1986.

Vegter, Anne. *Verse Bekken!* Amsterdam: Querido, 1991.

CHAPTER 2

Crosswriting as a Criterion for Canonicity
The Case of Erich Kästner

BETTINA KÜMMERLING-MEIBAUER

It cannot be denied that the interest in canons and canon formation has increased greatly in recent years.[1] By canon we typically mean those texts that are said to have an enduring quality by virtue of their universal themes, literary craft, and/or significant meaning. For a canon of literature is a selection of well-known texts, which are considered valuable, are used in education, and serve as a framework of reference for literary critics. A powerful example of the politics of children's literature is found in the exclusionary power of canons. Children's authors were accorded limited critical scrutiny in scholarly communities and excluded from the literary canon. The inclusion or exclusion of an author or group of authors from the canon is the result of a variety of factors. These factors include tradition, the literary knowledge of those who contribute to the canonizing process, the availability of literary works, awareness of the works, and sociocultural forces such as elitism and bias. Indeed, we need to perceive and acknowledge canons as essential components of sociocultural and historical forces. In simpler terms, canons do not appear as a result of spontaneous choice, they are engendered by institutions and by cultural phenomena. Now that the old canon is being questioned, it is necessary to examine under what conditions a canon can change or even be revised, as we cannot live without some sort of canon.[2] Because the appearance of deconstructive approaches in literary studies, the canonical works of so-called world literature and of national literatures are under close scrutiny. Reflection on the canon takes the place of the recognized canon insofar as it reflects the controversial ideas of values and literature in modern society. Scholars criticize the fact that the previous canon excludes too many groups of authors, world regions, and literary genres.[3] The new awareness of the literary domains heretofore neglected culminated in a call for the canon's extension and also for the nomination of "subcanons." This canon debate was hardly even taken up in children's literature research.[4] The argument that children's literature is not canonical has prevented a serious discussion of this topic up until now. Although children's literature mostly serves pedagogical purposes, one cannot pretend that it just excels through its practical values, but not through literary quality. As the adult literary canon is in general not accessible to children, they therefore have the right of their own children's literature canon, thus matching their demand for qualitative literature. The increasing literary quality of children's literature, but also the new theoretical approach to literacy, which is still in its infancy, moves the child's literary education to the fore. Furthermore, literary studies have not yet grasped that this subject is an important connection between children's and adult literature. By means of children's literature, the knowledge of poetical norms and features of literary genres can be taught.[5] Another decisive reason for establishing a children's literature canon is the growing tendency to choose children's books as reading matter in schools. Numerous scholars, however, denounce the fact that the selection of children's books is almost exclusively determined by pedagogical purposes. The demand for a completion of the curriculum by qualitative children's books, for example, the children's classics, has not yet been implemented. But who selects the children's literature canon and which works should be chosen?

Children read works of children's literature, but, on their own, cannot confirm them into the canon. It is the adult act of rereading that consecrates the masterpieces for children. Perhaps it is this double reading, by two distant, different but identical readers that affords a depth and a resonance to the best of children's literature, that sets them apart from works written for and read by adults alone. In this sense, the idea seems to be that classics or canonical works for children are those books that do not only appeal to children, but also have an underlying depth of meaning that is satisfying to a mature sensibility.

The establishment of the concept of a canon of children's literature ought not to be a matter of retreating to the supposed safety of older classics (the traditional canon), but rather a process of discovery and analysis of works that serve best to exemplify the possibilities and qualities of modern children's literature (the modern canon).[6] In addition, an adequate selection of recognized international children's classics offers a broad basis for the establishment of a comparative children's literature canon that did not previously exist.[7] In this regard, internationalism is an important dimension of children's literature too often neglected in many countries.[8]

As is shown in my encyclopedia of international children's classics, *Klassiker der Kinder- und Jugendliteratur*, crosswriting is—in addition to other aspects such as innovation, aesthetic style, polyvalence, and representation of the child's world of experience—a distinguishing criterion constituting the literary quality of children's classics.[9] In general, three types of crosswriting can be distinguished: first, the phenomenon that authors write both for children and adults; second, the finding that many children's books are directed at an implied audience that comprises children *and* adults; and third, the rewriting of a book for adults to turn it into a children's book and the reverse.[10] On closer examination, it is apparent that all three types of crosswriting are a common phenomenon among children's classics. Most of them are written by crosswriters, that is, authors of adult and children's literature. Among them one finds Nobel Prize winners (Rudyard Kipling, Selma Lagerlöf, Gabriela Mistral, Isaac Bashevis Singer, and others) and many famous authors of world literature.[11] Even the second aspect is common among the children's classics. From the beginning they were written for a double audience. This ambivalence reveals a complexity of structure and meaning that arouses the adult reader's interest.[12] The third type is not as common, but several children's classics are transformations of adult books, for example Italo Calvino's *Il barone rampante* (*The Baron in the Trees*, 1959), Noel Streatfeild's *Ballet Shoes* (1931), and Michel Tournier's *Vendredi ou la vie sauvage* (*Friday and Robinson: Life on Speranza Island*, 1971). T. H. White even wrote an adult version of his children's book *The Sword in the Stone* (1938) for his tetralogy *The Once and Future King* (1958).

One of the most outstanding German crosswriters is Erich Kästner, famous for his children's classic *Emil und die Detektive* (*Emil and the Detectives*, 1929).[13] The art of writing for a dual readership of children and adults, however, is not a new phenomenon in Germany. One is struck by the large number of famous authors of adult fiction who have written for children: Bertolt Brecht, Clemens Brentano, E. T. A. Hoffmann, Erwin Strittmatter, to name only a few. Their major works have become children's classics.[14]

Kästner began writing articles for renowned journals. He gained recognition with his satirical poems for adults and his *Fabian: Die*

Geschichte eines Moralisten (Fabian: The story of a moralist, 1931) was one of the canonical novels of the so-called New Realism *(Neue Sachlichkeit* in German), a new literary movement in Germany. Although Kästner already had contributed short stories for the children's supplement of the Dresden journal *Beyers für Alle*,[15] he did not at first consider writing children's books. An oft-cited anecdote reveals that Kästner made the crossover to children's literature at the initiative of Edith Jacobsohn, owner of the Jewish publishing house Williams & Co. in Berlin, well known for its qualitatively distinguished children's books. Kästner, who felt flattered by the prospect of being published alongside such famous children's authors as Hugh Lofting and A. A. Milne, accepted the offer immediately. 1929 saw the appearance of his first children's book, *Emil und die Detektive*, which was a world success and the model for eight film versions.[16] After Hitler's seizure of power in 1933, Kästner, because of his critical and satirical works, found himself among the condemned authors whose books were burned in public. His works—with the exception of *Emil und die Detektive*—were put on a so-called black list of forbidden books. Nevertheless, *Emil und die Detektive* was removed from public libraries. Its favorable reception in foreign countries still continued, however. In the 1930s and 1940s several school editions for teaching German appeared in the Netherlands, Sweden, and the United States. In addition, Kästner's novel inspired a new genre in children's literature: the detective novel for children.[17]

Contrary to many adult authors who wrote only one or two children's books, Kästner continued over the years to publish for children as well as adults. Even his other children's books have gained international acclaim and became well-loved favorites beyond German borders. His stories are widely read in the German-speaking countries and have been translated into at least forty foreign languages. The first English translation of *Emil und die Detektive* appeared in 1931, containing an enthusiastic foreword written by the famous poet and children's author Walter de la Mare.[18]

Kästner's keen understanding of the child's view of the world and the connection between modern urban life and childhood memory is what made his books so successful and contributed to their cross-generational appeal. Although Kästner did not rewrite his own adult works for children, he wrote abridged and simplified versions of two adult novels for children, Gottfried August Bürger's *Münchhausen* (1786) and Miguel de Cervantes Saavedra's *Don Quijote* (1605/1615). In addition, he often reflected on the relationship between children's and adult literature, arguing that authors should write for both audiences. In his speech *Jugend, Literatur, und Jugendliteratur* (Youth, literature, and youth literature), given at the Zurich town hall in 1953, he claimed that "writers who just write books for young people aren't really writers, and they certainly aren't at all writers for young people."[19] The author thus proposed a provoking thesis with the intention of encouraging the public to reflect on the status of children's literature in general. Kästner also stressed the lack of literary quality in most of the common children's books. In order to increase the importance of children's literature, Kästner turned to the writers of adult literature, proposing that they should consider writing books for children; in other words, he gave a speech in favor of crosswriting. Although Kästner is a good example for an author matching all three types of crosswriting, there is little theoretical research on this phenomenon. Scholars of children's literature have not recognized that a concise study of Kästner's books for adults will help to establish new insights into the author's purposes, namely the combining of modern narrative techniques with traditional narrative strategies.

Furthermore, in the case of Kästner, a fourth type of crosswriting is emphasized. I will argue that Kästner's adult works and his children's novels are complementary to each other, thus building a cluster of intertextual references.[20] This will be shown by a detailed comparison of Kästner's children's classic *Emil und die Detektive* with his adult novel *Fabian*.[21]

Kästner's children's book, which, together with Wolf Durian's *Kai aus der Kiste* (Kai out of the box, 1927),[22] pioneered a new realism in German children's literature, presents a socially and psychologically interesting portrait of children's street life in pre-World War II Berlin.[23] The story of Kästner's children's classic is certainly well-known: the pupil Emil Tischbein, who lives with his mother in poor conditions in a small town, is going to visit his grandmother in Berlin. On the train a thief, who offered Emil a candy with barbiturate, steals the money (140 marks) that Emil had fastened to his jacket lining with a safety pin. Emil pursues the thief through Berlin with the help of the boy Gustav and his gang. They catch the thief in a bank when he tries to change the money. Because he is a wanted bankrobber, Emil not only gets his money back, but also a thousand mark reward.

In the novel *Fabian*, the young scientist Jakob Fabian, who earns a living with casual jobs, roams around in Berlin, meeting representatives of different social groups. As a keen observer of modern society, he is disgusted by its decadence and indifference. He just finds support in his best friend Labude and his lover Cornelia. In the end, he loses his job, Labude commits suicide, and Cornelia becomes a film producer's lover. Fabian turns his back on Berlin and visits his parents in a small town. In his attempt to rescue a child who has fallen into the river, Fabian drowns, whereas the child gets safely to the bank.

At first sight, these novels seem to be representative of two antagonistic worldviews: *Fabian* is dominated by a feeling of moral despair, whereas *Emil und die Detektive* represents an optimistic attitude toward life, culminating in Emil's double reward. But this apparent contrast diminishes on closer examination. The importance of the child as a symbol of hope in both novels and the ironic moral implications expressed in each of the novels' last chapter reveal a continuing subtext of alternative perception that has thus far gone unnoticed and forces us to reconsider our conclusion.

Before going into more detail, I wish to outline my main points. First, I will explore the thematic and narrative elements that structure the novels and show the connection between the two works. A comparison of the two novels shows parallels in four main areas: the presentation of place (small town, Berlin), the dominant role of a dream that helps to provide insight into the protagonists' inner feelings, and the beginning and ending. These aspects occur in both novels, but manifest themselves differently in each. Second, I will concentrate on the overriding theme of the child as symbol of hope, a theme that is indicated in all four aspects.

We will begin with the presentation of place: Both novels are situated in Berlin and offer exact descriptions and names of places and streets. Using a big city as the setting was new in German children's literature. Kästner had several precursors, besides the already mentioned novel *Kai aus der Kiste*—Heinrich Scharrelmann's stories about the boy *Berni* (1908–), Hans Dominik's *John Workman, der Zeitungsboy* (John Workman, the paper boy, 1909), and Carl Dantz' *Peter Stoll: Ein Kinderleben* (Peter Stoll: A child's life, 1925)—but, in general, Kästner is regarded as the author who finally established this topic.[24] Although the metropolis enables children to act independently without parental supervision, the risk of a loss of control is recognized. The anonymity of the big city, the confusing traffic, and the noises are threatening to both children and adults:

> The city was so big. And Emil was so small. And nobody wanted to know why he had no money, and why he did not know where he should get off. Four million people lived in Berlin, and nobody was interested in Emil Tischbein.[25]

Even Fabian often feels lonely in the crowd, driven to despair by the people's ignorance and indifference. This feeling of helplessness that occurs in both novels is stressed by a cinematic narrative technique mainly consisting of quick changes of scene and changes in point of view. Whereas Emil, confronted with the big city, learns to recognize dangers, to reason, and to cooperate with children of the same age,[26] Fabian, who had already acquired these abilities (in some sense he could be seen as the adult version of Emil), loses faith in other people's good intentions. The protagonists' opposite development is particularly evident in their change of places. Emil leaves his home village, an idyllic small town where everybody knows everybody else, for the first time in his life, and is confronted with the problems of a big city. During his travel and his pursuit of the thief he undergoes an evolution leading to his acceptance as a leader in Gustav's gang.[27] Together with the "Professor," another gang member, he even establishes a sort of children's parliament in which everyone has the possibility to discuss justice and law. In this regard, the novel demonstrates that the social institutions of the Weimar Republic were rational and impartial.[28] In *Fabian*, an opposite itinerary is obvious. Fabian, who has lived for many years in Berlin, leaves the big city in order to return to his home village, where he visits his parents and his former school.[29] Fabian's travel does not lead to success and moral development, but to disillusionment and death. Is it any wonder that the social institutions, such as the press and the justice system, are characterized as corrupt? A comparison of the two novels thus reveals two different attitudes toward life and society: whereas in *Fabian* the social and economic problems of the Weimar Republic are told frankly, the perspective in *Emil und die Detektive* is guided by an utopian aim: The children's book intends to show a model (children's) society where the political and democratic ideas of the Weimar Republic come true.

Another important connection between the two novels is the central role of dreams which reveal the protagonists' inner feelings. In *Emil und die Detektive,* the theft of the money is not described in detail, but indicated only by means of a dream sequence. In this dream Emil digests his experiences of the past few days: his fear of the police, his curiosity about the unknown city Berlin, his anxiety concerning the money, and his longing for his beloved mother. Likewise, in *Fabian,* the hero confronts his experiences in a long and disturbing dream that reveals his fear of losing Cornelia, his longing for friendship and love, and his search for a meaning to life, culminating in the famous stair scene in which people standing on steps steal from each other. Only a little girl refuses to steal and gives confidence to Fabian, with whom she leaves the group. Both dreams, which contradict the poetics of New Realism, are inspired by the literary movement of Expressionism and the silent movie. Furthermore, Kästner integrated the latest findings of psychoanalysis. In this regard, the dreams with their surrealistic passages could be interpreted as the protagonists' psychological portraits. The link between the poetics of New Realism, elements inspired both by Expressionism and Surrealism, and psychoanalytical insights contribute to the modernity of the two novels.

Modern narrative techniques can also be found in the beginning and ending of both novels. One is struck by the fact that the first chapter of each novel contains a dialogue between the narrator (in *Emil und die Detektive*) or the protagonist (in *Fabian*) and a waiter who is a representative of the "people's voice." In both cases the waiter is asked for advice. Fabian indirectly asked whether he should go to a certain establishment of ill repute; the narrator, who later reveals himself as the author Erich Kästner, asked the waiter Nietenführ[30] what sort of children's book he should write. Whereas Fabian decided against the waiter's advice to visit the establishment, the narrator took to heart Nietenführ's proposal to write a real story about real children living in a town like Berlin, thus seemingly rejecting the idea of writing a fantastic adventure story with the title *Petersilie im Urwald* (Parsley in the jungle). Anyone familiar with Kästner's other children's books will recognize that the author published this book under the different title *Der 35. Mai oder Konrad reitet in die Südsee* (May 35 or Konrad rides to the South Seas) in 1931. This fact reveals that Kästner nonetheless ironically wrote the adventure story against which the waiter pleaded, thus casting his advice to the winds.

In retrospect, one observes that in both novels a decision is made contrary to public opinion. In *Fabian,* the protagonist, who is looking for the meaning of life, visits places and people avoided by the common public. In this regard, Kästner's adult novel is an unsparing representation of contemporary life in Berlin, guided by decadence and moral despair. In the case of his children's book, the situation is even more complicated. As the foreword indicates, the narrator first thought of writing a conventional adventure story that would satisfy the publishers' demand for children's books full of suspense and humor. After the discussion with the waiter, he began writing a realistic children's book situated in contemporary Berlin, which is regarded as the beginning of a "new realism" in German children's literature. The ironic implication of this decision consists in the feigned claim that the author thus serves public opinion concerning children's literature. In fact, he established a new literary genre and style inspired by modern adult literature.

In this regard, Kästner provides an important clue to his intentions in a three-part foreword that testifies to the book's obvious modernity. The first part, "Die Geschichte fängt noch gar nicht an" (The story does not yet begin), contains the dialogue between the narrator and the waiter, followed by the narrator's inner monologue: in a topsy-turvy perspective—the narrator is lying on the floor of his room, looking at his table from below—the connection between the table leg and the surname of the story's protagonist "Tischbein" (= table leg) inspired him to write a story about a real incident he had witnessed as a journalist. In this way fiction and reality seem to blend. Furthermore, this discovery is emphasized by Kästner's threefold role: He is at once the author, the narrator, and a figure in the story. The author thus evokes the reader's distance from the subsequent story, urging the latter to reflect upon the conditions that contribute to the origin of a fictional story. On closer examination, this first part of the foreword, which is often eliminated in foreign translations, plays an important role, revealing the author's ideas concerning a new poetics of children's literature. This poetics of the New Realism for children stresses three main points: the matter-of-factness of description, the reduction of moral judgements, and the apparent renouncement of the presentation of fantastic events.[31]

The foreword's second part, "Zehn Bilder kommen jetzt zur Sprache" (Ten images are now coming up), just consists of ten images by Walter Trier, introducing the main figures and giving hints about the subsequent story. The reader is thus invited to decode the story before reading it. The third part, "Die Geschichte fängt nun endlich an" (The story finally begins), leads to the story's actual beginning.

This often ignored structure of *Emil und die Detektive*, which reveals the book's modernity, contradicts the widespread opinion among children's literature researchers that Kästner's children's book is just an idyllic and humorous story. Furthermore, as the story unfolds, one notices that it is characterized by a dialogic interplay between two implied audiences. As a reader of this book, the child is invited to empathize with the protagonist and to share the process Emil undergoes when he is forced to catch a thief. The adult—and maybe even the sophisticated child—, by contrast, is encouraged, by concealed authorial cues, to decode Kästner's ironic references.[32] Crosswriting thus invites crossreading.

This also can be proved for the last chapter of the novels. A detailed analysis of these chapters will help to demonstrate the literary strategies necessary to write an ambiguous ending. The pessimistic ending of *Fabian* is unexpected and shocked many readers. The hero with whom the reader may sympathize has not overcome the obstacles. The ambiguity will convey doubt and an inability to make absolute assertions. Thus, the most interesting type of narrative fragment may be that which propels the reader into responsibility for the unwritten narrative conclusion. By leaving what follows to the reader's imagination, Kästner creates the necessity to come to terms with the substance of the story and with the problem of social responsibility for the future. No less subversive is Kästner's use of irony to undermine the dominant moralism of (children's) literature. A first hint of a deeper meaning is hidden in the chapters' titles. With the question "Läßt sich daraus etwas lernen?" (Can one learn something from that?) Kästner alludes to the common expectation that a children's book should be concluded with a moral aphorism. Emil and his aunt propose two different ideas,[33] but Emil's grandmother who had asked the question, rejects both proposals and suggests as the only rule: "Geld soll man per Postanweisung schicken!" (Money should be sent by postal order!). This pragmatic conclusion contradicts the reader's expectation of a general moral rule, ironically rejecting the implication that a children's book mostly has to serve pedagogical purposes.[34]

In *Fabian,* the implied ambivalent meaning of the ending is already indicated in the last chapter's title: "Lernt schwimmen!" (Learn to swim!). This title has a double meaning insofar as it insinuates, on the one hand, that one should know to swim before trying to save another person's life (the novel concludes with the sentence that Fabian drowns because he cannot swim), but it also alludes to the saying "to swim with/against the tide." Fabian fails in both senses because of his inability to swim *and* his refusal to fit into modern society. But it has thus far gone unnoticed that this sad ending finds its counterpart in a happy ending: the child's life is saved. The irony of Fabian's futile death arises from the fact that the child does not need to be rescued because, contrary to Fabian, the child can swim.

On retrospect, one notices that both books are determined by the overriding utopian idea of the child as symbol of hope. This is shown directly in *Emil und die Detektive,* but indirectly in *Fabian,* where this topic is revealed as an underlying thematic concern. Kästner, who felt indebted to the tradition of the Enlightenment, upheld values such as moral integrity, equality, democracy, and solidarity. He believed, however, that these values could be spiritualized by children, whereas he was skeptical about the adults' ability to keep them. For this reason Kästner intended, by means of his children's books, to boost the child's courage. Argumentation takes the place of affirmation and uncritical belief in authorities. Stressing the child's moral integrity and reason, the author pursued an utopian aim that points toward the future. Kästner does not seek refuge in the past or in the idea of a Golden Age that was upheld by the Romantics. On closer examination, these ideas appear clearly in *Fabian*. The protagonist meets children four times: the little girl in the department store, the same little girl in his dream, the pupils in the schoolyard, and the boy whom he wanted to rescue. Each scene stresses the child's innocence and confidence, thus creating a contrast to the adults' world view.

In this way, new aspects are added to both novels that change the meaning of them. Readers thus are encouraged to think of the new aspects as causes of events they did not as first acknowledge. By this choice, Kästner creates a change in point of view. Both novels complement one another; this aspect is mainly stressed by the common theme of the child as symbol of hope. This insight leads to the question of whether or not one needs to be familiar with both novels in order to understand their implied deeper meaning. As mentioned above, they can be read as independent novels. The reader does not necessarily have to have read the adult novel in order to understand the children's book and reverse. Nevertheless, I would argue that the background of one novel enables the reader to have a better and a more thorough understanding of the second.

The difference between the dominant mode of consciousness and the child's alternate vision may express itself through ironic passages. Kästner wrote his books for an implied audience of aesthetically sophisticated adults, whom he expected to be alert to his strategies of ironic reversal and indirection. Scholars in the field of children's literature have greatly underestimated the author's craft as a crosswriter who wishes both to explore and to test the shifting relation between the child and the adult reader. Kästner repeatedly blurs the binary oppositions upon which his contemporaries based their constructions of identity; thus he can be said to hover between two opposed states of perception—the innocent child's perception and the experienced adult's perception.

The network of intertextual references between both novels extends the scope of the author, because it makes the situation more meaningful, so that one can look back and interpret *Emil und die Detektive* in terms of the meaning of *Fabian* and the reverse. The effect is that each novel seems complete in itself, yet also seems to provide a slice of a much larger meaning.

It becomes clear that Kästner created, through a compact network of allusions and changing points of view, a complex structure that resists traditional ideas of children's literature. It is to be hoped that future studies will acknowledge the important impact of crosswriting and will reach beyond the borders of adult and children's literature. In this way, children's literature studies will eventually be recognized not as a peripheral field annexed to an established canon, but as a central core in its own right. In this spirit, this article feels indebted to Kästner's creed, which concluded his above mentioned essay *Jugend, Literatur, und Jugendliteratur*: "The future of youth, tomorrow and the day after tomorrow, will look like its literature? That's right. And what is more: it is true!"[35]

NOTES

1. A thorough discussion of this topic can be found in Renate von Heyde-brand, ed., *Kanon Macht Kultur* (Stuttgart: Metzler, 1998). Even there no attention is paid to children's literature.

2. Evidently, this interest in the canon is inspired by a serious problem. On the one hand—notwithstanding national differences between the European countries, or between Europe, America, Africa, and Asia—the teaching of literary history, including the teaching of a canon, has been rather neglected over the past ten or twenty years. On the other hand, it is difficult to imagine how literature can be taught without a canon, that is, a set of texts that must be read and studied.

3. See Janos Riesz, "Komparatistische Kanonbildung: Möglichkeiten der Konstitution eines Weltliteratur-Kanons aus heutiger Sicht," *Jahrbuch Deutsch als Fremdsprache* 13 (1987): 200–213.

4. An exception to the rule is Perry Nodelman, ed., *Touchstones: Reflections on the Best in Children's Literature* (West Lafayette: Children's Literature Association, 1985–1989); and John D. Stahl, "Canon Formation: A Historical and Psychological Perspective," in *Teaching Children's Literature: Issues, Pedagogy, Resources*, ed. Glenn E. Sadler, 12–21 (New York: Modern Language Association of America, 1992).

5. These aspects are discussed in Hans-Heino Ewers, "Kinderliteratur, Literaturerwerb und literarische Bildung," in *Kinderliteratur, literarische Sozialisation und Schule*, ed. Bernhard Rank and Cornelia Rosebrock, 55–74 (Heidelberg: Deutscher Studien Verlag, 1997).

6. For a comprehensive representation of the children's classics from sixty-five countries that build the core of the children's literature canon, see Bettina Kümmerling-Meibauer, *Klassiker der Kinder- und Jugendliteratur: Ein internationales Lexikon* (Stuttgart: Metzler, 1999). It includes more than more than 530 children's classics.

7. The need to constitute a comparative canon of children's literature is suggested in Bettina Kümmerling-Meibauer, "Comparing Children's Literature," *Compar(a)ison* II, special issue: *Current Trends in Comparative Children's Literature Research*, ed. Bettina Kümmerling- Meibauer (1995): 5–18.

8. John D. Stahl complains that "the exclusion of works translated from other languages from the American canon of children's literature is a form of cultural poverty and testifies to a lack of imagination in an information-rich-world" ("Canon Formation,"19).

9. A concise analysis of the elements which constitute the literary quality of children's classics can be found in the introduction to Bettina Kümmerling-Meibauer, *Klassiker der Kinder- und Jugendliteratur* (ix–xxvii).

10. A synopsis of criticism is found in U. C. Knoepflmacher and Mitzi Myers, "'Cross-Writing' and the Reconceptualizing of Children's Literature Studies," *Children's Literature* 25 (1997): vii–xvii.

11. Seventy-six percent of the authors mentioned in Bettina Kümmerling-Meibauer, *Klassiker der Kinder- und Jugendliteratur,* are crosswriters. For a detailed overview of English-speaking crosswriters, see Marilyn Faine Apseloff, *They Wrote for Children Too: An Annotated Bibliography of Children's Literature by Famous Writers for Adults* (Westport, Conn.: Greenwood Press, 1989).

12. Hans-Heino Ewers draws attention to this point. See "Das doppelsinnige Kinderbuch—Erwachsene als Mitleser und Leser von Kinderliteratur," in *Kinderliteratur—Literatur auch für Erwachsene?*, ed. Dagmar Grenz, 15–24 (München: Fink, 1990)

13. The *Encyclopedia Britannica* even called him "the dean of German children's literature." See the article "Children's Literature," in *Encyclopedia Britannica*, vol. 5 (Chicago: Benton, 1973), column 522B.

14. For detailed information about these authors and their classical works for children see Bettina Kümmerling-Meibauer, *Klassiker der Kinder- und Jugendliteratur.*

15. Jürgen Zonnefeld's dissertation, *Erich Kästner als Rezensent 1923–1933* (Frankfurt: Peter Lang, 1991), gives detailed information about Kästner's early works and thus complements Dirk Walter, *Zeitkritik und Idyllensehnsucht: Erich Kästners Frühwerk 1928–1933* (Heidelberg: Winter, 1977).

16. The most famous film version was directed in 1931 by the German filmmaker Günther Lamprecht.

17. For example, the German novel *Das Rote U* (The red U, 1932) by Wilhelm Matthießen and the Czech children's books *Kluci, hurá za ním!* (Stop, thief! 1933) by Václav Řezač and *Bileho Kliče* (*The league of the white key,* 1934) by Frantisek Langer. Even after 1945, many children's authors model their detective novels on Kästner's book: among them Paul Berna's *Le cheval sans tête* (*The horse without a head,* 1955), Astrid Lindgren's *Mästerdetektiven Blomkvist* (*Bill Bergson Master Detective*, 1948), and Alfred Weidenmann's *Gepäckschein 666* (*Baggage check 666,* 1959).

18. His children's books *The Three Mullah-mulgars* (1910) and *Peacock Pie* (1913) are now considered children's classics.

19. "Schriftsteller, die nur Jugendbücher schreiben, sind keine Schriftsteller, und Jugendschriftsteller sind sie schon gar nicht." Erich Kästner, "Jugend, Literatur und Jugendliteratur," in Erich Kästner, *Gesammelte Schriften*, vol. 7 (Köln: Kiepenheuer & Witsch, 1959), 216. All English translations of Kästner's texts are mine.

20. Another example is the Swedish author Peter Pohl, whose children's books—among them *Janne, min vän* (*Johnny, My Friend*, 1985) and the well-known Rainbow-trilogy (1986– 1990)—build a cluster, each of them referring to Pohl's other children's books. See Bettina Kümmerling-Meibauer, "Annäherungen von Jugend- und Erwachsenenliteratur: Die schwedische Jugendliteratur der 80er und frühen 90er Jahre," *Der Deutschunterricht* 46 (1996): 68–81.

21. Until now only Dagmar Grenz had tried to compare Kästner's adult novel *Fabian* with a children's book. Instead of *Emil und die Detektive,* she chose *Pünktchen und Anton* (1931). See "Erich Kästners Kinderbücher in ihrem Verhältnis zu seiner Literatur für Erwachsene." In *Literatur für Kinder*, ed. Maria Lypp, 155–169 (Göttingen: Vandenhoeck & Ruprecht, 1977). A more general view about the relationship between Kästner's adult works and children's books can be found in Andreas Drouve, *Erich Kästner—Moralist mit doppeltem Boden* (Marburg: Tectum, 1993) and Helmut Kiesel, *Erich Kästner* (München: C.H. Beck, 1981).

22. Helga Karrenbrock rightly stresses the importance of Durian's children's novel in *Märchenkinder-Zeitgenossen: Untersuchungen zur Kinder- und Jugendliteratur der Weimarer Republik* (Stuttgart: M & P, Verlag für Wissenschaft, 1995).

23. This idea is also expressed in John D. Stahl, "Moral Despair and the Child as Symbol of Hope in Pre-World War II Berlin," *Children's Literature* 14 (1986): 83–104.

24. See Miriam Mieles, "Zivilisationsraum Großstadt—Kinderliterarische Großstadtprosa in der Weimarer Republik." In *Naturkind, Stadtkind, Landkind: literarische Bilderwelten kindlicher Umwelt*, ed. Ulrich Nassen, 85–106 (München: Fink, 1995).

25. "Die Stadt war so groß. Und Emil war so klein. Und kein Mensch wollte wissen, warum er kein Geld hatte, und warum er nicht wußte, wo er aussteigen sollte. Vier Millionen Menschen lebten in Berlin, und keiner interessierte sich für Emil Tischbein." Erich Kästner, *Emil und die Detektive* (Hamburg: Dressler, 1970), 74–75.

26. Emil is the ideal pupil in the sense of Jean-Jacques Rousseau's philosophy, expressed in his famous *Émile ou de l'éducation* (*Emile*, 1762). Whether the name Emil is a direct allusion to Rousseau remains to be proved.

27. Luke Springman discusses the relationship between Emil and the children he meets in Berlin in detail in *Comrades, Friends, and Companions* (New York: Peter Lang, 1989).

28. For a detailed analysis of this topic, see Isa Schikorsky, "Literarische Erziehung zwischen Realismus und Utopie—Erich Kästners Kinderroman 'Emil und die Detektive.'" In *Klassiker der Kinder- und Jugendliteratur*, ed. Bettina Hurrelmann, 216–233 (Frankfurt: Fischer, 1995).

29. This passage where Fabian observes the pupils in the schoolyard is a reminiscence of Kästner's famous poem *Kinderkaserne* (*Children's barracks*). In this poem, the author criticizes the teachers' authoritative drill that is seen from the abused child's angle. An optimistic point of view is shown in Kästner's school story *Das fliegende Klassenzimmer* (*The Flying Class-Room*, 1931). The description of the schoolyard in the children's novel corresponds to that in *Fabian*.

30. In the first chapter of *Fabian,* the waiter is anonymous; however, a waiter called Nietenführ turns up in the second chapter.

31. See Volker Ladenthin, "Erich Kästners Bemerkungen über den Realismus in der Prosa: Ein Beitrag zum poetologischen Denken Erich Kästners und zur Theorie der Neuen Sachlichkeit," *Wirkendes Wort* 2 (1988): 62–77.

32. In general, children are able to decode ironic sentences at the age of nine. Nevertheless, irony often is presented in children's books, even in picture books for preschool children. A detailed analysis of whether younger children can grasp the meaning of ironic picture books is to be found in Bettina Kümmerling-Meibauer, "Metalinguistic Awareness and the Child's Developing Sense of Irony: the Relationship between Pictures and Text in Ironic Picture Books," *The Lion and the Unicorn* 23, no. 2 (April 1999).

33. Emil suggests: "Man soll keinem Menschen trauen" (One should not trust anybody), and his mother proposes: "Ich habe gelernt, daß man Kinder niemals allein verreisen lassen soll" (I have learned, that one should never let children travel on their own).

34. Klaus Doderer already pointed to the ironic meaning of this chapter. See "Erich Kästners 'Emil und die Detektive'—Gesellschaftskritik in einem Kinderroman," in *Erich Kästner: Leben—Werk—Wirkung*, ed. Rudolf Wolff, 104–117 (Bonn: Bouvier, 1983).

35. "Die Zukunft der Jugend wird so aussehen wie, morgen und übermorgen, ihre Literatur? Das stimmt. Und was mehr ist: Es ist wahr!" Erich Kästner, "Jugend, Literatur und Jugendliteratur," in Erich Kästner, *Gesammelte Schriften*, vol. 7 (Köln: Kiepenheuer & Witsch, 1959), 223.

REFERENCES

Apseloff, Marilyn Faine. *They Wrote for Children Too: An Annotated Bibliography of Children's Literature by Famous Writers for Adults*. Westport, Conn.: Greenwood Press, 1989.

Berna, Paul. *Le cheval sans tête.* Paris: Éditions G. P., 1955.

Bürger, Gottfried August. *Wunderbare Reisen zu Wasser und Lande, Feldzüge und lustige Abentheuer des Freyherrn von Münchhausen.* Göttingen: Dieterich, 1786.

Calvino, Italo. *Il barone rampante.* Turin: Einaudi, 1957.

Cervantes Saavedra, Miguel de. El ingenioso hidalgo *Don Quixote de la Mancha.* Madrid: Lumen, 1986.

Dantz, Carl. *Peter Stoll: Ein Kinderleben.* Berlin: Verlag J.H.W. Dietz, 1925.

De la Mare, Walter. *The Three Mullah-mulgars.* London: Duckworth, 1910.

———. *Peacock Pie.* London: Constable, 1913.

Doderer, Klaus. "Erich Kästners 'Emil und die Detektive'—Gesellschaftskritik in einem Kinderroman." In *Erich Kästner. Leben—Werk—Wirkung,* ed. Rudolf Wolff, 104–117. Bonn: Bouvier, 1983.

Dominik, Hans. *John Workman, der Zeitungsboy.* Leipzig: Koehler & Amelang, 1909.

Drouve, Andreas. *Erich Kästner—Moralist mit doppeltem Boden.* Marburg: Tectum, 1993.

Durian, Wolf. *Kai aus der Kiste.* Berlin: Franz Schneider, 1927.

Ewers, Hans-Heino. "Das doppelsinnige Kinderbuch—Erwachsene als Mitleser und Leser von Kinderliteratur." In *Kinderliteratur—Literatur auch für Erwachsene?,* ed. Dagmar Grenz, 15–24. München: Fink, 1990.

Ewers, Hans-Heino. "Kinderliteratur, Literaturerwerb und literarische Bildung." In *Kinderliteratur, literarische Sozialisation und Schule,* ed. Bernhard Rank and Cornelia Rosebrock, 55–74. Heidelberg: Deutscher Studien Verlag, 1997.

Grenz, Dagmar. "Erich Kästners Kinderbücher in ihrem Verhältnis zu seiner Literatur für Erwachsene." In *Literatur für Kinder,* ed. Maria Lypp, 155–169. Göttingen: Vandenhoeck & Ruprecht, 1977.

Heydebrand, Renate von. Ed. *Kanon—Macht—Kultur.* Stuttgart: Metzler, 1998.

Karrenbrock, Helga. *Märchenkinder—Zeitgenossen: Untersuchungen zur Kinder- und Jugendliteratur der Weimarer Republik.* Stuttgart: M & P, Verlag für Wissenschaft, 1995.

Kästner, Erich. *Pünktchen und Anton.* Berlin: Williams & Co., 1931.

———. *Das fliegende Klassenzimmer.* Stuttgart: Perthes, 1933.

———. *Der 35. Mai oder Konrad reitet in die Südsee.* Berlin: Williams & Co., 1933.

———. *Emil and the Detectives.* Trans. Eileen Hall. London: Jonathan Cape, 1959.

———. *Fabian: Geschichte eines Moralisten.* In Erich Kästner: *Gesammelte Schriften.* vol. 2. Köln: Kiepenheuer & Witsch, 1959.

———. "Jugend, Literatur und Jugendliteratur." In Erich Kästner: *Gesammelte Schriften.* vol. 7. 216–223. Köln: Kiepenheuer & Witsch, 1959.

————. *Emil und die Detektive.* Hamburg: Dressler, 1970.

Kiesel, Helmut. *Erich Kästner.* München: C.H. Beck, 1981.

Knoepflmacher, U.C., and Mitzi Myers. " 'Cross-Writing' and the Reconceptualizing of Children's Literary Studies," *Children's Literature* 25 (1997): vii–xvii.

Kümmerling-Meibauer, Bettina. "Comparing Children's Literature." *Compar-
(a)ison II,* special issue: *Current Trends in Comparative Children's Literature Research,* ed. Bettina Kümmerling-Meibauer (1995): 5–18.

————. "Annäherungen von Jugend- und Erwachsenenliteratur: Die schwedische Jugendliteratur der 80er und frühen 90er Jahre," *Der Deutschunterricht*
46 (1996): 29–45.

————. *Klassiker der Kinder- und Jugendliteratur: Ein internationales Lexikon.*
2 vols. Stuttgart: Metzler, 1999.

————. "Metalinguistic Awareness and the Child's Developing Sense of Irony:
the Relationship between Pictures and Text in Ironic Picture Books," *The
Lion and the Unicorn* 23, no. 2 (April 1999): 157–183.

Ladenthin, Volker. "Erich Kästners Bemerkungen über den Realismus in der
Prosa: Ein Beitrag zum poetologischen Denken Erich Kästners und zur
Theorie der Neuen Sachlichkeit." *Wirkendes Wort* 2 (1988): 62–77.

Langer, Frantisek. *Bileho Klice.* Prague: Artia, 1934.

Lindgren, Astrid. *Mästerdetektiven Blomkvist.* Stockholm: Rabén & Sjögren,
1946.

Matthießen, Wilhelm: *Das Rote U.* Köln: Hermann Schaffstein Verlag 1932.

Mieles, Miriam. "Zivilisationsraum Großstadt—Kinderliterarische Großstadtprosa in der Weimarer Republik," In *Naturkind, Stadtkind, Landkind: literarische Bilderwelten kindlicher Umwelt,* ed. Ulrich Nassen, 85–106.
München: Fink, 1995.

Nodelman, Perry. Ed. *Touchstones. Reflections on the Best in Children's Literature.* 3 vols. West Lafayette: Children's Literature Association, 1985–1989.

Pohl, Peter. *Janne, min vän.* Stockholm: AWG, 1985.

Řezáč, Václav. *Kluci, hurá za nim!* Prague: Artia, 1964.

Riesz, Janosz. "Komparatistische Kanonbildung: Möglichkeiten der Konstitution eines Weltliteratur-Kanons aus heutiger Sicht." *Jahrbuch Deutsch als
Fremdsprache* 13 (1987): 200–213.

Rousseau, Jean-Jacques. *Émile ou de l'éducation.* Paris: Gallimard, 1977.

Scharrelmann, Heinrich. *Ein kleiner Junge. Was er sah und hörte, als er noch
nicht zur Schule ging.* Hamburg: A. Jansson, 1908.

Schikorsky, Isa. "Literarische Erziehung zwischen Realismus und Utopie—
Erich Kästners Kinderroman 'Emil und die Detektive.' " In *Klassiker der
Kinder- und Jugendliteratur,* ed. Bettina Hurrelmann, 216–233. Frankfurt:
Fischer, 1995.

Springman, Luke. *Comrades, Friends, and Companions.* New York: Peter Lang, 1989.

Stahl, John D. "Moral Despair and the Child as Symbol of Hope in Pre-World War II in Berlin." *Children's Literature* 14 (1986): 83–104.

———. "Canon Formation: A Historical and Psychological Perspective." In *Teaching Children's Literature. Issues, Pedagogy, Resources,* ed. Glenn E. Sadler, 12–21. New York: The Modern Language Association of America, 1992.

———. *Friday and Robinson: Life on Speranza Island.* Trans. Ralph Manheim. New York: Alfred A. Knopf, 1971.

Streatfeild, Noel. *Ballet Shoes.* London: Dent, 1936.

Tournier, Michel. *Vendredi ou la vie sauvage.* Paris: Gallimard, 1977.

Walter, Dirk. *Zeitkritik und Idyllensehnsucht. Erich Kästners Frühwerk 1928–1933.* Heidelberg: Winter, 1977.

Weidenmann, Alfred. *Gepäckschein 666.* Bayreuth: Loewes, 1959.

White, T(erence) H(anbury). *The Once and Future King.* New York: Putnam, 1958.

———. *The Sword in the Stone.* New York: Putnam, 1963.

Zonnefeld, Jürgen. *Erich Kästner als Rezensent 1923–1933.* Frankfurt: Peter Lang, 1991.

CHAPTER 3

Crosswriting Child and Adult in France

Children's Fiction for Adults? Adult Fiction for Children? Fiction for All Ages?

SANDRA L. BECKETT

> *[. . .] sometimes I apply myself so well and have so much talent that what I write can also be read by children. When my pen is less lucky, what it writes is only good enough for adults.*
> —MICHEL TOURNIER, "MICHEL TOURNIER: AVANT TOUT, PLAIRE AUX ENFANTS."

The art of crosswriting child and adult has had particular appeal in twentieth-century France. The list of mainstream French authors who have written for a juvenile audience is extensive, varied, and prestigious. It includes the names of some of the country's most prominent poets, playwrights, and novelists, such as Max Jacob, Paul Eluard, Jules Supervielle, Jacques Prévert, Eugène Ionesco, Colette, Antoine de Saint-Exupéry, Georges Duhamel, Marcel Aymé, André Maurois, François Mauriac, Jean Giono, Henri Bosco, Marguerite Yourcenar, Julien Green, Marguerite Duras, Michel Butor, Michel Tournier, Claude Roy, Daniel Pennac, and J. M. G. Le Clézio.[1] This essay focuses particularly on authors who have published the same texts for a dual audience of children and adults. It examines the different ways in which they transcend or transgress the so-called borders between adult and children's fiction in order to address readers of all ages.

As is often the case in other countries as well, many French authors feel that good children's literature also must appeal to adults. Henri Bosco echoed C. S. Lewis's much cited maxim when he wrote, also in the 1950s, that "great children's books are those that touch childhood and adulthood." What Bosco calls a "livre d'enfants" is not a book written exclusively for children. The target age group of his children's books is ten to twelve, but he writes his books with grown-ups in mind, those who have not forgotten that they once were children. Some of Bosco's reflections on what constitutes a children's book actually seem to give greater importance to the adult addressee than to the child. An entry in his diary in 1957 states: "It is rare that good children's books aren't also—and perhaps especially—books for grown-ups."[2] A good children's book is thus paradoxically defined as a book for adults. In 1971, a journalist interviewing Michel Tournier questioned the existence of "children's literature" and suggested that, apart from a very few exceptions—he names only Bosco, but obviously includes Tournier as well—authors who write for young readers are not so much "writers" as "manufacturers of a functional, sterilized, and vaguely educational literature."[3] In the eyes of some authors and critics, children's literature that is not read and enjoyed by adults is not worthy of the name. Much of the problem obviously lies in the controversy over what constitutes children's literature, and many French authors have expressed their dissatisfaction with the connotations often attributed to the term "children's book." Samivel, who also wrote for both children and adults, called Bosco's *Barboche* a "false 'children's book,' " in the common sense of the term that he feels ignores the "true genius" of childhood, in certain respects quite superior to that of adulthood.[4]

Some authors approach the border from the opposite direction, maintaining that good adult literature also can be read by children. Michel Tournier, one of Gallimard's bestselling authors for both children and adults, told a group of students at a French lycée in 1986 that he "never" writes for children, that he would be "ashamed" to do so, and that he "doesn't like books written for children." During a discussion, in 1993, of his fiction marketed for children, Tournier told me insistently that his books do not fall within the category of "children's literature, even when they are read by children." The afterword in one of his books published for children, titled "Écrire pour les enfants," begins with the paradoxical statement: "I don't write children's books."[5] That has not prevented the author from devoting numerous articles to the subject of writing for children. Can an author write for children without writing children's books, as Tournier claims to do?

Another contemporary author, J. M. G. Le Clézio, goes even further than Tournier, declaring that there is no such thing as "children's literature." He claims to write without having a specific audience in mind, but admits that he would like to write "for everyone."[6] The readers that interest him most, however, are preadolescents. Many mainstream authors would like their novels to be accessible to a juvenile audience. Very early in his career, Tournier questions the worth of a book—especially a novel—"if its author cannot communicate its substance to an audience of ten-year-olds." That is why he subjected two of his own novels to what he calls the "crible enfantin," the ultimate test of a children's screening.[7] Over the years, Tournier has increasingly turned to children as the ultimate critics of a literary text, and he now considers any work that does not meet with their approval to be a failure. In an article with the apposite title "Writing for Children is No Child's Play," Tournier claims that Shakespeare, Goethe, and Balzac are all "marred" by an "unforgivable" defect, namely "children cannot read them." Perrault, on the other hand, is one of the authors he most admires; he considers *Le chat botté* "a wonderful masterpiece," ranking it above Racine's tragedies and admitting quite frankly that he would exchange all of Corneille's theatre for that one tale.[8] He claims to judge the value of a book "inversely according to the age of its readers," that is to say "the more a book can be read by young people, the better it is." An author can have no higher goal, in his mind, than to strive to emulate those great "geniuses" of world literature who wrote so well that they could be read "by everyone, *even children!*"[9]

In France, as in many other countries, children's literature is often still regarded as a minor, insignificant genre, a "pseudo-literature" to quote Tournier, who feels that "a children's book is not considered a literary work."[10] Mainstream authors who make a foray into the domain of children's literature do run the risk of being excluded from the canon and irreparably compromising their rank in literary history. The example of Jules Verne still serves as a warning to contemporary novelists who are tempted to address a young public. The rather low status of children's literature no doubt explains, at least in part, why authors such as Tournier and Le Clézio, who have quite successfully published for children, deny vehemently that they write deliberately for that audience, and take care not to allow themselves to be catalogued as "children's authors." Other writers, such as Henri Bosco, who have more willingly embraced the label "children's author," have sometimes been marginalized, even completely excluded from the canon.

The widespread phenomenon of crosswriting child and adult in twentieth-century France can no doubt be traced back to the end of World War II, when a new interest in children and children's literature led major authors of adult fiction to write for young readers, often at the demand of prestigious publishers who had finally begun to take the juvenile market seriously. Antoine de Saint-Exupéry's *Le Petit Prince* was published in France with illustrations by the author in 1946, after first appearing in New York in 1943. A classic dual-audience text, *Le Petit Prince* is the number one bestseller for children in France[11] and an international favorite with readers of all ages. Saint-Exupéry's double dedication "to Léon Werth" and "to Léon Werth when he was a little boy," clearly suggests an implied dual audience. Although the second dedication is supposedly a "correction" of the first, the author leaves both, as well as his apology to young readers for dedicating the book to a "grown-up," his reasons for doing so, and his explanation that "all grown-ups were once children," so that the dedication page reads like a transparent palimpsest.[12] *Le Petit Prince*, like other "children's books" written by mainstream authors in the 1930s and 1940s, for example André Maurois's *Patapoufs et Filifers* (1930) and Jacques Prévert's *Contes pour enfants pas sages* (1947), appeared outside of any regular series, a further indication of their ambivalent status.

The major French publishing house, Gallimard, launched La Bibliothèque blanche series for children in 1953, with the intention of helping children build a library of works of "indisputable literary value" that would parallel their parents'. Convinced that many "renowned" authors often have had the urge to write for young readers, Gallimard deliberately chose not to turn to "specialists of children's literature," but rather to call upon "writers 'for grown-ups,'" "authors of serious books." Targeted at readers between the ages of nine and fifteen, these "children's books" were seen to constitute a transition from picture books to "the 'serious' books" of their parents' library, but the intention was that they would continue to find a place on their bookshelves even when they had grown up.[13] It is therefore not surprising that very little distinguished the books in La Bibliothèque blanche series from the adult novels in the prestigious parent series, the Collection blanche, with which they shared the same format (the typography is slightly larger) and the same familiar cover (with the addition of a slight finish and a small vignette, the book's only illustration). Gallimard offers an excellent example of the fundamental role publishers often play in determining a book's audience. In the case of "crossover" texts, the publishing history is often crucial in understanding how they transcend the sometimes rigid boundaries between children's fiction and adult fiction in order to address all ages.

One of the first authors chosen for Gallimard's La Bibliothèque blanche series was Henri Bosco, who had won the prestigious Prix Théophraste Renaudot in 1945 for his adult novel *Le Mas Théotime* (*The Farm Théotime*). The same year the novelist published his best-known and most translated work, *L'enfant et la rivière* (*The Boy and the River*), which has sold more than three million copies and ranked fourth on Gallimard Jeunesse's 1993 list of children's bestsellers.[14] The original edition of *L'enfant et la rivière* was not published for a young audience, however, and it wasn't until the 1953 Gallimard edition that this "classic" of French children's literature actually became a children's book. The success of the children's edition seems to have directly inspired Bosco to write a sequel. Between 1956 and 1958, he published four novels that, along with *L'enfant et la rivière*, constitute the children's series known as the Pascalet cycle. Three of the sequels, *Le renard dans l'île* (*The Fox in the Island*, 1956), *Barboche* (1957)— later published as *Le chien Barboche* (The dog Barboche)—and *Bargabot* (1958), were undoubtedly written specifically for Gallimard's children's series and have appeared only in children's editions. But the last book in the cycle, *Pascalet*, published together with *Bargabot* in a single volume bearing only the title of the latter, first appeared under the title *La clef des champs* (The key to the fields, 1956) in Algiers, in an edition that was not intended for children. Thus the opening and closing stories of the series both have a dual readership. Unlike *L'enfant et la rivière,* however, that has continued to be reprinted for both children and adults, *La clef des champs* was eliminated from the adult catalogue when it was integrated into the children's series under the new, eponymous title that seemed to bind it inseparably to the Pascalet cycle.

In a similar manner, an earlier 1937 novel, *L'Âne Culotte* (The donkey Culotte), was appropriated for children thanks to the 1956 edition by the Club des Jeunes Amis du Livre. Like *L'enfant et la rivière*, it continues to be reprinted regularly for both children and adults. Its status as a children's book, however, is even more problematic. Whereas the crossover text *L'enfant et la rivière* introduced a cycle in which all the novels were published in children's editions, *L'Âne Culotte* is the first book in a trilogy in which the other two are indisputably adult-only novels. Although adults are unlikely to read the sequels to *L'enfant et la rivière* and may not even know of their existence, they do have access to the entire Pascalet cycle, whereas children cannot read the whole Hyacinthe trilogy and will definitely be unaware of the sequels.

Although Bosco often calls *L'Âne Culotte* his first children's book, there is no proof that he wrote it deliberately for children. A letter written about the time of *L'enfant et la rivière*'s publication classifies the new book as the same "type" as *L'Âne Culotte* and goes on to describe it as "a novel as well, but short and illustrated, [. . .] for children, adolescents, and poets." The first novel in the cycle seems indisputably to have been a deliberate attempt to crosswrite child and adult, but the author also seems to consider *L'Âne Culotte*, at least retrospectively in 1945, as a dual-readership text. Although Bosco insists in later years that *L'Âne Culotte* is a children's book, it is always with the understanding that it will be read by grown-up children as well. In an article published as he was completing the Pascalet cycle, Bosco had this to say about the readership of the earlier *L'Âne Culotte*: "If the tale [. . .] appeals, by a stroke of great luck, to grown-ups, have no fear. It is nonetheless a children's book."[15] It is possible, of course, that *L'Âne Culotte* did not appear as a children's book from the outset simply because the area of children's fiction remained quite undeveloped at Gallimard in the 1930s. The fact that the author began almost immediately to write a sequel that is a very difficult novel even for adults, however, clearly indicates that *L'Âne Culotte* was not written exclusively for young readers. Furthermore, long before the novel was ever published for children, the author seems to encode its dual implied reader into the adult novel, *Un rameau de la nuit* (*The Dark Bough*). The little book that the adult hero carries in his knapsack is *L'Âne Culotte*, and when he introduces the cherished book to a café proprietor and her nephew, we are told it enchanted both Rose and the child. This *mise en abyme* suggests that *L'Âne Culotte* was originally intended for a dual audience of children and adults, in spite of the author's later claims to the contrary. Likewise, in *L'enfant et la rivière*, the reception of Grandpa Savinien's simple tale by the villagers of all ages—from the village elders to the youngest child—can be seen as a *mise en abyme* of the reception of the frame story, destined to delight both children and adults. It was not until after the appearance of the first children's editions of *L'enfant et la rivière* and *L'Âne Culotte* in the 1950s that Bosco began to speak of his "children's books" and his status as a children's author.

     L'Âne Culotte is a unique example of a "border" text because its equal appeal for adult and child readerships seems to have engendered a series for adults (the other volumes of the Hyacinthe trilogy) and a series for children (the Pascalet cycle). Although the true sequels to *L'Âne Culotte* seem to be *Hyacinthe* and *Le jardin d'Hyacinthe*, Bosco tends to include it in the children's cycle and thus to favor the sequels accessible to young readers. An unedited letter he wrote in 1963 mentions the cycle that goes from *L'Âne Culotte* to *Bargabot*, and a footnote in the French edition of *L'enfant et la rivière* refers readers who want to get to know

Hyacinthe better to *L'Âne Culotte*, suggesting that the latter initiates the cycle. English-speaking children, however, will have no knowledge of the earlier novel, as the footnote was omitted from the translation, undoubtedly because *L'Âne Culotte* has never appeared in English.

In 1959, Bosco received the Grand Prix de la Littérature pour les Jeunes for *Barboche*, a novel that, although published only for children, has often been considered the least suitable for a young readership. My conviction that *Barboche* was meant to be a dual-audience text was confirmed in the summer of 1997, when an examination of the manuscript revealed a page titled "Foreword for grown-ups." Although the foreword was eliminated when the book was published, its existence clearly indicates that the author's intended readership included adults. The fact that the manuscript contains three versions of the foreword, including a good, typed copy, suggests that it was the publisher rather than the author who decided to omit it, feeling no doubt that a text addressed specifically to adults had no place in a book that was part of a children's series. The foreword treats the trilogy and the cycle as if they were part of the same series, and an entry in Bosco's journal (1958) states that "a single, more or less coherent cycle" could be created by placing "series II," in other words the Pascalet cycle, immediately after the last novel of the Hyacinthe trilogy. When Bosco set about writing "a sequel (and an ending) to the white Cycle that goes from *L'Âne* to *Bargabot*,"[16] the result was an adult novel, *Mon compagnon de songes* (My dream companion), which did not in fact end the series as Pascalet's story would be continued in another adult novel titled *Tante Martine* (Aunt Martine), the last book published before the author's death in 1976. What makes Bosco's work unique is his persistent and deliberate refusal to limit a cycle of works to a single, or even a uniform, readership; for more than thirty-five years, the author continued the haunting story of Pascalet and Hyacinthe in books published sometimes for children only, sometimes for adults only, and sometimes for a dual readership.

From the 1960s onward, juvenile books such as Bosco's began to appear in editions that were quite different from those for adults. In an attempt to address more closely the needs and tastes of young readers, La Bibliothèque blanche series, for example, took on a new, more modern look in the mid-1960s, with a glossy hardcover and black and white illustrations. The series now targeted a younger readership of eight to twelve years of age. Although Gallimard maintained that its goal was still to offer young readers texts written "by real writers" so that they acquire from the outset a taste for "good literature," the paratextual changes these works had undergone meant that adults were no longer likely to buy them for their own libraries.[17] The scope of this chapter does not allow us to examine the role of the paratext in dual-audience texts, but the example of Bosco's *L'enfant et la rivière* clearly shows that it can be crucial.[18]

Some crossovers have been the result of novelists adapting for a young audience texts originally written for adults. As Le Clézio often designates his adult novels as adventure stories, I asked him whether he had ever contemplated rewriting any of them for children, but he feels that such a project would be impossible for him because the adaptation of a text for young readers would necessarily imply the existence of a separate literature for children, a genre that he denies.[19] It is Michel Tournier's name that most French readers associate with the art of rewriting adult novels for children, although he has only published two such adaptations. A member of the Académie Goncourt, Tournier won the Grand Prix du Roman de l'Académie Française in 1967 for his first novel, *Vendredi ou les limbes du Pacifique* (*Friday*), a retelling of Defoe's *Robinson Crusoe*. Four years later, he rewrote his Robinsonade for children, and the new version, titled *Vendredi ou la vie sauvage*, has become one of the bestselling children's books in France, surpassed only by *Le Petit Prince*. Thus Tournier began his career as a novelist by retelling, first for adults and later for children, a story that already had a long-established tradition of dual readership.[20]

Soon after the publication of his first novel, Tournier felt the need to rewrite it in a more concise, less abstract form, but he was surprised to learn on the completion of *Vendredi ou la vie sauvage* that he had written "a children's book," and furthermore, that no publisher wanted to touch it. When Flammarion finally published it, reluctantly, the book was a dismal failure. At the time, Gallimard, who had published Tournier's acclaimed adult novel, still did not have a children's department and was not in the least interested in the adaptation. When their children's department was founded later in the 1970s, however, *Vendredi ou la vie sauvage* was chosen to be one of the first books published in the new Folio Junior series, in spite of the fact that Flammarion still held the copyright. Tournier finds it highly amusing that a pirate edition of the book Gallimard once flatly turned down has sold millions of copies. The publisher now claims that by the year 2000 the book will no doubt have been read by every living French person![21]

Tournier originally called *Vendredi ou la vie sauvage* "the children's version" of the first *Vendredi* and an article he wrote at the time of its publication was titled "Quand Michel Tournier récrit ses livres pour les enfants" (When Michel Tournier rewrites his books for children). The somewhat ambivalent status of the two *Vendredi*, even in the author's mind, is clearly reflected in the article, which describes a rather complicated process of double crossover:

> [. . .] translating *Les Limbes du Pacifique* into *Vie sauvage*, I had the definite feeling I was taking a path already traveled in the opposite direction. [. . .] in a sense, I was only able to derive a novel for children from an adult novel because the latter had itself in a way been taken from the former in the first place. Aside from the fact, however, that the original novel for children had initially remained unformulated.

Although he felt that it would be worthwhile experimenting with writing the "children's novel" first, he feared that it might prevent the subsequent unfolding of the "adult book." Tournier would eventually reject his earlier view that an adult version might somehow be richer, and aspire to the "simpler" text from the outset, no longer seeing it as a children's book, but as a superior work.[22] The author now maintains that the shorter *Vendredi* is not a children's book, but rather the result of an evolution of his craft toward the superior text that appeals to a dual readership. Almost twenty years after the publication of the first *Vendredi*, the novelist reflects on the changes his art has undergone and states unequivocally:

> The gibberish is finished. This is my true style aimed at twelve-year-old children. And so much the better if it appeals to adults. The first *Vendredi* was a rough draft, the second is the good copy.[23]

His remarks to a class of high school students in 1986 clearly reveal that the author, his own severest critic, judges all of his work by what we could call the dual-audience criterion:

> When I write, one of three things occurs: in the exceptional case, I am brimming over with talent, with genius, [. . .] and I write straightaway a work so good that children can read it. Or, I don't carry it off and I write *Vendredi ou les limbes du Pacifique*, but I have the strength to begin again, and that produces *Vendredi ou la vie sauvage*, which is not at all a version for children but simply a better version. Or I don't pull it off, and the undertaking seems hopeless, beyond saving, and that results in *Le Roi des aulnes*.[24]

Although Tournier sees *Vendredi ou la vie sauvage* as the improved version aimed at readers of all ages, he has not disowned the "inferior" adult novel nor taken any steps to prevent reprintings. On the other hand, the second *Vendredi*, despite the author's claim that it is not a children's book, has not been published in an edition for adults. Tournier insisted, however, on adding some of the new episodes from the "children's version" to the new paperback edition of the adult novel in 1972. In spite of Tournier's claims, adults—publishers, critics, and readers alike—seem almost without exception to prefer *Vendredi ou les limbes du Pacifique* to the condensed, more concrete, less explicitly philosophical version published only for children. Gérard Genette, for example, refuses to consider *Vendredi ou la vie sauvage* as anything but a children's text in the pages he devotes to the novel in *Palimpsests*. It is significant, however, that it is the only "children's book" that the critic deigns to mention in his groundbreaking work on "transtextuality," suggesting perhaps that the second *Vendredi* does indeed transcend boundaries. Genette speaks of the "double 'reception'" that the text engenders, but he is not referring to a dual audience of children and adults, but rather to the reception on two levels by the intrusive adult reader "superimposed" upon the intended child addressee, in what the critic calls "a palimpsest of reading." In Tournier's eyes, however, the adult reader is not the unforeseen and importunate reader portrayed by Genette, but has the same addressee status as the child.[25]

Shortly after unanimously winning the Prix Goncourt for *Le roi des aulnes* (*The Erl-King*) in 1970, Tournier indicated his intention to rewrite the lengthy and difficult novel about Nazi Germany for children. Such a project would seem infeasible, and no doubt undesirable, to most adult readers familiar with the work. Although Tournier himself described such an undertaking as "hopeless" in 1986, he told me several years later that he still felt the novel could be rewritten for nine-year-olds, but admitted that he had no desire to do so because of the somber nature of the subject matter. *Le roi des aulnes* is the novel from which he now feels the most removed; in spite of its award-winning status, it is a second-rate novel in the author's eyes because it cannot be read by a juvenile audience.[26] Tournier even had envisaged a children's adaptation of his most ambitious and complex novel, *Les météores* (*Gemini*). Recognizing his inherent laziness, the author nonetheless denies that this was what kept him from rewriting further novels: "For my part, I would gladly sharpen my pen and recast my other novels [. . .] in purer, less cluttered and more chiselled form; in a word, so that even children could read them." What prevented the novelist from doing so was his conviction that he would never find a children's publisher willing to go out on a limb and take on such "non-

standard" books nor an adult public willing to read these "children's stories."[27] Tournier did adapt a second novel, *Gaspard, Melchior et Balthazar* (*The Four Wise Men*), for young readers under the title *Les Rois
Mages racontés par Michel Tournier* (The Three Wise Men told by
Michel Tournier, 1983). As the adult novel was hitting the bookstores, the
author was already expressing his dissatisfaction with it: "I didn't go far
enough, I didn't have enough talent or genius for the book to be accessible
to ten-year-old children, but that is what one must strive toward."[28] One
critic, no doubt influenced by Genette's comments in *Palimpsests*, compares the reception of Tournier's two rewritings by adult readers and concludes that the more recent adaptation is superior because the adult reader
of the second *Vendredi* has "an awkward sensation of being alternately
adult and child," whereas the second Magi story produces the feeling of
being "simultaneously adult and child."[29] *Les Rois Mages,* nonetheless,
also remains a book published exclusively for children.

Even more remarkable than these ambitious projects of adapting
major adult novels for children are those that Tournier claims to have in
progress involving the rewriting for adults of texts originally addressed
to children, or what he calls "expansions," an undertaking that seems to
be unique in French literature. In 1994, Tournier told me how much he
was enjoying rewriting *La couleuvrine* (The culverin), a short novel or
novella published earlier that year in a children's journal, and in our en-
suing conversations he outlined a few of the developments that would
transform it into an adult novel. In June 1996, however, he admitted that
he hadn't even started writing the second version, and to date the adult
novel has not been published. Has the "expansion" project proven too
difficult even for Tournier? *La couleuvrine* was not the only expansion
the novelist was contemplating at the time. He also mentioned a "religious western" inspired by the story of Moses and later showed me the
manuscript of what was supposed to be the "children's version" that he
would later rewrite for adults.[30] To my surprise, *Éléazar ou la source et le
buisson* (Eleazar, or The spring and the bush) appeared in 1996 for
adults. Apparently Gallimard had decided the religious western was not
appropriate for young readers, although Tournier has since expressed his
hope that it will be appreciated by eleven-year-olds. This incident is an
important reminder that it is not always the author who determines the
readership of his or her texts. It remains to be seen whether *Éléazar ou la
source et le buisson* will ever be published for children.

In a similar vein, Le Clézio admitted to me that what appeals to him
is the idea of rewriting for an adult audience texts he wrote as a child (he

claims to have started writing at the age of seven), but no such work has as yet appeared in print. The author claims to have written approximately one hundred tales of imaginary journeys in the manner of *Voyage au pays des arbres*, but unfortunately they were lost. Perhaps some of these missing tales were, in fact, rewritings of texts Le Clézio had composed as a child; however, as they were written, like *Voyage au pays des arbres*, specifically for young children, they would probably never have been published for an adult readership.

To the best of my knowledge, the only other contemporary French author to have rewritten her fiction for children is Marguerite Yourcenar, the first, and so far only, woman to be elected to the Académie française, in 1980. The one book she addressed to children was a rewriting of a short story titled "Comment Wang-Fô fut sauvé" ("How Wang-Fo Was Saved"), originally published in 1938 in the adult collection *Nouvelles orientales* (*Oriental Tales*). The children's version, with beautiful illustrations by the celebrated illustrator, Georges Lemoine, did not appear until 1979, only a few years before the author's death. It was first published in the Enfantimages series and, more recently, in the Folio Cadet Rouge series for very young children. Whereas Tournier modified the title of the second version of *Vendredi*, Yourcenar retained the title of the adult text for the children's version. Much to my surprise, the Yourcenar specialists at a conference in Mendoza in 1994 admitted that they hadn't realized the two texts differed.[31] *Comment Wang-Fô fut sauvé* is a crossover text that takes a slightly different form for the two readerships.

It wasn't until 1972 that Gallimard officially created a children's department, in recognition of the fact that "the rules of children's literature are totally different from those of general literature."[32] This stance may seem rather contradictory on the part of a publishing house that consistently has published some their most eminent authors in children's editions. Ever since the inception of Folio Junior, well-known mainstream authors have published in the popular paperback series for children, not only texts written specifically for children, but often poetry, short stories, tales, or extracts of novels originally written for adults. In recent years, Gallimard continues to encourage ever younger children to read their most renowned authors. The Folio Cadet series claims to allow very young children "to learn to love reading while learning to read," by offering them texts previously addressed to adults by some of France's most prominent literary figures, including Giono, Le Clézio, Tournier, and Yourcenar.[33]

Numerous authors have acquired a dual audience of adults and children by publishing for young readers stories taken from collections of short fiction for adults. The conciseness of the short story genre lends itself to such a transposition and generally only paratextual changes are made to facilitate the crossover. Following the creation of their children's department in 1978, Gallimard published quite a number of adult short stories by some of their most renowned authors in editions for children. Thus, both Marguerite Yourcenar and Jean Giono have two children's books each to their credit, although, in fact, they addressed only one deliberately to young readers. Like *Comment Wang-Fô fut sauvé*, Yourcenar's *Notre-Dame des Hirondelles* ("Our-Lady-of-the-Swallows," 1982), was taken from the collection *Nouvelles orientales*, but this time it was not rewritten for the new readership. Perhaps this explains why *Notre-Dame des Hirondelles* has not been as successful with a juvenile audience as *Comment Wang-Fô fut sauvé*. Whereas the first appeared only in the Enfantimages series in the early 1980s, the latter was republished in 1990 in the popular new Folio Cadet series for young children. Conversely, Jean Giono's *L'homme qui plantait des arbres* (*The Man Who Planted Trees*, 1983), which was likewise published for children without any modification, has been more popular with young readers than the text he wrote specifically for them, *Le petit garçon qui avait envie d'espace* (The little boy who longed for space, 1949). The success of the former could be due largely to the highly acclaimed animated short children's film adapted from the book in 1987 by Frédéric Back.

Marcel Aymé's *Les contes du chat perché* (*The Animal Farm*, 1939) is another French children's classic by an author who denies having written for children. He claims to have written the first tales merely for his own pleasure, and even after the first volume was published for children, he did not concern himself with the question of addressee. Elsewhere, however, he has identified his readership as children "from four to seventy-five."[34] Some of his adult short stories seem to appeal to an audience almost as broad. A number of them were published in collections for children during Aymé's lifetime and more recently, Gallimard grouped three of them in a volume of their Folio Junior series. The title story, "Les bottes de sept lieues" ("The Seven League Boots"), taken from the adult short story collection *Le passe-muraille* (The man who could pass through walls, 1943), was no doubt chosen to facilitate the crossover, as it links the volume to the world of fairy tales, even though, like Tournier's retelling of *Le Petit Poucet*, it is a *nouvelle* rather than a *conte*. In Aymé's work, there is no division between writing for adults and writing for children. As he puts it, a book that is "deadly boring for middle-aged people is for children as well."[35]

Of the numerous contemporary authors of short fiction who have published for a dual readership of children and adults, Tournier and Le Clézio are among the most prolific. The year that Gallimard launched its children's department, both authors published short story collections for adults, from which a number of texts were later extracted and published for children. Five stories from Tournier's *Le coq de bruyère* (*The Fetishist*) were included, along with two other tales, in the children's collection *Sept contes* (Seven tales). Genre seems to have dictated the selection, as *Le coq de bruyère* was a collection of "contes et récits," but only the "contes" were retained for the children's collection, as its title clearly indicates. Among the adult stories published separately as children's books, however, there is also a "nouvelle," *L'aire du Muguet* (The Lily of the Valley Rest Area). Many readers will be shocked to learn that another "nouvelle," "Tupick," the grim story of a boy who castrates himself, was actually intended to be "a tale for children."[36] The only tale from *Sept contes* that has not also been published individually in at least one children's edition is "La Fin de Robinson" ("The End of Robinson Crusoe"), a somber, cynical third variation on the Crusoe myth, which is apparently Tournier's least successful dual-audience text.

Le Clézio, who achieved instant acclaim by winning the Prix Théophraste Renaudot for his first novel, *Le procès-verbal* (*The Minutes*, 1963), at the age of twenty-three, is an excellent example of a mainstream author who made the crossover to children's literature at the initiative of an enterprising publisher eager to capitalize on its bestselling authors. Pierre Marchand, the director of Gallimard Jeunesse, felt that the author wrote more for young readers than for adults, and suggested that he publish some of his texts in children's editions. Almost all of Le Clézio's titles published for children are taken from either the 1978 short story collection for adults, *Mondo et autres histoires* (Mondo and other stories) or a later collection, *La ronde et autres faits divers* (The round and other trivial events, 1982). With the exception of the rather lengthy *Lullaby*, Le Clézio's stories have all appeared for young readers in pairs, although the title of both stories is indicated on the cover of only one of the books: *Celui qui n'avait jamais vu la mer* (The boy who had never seen the sea, 1982), *Villa Aurore* (1985), and *La grande vie* (The good life) followed by *Peuple du ciel* (Sky people, 1990). *Peuple du ciel* also was published as a beautifully illustrated hardcover book in 1991. Paradoxically, the only text that Le Clézio wrote intentionally for children, *Voyage au pays des arbres* (Voyage to the land of trees, 1978), has not been as well received as his "children's books" that were published first for adults.

Although the phenomenon is much less common, some books make the crossover in the opposite direction, appearing first for children and then for adults. It is highly significant that Tournier's favorite and, in his mind, best work, *Pierrot ou les secrets de la nuit* (Pierrot or The secrets of the night), was initially published for children in 1979. The author claims that he would gladly give up all of his other works for these few pages that he believes will outlast all of them.[37] *Pierrot* gained international acclaim as a children's book when it was awarded the prize for best foreign book at the Leipzig Fair. Ten years later Tournier included the short tale, in which three characters from the *commedia dell'arte* play out the eternal love triangle, in *Le médianoche amoureux* (*The Midnight Love Feast*), a collection of "contes et nouvelles" for adults, in which the first story provides a rather ingenious frame for the others.

Later that year Tournier would publish what could be considered the children's version of *Le médianoche amoureux*, titled *Les contes du médianoche* (Tales of a midnight feast). These works, with their strikingly similar titles and their almost simultaneous publication dates, offer a particularly interesting example of crosswriting child and adult. The parallel titles remind us of Tournier's two *Vendredi*, but, as I have mentioned elsewhere, *Les contes du médianoche* is neither a rewriting for children nor a new and improved version of *Le médianoche amoureux*; nor has the first volume merely undergone paratextual and cosmetic changes to turn it into a children's book.[38] Although a glance at the table of contents of the two books immediately reveals a great deal of overlap, they are far from being identical. The same genre criterion utilized for his first collection of short fiction for children was applied here, that is to say the contes were retained and the nouvelles were eliminated. Whereas Tournier considers the nouvelle inappropriate for children, the conte, due to its "mythic dimension," is, in his eyes, the dual-audience genre par excellence.[39] One tale was nonetheless omitted from the children's version, and it may surprise many readers to learn that it was *Pierrot*, precisely the one that Tournier considers his finest. The author told me that it was not included in *Les contes du médianoche* because it had already appeared in *Sept contes* and he didn't want to include it in two collections. He seems to have had no such scruples with regard to *Amandine ou les deux jardins* ("Amandine, or The Two Gardens") or *La fugue du petit Poucet* ("Tom Thumb Runs Away"), however, which were published in both *Sept contes* and *Le miroir à deux faces* (The mirror with two sides), although the latter did appear with a different publisher.

Le médianoche amoureux and its counterpart for children both contain a tale in which Tournier revisits once again the myth of the Magi. After having developed the legend of the fourth Wise Man in his two previous retellings, the author invents the tale of a fictional fifth Wise Man inspired by Goethe's *Faust*. Although the text itself is identical in both collections, the original title, "Le roi mage Faust" (translated in the English edition as "Faust I, King and Magus") became "Le roi Faust" (King Faust) in the children's book, a simplification that rendered the dual intertext less transparent. Another hypertext that appears in both volumes is "Angus," inspired by a passage from Victor Hugo's famous epic poem *La légende des siècles* (*The Legend of the Centuries*). Written to mark the hundredth anniversary of Hugo's death, *Angus* had previously been published as a children's picture book. It appears unchanged in the two short fiction collections, followed by a long note that reproduces the author's original afterword explaining the text's genesis. By including the note, Tournier invites readers, both young and old, to read or reread Hugo's famous hypotext. But the addition of Hugo's *L'aigle du casque* ("The Eagle on the Helmet") after the note in the children's collection, changes the context of "Angus" and reflects the author's desire to adapt his text to a juvenile readership and to give it curriculum value by facilitating an intertextual reading.

Another widespread phenomenon in crosswriting child and adult are the large, lavish, and relatively expensive illustrated books that seem to target the adults who buy children's books rather than the children who are the official implied addressees. Although illustrations often are the means by which an adult text becomes a children's book, the aesthetic quality of many picture books makes them irresistible to adult readers. The status of these books is particularly ambiguous when the texts were originally published for adults. In 1977, Bosco's *L'enfant et la rivière* was published in Gallimard's children's series, Grands Textes Illustrés, designed to offer lengthy, unabridged novels in a large illustrated format for "the pleasure of lovers of fine books."[40] Either the publisher is acknowledging that children are already bibliophiles, or they are pitching the series to adults who can't resist buying "fine books" for their children. The bold, vivid, and contemporary pictures by Georges Lemoine tend to appeal more to adults than to children. Lemoine plays with the "intratextual" nature of Bosco's works to further intermingle the two readerships: the illustration of the enchanted donkey, Culotte, in the picture book is almost identical to the one on the cover of *L'Âne Culotte* in the popular Folio paperback series for adults.

Even more complex and ambivalent is the status of Tournier's *Le miroir à deux faces*, a large format, stunningly illustrated collection of tales published by Seuil Jeunesse in 1994. It contains *Amandine ou les deux jardins*, Tournier's first text to appear for a dual readership of children and adults, and a tale that shows clearly how easily, almost dizzyingly, his texts cross over from adult literature to children's literature, or the reverse, and back again. *Amandine* originally was published in the women's magazine *Elle* in 1974, then appeared as a children's picture book in 1977, before being included a year later in the adult short story collection *Le coq de bruyère*, and then in the children's collection *Sept contes* in 1984. For English-speaking readers, however, it is a text accessible only to adults.[41]

The destiny of one of the other four tales in *Le miroir à deux faces* began in the same manner, but subsequently followed the reverse itinerary. *La fugue du petit Poucet*, a modern retelling of Perrault's famous tale, initially was published in *Elle* in 1972 under a slightly different title, but then appeared for adults in *Le coq de bruyère*, before coming out a year later as a children's picture book, and more recently in *Sept contes*. Without a doubt, Tournier is a master of the art of recycling fiction for multiple readerships. Few contemporary authors have demonstrated the versatility of the French novelist, who has ingeniously managed to publish the same texts as magazine articles, as children's books (both separately and in one or more regular series), as well as in one or more short story collections for both children and adults. The tale that gave its title to the collection *Le miroir à deux faces* had previously only been published in a journal for adults, and the author told me he was contemplating embedding it in the adult version of *La couleuvrine*, a story first published in a children's journal. The remaining tale, "Ikonut ou L'infini et les Eskimos" (Ikonut, or Infinity and the Eskimos), is the only one previously unpublished, and it remains thus far a text published only for children, if indeed we consider *Le miroir à deux faces* a children's book. Tournier, himself, expressed his doubts when he told me that he felt Alain Gauthier's illustrations, reminiscent of Chagall, Picasso, and other prominent twentieth-century artists, were not at all appropriate for children. A comparison of this sumptuous and sensuous book and the first children's edition of *La fugue du petit Poucet*, illustrated by the same author fifteen years earlier in a much more childlike style, highlights the recent trend toward sophisticated picture books for all ages.

Certain dual-audience texts are the result of commissions that authors have received, sometimes from very strange quarters. Jean Giono, a member of the Académie Goncourt, wrote only one book deliberately for children. It was commissioned by a Swiss chocolate company in 1949 for a series of books whose illustrations took the form of stickers to be found inside chocolate bar wrappers. During a conversation in June 1995, the author's daughter, Sylvie Durbet-Giono, told me she remembers sticking them into their copy as a little girl. *Le petit garçon qui avait envie d'espace* later was published as a picture book by Gallimard, and eventually made its way into the prestigious Pléiade edition of Giono's complete works of fiction. As the Pléiade publishes the complete works of an author, it also includes texts written only for children, but in so doing it extends their readership to adults. Children's authors are not generally among the hallowed ranks of those published in the Pléiade, but crosswriters who have entered the canon as authors for adults bring children's texts in by the back door.

During an interview, Tournier told me that his short story, *L'aire du Muguet*, was the fruit of a strange and rather disconcerting commission he had received from a luxury journal to write a page about an aerial photograph of a highway cutting across a plain in Normandy. He showed me the photograph that had been published in the journal with his text (Tournier himself is a fine photographer). After he had completed the commission, the idea continued to haunt him and he eventually wrote "L'aire du Muguet," which has appeared for both children and adults. Tournier claims that commissions force an author to change tracks; in some cases, this change in direction results in a dual-audience text. Like Giono, Tournier enjoys the challenge of specific commissions, and his most recent children's "novel," *La couleuvrine*, was originally commissioned by *Je bouquine*, to mark the tenth anniversary of the children's journal.[42]

In a few instances, excerpts from adult novels have been repackaged for young readers in a children's edition, sometimes on the publisher's initiative, sometimes on the author's. One of the seven chapters of Tournier's *Gaspard, Melchior et Balthazar* is an oriental tale titled "Barbedor" ("King Goldbeard"), told to Herod and the Magi by an Indian storyteller. Tournier did not include it when he retold the story of the Magi for children in *Les rois mages*, perhaps because it had already been extracted from the adult novel and published separately as a children's book in 1980. *Barbedor* is an interesting example of a text that has been diverted from an adult novel and addressed to an ever younger readership. After appearing in Gallimard's Enfantimages series and in *Sept contes* in the Folio Junior series,[43] it was published in the Folio Cadet series for the very young. As Tournier seeks to efface all borders between different readerships with crossover texts like *Barbedor*, it is somewhat paradoxical that Gallimard publishes them in series for ever more age-specific categories of readers.

On more than one occasion, Tournier has pointed out that *Gaspard, Melchior et Balthazar* is not his only adult novel that includes interpolated stories that could be isolated and published for a young readership. He feels that the two oriental tales embedded in *La goutte d'or* (*The Golden Droplet*), "Barberousse" (Redbeard) and "La reine blonde" (The blond queen) are particularly suited to such a transposition, but also mentions the two tales embedded in the first part of *Le roi des aulnes*.

Another novel published by Gallimard the same year as *Gaspard, Melchior et Balthazar* underwent an identical process of crossover. Le Clézio's *Désert* (Desert), which received the Académie Française's Grand Prix Paul Morand in 1980, also contains an oriental tale, titled *Balaabilou*. At Gallimard's suggestion, it was extracted from the adult novel and "made into a children's book" with exquisite illustrations by Georges Lemoine.[44] It seems that oriental tales embedded in novels lend themselves particularly well to this type of transposition, no doubt due to the popularity of individual tales from *The Arabian Nights*.

For many years, abridged versions of the great classics of world literature accounted for a large number of children's books. Thus *Robinson Crusoe*, *Treasure Island*, *Don Quijote*, *Les trois mousquetaires*, and so forth, were appropriated by children and became dual-audience texts. In the latter half of the twentieth century, editors still use this process to turn adult fiction into children's fiction. Critics have given a great deal of attention lately to what they call the process of "dumbing down."

Although the first children's edition of Bosco's *L'Âne Culotte* was unabridged, successive editions do not contain the final eighty-one pages of the original text, notably the lengthy, enigmatic, and disturbing journal of the magician, Cyprien. As is generally the case when adult texts are abridged for young readers, it was the publisher who was responsible for the shortened version of Bosco's novel. The author's journal contains an entry on 2 March 1967 mentioning the fact that he had received the abridged version of *L'Âne Culotte* in La Bibliothèque blanche series, and although he does not express his opinion explicitly, one senses disapproval, or perhaps resignation, in the terse notation. Bosco no doubt had a predilection for the first children's edition of the novel, in which he had actively participated. The 1956 edition by the Club des Jeunes Amis du Livre was not only "integral," but "augmented" by an unedited preamble and a pen and ink drawing by the author. It had been expanded further by other paratextual elements, namely a lengthy preface by Gabriel d'Aubarède and original photographs of Provence by Paul Bertrand, all of which probably appealed more to adults than to children.

Michel Tournier's adaptation of *Gaspard, Melchior et Balthazar* is a rare example of an abridgement done by the author himself on his own initiative. Whereas his adaptation of *Vendredi ou les limbes du Pacifique* was a complete rewriting, in which the author claims not to have retained a single line, the children's version of the story of the Magi involved more elimination than rewriting, as four of the original seven chapters were omitted in *Les Rois Mages*. Tournier admits that he is very dissatisfied with the second retelling of the story of the Magi and compares it unfavorably with the second *Vendredi*. The huge success of the first children's novel and the relatively limited success of the second confirm the author's own assessment, and clearly show, quite unsurprisingly, that a complete rewriting by the author is highly superior to the simple process of elimination, even when it is the author who wields the scissors.

Children have long laid claim to adult novels, and not just abridged versions. Some novels have been so completely appropriated by a juvenile audience that they actually disappear from adult catalogues. Many authors who crosswrite child and adult insist on the fact that their own writing is profoundly influenced by the books they read as children, books that were often not written specifically for a juvenile audience. Both Tournier and Le Clézio stress the fact that children's literature was virtually inexistent when they were young. Reminiscing about the books he read as a child, Le Clézio recalls that they weren't "children's literature," but were "largely read by children," books like Jack London's *The Call of the Wild*. He claims that, at the age of ten, he borrowed from his grandfather's library "the major part of adult literature [. . .] from Robinson Crusoe to Stevenson."[45]

When Tournier published *La goutte d'or* in 1986, his aspiration was that twelve-year-olds would be able to read it. He traces the evolution of his craft toward purification and simplicity in the following terms: "At the outset of my work, I had Thomas Mann for ideal, today it is Kipling and London." The author believes he achieved his goal; he told me in 1993 that there was no need to consider rewriting *La goutte d'or,* because it is already accessible to twelve-year-old children. Speaking with a group of high-school students, he lowers the age bracket even further, claiming the novel is "so good" it can be read "from ten-years-old onwards." "*Fabricando*, I learned to write," he declares rather flippantly.[46]

Three years earlier, Tournier's previous pattern of lengthy novels had been broken by the novella *Gilles et Jeanne* (1983), considered by some to be the long-promised children's version of *Le roi des aulnes*. During our discussion of dual-audience texts in 1994, Tournier mentioned *Gilles et Jeanne*, which has never been published for children, but whose clear and concise style could easily be understood by a juvenile audience. Tournier admitted refusing categorically to send the macabre novella to his nine-year-old nephew, under the pretext that it wasn't suitable reading material for a child his age, but this led the author subsequently to reflect seriously on whether or not the cruel story about Gilles de Rais' victims, which was after all a story about children, could in fact be read by a juvenile audience. Although he felt that it was accessible to young readers, he hadn't been able to bring himself to send a copy to a child.

When *Éléazar ou la source et le buisson* came out, one journalist described it as "a tale to read with the family." She reported that the only verdict that was of interest to the seventy-one-year-old Tournier was "that of children from six to twelve years old." The author had stated his intention of judging *Éléazar* according to its reception by the eleven-year-old girl to whom it is dedicated: "If it falls from her hands, I will consider it a failure."[47] Tournier's adult novels that predate *La goutte d'or* seem to constitute a preliminary stage in his quest for the ultimate text that appeals to all ages. However, neither *La goutte d'or* nor *Éléazar* has actually been published for a juvenile readership.

Many adult novels by authors who have written at least one children's book could probably be edited for a juvenile audience, as many mainstream authors who have crossed over even briefly seek to simultaneously address a dual audience in their subsequent works. One novel that comes to mind is Le Clézio's *Le chercheur d'or* (*The Prospector*). When the novelist attended the International Festival of Authors at Harbourfront Centre in Toronto in 1993 to promote the English translation of his novel, he told me that it could no doubt be read by a juvenile audience, but reminded me that he makes no distinction between children's and adult literature. Whereas he would like to appeal to all readers, Le Clézio is particularly interested in readers aged ten to twelve, who should be addressed, he feels, in the same manner as adults. He insists that writers must never lose sight of the fact that they are always also addressing "children on the threshold of adolescence," whom he considers to be the only "true readers."[48]

One is struck by a similar evolution in the adult novels of authors like Le Clézio and Tournier, who seem to be moving toward a simpler, more elemental narrative that appeals to young readers. That is one of the reasons why novels published for adults in one country sometimes appear for a juvenile audience in another. In the eyes of a Tournier or a Le Clézio, novels like *Treasure Island* and *Robinson Crusoe*, that is to say, novels that were not aimed at young readers but were appropriated by them, represent the ideal toward which novelists should strive. Le Clézio's childhood ambition to write an adventure story in that vein still haunts him. *Pawana*, a whaling story reminiscent of Melville's *Moby Dick*, no doubt came closer to that goal than *Le chercheur d'or*, because it was published in a series for children nine years and older within three years of its publication for adults in 1992. Furthermore, *Pawana* has been far more successful in the children's edition illustrated by Georges Lemoine than as a text for adults. Like Tournier's *Gilles et Jeanne* and *Éléazar*, *Pawana* is much shorter than Le Clézio's other novels, comprising only fifty-five pages in the adult edition. It is certainly much shorter than the novels that Le Clézio liked to read as a child, but the author recognizes that today's children are no longer used to reading lengthy novels.

Often the audience that crosswriters seek first and foremost to please is that of young readers. In his journal, Bosco confesses his desire to be "liked by all, but especially by young boys and girls."[49] Tournier's motto as a writer is: "Above all, please children." He feels that an author only can write texts accessible to a dual readership of children and adults when he or she is truly inspired: "Sometimes I apply myself so well and have so much talent that what I write can also be read by children. When my pen is less lucky, what it writes is only good enough for adults." Tournier continually reminds us that his models are the great masterpieces of world literature that are so well written that they can be read by children as well, in particular Perrault's *Le chat botté*, Andersen's *The Snow Queen*, Selma Lagerlöf's *The Wonderful Adventures of Nils*, Kipling's *Just So Stories*, and Saint-Exupéry's *Le Petit Prince*. Tournier points out that these works are "generally said to be 'for children,'" which he claims is "to pay a very great tribute to children." It concurs with his view that "a work can be addressed to a young public only if it is perfect" and that "every shortcoming lowers it to the level of adults alone."[50]

The importance given to the child addressee by these authors does not mean that they completely ignore the adult addressee. For Tournier, the proof of a novel's success is the reponse that it is able to elicit "from two readers at opposite poles of sophistication: a child at one end of the scale, a metaphysician at the other." Many crossover texts could be described in the terms Tournier uses to depict myth, that is to say "a multi-storied structure" with "a children's tale" as its "ground floor" and "a metaphysical summit." In this light, Tournier's *Pierrot ou les secrets de la nuit*, "an onthological treatise that has all the appearance of a children's tale," is an exceptionally fine example of crosswriting child and adult.[51] Dual-audience texts often have the veiled, deceptive simplicity of myth and parable that conceals multiple levels of meaning for readers of all ages.

In the works of many mainstream twentieth-century French authors, the border between adult and children's fiction seems to disappear entirely. Although the collapse of these boundaries seems to be very widespread in the contemporary literature of numerous countries, as this volume clearly illustrates, the phenomenon seems to be particularly pronounced in France. Although numerous authors have only one or two dual-audience texts to their name, many others continued, after their first successful crossover, to publish for both children and adults. Some of these authors are among the world's great masters of the art of crosswriting child and adult. They are satisfied only when a text appeals to both audiences, regardless for which one it happens to be marketed. Whether it be a commission, a whim, happenstance, or even a good business mind that provokes the initial crossover, an author who has successfully addressed a dual audience is often not content to return to writing for a single readership.

NOTES

1. Although many of their works have become children's classics in France, surprisingly few are familiar to a non-French-speaking audience. Most have never been translated into English, but even those that have rarely reach a wide readership. The notable exception is Saint-Exupéry's *Le Petit Prince* (*The Little Prince*).

The first time a French title is cited, an English translation will follow in parentheses. If an English translation exists, the English title will be given in italics for a book and in roman type with quotation marks for texts published in journals or elsewhere; otherwise, the translation of the title is mine and will appear in roman type only. Translations of texts in French are mine unless otherwise indicated.

I have devoted an entire book to the works that five major French novelists have published for children; see *De grands romanciers écrivent pour les enfants* (Montréal: PUM; Grenoble: ELLUG, 1997). For a more detailed study of the children's books of Tournier and Le Clézio, see my article "Crossing the Borders: The 'Children's Books' of Michel Tournier and Jean-Marie Gustave Le

Clézio," *The Lion and the Unicorn* 22.1 (January 1998): 44–69. An article I published in Lithuanian offers a brief introduction to several of the authors dealt with
in this essay; see "Adresato dvejinimas dabartineje prancuzi literaturoje" (Contemporary French children's books), *Rubinaitis* (Vilnius) 2, no. 7 (1997): 13–18.

    2. Henri Bosco, "Les enfants m'ont dicté les livres que j'ai écrits pour eux,"
Les Nouvelles littéraires 4 December 1958: 4; Henri Bosco, *Diaire*, between July
and October 1957, unpublished. Bosco's journal, manuscripts, and other writings
are kept at the Fonds de documentation Henri Bosco at the Université de Nice. I
wish to express my sincere thanks to Claude Girault, who generously permitted
me to quote these documents.

    3. Jean-François Josselin, "Les enfants dans la bibliothèque," *Le Nouvel
Observateur* 6 December 1971: 56.

    4. Samivel, "*L'Âne Culotte* et l'univers onirique d'Henri Bosco," *Les
Cahiers de l'Amitié Henri Bosco* 11 (April–October 1976): 77.

    5. Michel Tournier, "Michel Tournier face aux lycéens," *Le Magazine littéraire*
226 (January 1986): 21; Sandra L. Beckett, *De grands romanciers écrivent pour les
enfants* (Montréal: PUM; Grenoble: ELLUG, 1997), 265; Michel Tournier, "Écrire
pour les enfants," in *Pierrot ou les secrets de la nuit* (Paris: Gallimard, 1979), n.p.

    6. Beckett, *Romanciers*, 296. He did qualify that assertion somewhat, however,
when he told me that he believes "that one doesn't write deliberately for young people, except when one writes tales that are intended for tiny tots" (293). Pierre Lhoste,
Conversations avec J.M.G. Le Clézio (Paris: Mercure de France, 1971), 30.

    7. Michel Tournier, "Quand Michel Tournier récrit ses livres pour les en-
fants," *Le Monde* 24 December 1971: 7.

    8. Michel Tournier, "Writing for Children is No Child's Play," *UNESCO
Courier* (June 1982): 34; Beckett, *Romanciers*, 266; Serge Koster, *Michel
Tournier* (Paris: Henri Veyrier, 1986), 158.

    9. Beckett, *Romanciers*, 266; Tournier, "Writing for Children is No Child's
Play," 34.

    10. Tournier, "Lycéens," 21; Josselin, "Enfants," 55.

    11. *Histoire du livre de jeunesse d'hier à aujourd'hui, en France et dans le
monde* (Paris: Gallimard Jeunesse, 1993), 73.

    12. Antoine de Saint-Exupéry, *The Little Prince* (San Diego: Harcourt
Brace Jovanovich, 1971): 5.

    13. "Bibliothèque blanche," *Bulletin de la NRF* 75 (November 1953): 16;
Jacques Lemarchand, "Livres pour enfants," *Bulletin de la NRF* 144 (December
1950): 13b–14a.

    14. *Histoire*, 73. For a more detailed study of the novel, see my article
"Crosswriting Child and Adult: Henri Bosco's *L'enfant et la rivière*," *Children's
Literature Association Quarterly* 21, no. 4 (Winter 1996–97): 189–198.

15. Bosco, Letter to Armand Guibert, 11 July 1945; Bosco, "Enfants," 4.

16. Henri Bosco, Letter to Henri Ehret, 27 July 1963, in "Henri Bosco voyageur. Le séjour en Grèce (juin–juillet 1963)," critical edition by Claude Girault, *Cahiers Henri Bosco* 21 (1981): 28–29.

17. "Bibliothèque," [1966].

18. See Beckett, "Crosswriting," 192–196.

19. Beckett, *Romanciers*, 296.

20. Although the scope of this essay does not allow us to examine the role of intertextuality in dual-audience texts, I have suggested elsewhere that in the case of Tournier, whose craft is based on a bricolage of Western culture's myths, legends, and tales, intertextual play explains to a great extent his success at crosswriting child and adult. See "From the Art of Rewriting to the Art of Crosswriting Child and Adult: the Secret of Michel Tournier's Dual Readership," in *Voices from Far Away: Current Trends in International Children's Literature Research* 24, ed. Maria Nikolajeva (Stockholm: Centrum för barnkulturforskning, 1995), 9–34.

21. *Histoire*, 88.

22. Michel Tournier, "Quand Michel Tournier récrit ses livres pour les enfants," *Le Monde* 24 December 1971: 7.

23. Jérôme Garcin, "Interview avec Michel Tournier," *L'Événement du jeudi* 9–15 January 1986. Tournier nonetheless told me in 1993 that he felt the failure of the novel's English translation partly was due to the fact that it was not published by a children's publisher in the United States, and therefore constituted more of "an intellectual curiosity than a true children's book" (*Romanciers*, 265–266).

24. Tournier, "Lycéens," 21.

25. Gérard Genette, *Palimpsests: Literature in the Second Degree* (Lincoln: The University of Nebraska Press, 1997), 374. For a more detailed analysis of Genette's interpretation of *Vendredi*, see Beckett, "Art," 15.

26. Tournier, "Lycéens," 21; Beckett, *Romanciers*, 267–268.

27. Tournier, "Writing," 34.

28. Gilles Lapouge, "Michel Tournier s'explique," *Lire* 64 (December 1980): 45.

29. Michael Worton, "Michel Tournier and the Masterful Art of Rewriting," *PN Review* 11, no. 3 (1984): 25.

30. Sandra L. Beckett, "Entretien avec Michel Tournier." *Dalhousie French Studies* 35 (Summer 1996): 67; unpublished interview with Michel Tournier, 7 July 1995.

31. The paper I gave at the conference "Réécriture et les *Nouvelles orientales*" was published under the title "La Réécriture pour enfants de *Comment Wang-Fô fut*

sauvé" in the proceedings, *Lectures transversales de Marguerite Yourcenar*, ed. Rémy Poignault and Blanca Arancibia (Tours: Société Internationale d'Études Yourcenariennes, 1997), 173–185. A lengthier, revised version of the paper was published in *De grands romanciers écrivent pour les enfants* (169–193).

32. *Histoire*, 69.

33. *Catalogue lectures cadet* (Paris: Gallimard Jeunesse, n.d.), 2. Poems by poets who in some cases have never published children's poetry have appeared for a juvenile audience, notably in Gallimard's Folio Cadet series. Jacques Prévert seems to be a particular favorite of publisher and reader alike. Prévert's *Contes pour enfants pas sages* (Tales for naughty children), published for young readers in 1947, is a children's classic in France. *Paroles* (*Words for All Seasons*), Prévert's highly acclaimed first collection of poetry for adults, has always been popular with a juvenile audience. In more recent years, however, several of his poems have been published in Gallimard's Folio Benjamin series for tiny tots, for example, *En sortant de l'école* (Getting out of school), *Page d'écriture* (Page of writing), *Chanson pour chanter à tue-tête et à cloche-pied* ("Song for Singing at the Top of Your Lungs and from the Bottom of Your Heart"), and *Le gardien du phare aime trop les oiseaux* (The lighthouse keeper loves birds too much).

34. Quoted in Jacques Demougin, ed., *Dictionnaire de la littérature française et francophone*, vol. 2 (Paris: Larousse, 1987), 100.

35. D'Aubarède, "Écrire," 4; Jacques Demougin, ed., *Dictionnaire de la littérature française et francophone*, vol. 1 (Paris: Larousse, 1987), 100; quoted in François Caradec, *Histoire de la littérature enfantine en France* (Paris: Albin Michel, 1977), 219.

36. Joseph H. McMahon, "Michel Tournier's Texts for Children," *Children's Literature* 13 (1985): 168.

37. Tournier, "Writing," 34.

38. See Beckett, "Crossing," 56.

39. A chapter of Tournier's autobiography *Le vent Paraclet*, "La dimension mythologique" ("The Mythic Dimension"), is devoted to this essential element of his writing.

40. *Histoire*, 70.

41. For a more detailed study of *Amandine*, see my article, "Amandine through the Looking Glass: Michel Tournier's 'Initiatory Tale' for Children," *Bookbird* 35, no. 2 (Summer 1997): 12–15

42. Beckett, "Entretien," 68.

43. A footnote was added to later reprintings of *Les Rois Mages* to refer readers to the new book in which they could read the tale that is only mentioned in the novel.

44. Beckett, *Romanciers*, 295.

45. Ibid., 290, 298.

46. Garcin, "Interview"; Beckett, *Romanciers*, 267; Tournier, "Lycéens," 21.

47. Marianne Payot, "Entretien: Michel Tournier," *Lire* (October 1996): 32.

48. Beckett, *Romanciers*, 293, 299. Censorship can be a major obstacle for authors who wish to address their texts to a dual audience, especially in the case of texts originally published for adults. The limited success of Yourcenar's *Notre-Dame des Hirondelles* as a children's book may be due in part to the illustrations of the nude nymphs that tease the old monk. Elsewhere I have examined briefly this very important question of the censorship of dual-audience texts (see "Crossing," 62–64). It is undoubtedly Tournier who has denounced most bitterly the censorship of conservative adults—parents, editors, librarians, and educators—that he feels prevents many of his texts from reaching a wide juvenile readership. He insists that his books are censored because he introduces subjects considered taboo in children's literature, namely money, politics, cruelty, and sex. With regard to the latter, he has provocatively suggested that "children's books should be eroticised, perhaps even in a more intense manner than adult books" (Josselin, "Enfants," 75).

49. Bosco, *Diaire*, between July 1962 and October 1963.

50. Tournier, "Plaire"; Tournier, "Comment," 19.

51. Michel Tournier, *The Wind Spirit: An Autobiography* (Boston: Beacon Press, 1988), 29, 156; Koster, *Tournier*,150.

REFERENCES

Aubarède, Gabriel d'. "Écrire pour les enfants." *Les Nouvelles littéraires* 22 March 1956: 4.

Aymé, Marcel. *Les contes du chat perché*. Paris: Gallimard, 1939.

———. *Les bottes de sept lieues et autres nouvelles*. Folio Junior. Paris: Gallimard, 1988.

Beckett, Sandra. Unpublished interview with Michel Tournier, 7 July 1995.

———. "From the Art of Rewriting to the Art of Crosswriting Child and Adult: the Secret of Michel Tournier's Dual Readership." In *Voices from Far Away: Current Trends in International Children's Literature Research* 24, ed. Maria Nikolajeva, 9–34. Stockholm: Centrum för barnkulturforskning, 1995.

———. "Entretien avec Michel Tournier." *Dalhousie French Studies* 35 (Summer 1996): 66–78.

———. "The Meeting of Two Worlds: Michel Tournier's *Friday and Robinson: Life on Speranza Island*." In vol. 2 of *Other Worlds, Other Lives: Children's Literature Experiences*, ed. Myrna Machet, Sandra Olën, and Thomas van der Walt, 110–127. Pretoria: Unisa Press, 1996.

————. "Crosswriting Child and Adult: Henri Bosco's *L'Enfant et la rivière*." *Children's Literature Association Quarterly* 21, no. 4 (Winter 1996–97): 189–198.

————. *De grands romanciers écrivent pour les enfants*. Montréal: PUM; Grenoble: ELLUG, 1997.

————, ed. *Reflections of Change: Children's Literature Since 1945*. Westport, Conn.: Greenwood, 1997.

————. "Adresato dvejinimas dabartineje prancuzi literaturoje" (Contemporary French children's books). *Rubinaitis* (Vilnius) 2, no. 7 (1997): 13–18.

————. "Amandine through the Looking Glass: Michel Tournier's 'Initiatory Tale' for Children," *Bookbird* 35, no. 2 (Summer 1997): 12–15

————. "La Réécriture pour enfants de *Comment Wang-Fô fut sauvé*." In *Lectures transversales de Marguerite Yourcenar*, ed. Rémy Poignault and Blanca Arancibia, 173–185. Tours: Société Internationale d'Études Yourcenariennes, 1997.

————. "Crossing the Borders: The 'Children's Books' of Michel Tournier and Jean-Marie Gustave Le Clézio." *The Lion and the Unicorn* 22, no. 1 (January 1998): 44–69.

"Bibliothèque blanche." *Bulletin de la NRF* 75 (November 1953): 16.

"La Bibliothèque blanche." *Bulletin de la NRF* [1966].

Bosco, Henri. *L'Âne Culotte*. Paris: Gallimard, 1937.

————. *L'Âne Culotte*. Paris: Club des Jeunes Amis du Livre, 1956.

————. *L'Âne Culotte*. Folio Junior. Paris: Gallimard, 1983.

————. *L'enfant et la rivière*. Illus. E. Jalabert-Edon. Algiers and Paris: Charlot, 1945.

————. Letter to Armand Guibert, 11 July 1945.

————. *The Boy and the River*. Trans. Gerard Hopkins. New York: Pantheon Books, 1956.

————. *The Fox in the Island*. 1956. Trans. Gerard Hopkins. London: Oxford University Press, 1958.

————. "Les enfants m'ont dicté les livres que j'ai écrits pour eux." *Les Nouvelles littéraires* 4 December 1958: 4.

————. *Bargabot* [followed by] *Pascalet*. Paris: Gallimard, 1958.

————. *Barboche*. 1957. London: Oxford University Press, 1959.

————. Letter to Henri Ehret, 27 July 1963, in "Henri Bosco voyageur. Le séjour en Grèce (juin–juillet 1963)." Critical edition by Claude Girault, *Cahiers Henri Bosco* 21 (1981): 28–29.

Caradec, François. *Histoire de la littérature enfantine en France*. Paris: Albin Michel, 1977.

Catalogue lectures cadet. Paris: Gallimard Jeunesse, n.d.

Demougin, Jacques, ed. *Dictionnaire de la littérature française et francophone*. Vol. 1. Paris: Larousse, 1987.

Garcin, Jérôme. "Interview avec Michel Tournier." *L'Événement du jeudi* 9–15 January 1986.

Genette, Gérard. *Palimpsests: Literature in the Second Degree.* Trans. Channa Newman and Claude Doubinsky. Lincoln: The University of Nebraska Press, 1997.

Giono, Jean. *Le petit garçon qui avait envie d'espace.* In *Les jolis contes N.P.C.K.* Vol. 6. Vevey (Switzerland): Société des Produits Nestlé S.A., 1949.

———. *Le petit garçon qui avait envie d'espace.* Illus. Gilbert Raffin. Enfantimages. Paris: Gallimard, 1978.

———. *L'Homme qui plantait des arbres.* Paris: Gallimard, 1983.

Histoire du livre de jeunesse d'hier à aujourd'hui, en France et dans le monde. Paris: Gallimard Jeunesse, 1993.

Josselin, Jean-François. "Les enfants dans la bibliothèque" [Interview with Michel Tournier]. *Le Nouvel Observateur* 6 December 1971: 56–57.

Koster, Serge. *Michel Tournier.* Paris: Henri Veyrier, 1986.

Lapouge, Gilles. "Michel Tournier s'explique." *Lire* 64 (December 1980): 28–46.

Lemarchand, Jacques. "Livres pour enfants." *Bulletin de la NRF* 144 (December 1950): 13b-14a .

Le Clézio, J. M. G. *Le Procès-verbal.* Paris: Gallimard, 1963.

———. *Mondo et autres histoires.* Paris: Gallimard, 1978.

———. *Désert.* Paris: Gallimard, 1980.

———. *Lullaby.* Folio Junior. Paris: Gallimard, 1980.

———. *Balaabilou.* Paris: Gallimard, 1985.

———. *Celui qui n'avait jamais vu la mer.* Folio Junior. Paris: Gallimard, 1988.

———. *La grande vie* [followed by] *Peuple du ciel.* Folio Junior. Paris: Gallimard, 1990.

———. *Villa Aurore.* Folio Junior. Paris: Gallimard, 1990.

———. *Voyage au pays des arbres.* Folio Cadet Rouge. Paris: Gallimard, 1990.

———. *Peuple du ciel.* Paris: Gallimard, 1991.

———. *Pawana.* Paris: Gallimard, 1992.

———. *Pawana.* Lecture Junior. Paris: Gallimard, 1995.

Lhoste, Pierre. *Conversations avec J.M.G. Le Clézio.* Paris: Mercure de France, 1971.

Magnan, Jean-Marie. "Écrire pour les enfants" [Interview with Michel Tournier]. *La Quinzaine littéraire* 16–31 December 1971: 11–13.

McMahon, Joseph H. "Michel Tournier's Texts for Children." *Children's Literature* 13 (1985): 154–168.

Payot, Marianne. "Entretien: Michel Tournier." *Lire* (October 1996): 32–40.

Petit, Susan. "An Interview with Michel Tournier: 'I Write Because I Have Something to Say.'" In *Michel Tournier's Metaphysical Fictions*, 173–193. Amsterdam and Philadelphia: John Benjamins Publishing Co., 1991.

Prévert, Jacques. *Contes pour enfants pas sages*. Paris: Gallimard, 1977.

———. *Words for All Seasons*. Trans. Teo Savory. Greensboro, N.C.: Unicorn Press, 1980.

Saint-Exupéry, Antoine de. *The Little Prince*. San Diego: Harcourt Brace Jovanovich, 1971.

Tournier, Michel. *Vendredi ou les limbes du Pacifique*. Paris: Gallimard, 1967.

———. *Friday*. Trans. Norman Denny. Garden City, N. Y.: Doubleday, 1969.

———. *Friday and Robinson: Life on Speranza Island*. Trans. Ralph Manheim. New York: Alfred A. Knopf, 1971.

———. "Quand Michel Tournier récrit ses livres pour les enfants." *Le Monde* 24 décembre 1971: 7.

———. *Vendredi ou la vie sauvage*. Paris: Gallimard, 1977.

———. *Le vent Paraclet*. Paris, Gallimard: 1977.

———. *Le coq de bruyère*. Paris: Gallimard, 1978.

———. *La fugue du Petit Poucet*. Paris: Éditions G. P., 1979.

———. "Michel Tournier: comment écrire pour les enfants." *Le Monde* 24 December 1979: 19.

———. "Écrire pour les enfants." In *Pierrot ou les secrets de la nuit*. Enfantimages. Paris: Gallimard, 1979.

———. *Gaspard, Melchior et Balthazar*. Paris: Gallimard, 1980.

———. *Barbedor*. Enfantimages. Paris: Gallimard, 1980.

———. "Michel Tournier: avant tout, plaire aux enfants." In *Barbedor*. Enfantimages. Paris: Gallimard, 1980.

———. "Writing for Children is No Child's Play." *UNESCO Courier* (June 1982): 33–34.

———. *Les Rois Mages*. Folio Junior. Paris: Gallimard, 1983.

———. *Sept contes*. Folio Junior. Paris: Gallimard, 1984.

———. "Pierrot, or The Secrets of the Night." Trans. Margaret Higonnet. *Children's Literature* 13 (1985): 169–172.

———. "Michel Tournier face aux lycéens." *Le Magazine littéraire* 226 (January 1986): 20–25.

———. *The Golden Droplet*. Trans. Barbara Wright. New York: Doubleday, 1987.

———. *Angus*. Paris: Signe de Piste Éditions, 1988.

———. *The Wind Spirit: An Autobiography*. Trans. Arthur Goldhammer. Boston: Beacon Press, 1988.

———. *Les contes du médianoche*. Folio Junior. Paris: Gallimard, 1989.

———. *The Midnight Love Feast*. Trans. Barbara Wright. 1989. London: Collins, 1991.

———. *La couleuvrine*. Lecture Junior. Paris: Gallimard, 1994.

————. *Le miroir à deux faces*. Paris: Seuil Jeunesse, 1994.

————. *Éléazar ou la source et le buisson*. Paris: Gallimard, 1996.

Yourcenar, Marguerite. *Notre-Dame des Hirondelles*. Illus. Georges Lemoine. Enfantimages. Paris: Gallimard, 1963.

————. *Comment Wang-Fô fut sauvé*. Illus. Georges Lemoine. Folio Cadet Rouge. Paris: Gallimard, 1990.

Worton, Michael. "Michel Tournier and the Masterful Art of Rewriting." *PN Review* 11, no.3 (1984): 24–25.

CHAPTER 4

Children's, Adult, Human . . . ?

MARIA NIKOLAJEVA

This chapter will examine three novels that address an ambivalent audience. *Skriket fra jungelen* (A cry from the jungle, 1989),[1] by Norwegian Andersen Medal winner Tormod Haugen, was published and marketed as a children's novel, although many critics have expressed doubts about its address. *Northern Lights* (1995), by British author Philip Pullman, winner of the 1996 Carnegie Medal and a number of other distinguished British children's book awards, has been marketed in the United States and Sweden as a novel for adults.[2] Finally, the international bestseller *Frøken Smillas fornemmelse for sne* (*Miss Smilla's Feeling for Snow*, 1992), by the Danish author Peter Høeg, has only been marketed for adults, but also can be enjoyed by young readers. The three novels have as a common theme adults' abuse of children for dubious scientific purposes. Traditionally, this theme would be considered as "not suitable" for a young audience. Recent children's and young adult fiction seems, however, to question all the earlier thematic taboos, often reflecting on extreme violence. The difference between the novels—either their intrinsic qualities or their social function—therefore is not determined in the first instance by the theme itself, but rather by the way the theme is treated. My analysis therefore will begin with the questions of address and genre, and then focus on the narrative aspects of the novels: plot, setting, character, perspective, and temporality.

ADDRESS

There are certain prejudices about young readers and their comprehension of particular narrative structures governing the marketing of books that otherwise target both child and adult audiences. Contemporary children's literature often questions the artificial boundaries created by these prejudices, showing a considerable sophistication in narrative structure. To begin with, a children's novel is supposed to have a clear and unambivalent address, that is, can be easily identified as a children's book. Children's novels usually are shorter than adult novels, they have larger print, they often are illustrated, and they have a specific cover layout that is supposed to be attractive for young readers. Children's book titles traditionally are either nominative (that is, having the protagonist's name in it) or narrative (emphasizing the main event or conflict of the plot).[3] Children's novels also may be recognized by the fact that they are brought out by a publishing house specializing in children's literature.

In the case of the three novels discussed here, none of these superficial criteria is applicable. They are about the same length (between four hundred and five hundred pages) and have similar, rather small print; they have no illustrations, and although the covers of some editions of Haugen and Pullman may suggest a child addressee, most of them have symbolic connotations that can address an adult or a sophisticated child equally. The titles of the novels are not traditional children's titles either. Instead they are all slightly enigmatic, focusing on the central image of the novel (jungle, "dust," snow) rather than on the protagonist or the events.

These superficial features of the three novels, however, probably are less interesting than the more profound characteristics of their implied audience. Traditional children's fiction makes use of either single or double address (in the sense that Barbara Wall attributes to these terms[4]), that is, either pretends to be addressing the child audience and ignoring the adult coreader, or addresses the adult at the child's expense. Haugen's novel, featuring both child and adult characters in equally central roles, allows identification for readers of all ages. It would match Barbara Wall's definition of dual address, in which child and adult are addressed on different levels, but on equal terms. In plain words, it means that a child and an adult reader will probably read and understand the novel differently, but enjoy it equally; that neither the child nor the adult has priority to a "correct" interpretation. The same is true for *Northern Lights*. Most young readers probably will read the novel as a fantastic adventure, recognizing patterns and characters from Tolkien, C. S. Lewis, or other predecessors. Adult readers will read it as an allegory, perhaps with Milton's *Paradise Lost* as an intertext. *Miss Smilla* has an adult protagonist, but the same is true not only for most formula stories, but also for most fairy tales that, for various reasons, been accepted as part of children's reading.

GENRE

Another common characteristic of children's fiction is clear-cut generic features. In most studies of children's fiction we meet chapters or sections devoted to family stories, school stories, animal stories, fantasy, detective stories, adventure stories, and so forth. No mixing of genres is acknowledged in children's novels, mainly for pedagogical purposes: supposedly, children wish to know from the start what kind of story they are dealing with. In contemporary adult fiction, genre eclecticism, most notably the blending of "high" and "low" genres, has become one of the most prominent features, and *Miss Smilla* is an excellent illustration of this phenomenon. Superficially, it is a crime novel or thriller, which at the end also appears to have distinct traits of science fiction. These popular genres often are assumed to be suitable for young readers, especially as children's fiction, too, is sometimes treated as formula literature. *Miss Smilla,* however, lacks the essential components of the traditional crime or adventure novel, because the villains are never exposed, let alone punished, and the open ending leaves the reader in doubts as to whether the heroine has indeed won her battle. In fact, she may be dying or dead. Although the structure of the novel follows the prescribed scheme,[5] the characterization goes far beyond the usual in entertainment literature. The novel thus is more than merely formula fiction.

Northern Lights may, from the genre viewpoint, seem embarrassingly traditional. In the late 1990s, it is hard to imagine a successful new variation on the theme of the struggle between good and evil in an alternative world in which magic is part of the everyday. In a simple plot summary, the novel would indeed appear banal and colorless, with a number of familiar elements, such as a chosen child or a gate between worlds. It is essential, however, to remember that fantasy has never been a genre exclusively for young readers; indeed, some of its masterpieces, like George Macdonald's *Phantastes*, were never intended for children and never have become part of children's reading. Recently, fantasy has become a popular genre in adults' reading, alongside other types of formula literature.

Whereas *Miss Smilla* can, apart from the sci-fi ending, be described as "realistic," and *Northern Lights* is unmistakably "fantasy," *A Cry from the Jungle* questions the distinction itself, as well as the traditional—mimetic—view of literature as an immediate reflection of reality. The novel only is comprehensible if we abandon the mimetic reading and interpret its events and characters metaphorically, which is the main premise of the so-called postmodern approach to fiction. *A Cry from the Jungle* is almost impossible to ascribe to a particular genre. One cannot help but notice its unusual form already in the layout: the story begins before the title page. The book bears the subtitle "A film novel," and its "prologue" corresponds to the common device borrowed from film of an initial sequence followed by the title and credits. The quick succession of relatively short episodes ("montage") reminds one of film technique, notably in contemporary entertainment genres, such as sitcoms and soap operas. The text pretends to be a film script but would apparently be unsuitable for filming; for one thing, it has almost no dialogue. There are other cinematic elements in the narrative—for instance, concrete time indications (characters consult their watches so that the temporal relation between separate episodes is established). A character can feel "like a heroine in a bad movie," something can feel "as if watching a video," something looks "like a movie set."[6] These are metafictive comments, reminding the reader that the narrative is fiction, a literary construction.

The descriptive chapter headings ("Chapter 1, in which . . .") may remind us of the traditional epic novel, such as *David Copperfield*; however, at closer examination, they prove to be confusing rather than informative, and they are obviously ironic. This is parody of a genre rather than a generic feature. The novel is not "epic" (in Mikhail Bakhtin's sense, that is, it is not a life story[7]), and the chapter headings function as metapoetic comments on the narrative.

A closer look at the generic features of the novel reveals elements from many different genres, primarily formula fiction: crime and mystery novel, thriller and also science fiction, that is, more or less the same blending of genres we encounter in *Miss Smilla*. The major sci-fi element is the villain's invention that threatens to destroy the world: He has built a machine that can extract dreams and hopes from people's minds and transform them into energy. In other words, it is similar to the scientific experiment in *Northern Lights*, where we, because of our generic expectations, do not see it as science fiction but rather as magic. Thriller is parodied in Haugen's book not only through stereotypical characters (a mad scientist, a Russian spy, and an American spy, and so forth), but through the composition as well: the reader is faced with a number of mysterious facts. As in most modern thrillers, relatively early in the book the villain himself explains his wicked plans. Many chapters in the book conclude with cliffhangers. The spy story is parodied because the mystery is being investigated on two levels, by two "real" agents and by a girl detective, Veronica, an obvious intertextual reference to Nancy Drew. Furthermore, the female American agent's name is Lyn Keene (truncated "Carolyn Keene," the pseudonym used by the writer team of the Nancy Drew novels). The explicitly children's novel appears at a closer view to have the least distinct generic characteristic, the most prominent genre blending, and the most ironic attitude toward established genres.

PLOT

Among the characteristics of children's fiction, we also find concrete and familiar subject matter and a clearly delineated plot. Of the three novels discussed, Haugen's matches this description least. In fact, it would be impossible to give a plot summary of the novel. There are two main parallel plots, one involving the mad scientist, and the other the emergence of a jungle in the streets of Oslo; but there are several subsidiary plots, some of which are never resolved. The plot of *Northern Lights* is extremely complicated, too, and it demands a keen reader to follow its intricate patterns (this is even truer of the sequel). The main conflict concerns a dubious scientific project based on the specific feature of the imaginary world. In this world, people's souls are fully visible and assume the forms of different animals, which reveal the person's true nature. The soul, called daemon, is a person's closest friend and assistant, and it is virtually impossible to part with it, even for a distance of a few steps. When the dark forces capture children and cut the invisible bonds between the child and its soul, it is not only a cruel detail in a dynamic adventure, but an ethical dilemma, which has clear parallels in the contemporary world. Female circumcision is merely one possible example (suggested also by the coinage of the term "intercision," used to describe the operation performed on children).

The plot of *Miss Smilla* may be seen as relatively straightforward, and it is typical of crime novels, as it starts with the crime and then goes back to events and circumstances leading up to it. On the other hand, it is overcrowded with details, secondary characters, names, and subsidiary plots, which are, however, all subordinated to the main plot. For trained thriller readers (or film, television, or video viewers), which young audiences often are, there are few difficulties in following the story.

SETTING

In traditional children's fiction, we encounter two basic types of setting: the familiar (home, school, countryside during summer holidays) in "realistic" stories and the abstract fairy tale setting in fantasy. Traditional settings provide some form of rural, idyllic, autonomous environment.

A Cry from the Jungle very clearly eradicates the boundary between fantasy and realism. The spatial indications are so concrete that we could follow the events with the help of a city map of Oslo. The setting is thus neither the traditional rural idyll, nor a fairy tale realm. When the events take place in a "real" city, the threat from mysterious forces, both the mad scientist and the invading jungle, becomes much more tangible. With regard to the events described, the writer says explicitly that "there has been a synthesis of fantasy and reality."[8]

Miss Smilla operates with three settings, all in sharp contrast with one another: modern urban ("realistic" Copenhagen), the secluded setting on board the ship—one of the favorite settings for crime novels (other variants are a train, a house isolated by a storm, or an island)—and the half-exotic, half-mythic setting on Greenland in the last part of the novel. The intriguing exoticism of the far North echoes strongly in Pullman's novel, set largely in Lapland and on Svalbard, which for the British author must be even more exotic than for Høeg. Pullman does not rely on Norse mythology, but instead weaves shamanism and other archaic religions into his narrative, in a similar manner to Høeg's novel. I am not, however, inclined to suggest influence, although it is not improbable, given the success of *Miss Smilla* in the English-speaking world. Rather, I would point to the general "lure of the North," which seems to be common to British and Scandinavian cultures. The North, associated with winter and thus with death, has a specific symbolic connotation in these countries' literature (for example, George Macdonald's *At the Back of the North Wind*).

Pullman's novel, however, does not merely depict an exotic setting for adventure, neither does it create a traditional fairy tale realm. His universe may best be described by the notion of heterotopia, although the multitude of worlds is implied only at the end and not fully developed until the sequel. The novel's initial setting is specified as Oxford, but it very soon appears to be taking place in a world that is similar to our own, but not identical with it. This, among other things, allows the author to play with language, geography, and history. In this alternative world, the Inquisition still exists in the twentieth century, the Pope has his seat in Geneva, the Tartars ravage in Muscovy, quantum physics are called "experimental theology," America is "New Denmark," and the fastest means of transportation is by zeppelin. All this invites reflections on the random nature of Fate.

CHARACTER

Occasionally, children's fiction is defined by its protagonist; that is, "children's literature is about children."[9] Naturally, a child protagonist does not automatically make a novel a children's book. As already mentioned, *Northern Lights* is marketed in some countries as an adult novel, although the main character is obviously a child. In *Miss Smilla*, the child is dead before the novel starts, and all the events involving him take place in the flashbacks. In *A Cry from the Jungle*, it is almost impossible to decide who the protagonist is, which also raises the question of a clear denotation of the protagonist as one of the possible criteria for children's fiction. The postmodern view of literature rejects the idea of a fixed and homogeneous subject in a literary work; instead, the idea of dialogics and intersubjectivity is put forward. Haugen's novel is a perfect illustration of this point. The number of characters is extremely large for a children's book; but more important is the fact that at least twenty of them are used as focalizers, that is, characters with whom the reader is supposed to share the point of view and thus the information. Fourteen of these focalizers are adults, which means that adult perspective is, if not overwhelming, then at least prominent.

Our apprehension of the eleven-year-old Miki as the main character is prompted by the prologue, where we are manipulated to assume that the rest of the novel will be about Miki—an interpretative strategy based on previous experience. Miki appears as a focalizing character in fourteen episodes, followed by the Zhahdine priest Ibon Arah (adult) in eight episodes, and Veronica (child) and Miki's father in seven each. The fact that we primarily notice the child perspective is the result of the subject matter as well as our general expectations: we are dealing with a children's book. If we liberate ourselves from this assumption, the question of the main character is no longer self-evident.

The prescribed limited number of secondary characters in children's fiction does not match the structure of *A Cry from the Jungle*, nor does it in *Northern Lights*, in which a great number of secondary characters are introduced, only a few reappearing as the plot progresses. A common prejudice is that young readers cannot retain a large number of characters in their memory.

Another unwritten rule is that the characters in children's fiction have a flat and static orientation, among other things demonstrating a clear distinction between good and evil. In both Haugen's and Pullman's novels, however, the characters show a great deal of complexity and can definitely not be ascribed the quality of good or evil. In Haugen's novel, there is, of course, a human villain, but the jungle, the main threat, is ambivalent and mystifying. The characters are neither heroes nor cowards; the adults are unreliable and provide no support. The same is true of

Northern Lights: the actions of both of Lyra's parents have equally dubious motives; the fairy tale "helper," Iorek the bear, is basically helping the protagonist out of self-interest; and even Lyra's own actions and opinions are far from clear-cut.

In *Miss Smilla*, on the other hand, we have relatively simple roles: the noble detective, the innocent victim, and a vast number of villains in conspiracy. Smilla herself, however, is much too complex to be "merely" a detective; her investigation of the mysterious murder is at the same time her quest for identity. She feels connected with the murdered boy because of their common ancestry on Greenland and their similar displacement in modern urban Denmark. Although Smilla is thirty-seven years old, she is in fact a lonely, abandoned, and betrayed child, much like Lyra, Miki, or the other characters in *A Cry from the Jungle*, children and adults alike.

PERSPECTIVE

The complexity of the characters in all three novels is further emphasized by the narrative perspective. Traditional children's fiction presupposes a distinct narrative voice, often an omniscient, didactic (presumably adult) narrator. At first sight it may seem that in *A Cry from the Jungle* we are dealing with just such an omniscient and omnipresent narrator. The main narrative device, however, is polyfocalization. In each episode, only one character is focalized externally as well as internally, which means that the final picture of what is happening at the same time in different places and in the different characters' minds can only be assembled by the reader. With very few exceptions, the narrator refrains from direct comments on the events or characters. It takes a long time before the reader understands how the characters and the different plots are related to each other (here again we must depend on our previous reading experience to assume that they are). There are evident gaps in the parallel plots. Sometimes they overlap, but more often they interrupt each other. This discontinuity creates a sense of uncertainty, and the strong focalization of characters implies that as readers we cannot be sure whether the described events actually take place. We witness a number of subjective experiences, rather than an objective account of events.

On the other hand, the narrator pretends to be objective by inserting a number of "reports" from newspapers, quotations from encyclopedias, and excerpts from what are supposed to be ancient sacred scripts of the imaginary Zhahdine tribe. The latter are parodic in themselves, starting with "In the beginning was the Jungle . . ."[10] At the same time, the reader has the advantage of having access to all information and all the characters' thoughts. As in all good thrillers, we are allowed to be ahead of the protagonists in solving the mystery. We get a clear clue in the concrete place, Oscar Street 25B, which from the beginning appears to be the axis of the narrative. As readers, we are superior to all characters in the story and can penetrate the villains' evil intentions. All the parallel plots are finally brought together in Part 3 of the novel, which is extremely dynamic and action-oriented, much more "objectively" narrated, and may seem to be the culmination of the plot leading to a resolution. Evil is punished, and the kidnapped children are set free. Part 4 may be seen as a quiet epilogue told by an objective, omniscient narrator. But in fact the first three parts, comprising three-fourths of the book, are merely a prolonged introduction of the real protagonist: the jungle.

By comparison with the complicated narrative perspective of *A Cry from the Jungle, Northern Lights* may seem relatively simple. There is, however, no omniscient narrator either. Instead, the child protagonist is focalized internally, which means that we perceive the events and other characters exclusively though her naïve, immature, and often biased mind. The narrator does not give us access to more information than Lyra has. As in Haugen's novel, however, a keen reader may make inferences beyond the protagonist's ability. As readers, we are again superior to the protagonist and can see through her weak points and false steps. Moreover, the fantasy frame allows the author to play with language, for instance, calling electricity "anbaric light," and encouraging the reader to substitute the "correct" notion that Lyra is not familiar with. It also is worth mentioning that in the sequel, *The Subtle Knife*, Pullman makes use of polyfocalization in much the same manner as Haugen, allowing the readers to know and understand more than any of his several focalizing characters. In the sequel, our own world is described partially through Lyra's eyes by means of estrangement, that is, by presenting familiar things as if they were unfamiliar.

Miss Smilla has a first-person narrator. There is a very strong prejudice against first-person narrators in children's fiction (which, among other things, accounts for the fact that most adaptations of adult novels to child reading, such as *Robinson Crusoe* or *Gulliver's Travels*, involve a transposition from first to third person). There are many reasons for this prejudice, all mostly of a pedagogical–psychological nature, that assumes that young readers have difficulty identifying with the abstract "I" of the story. One aspect of this is that a first-person narrator is unreliable by definition. We have only the narrator's point of view on the events, both perceptional and conceptional point of view. Smilla may be wrong in her apprehension of events and other people, she may be influenced by the traumatic memories of her childhood. Moreover, we cannot be sure how much Smilla the narrator is actually sharing with us. It is apparent throughout the novel that she is withholding information from the reader; she never tells us exactly what she finds out in the archives she visits; her accounts of her meetings with people are fragmentary. This is, of course, a deliberate narrative device: the reader is encouraged to conduct the investigation parallel to Smilla and independently of her.

One of the most revolutionary ideas proposed by Gérard Genette in his *Narrative Discourse* is that there is no radical difference between first- and third-person narrators; whereas the so-called third person narrator focalizes another character, the first-person narrator focalizes himself or herself. Smilla the narrator focalizes Smilla the character, just as the covert narrator of *Northern Lights* focalizes Lyra, the result being in both cases that we receive only limited and distorted information. This leads me to suggest that there is no principal difference between the narrative perspective in the three novels I am discussing. All three deviate from the traditional omniscient narrator, instead using with sophisticated focalization patterns, which work to conceal the events rather than to account for them. All three put very high demands on the reader who is supposed to fill the textual gaps, make connections, and draw conclusions that the authors have chosen to omit.

All this illustrates very well the general shift in narrative technique in contemporary literature, which also has now entered children's fiction. Although a traditional epic narrative, including traditional children's literature, presupposes a single subject in unity with the world, in "contemporary" narrative this unity is disturbed, resulting in polyphony, intersubjectivity, unreliable narrators, multiple plots and endings, and so forth. As Linda Hutcheon remarks, contemporary literature "refuses the omniscience and omnipresence of the third person and engages instead in a dialogue between a narrative voice . . . and a projected reader."[11] This narrative mode creates (as well as reflects) a chaotic view of the world, as opposed to the ordered (structured) universe of a traditional narrative, based on nineteenth-century positivistic philosophy.

TEMPORALITY

The last narrative feature I would like to discuss is temporality, the relation between story time and discourse time. Children's fiction is supposed to use chronological narrative, rendering the events more or less in the same order they have taken place. Anachronies, that is, different types of deviations from the chronological order of events, are avoided. Further, children's fiction seldom has prolonged textual duration, because children are assumed to lack a fully developed sense of time, they live "here and now."

As should be clear from the discussion of perspective in Haugen's novel, its temporal pattern is extremely complicated, and the indications of physical time confuse rather than clarify the flow of time. Moreover, in Part 4, the novel emerges into an eternal, mythical time or, rather, timelessness, a sort of fairy tale "lived happily ever after." Although there are no formal indicators of it, this part is narrated in what Genette calls the iterative frequency: the events are described once, but are supposed to be taking place over and over again.

Northern Lights has no sophisticated temporal deviations, but as the whole story is taking place in an alternative world, the question of time is inevitable for anyone even slightly familiar with fantasy codes. This question does not, however, arise explicitly until the sequel, which recurrent transportations between parallel worlds makes time disturbance a major narrative element. *Miss Smilla*, finally, shows an intricate pattern of analepses, that is, flashbacks involving memories or previously omitted details. As mentioned earlier, this is a common narrative device in the thriller genre and is perhaps not seen as complex. Once again, the explicitly children's novel, *A Cry from the Jungle*, proves to be the most complicated in its narrative structure.

IDYLL OR DYSTOPIA?

From the discussion above we must draw the conclusion that, at least as far as these three concrete texts are concerned, there is no radical difference in the way the stories are narrated. Moreover, we also must agree that the novels intended, or at least marketed for young readers, show no less sophistication in their narrative structure than the novel apparently written and marketed for a general audience (it was proclaimed "The Book of the Year" by *Time* magazine). Are we obliged to accept that in contemporary literature the boundaries between children's and adult fiction are completely obliterated?

Let us return to the thematic aspects of the novels and see where the plot leads the characters. Children's fiction sometimes is defined as literature based on idyll.[12] The concept of childhood and innocence often is used to distinguish between children's fiction and adult fiction. Not only literature written specifically for children, however, but also general literature often has used the child as an image and a symbol of purity and innocence. It is a commonplace to point out that in the Romantic tradition childhood is equal to idyll, whereas growing up is equal to loss of Paradise. Traditional children's fiction creates and preserves what may be called a pastoral convention.[13] As a consequence, it maintains the myth of a happy and innocent childhood, apparently based on adult writers' nostalgic memories and bitter insights about the impossibility of returning to the childhood idyll.

Children's fiction is written—with very few exceptions—by adult writers for young readers. Consequently, the notion of childhood and the ideas about growing, procreation, and death that we meet in children's fiction reflect adults' views, which may or may not correspond to the real status of children and childhood in any given society. The central concept is that childhood is something irretrievably lost for adults, and this lost Arcadia can only be restored in fiction. With this premise, children's fiction is not, as it is commonly defined, literature addressed to children, but a sort of storytelling therapy for frustrated adults.[14]

Haugen's novel subverts the myth of happy childhood, but at the same time preserves it. The adventure plot of the first three parts of the novel is merely a preparation for the characters' encounter with the jungle. Who is allowed to enter the jungle and why? Where does the jungle come from and what does it symbolize? It would be much too simple to consider the jungle merely as an element of popular culture, a horror story, a variation of aliens, dinosaurs, giant bees, or killer tomatoes.

The subject of the novel can be viewed within several discourses, such as world politics, children's rights, or ecology. Haugen is trying to give us the illusion that the jungle is about anything other than the individual, that it is a global matter, that it "would change the whole nation."[15] As a symbol, the jungle may signify a number of things, such as drugs or cyberspace (which, however, became a social factor several years after the publication of the novel). Most critics have interpreted the jungle positively, as a "sanctuary,"[16] "a happy return to nature, which surpasses anything that Rousseau could imagine . . . evidence of the creative power of imagination."[17] To my mind, the jungle is much more complicated and ambivalent, as is clearly reflected in the various characters' attitudes toward it. The jungle is wild and uncontrollable, but natural. Is it a threat to civilization or a "happy return to nature"? Haugen portrays the attack of the jungle in a contradictory manner. He is trying to give us a sense of peace, saying for instance: "The strangest thing was that there was no panic," but the description of the jungle encroaching on Oslo is nightmarish, like something out of a horror movie, and the repetition of the words "homeless" and "fugitives" does not create a sense of security, but rather evokes reality with its wars, hunger, and natural catastrophes. I cannot unequivocally accept the jungle as positive. It is undoubtedly destructive. Haugen also shows the difference in children's and adults' attitudes: the adults are thinking about various methods of "coping with" the jungle, struggling against it, stopping it, or the other way round, rather rationally "releasing our inner jungle." They also create "a new, extraordinarily efficient jungle committee."[18] Children become curious and run away from home.

At the same time, the jungle is definitely a liberation (as drugs and computer games can be), and it is summoned by the imagination. Miki and the other children literally sing forward the jungle landscape, which becomes more real with every minute. It is first described as a mirage, but very soon the children can enter it. The motif of entering a landscape created by the imagination evokes the myth of Wu Lao-Tsu, the artist who enters his own picture. But who is the artist, the creator? We can suspect that it is Miki, because we consider him as a protagonist (subject); he is the one who encourages the other children to enter the jungle. But it turns out that the jungle is a collective creation (intersubjective), because everybody recognizes their own fantasy plants and animals in it.

We can thus view the characters of the novel as parts of the collective protagonist, a split personality longing to become whole again. Parts of the split character gather in the jungle, but some parts stay outside. What is the passkey into the jungle? Is it every child's paradise? It appears to be more complex than that. The word "betrayal" is one of the most frequent in the text ("lonely" and "loneliness" are two more). Miki's parents have betrayed him, each in their own way. The other children also are described as having been betrayed by adults. Adults' betrayal of children is depicted in detail in the learned manuscripts of the Zhahdines, the fictitious archaic tribe that plays an important role in the story. A feminist activist sums it up in a lecture as: ". . . children who are not loved for what they are, who are not seen as the children they are, who are given the responsibility that they do not feel they can cope with." The jungle is a compensation for the lack of love and for the colorless, hopeless reality. It is open for both children and adults who have been betrayed and who are trying to forget their bitterness: ". . . dreaming, longing, but abandoned, *invisible*, lonely."[19] Invisibility as a consequence of betrayal is a recurrent motif in Haugen's books.[20]

Is the jungle a symbol of the subconscious? Is it the dark, suppressed corner of our psyche that lies in wait and attacks us when we least expect it, and that feeds our dreams and fancies? We read, for instance: "Miki felt the jungle inside himself" or "Somebody spoke of the jungle deep inside me." In addition, "an inner landscape similar to a jungle" is mentioned.[21] The jungle is thus a part of the psyche. Is Haugen saying that we have to meet our subconscious in order to become whole? But in this case there must be a way out of the jungle. If the Zhahdine messenger is The Wise Old Man, he should not only lead the children into the jungle, but also out of it. Instead he abandons them. Haugen never says that the ultimate goal is to leave the jungle with a better understanding of life and one's own personality. For those who have chosen the jungle it seems to be the final destination.

The jungle is thus preventing people from developing; to enter the jungle is not simply escape, it is regression, a frustrated attempt to return to the sorrowless idyll of childhood. If the jungle represents the Goddess, the good Progenitrix, then the children stay unborn in her womb. "A child must always be a reminder of man's wholeness," says a proverb from Zhahdine legends.[22] But a man cannot be whole if the child is not allowed to grow up.

In another novel by Haugen, a young boy tries to avoid taking the decisive step into adulthood by committing suicide. A young person's suicide becomes, strangely enough, a way to escape death. *A Cry from the Jungle* starts with Miki's—then later Michael's—first encounter with death. "To be dead is the same as not being any more," he learns. At this moment Michael changes his name—a symbolical death and rebirth in a rite of passage—and also hears a cry from the jungle for the first time. The jungle has promised freedom but turns out to be a trap. After this first cry Miki enters "a new phase of his life," a phase in which he is aware of his own mortality. After this, "nothing can be as it was before."[23] The jungle calls him, and Miki, unable to cope with life and without help from adults, succumbs. Miki's father cannot accept death either—his mother's (Miki's grandmother's) death—and is prepared to let the mad scientist free him from dreams or else to enter the jungle where death does not exist.

Entering the jungle is thus a circumlocution of suicide. In this case, the practical Veronica, who stays outside the jungle, is both cleverer and more mature. Instead, she starts "a painful wandering which she would not like to be without," that is, movement toward adulthood. A positive example? The children who enter the jungle, however, haven't much choice. The alternative is "to come home and be taken care of," that is to get socialized and to adopt the norms prescribed by adult life.[24] And this is exactly what the children are trying to avoid. Entering the jungle they believe that they are going home. They wish to stay in the jungle forever and ever, while life outside the jungle goes on, with its light and dark sides.

Thus I view the jungle as a regression, a dystopia rather than "the happy return to nature." Haugen's sense of resignation when confronted with the great mystery of life is something that he shares with many contemporary children's writers. Adults' oppression of children has become a commonplace, and the earlier happy endings have become unusual in serious children's fiction.

In Pullman's novel, the notion of the child as innocent is the basic premise. The anticipation of Lyra's role as the new—female—Savior is amplified in the sequel, but already in *Northern Lights* she is given a special role: She is the only one who can read and interpret the signs of the alethiometer, the magical truth machine. The firm Romantic belief that the child is good by nature and therefore more suitable to struggle against evil is central in all fantasy novels. Pullman's heroine, however, is more subtly portrayed. She has in fact caused the death of her best friend. Morally, she is not as pure and innocent as traditional fantasy prescribes. On the other hand, even traditional fantasy presupposes the moral growth of the protagonist, and Lyra's development matches this criterion.

As for *Miss Smilla*, this novel leaves no doubts as to the moral regression of the individual as well as society. An innocent child is brutally murdered. The protagonist/narrator, once an oppressed and spiritually deprived child herself, is disillusioned and, as I see it, suffers total defeat. The main feeling of the novel is hopelessness. Snow becomes a powerful symbol of human cold and indifference. There is no salvation for humanity, and no grand happy endings à la *Independence Day* are in view.

Tormod Haugen is not alone in his pessimistic view of the world and far from the only contemporary children's writer who subverts the myth of happy childhood. Many critics question the status of his novels as children's literature, presumably because they are imprisoned in the view of children's fiction as Arcadia. *Miss Smilla's Feeling for Snow* shows clearly that contemporary formula fiction no longer makes use of traditional plot structures or stereotypical characters, and in the first place it does not operate with clear-cut categories, such as good and evil, always letting the good win over the evil in the end. We can perhaps treat traditional formula fiction, including the crime novel, as a kind of idyllic literature for adult audiences, in the sense that it does not question our standard notion of justice and always brings things back to initial harmony. Peter Høeg's novel has definitely broken this rule.

Pullman's book appears to be the most Arcadian in its treatment of the child as innocent and therefore capable of struggling against global evil. The sequel, however, shows a tendency toward loss of innocence. Moreover, the very category of evil seems to be getting quite vague. Apparently it is this uncertainty that has determined the status of *Northern Lights* as an adult novel in some countries. Until the trilogy is completed, it is impossible to say whither Pullman is heading. His work, however, is the best illustration of the growing number of novels which bridge the gap between young and adult audiences and question the distinction itself. Whether this trend is desirable is another question.

NOTES

1. Tormod Haugen, *Skriket fra jungelen* (Oslo: Gyldendal, 1989). This novel has not been translated into English. All translations from the novel are mine, and it will be referred to throughout this chapter as *A Cry from the Jungle*.

2. *Northern Lights* is the first part in an announced trilogy, of which the second part, *The Subtle Knife*, appeared in 1997. I will concentrate on the first novel, but will take into consideration some features of the sequel.

3. See Maria Nikolajeva, "Reflections of Change in Children's Book Titles," in *Reflections of Change: Children's Literature Since 1945*, ed. Sandra L. Beckett (Westport, Conn.: Greenwood, 1997): 85–90.

4. Barbara Wall, *The Narrator's Voice: The Dilemma of Children's Fiction* (London: Macmillan, 1991).

5. See John G. Cawelty, *Adventure, Mystery and Romance: Formula Stories as Art and Popular Culture* (Chicago: University of Chicago Press, 1976).

6. Tormod Haugen, *Skriket fra jungelen*, 187, 263, 299.

7. Mikhail Bakhtin, *Problems of Dostoyevsky's Poetics* (Minneapolis: University of Minnesota Press, 1984): 6.

8. Haugen, *Skriket fra jungelen*, 322.

9. Perry Nodelman, *The Pleasures of Children's Literature* (New York: Longman, 1992): 190.

10. Haugen, *Skriket fra jungelen*, 65.

11. Linda Hutcheon, *A Poetics of Postmodernism: History, Theory, Fiction* (New York: Routledge, 1988): 10.

12. See Humphrey Carpenter, *Secret Gardens: The Golden Age of Children's Literature* (London: Unwin Hyman, 1985).

13. See Alison Lurie, *Don't Tell the Grownups: Subversive Children's Literature* (Boston: Little, Brown, 1990): xiii.

14. See Jacqueline Rose, *The Case of Peter Pan, or The Impossibility of Children's Fiction* (London: Macmillan, 1984).

15. Haugen, *Skriket fra jungelen*, 10.

16. Else Breen, *Slik skrev de. Verdi og virkelighet i barneböker 1968–1983* (Oslo: Aschehoug, 1988): 298.

17. Ying Toijer-Nilsson, "Tormod Haugen," in *De skriver för barn och ungdom* (Lund: Bibliotekstjänst, 1991): 176.

18. Haugen, *Skriket fra jungelen*, 314, 352.

19. Ibid., 245, 55; italics mine.

20. See Eva-Maria Metcalf, "The Invisible Child in the Works of Tormod Haugen," *Barnboken* 1 (1992): 15–23.

21. Haugen, *Skriket fra jungelen*, 303, 329, 351.

22. Ibid., 155.

23. Ibid., 4, 9.

24. Ibid., 376, 297.

REFERENCES

Bakhtin, Mikhail. *Problems of Dostoyevsky's Poetics*. Minneapolis: University of Minnesota Press, 1984.

Breen, Else. *Slik skrev de. Verdi og virkelighet i barneböker 1968–1983*. Oslo: Aschehoug, 1988.

Carpenter, Humphrey. *Secret Gardens: The Golden Age of Children's Literature*. London: Unwin Hyman, 1985.

Cawelty, John G. *Adventure, Mystery and Romance: Formula Stories as Art and Popular Culture*. Chicago: University of Chicago Press, 1976.

Genette, Gérard. *Narrative Discourse: An Essay in Method*. Ithaca, N.Y.: Cornell University Press, 1980.

Haugen, Tormod. *Skriket fra jungelen*. Oslo: Gyldendal, 1989.

Høeg, Peter. *Miss Smilla's Feeling for Snow*. Trans. F. David. New York: Farrar, Straus & Giroux, 1993 (published in the United States. as *Smilla's Sense of Snow*).

Hutcheon, Linda. *A Poetics of Postmodernism: History, Theory, Fiction*. New York: Routledge, 1988.

Lurie, Alison. *Don't Tell the Grownups: Subversive Children's Literature*. Boston: Little, Brown, 1990.

Metcalf, Eva-Maria. "The Invisible Child in the Works of Tormod Haugen." *Barnboken* 1 (1992): 15–23.

Nikolajeva, Maria. "Reflections of Change in Children's Book Titles." In *Reflections of Change: Children's Literature Since 1945*, ed. Sandra L. Beckett, 85–90. Westport, Conn.: Greenwood, 1997.

Nodelman, Perry. *The Pleasures of Children's Literature*. New York: Longman, 1992.

Pullman, Philip. *Northern Lights*. London: Scholastic, 1995 (published in the United States as *The Golden Compass*).

_____. *The Subtle Knife*. London: Scholastic, 1997.

Rose, Jacqueline. *The Case of Peter Pan, or The Impossibility of Children's Fiction*. London: Macmillan, 1984.

Toijer-Nilsson, Ying. "Tormod Haugen." In *De skriver för barn och ungdom*, 169–178. Lund: Bibliotekstjänst, 1991.

Wall, Barbara. *The Narrator's Voice: The Dilemma of Children's Fiction*. London: Macmillan, 1991.

PART II

Ages All? Parents, Play, and Picturebooks

CHAPTER 5

The Double Attribution of Texts for Children and How It Affects Writing for Children

ZOHAR SHAVIT

The most characteristic feature of children's literature is its double attribution. By definition, children's literature addresses children, but always and without exception, children's literature has an additional addressee—the adult, who functions as either a passive or an active addressee of texts written for children. This is because:

(a) as the modern notion of the child was more widely accepted by Western society, the child's culture gradually began to develop into an autonomous domain in which the needs of the child and his/her well-being were taken care of by adults, under their strict supervision. As we approach the end of the century, this supervision appears to be becoming increasingly more rigid.

(b) the opposition between adults and children has become one of the most conspicuous societal oppositions of modern times. It is one of the first a child learns to respect and submit to in the process of socialization; it also is one of the basic cultural notions that organizes the lives of all adults who are members of a modern community.

(c) the opposition between adults and children does not entail a solid untransferable border between the two. On the contrary, each of these social systems determines not only the other's boundaries, but defines its own patterns of behavior and derives its own societal meanings from the existence of the other.

(d) over the past decades, adult involvement in the child's culture continuously has grown, with the result that children's literature needs to be approved by two groups of readers, which by definition exclude each other.

This double attribution has far-reaching implications on writing for children, on the status of writers for children as well as on the nature of the texts produced for the child. Children's literature must cater for adult approval in order to secure its existence, even its physical existence.

Every book for children is first read by adults. If adults don't approve of a certain text, the author may find it extremely difficult to reach an audience, let alone find his/her way to being published. It is the adults who have the right and the obligation to provide for children and it is the adults who, in the framework of these obligations, produce books for children.

Adults not only write books for children, they also publish, evaluate, interpret, and distribute them. Adults also are the only ones in a position to decide whether a book will be published, how it will be published, and how it will be distributed to its official readership of children.

As is well known, this has not always been the case. Because we have become accustomed to the modern societal understanding of childhood, and to the overall existence of books for children, we tend to forget that both concepts, that of childhood itself and that of books for children, are relatively new. The connection between them is inseparable. It has repeatedly been noted by several scholars that the creation of the notion of childhood was an indispensable precondition for the production of children's books and to a large extent determined the course of development and specific options within the development of children's literature.

Before children's literature could begin to develop, a total reform in the notion of childhood had to take place; this reform has been described in the well-known, pioneering study by Philippe Ariès.[1] Children's literature could not have existed before children's needs in themselves were legitimately recognized as distinct from the needs of adults. As John Rowe Townsend states: "Before there could be children's books, there had to be children—children, that is, who were accepted as beings with their own particular needs and interests, not only as miniature men and women."[2]

Ariès and his followers have taught us that, until the seventeenth century, children were not considered to have had needs that were any different from the needs of adults. Subsequently, there was no such thing as children's literature, that is, if we perceive children's literature as a steady and continuous flow and not as a sporadic activity. Books written specifically for children were seldom published until the eighteenth century, and the whole industry of children's books began to flourish only in the second half of the nineteenth century. Children's literature became a culturally recognized field only in the eighteenth century, and a prominent field within the publishing establishment only from the middle of that same century.

The reading of the few children's books that were published during the sixteenth and seventeenth centuries was not regarded as part of the "leisure time" of the child, nor did they encourage further education by means of books; moreover, these books lacked the recognition that became part of the conceptual cultural framework of the eighteenth century—the recognition that children needed books of their own that could be distinguished from books read by adults.

The basic idea was that through books the child would be disciplined along the paths of learning and godliness. In an unprecedented way, schooling and education were given pride of place in the life of an individual; moreover, the more they were perceived as indispensable tools for carrying out the process of education, the overall demand for children's books, providing encouragement and fresh turf for writers of children's books. The latter all shared the view that in the process of their education, children needed books, and agreed that these books should be distinguished from adult books principally through their fundamental attachment to the educational system itself.

Thus, it was within the framework of the new concept of childhood, evolved in Western society since the seventeenth century, that children's literature began to emerge, and it was this new concept of childhood that determined the terms of existence for children's literature. Since its initial stages of conceptualization, the notion of childhood may well have changed considerably, but the linkage between children's literature, notions of childhood, and the child's education remained crucial factors in determining the nature of children's literature. In fact, the notion that children's literature is the outcome of a specific notion of childhood dominant at the time of its construction can be formulated as a universal.

Never has the notion of childhood been as dominant as it is today, nor has the presence of the child in Western culture been so striking. This is of course in contradistinction to Neil Postman's ideas in *The Disappearance of Childhood*.[3] To my mind, Postman errs in assuming that childhood has disappeared from modern Western society, largely because he seems to confuse the changing nature of childhood with the existence of childhood as a cultural institution. He is right, however, in pointing out the changes undergone by the notion of childhood in terms of the changing borders between children and adults. In this process, childhood has indeed shed some of its older characteristics and has taken on new ones, but the notion of childhood itself remains one of the more significant organizing principles within Western society. The past few decades have placed increasing emphasis on the notion of the child's well-being as central to both the private and the public spheres, even as it determines adult agendas and specifies divisions of labor.

Within this framework of shared labor and responsibilities, children's literature has come to occupy a special position in-the-culture. It is, in fact, this framework that authorizes children's literature and legitimizes it, even as it determines its social mandate. This social mandate expects children's literature to function as one of several tools in a conglomerate of social institutions, all seeking to supply the needs of the child as understood by society at a given point in time.

Writers of children's books seem to regard as increasingly disturbing the social mandate given to them, and consequently the demand that children's literature must respond to the needs of the child. Where previously writers for children were willing to accept their instrumental task, in recent decades they seem to wish to challenge the responsibility they are ascribed as writers of books for children, and the educational idea of children's literature as a device for the proper raising of children.

Jill Paton Walsh speaks for many writers when she says protestingly:

> Many teachers see the children's writer, like the children's doctor, the children's psychiatrist, the children's teacher, the children's home, as part of the apparatus of society for dealing with and helping children, as a sort of extracurricular psychiatric social worker.[4]

The result of viewing children's literature as an agent of other systems is that each children's book must meet social expectations, determined by a group of adults, whose social mandate is to approve or disapprove of books for children. In fact, this is the whole raison d'être of modern society. Based on the assumption that the needs of children and young people as distinct social groups are different from those of adults, members of modern Western society believe that children's needs should be determined by adults because they always know better what is best for children.

Adults pretend to know and to understand what children like and what is good for them. Moreover, adults presume to know *better* than children what is good for them. Not only do children's evaluations of books for children not count, they can even be counterproductive. If children find a certain book attractive or good or interesting—their assessment is ascribed very little value or authority, and often none at all, and may even prompt a negative assessment of a book by adults. This is so because children's understanding and children's taste are perceived as having far less value than adult taste and understanding. Unless a book is approved of by adults, it will not be introduced into the official system of the child. Nor will a book for children stand a chance of being evaluated as "good" if "only" children like it or find it a "good book"; to this end, it always needs to be authorized by adults.

This leads to the well-known formulations about what good children's literature is all about. Widely accepted, for instance, is the conviction that: "Good literature is good literature; it satisfies both children and critics," as formulated by the critic Rebecca Lukens.[5]

Here, I must say, I have my doubts. To begin with, I doubt whether "good literature" exists at all—good literature, that is, in the sense that "good literature" is not a cultural construct, but a substantial entity. As we all know, what a given generation regards as "good literature" may well be regarded by the next generation as "bad" or unworthy literature. Adults all too easily hasten to agree with the famous writer C. S. Lewis, who made the following, oft-cited statement:

> I am almost inclined to set it up as a canon that a children's story which
> is enjoyed only by children is a bad children's story.[6]

But what is the real implication of a statement such as this? Is it not like saying a child's game enjoyed only by children is a bad children's game, or even, a child's dress worn only by children is a bad/ugly child's dress? Lewis's words are not only patronizing—which is always the case when adults refer to the child's culture—but they deny children any right to cultivate their own taste or preferences.

What do adults really know about children's culture and about what children enjoy? Only the following: Were children the only ones to enjoy something, adults would most probably not approve of it. I believe that adults should at least be aware of the irreconcilable differences between adult and children's tastes and sources of pleasure. Nowadays, adults in Western society have the privilege of determining what children should like, but have very little knowledge of what children actually do like. I don't think it is for us to try and change this situation, nor do I believe this disparity can be reconciled. After all, this is the very basis for the cultural opposition in the West between children and adults; I do believe, however, that adults should be more modest and question their own ideas of what children prefer and like.

On the other hand, I have no doubts whatsoever about the implications of these convictions as far as writers for children are concerned.
With the increased autonomization of children's literature, writers for
children have become less reluctant to submit to their inferior status. Any
field of culture whose autonomy is undermined is less appreciated by the
comprehensive cultural system. The need to be evaluated and appreciated by a different group of readers than the official addressee of children's literature ultimately results in lowering the status of children's
literature, as compared to adult's literature.

In his Nobel Prize address, Isaac Bashevis Singer cited ten reasons
why he wrote for the young.[7] Why Bashevis Singer chose to address children's literature on such a prestigious occasion is indeed unclear. Was he
interested in improving the status of writing for children? I hardly think
so. Perhaps he was simply using the case of children's literature to make
a statement about adult literature and thus to add a flare of irony to the
rather pompous circumstances in which the Nobel prize is awarded. At
any rate, Bashevis Singer characterizes the child reader in ten points, of
which the following are relevant in the context of our discussion:

1. Children read books, not reviews. They don't give a hoot about
   the critics.
2. Children don't read to find their identity.
3. They don't read to free themselves of guilt, to quench their thirst
   for rebellion. or to get rid of alienation.
4. They have no use for psychology.
5. They detest sociology.
6. They don't try to understand Kafka or *Finnegan's Wake*.
7. They still believe in God, the family, angels, devils, witches,
   goblins, logic, clarity, punctuation, and other such obsolete stuff.
8. They love interesting stories, not commentary, guides, or foot-
   notes.
9. When a book is boring, they yawn openly, without any shame or
   fear of authority.
10. They don't expect their beloved writer to redeem humanity. Young
    as they are, they know that it is not in his power. Only adults have
    such childish illusions.

Well, perhaps one could say that children read books (not reviews),
but writers of children's books, like all writers, do read reviews. Furthermore, although children may not give a hoot about critics, writers for

children most certainly do. Like all other writers, writers for children wish to be well received, they hanker after good reviews, and hope to be acknowledged as worthy writers by the literary elite. If they are accepted "merely" as writers for children, however, their chances of acquiring recognition are rather poor. Writing for children is located on a lower rung of the cultural ladder, on which writers can only aspire to climb upward, as Patricia Wrightson openly admitted:

> So I ventured to try my hand at a novel for children, very deliberately making my work into a course of training; requiring that in each book I should break new and (for me) difficult ground, and hoping to graduate to adult novels some day.[8]

But writers for children are often confined to their own territory and are not easily permitted to leave it, as Maurice Sendak confirmed in an interview he gave in 1980:

> We who work on children's books inhabit a sort of literary shtetl. When I won a prize for *Wild Things,* my father spoke for a great many critics when he asked whether I would now be allowed to work on "real" books.[9]

The sense of this shtetl results almost immediately in a shared denial on the part of writers for children of the fact that they write children's books. Absurd as it may sound, I have seldom read an interview with a writer for children in which their position as writers for children, or the standing of their addressees, was not denied.

Madeleine L'Engle recalls that when asked why she writes for children she answered: "I don't." Rosemary Sutcliff proclaims: "I have never written for any age-group,"[10] while Jane Gardam has said: "Each book I have written I have desperately wanted to write. Whether or not they had anything to do with children has never occurred to me. I have never liked children's books very much, I don't read very many."[11] L. M. Boston, for her part, has claimed: "I could pick out passages from any of the books and you would not be able to tell what age it was aimed at"[12] and Pamela Travers assures us that her books do not have "anything to do with that other label: 'Literature for children.' "[13] Scott O'Dell even seems to be protesting when he claims: "Books of mine which are classified officially as books for children were not written for children."[14]

This, it must be admitted, reveals a strange disposition: In most cases the writers at stake are highly praised and acclaimed figures who have acquired their high social position because they write for children. Despite this, they not only deny that they themselves have written for children, but also that there even exists an opposition between children's literature and literature for adults.

This denial has nothing whatsoever to do with being familiar with the literary field. As themselves people in-the-culture, writers for children know that children's literature and writing for children are strong societal forces. Their attempts to deny the existence of an opposition between adults and children's literature are actually a protest against both the inferior status of writers for children, and against the textual implications of this systemic opposition.

By admitting to writing "merely" for children, a writer automatically acknowledges his or her lesser status. Since the wide acceptance of C. S. Lewis's statement about "good" children's literature, writers for children are afraid that if only children accept their books they will be confined to a cultural Ghetto, and will be committed to social responsibilities that will seriously constrain their options of writing. In addition, they are afraid that this commitment also will implicate them in the system's reluctance to admit new models, its preference for simplified and reductive models over more sophisticated ones, and its assumption of the limits of the possible realizations of texts. The textual implication of the double attribution of children's literature lies in the fact that a writer for children has a more limited mandate than that enjoyed by a writer for adults. In denying their status as writers for children, writers of books for children are in fact trying to deny the limits of this mandate.

I would like to turn now to the texts themselves, and briefly address the textual implications of the limitations mentioned above. In discussing the texts, I will briefly refer here to three well-known cases of writing for children. In the first, that of Lewis Carroll's three versions of *Alice*, I will point to the writer's different strategies in appealing either to adults or "merely" to children. In the two other cases, those of Maurice Sendak and Shel Silverstein, I will point to a new genre of writing for children, one which addresses the parents, very often at the expense of their children, or as Astrid Lindgren puts it:

> Many who write for children wink slyly over the heads of their child-readers to an imaginary reader; they wink agreeingly to the adults and ignore the child.[15]

FROM LEWIS CARROLL'S OWN ADAPTATION OF *ALICE'S ADVENTURES IN WONDERLAND* TO MAURICE SENDAK'S *HIGGLETY PIGGLETY POP!*

As we all know, Carroll wrote three different versions of *Alice's Adventures in Wonderland*. After the unprecedented success of *Alice's Adventures in Wonderland*, followed by *Alice's Adventures Underground*, which primarily addressed adults, Carroll published a third version of the story, *The Nursery Alice*, which addressed children and children only.[16] Carroll eliminated and deleted all the elements that he had elaborated in *Alice's Adventures in Wonderland* in order to make sure that his text would appeal to adults as well: He totally changed the tone of the text, omitting all its satirical and parodical elements, renouncing his previous attempt to blur the relations between reality and fantasy, thus transforming *The Nursery Alice* into a simple fantasy story, based on the conventional model of the time. Fantasy is motivated in the *Nursery* version as something that happens in a dream; a logical explanation exists for each event. In the *Nursery* version, Carroll made clear-cut distinctions between reality and fantasy and allowed for no confusion between them.

The distorted relations between space and time, fantasy and reality, so typical of *Alice's Adventures in Wonderland,* were unacceptable for the *Nursery* version, written especially for children. Thus, for example, in *Alice's Adventures in Wonderland*, Carroll deliberately confuses the two worlds and at the most decisive points of the text; that is, he does this not only at the beginning of the story, but at the end as well. For example, Alice grows back to her normal size while she is still with the cards. In other words, she comes back to the "real" world when she is still in the world of fantasy. This confusion of the two worlds is described in detail as a long process, extending the coexistence of the two worlds for quite a long time:

> "If any one of them can explain it," said Alice, (she had grown so large in the last few minutes that she wasn't a bit afraid of interrupting him). . . .
>
> "Who cares for you?" said Alice, (she had grown to her full size by this time). "You're nothing but a pack of cards!"[17]

To confuse matters even more, Carroll does not end the story when Alice wakes up; rather, he leaves open the question of whether or not it was a dream, and even makes Alice's sister dream the whole story again. Thus, while he opened the story by framing it within another story, he uses the sister's dream to reframe the entire text into "a dream within a dream":

> But her sister sat still just as she left her, leaning her head on her hand, watching the setting sun, and thinking of little Alice and all her wonderful Adventures, till she too began dreaming after a fashion, and this was her dream. . . .[18]

This complicated technique totally blurs the relations between the two worlds. Alice's sister dreams about Alice's adventures, as if they were of real substance, belonging, as it were, to the same ontological order of the real world. In this way, Carroll questions the boundaries between the two dimensions. If a dream can be dreamed about, as if it were real, conversely, reality can be described as if it were a dream. The two dimensions exist equally and are equally "real." Evidence of this can be seen when Alice's sister dreams about Alice and about her adventures in the same sequence, without distinguishing between them at all.

On the other hand, when Alice wakes up in the *Nursery* version, she finds "that the cards were only some leaves off the tree, that the wind had blown down upon her face." Furthermore, Carroll makes sure to stress once again that the whole story is a dream: "*Wouldn't* it be a nice thing to have a curious dream, just like Alice? (56).

Carroll further adjusted the tone of the narrative to take on a condescending authoritative tone, which was typical of conventional didactic stories of the time, especially those intended to be read to, not by, children. The difference between the two versions, the conflicting narrative tones, the lack of parody and satire in the *Nursery* version, the different handling of space and time, and the relations between reality and fantasy, all indicate that in the *Nursery* version Carroll was indeed well aware of the child as the text's sole addressee.

Many famous writers for children who followed Carroll preferred to adopt his version of *Alice's Adventures in Wonderland* as a model of imitation, rather than the *Nursery* version that Carroll transformed into a "pure" children's story. What writers such as Maurice Sendak in his *Higglety Pigglety Pop!*, or Shel Silverstein in his *The Giving Tree*, have decided to do, is to maintain a dialogue with the adult reader in their illustrated texts for preschool children. The process of reading these texts always involves adults as active coreaders (a notion coined by H.-H. Ewers[19]). This tendency to maintain a dialogue with the adult reader appears to be on the rise over the past few decades.

Let's take a look first at Maurice Sendak's *Higglety Pigglety Pop!,* a highly successful and well-loved children's book that has dominated the bestseller list for children for several years. The protagonist's name is borrowed from a nonsense rhyme that is well known, and remembered by heart, by almost every literate native-speaker of English in the Anglo-American world. This nonsense rhyme was not originally included in the collection of *Mother Goose*, as is occasionally assumed. It was written as a parody on *Mother Goose* "stupid" poems by Samuel Goodrich, a serious American writer and educationalist. He wrote this poem as part of a campaign against nonsense writing for children, in order to illustrate how ineffectual this kind of verse actually is. Ironically, Samuel Goodrich, who advocated rationalistic writing for children, was destined to leave to posterity nothing but this very poem, "Higglety Pigglety Pop," which, against his every will and intention, was ultimately included in *Mother Goose*.

Sendak, who was probably well aware of the history of the poem/rhyme, and probably assumed that highbrow readers were well aware of it, too, drew on its history and in so doing transformed it into a base from which he navigated into the cultural repertoire of his highbrow adult reader; most notable are the literary, historical, and psychological aspects of this repertoire.

Higglety Pigglety Pop! recounts the adventures of Jennie, a dog who leaves the cozy and comfortable home where she is well taken care of, and sets off on an instructive tour, which alludes to the tradition of the *Erbaaungsliteratur*. Jennie wishes to become a star, the main actress in Mother Goose's theater, and gets involved in strange and eccentric adventures, modeled at once on the theater of life, the theater of the stage, and the theater of the absurd.

Jennie leaves home not because she wants for anything, but because she believes that:

> There must be more to life than having everything! (5)

Or, in other words, money and property are not everything in life. Between being a dog who has everything and being a dog who has nothing, she loses everything she has, which leads her to say:

> There must be more to life than having nothing. (39)

She risks her own life and almost loses it, fails as a nanny (or almost fails), but eventually gets what she wants: the part of the main actress in a play staging the five lines of *Higglety Pigglety Pop!*

Her long and complicated adventures, and especially their interpretation by Jennie's aphorisms, leave lots of room for the adult reader, and especially the adult critic, to delve deeply into the text and come up with piles of fertile soil for interpretation.

What *Higglety Pigglety Pop!* offers, as does Shel Silverstein's *The Giving Tree*, is a philosophical story about the value of life and what makes life worth living. Like other books of this genre, this illustrated book, which is allegedly intended for preschool children is jam-packed with prevailing psychological and philosophical cliches, also to be found in the commonplace highbrow narrative.

Silverstein's *The Giving Tree* conveys a similar message to Sendak's, though the story is far less adventurous and Silverstein's message is much simpler than Sendak's. Sendak deliberately leaves unresolved the question of what gives life its value, suggesting that the answer is ambiguous and open to various interpretations. In addition, *Higglety Pigglety Pop!* is loaded with metaphors on life and death and with allusions to Freudian–psychological traumas such as the fear of rejection and the fear of death. In order to occupy the adult highbrow reader, it also alludes directly to Sendak's own private life—the baby illustrated on the cover is modeled on an old portrait of a child in the Sendaks' family album, and he himself had a dog named Jennie of whom he was very fond.

The combination of worldly and unworldly experiences results in an adventurous, fantastic story with a philosophical flavor, which addresses adults and children; it appears to be based on C. S. Lewis's assumption that this is the only kind of text for a "good" children's book.

It seems that this formula, used both by Silverstein and Sendak, has become a model in its own right, for by now there are many texts for children that address adults, as it were, over the shoulder of their child addressees. They are all rife with pseudophilosophical and pseudopsychological statements, which adults allegedly like to find in books for children. I doubt very much whether these statements would be at all acceptable in books for adults; I have a strong hunch that they would not. They have become almost mandatory, however, in children's books whose writers think that they should address parents or other adults who might read the text to the child. Personally I must admit that I find this thinly disguised genre of books for children that actually address adults quite tiresome. It appears to have become a channel for conveying simple and oversimplified messages, which seemingly conceal deeper thoughts that secure adult enjoyment of the texts but cannot be conveyed in books for adults.

This tendency goes back as far as the Victorian era, as the Victorians were the first to explore the magic of childhood, though in its abstract sense. As the terra incognita of every English gentleman, this aspect emphasized the beauty and the innocence of childhood, presenting it as the lost paradise from which adults are driven away at an early stage and to which they can never return. Ever since adults discovered both the existence of childhood as well as its sealed doorways, they have realized that they need a well-grounded excuse for entering the closed gates of the child's culture. Nineteenth-century texts, such as *Alice,* and twentieth-century texts, such as *Higglety Pigglety Pop!* and *The Giving Tree,* supply the key for catching a glimpse of this lost childhood. Texts for children that maintain a dialogue with adults supply this precious asset. Their inherent double attribution enables adults briefly to reexperience aspects of a lost childhood, though this is no longer a "pure" childhood, but rather an image of childhood that adults wish to reconstruct. Texts that address both children and adults make it possible to reenter a fabricated childhood—one that never really existed, but nonetheless pretends to be the nostalgic childhood adults always love to remember. Texts that merely address children could not fulfill this need. Only texts for children that also make sure to appeal to adults can repeatedly try to recall the illusion of experiencing childhood time and time again.

The double attribution of children's literature is used in this genre as a means of bypassing the limitations of writing for children without risking being rejected by adults. A writer for children can thus still write in the framework of children's literature without having to pay the price of being ascribed an inferior status and placing severe limitations on his or her writing. Combining the longing for a lost childhood with the attempt to secure the appeal of an adult readership has resulted in this new genre of books for children. Subsequently, more and more texts nowadays are less interested in appealing to the child, and indeed seem to forget that the child is, after all, their official addressee.

As much as adults enjoy this kind of literature, they should ask themselves whether children's literature is not reaching a point where the child-reader is being abused in favor of the child's parents. Perhaps the time has come to be more conscious of how the cultural differences between children and adults are used strategically by writers, readers, and critics of children's literature. Paradoxically, the process through which children's literature became an autonomous cultural system, defined by children as its addressee, led writers to clearly define the boundaries between children and adults in order to gain the support of the adult reader. Adults always will remain involved in the writing for children, but they must remember that children's literature is, after all, written not for them, but for children. Like a doting father who buys himself an electric train in order to fulfill his own childhood dream that never came true, more and more recent books for children seem intent on satisfying adult wishes and, in this sense, often appeal to adults at the expense of the child-reader. For adults seem to find it difficult to accept that once their own childhood is over, it is over for good. Sadly, the loss of childhood is irreversible, for childhood can never be recovered, even in books for children.

NOTES

1. Philippe Ariès, *Centuries of Childhood* (London: Jonathan Cape, 1962).

2. John Rowe Townsend, *Written for Children* (London: Penguin, 1977), 17.

3. Neil Postman, *The Disappearance of Childhood* (New York: Delacorte Press, 1982).

4. Jill Paton Walsh, "The Writer's Responsibility," *Children's Literature in Education* 4 (1973): 32.

5. Rebecca Lukens, "The Child, the Critic and a Good Book," *Language Arts* 55 (1978): 452.

6. C. S. Lewis 1969 [1952], "On Three Ways of Writing for Children," in *Only Connect*, ed. Sheila Egoff, G. T. Stubbs, and F. Ashley (New York: Oxford University Press, 1969), 210.

7. Isaac Bashevis Singer, "Isaac Bashevis Singer on Writing for Children," *Children's Literature* 6 (1977): 9–16.

8. Quoted in John Rowe Townsend, *A Sense of Story* (London: Longman, 1971): 212.

9. Stefan Kanfer, "A Lovely, Profitable World of Kid Lit." [interview with Maurice Sendak], *Time* 29 December 1980: 41.

10. Quoted in Townsend, *A Sense of Story*, 127, 201.

11. Jane Gardam, "On Writing for Children: Some Wasps in the Marmalade," part 1, *Horn Book Magazine* 60 (1978): 489.

12. Quoted in Townsend, *A Sense of Story*, 36.

13. Pamela Travers, "On Not Writing for Children," *Children's Literature* 5 (1975): 21.

14. Quoted in Townsend, *A Sense of Story*, 160.

15. Astrid Lindgren, "A Small Chat with a Future Children's Book Author," *Bookbird* 16 (1978): 12.

16. Lewis Carroll, *Alice's Adventures in Wonderland* (New York: Macmillan, 1968 [1865]); *Alice's Adventures Underground* (New York: Dover, 1965 [1886]); *The Nursery Alice* (New York: Dover, 1966 [1890]).

17. Martin Gardner, ed., *The Annotated Alice* (London: Penguin, 1977), 159, 161.

18. Ibid.,162.

19. Hans-Heino Ewers. "Das doppelsinnige Kinderbuch: Erwachsene als Leser und als Mitleser von Kinderliteratur." *Fundevogel*, 14, no. 42 (1987): 8–12.

REFERENCES

Ariès, Philippe. *Centuries of Childhood*. London: Jonathan Cape, 1962.

Carroll, Lewis. *Alice's Adventures in Wonderland*. New York: Macmillan, 1968 [1865].

———. *Alice's Adventures Underground*. New York: Dover, 1965 [1886].

———. *The Nursery Alice*. New York: Dover, 1966 [1890].

Egoff, Sheila, G. T. Stubbs, and F. Ashley. *Only Connect*. New York: Oxford University Press, 1969.

Ewers, Hans-Heino. "Das doppelsinnige Kinderbuch: Erwachsene als Leser und als Mitleser von Kinderliteratur." *Fundevogel* 14, no. 42 (1987): 8–12.

Gardam, Jane. "On Writing for Children: Some Wasps in the Marmalade." Part 1. *Horn Book Magazine* 60 (1978): 489–496.

Gardner, Martin, ed. *The Annotated Alice*. London: Penguin, 1977.

Kanfer, Stefan. "A Lovely, Profitable World of Kid Lit" [Interview with Maurice Sendak]. *Time* 29 December 1980: 38–41.

Lewis, C. S. "On Three Ways of Writing for Children." In *Only Connect*, ed. Sheila Egoff, G. T. Stubbs, and F. Ashley, 207–220. New York: Oxford University Press, 1969 [1952].

Lindgren, Astrid. "A Small Chat with a Future Children's Book Author." *Bookbird* 16 (1978): 9–12.

Lukens, Rebecca. "The Child, the Critic and a Good Book." *Language Arts* 55 (1978): 452–454, 546.

Postman, Neil. *The Disappearance of Childhood*. New York: Delacorte Press, 1982.

Sendak, Maurice. *Higglety Pigglety Pop!*. New York: Harper & Row, 1967.

Silverstein, Shel. *The Giving Tree*. New York: Harper & Row, 1964.

Singer, Isaac, Bashevis. "Isaac Bashevis-Singer on Writing for Children." *Children's Literature* 6 (1977): 9–16.

Townsend, John Rowe. *A Sense of Story*. London: Longman, 1971.

———. *Written for Children*. London: Penguin, 1977.

Travers, Pamela. "On Not Writing for Children." *Children's Literature* 5 (1975): 15–22.

Walsh, Jill Paton. "The Writer's Responsibility." *Children's Literature in Education* 4 (1973): 30–36.

CHAPTER 6

Dual Audience in Picturebooks

CAROLE SCOTT

The cityscape Maurice Sendak presents as the backdrop to his 1993 work, *We Are All in the Dumps with Jack and Guy*, is depicted with a condemnation whose harshness recalls Dickensian descriptions of nine- teenth-century London characterized by grime, want, and hunger, per- meated with crime, yet still seeking a benevolent power that might bring help and succor to its children. Whereas the Victorian imagination was captured by the child bent to economic gain—in the street, in the facto- ries, and still, like Blake's recurrent image of child despoliation, sweep- ing chimneys—Sendak's eye is caught by the city child as detritus, swept into odd corners, sheltering in cardboard boxes, the flotsam and jetsam of so-called civilized society, useless, uncared for, and prey to whatever the forces of evil portend. The passion with which Sendak presents the chil- dren's marginal world finds expression not only in the depiction of their plight, but in the impact of the turbulent relationship between text and il- lustration that becomes evident as he experiments with the genre.

This picturebook with its somber message—that the children will have to look out for themselves because there is no one else willing to do it—clearly fuels two of the most significant (and related) conversations currently occurring among children's literature critics. The first is the question of audience: For whom is this book intended? If this is a chil- dren's book, what does Sendak hope to communicate to them: that they are entering a world that does not value them and has no place for them? He depicts a society that no longer recognizes children's needs, grants them no love or care, and expects them to act as miniature adults who must struggle for their own survival. Or is the book intended for adults, signaling that the special status accorded to childhood, itself a relatively recent concept, no longer exists, and that those aspects of childhood that have been venerated—innocence, wonder, trust, creativity—are out of date and defunct? If it is a book for adults, does it speak to those "child-like" qualities that persist within the heart of the sensitive adult charac-terized as "the inner child"? Or is the book truly a dual-readership work, safe to be read by children only in the presence of an adult who can me-diate the message of the world's indifference by providing the security and permanence that the child needs to bear the hurtful message?

Regarding these dilemmas from a slightly different point of view suggests the semiotic approach to changes in norms and expectations for children's literature, especially the inclusion of themes earlier considered inappropriate to the genre. Historic approaches to the nature and scope of children's literature have revealed the changes in purpose, from didactic tales that sought to control and shape the emerging individual's moral de-velopment, to stories intended to delight, to appeal to children's imagina-tion and sensitivity, and to stimulate creativity and individuation. Early American tales for children that might characteristically feature a highly religious and moral child whose early death was heaven's reward for goodness, soon gave way to more entertaining stories. The codes that de-termine the field are constantly in flux as peripheral codes move over the boundary of the semiosphere toward its center, displacing earlier codes and forcing a new definition of the genre as it responds to the cultural con-text at large.[1] Recent works that allude to the impossibility of children's literature or to the death of the genre signal the striking changes that are occurring and dramatize the need for our reevaluation of what is appropri-ate.

In the 1997 *Children's Literature* volume dedicated to "Cross-Writing Child and Adult," Knoepflmacher's essay on Kipling's combining of vi-sual and verbal expression in his *Just So Stories* emphasizes the partner-ship with his daughter, real and remembered, in the creation of the work. This approach is in contrast to many of the others that focus upon the un-even distribution of power and knowledge between children and adults that is exemplified in many narratives. For example, in her article considering "E. Nesbit's Cross-Writing of the Bastables," Erika Rothwell speaks of "children's inability to understand what is easily apparent to adults" and the undermining of "the child's autonomy and status through sentimental and condescending attitudes,"[2] while Julia Briggs discusses "the persua-sion or even coercion implicit in the adult writer's address to the child reader" and makes the significant assertion that "positioning the nostalgic adult reader over the child's shoulder decisively alters the narrative voice and the angle of address."[3]

As readers, children do not have the experience, the knowledge, or the sophistication to unravel the nature of the dual address, and may either be unaware or it, or bewildered by the sense that they are missing something; in this way they reflect the feelings and perceptions of the child characters within the books. Not all dual-address books share the schismatic subtleties of E. Nesbit, where the children's naivete and uncertain attempts to be "grown up" are made fun of. Lorraine Janzen Kooistra's analysis of the careful choice of illustration to define Rossetti's *Goblin Market* as either a children's fairy tale or an adult erotic fantasy, thus targeting its intended audience, dramatizes what Jacqueline Rose, in her groundbreaking work *The Case of Peter Pan, or, The Impossibility of Children's Fiction*, cites as the necessity of using "knowledge to hold the two instances safely apart."[4] Lewis Carroll's *Alice In Wonderland*, a classic dual-audience work, is more even-handed, making fun of adults and children alike, and allowing numerous strata of interpretation that offer a sense of understanding regardless of the reader's age.

Whereas many of the works that have drawn the attention of critics fascinated by the dual-audience or cross-audienced phenomenon offer opportunities for intricate analysis of narrative technique, perspective, symbolism, and characterization, I believe that picturebooks give a unique opportunity for what I consider a collaborative relationship between children and adults, for picturebooks empower children and adults much more equally. Although illustrated books certainly encourage the less experienced child reader, picturebooks are specifically designed to communicate by word, by image, and by a combination of both. This form has redrawn boundaries, and in so doing has challenged accepted forms and learned expectations. Those less bound to the accepted conventions of decoding text are freer to respond to less traditional work, so children's very naivete serves them well in this arena, making them truer partners in the reading experience. As in the "find Waldo" books, children's ability to perceive and sift visual detail often outdistances that of the adult.

I will consider three examples of picturebooks that exemplify various levels of collaborative child-adult interpretation and help us to explore the tensions and relationships inherent in cross-writing: the Sendak book already mentioned, the British author/illustrator Colin Thompson's *Looking for Atlantis*, and the Swedish picturebook maker Tord Nygren's *The Red Thread* (originally titled *Den röden tråden*). Although Thompson's work can be packaged by Knopf as part of its Dragonfly series, complete with practical exercises in "how to look at things more closely" with a list of questions to promote observation,[5] Sendak's and Nygren's books are less easily categorized, and suggest some degree of uncertainty in their projected audience. Sendak's in particular raises questions very pertinent to Rose's tracing of the history of *Peter Pan,* which communicates that, although the story centers upon children, it was directed initially and primarily to adults.[6]

"Reading Level Ages 4–8" states the Amazon.com web page description of *Looking for Atlantis.* Yet the adult reader who ventures into Colin Thompson's 1993 "learn how to look" picturebook will find verbal and visual jokes and allusions dependent on a far greater sophistication. Besides the watery play on classical titles such as Finnegan's Whale, Moll Flounders, Cyrano de Bladder Wrack, and The Merry Whelks of Windsor, Thompson includes allusions to more popular adult fiction or movies: The Brine of Miss Jean Brodie, All Quiet on the Waterfront, and Kind Hearts and Cormorants. Adults also will respond to the sly cynicisms that rely on life experience: The Sip and Sigh diet, anti-accountant pills, and The Di-Milo Arms, which advertises "Get legless too!!" Unless the 4- to 8-year-old has some foreign language ability, he or she will probably miss the linguistic play involved in the house named Chez Mon You, or the multiple play on a bottle of wine labeled vin d'or leaning next to a toy vehicle door named van door.

Though *Atlantis* may be less sophisticated in theme than the other two works selected, its dialog between text and illustration is complex. As in Sendak's *In the Night Kitchen,* although the division between the true "text" and the illustration is relatively conventional, Thompson feels no need to restrict all his words to this textual aspect, but allows a tangential subtext to operate throughout his illustrations. While the progression of the story takes place in identified textual blocks on most, but not all, of the doublespreads, other stories and other lives, presented in a complex pastiche of pictures and individual words and phrases, offer a byzantine pattern of activity, word play, and image/word tension and interplay directed sometimes to adults, sometimes to children, and sometimes to both. The richness of this experience contrasts strongly with the shallow linear quality of the "learn how to look" pedagogical exercises already cited.

The title page precedes the beginning of the story, but it provides an immediate definition of multiple levels of sophistication. It also alerts us to the fact that the child-adult reader distinction is not a schismatic division, but a continuum of understanding. The nonreader can perhaps recognize that the sea depicted, complete with sailing vessel, waves, water lilies, and bulrushes, is in fact housed in a toilet tank, at the bottom of which is a shadowy city, surveyed by a mermaid; can see that there are eyes peering out from, and a hand emerging from a half sandwich; and can immediately recognize a variety of objects. The reader can identify some word play such as *Atlantis*, Antlantis (on a jar of ants), and Artlantis on a palette, as well as more complex sea-related equipment, such as the scuba diver's pressurized tank or the ship's cannon. But it takes more sophistication to articulate the discrepancies between the objects, and such visual gags as the broken sections of numbers, which translate into "pieces of eight."

Most of Thompson's illustrations in this book are characterized by a split page organization: the ordinary world dominates the upper part of the image, but under the floor lie all kinds of objects, and tiny people and animals carrying on their lives, hidden from the people living above. This concept of the hidden world also is injected into the world above the floor. For example, the front of the cabinets in the kitchen scene are removed so that we see, as if in cross section, all of the objects and activity taking place: besides all kinds of boxes, jars, vegetables, and cans (including a can of "Hoggett's Wholemeal Horse Fly Pâté") are mice blowing up the mousetrap; an aquarium with a mermaid in it; a little house named Pirate's Rest; water from the sink flowing into an underground lake with a river road, and a sailing boat crossing *over* a bridge. This cross section technique is multiplied as in the case of the egg box, whose side is cut off, and in which the eggs are also cross-sectioned, revealing three with yolks inside, and a fourth in which the yolk is replaced by a crown.

Another example of this technique invading the upper world is in the sitting room scene in which, amidst the ordinary perspective of the room, stands a chair in cross section, revealing four stories of mouse-house erected inside, as well as a rural scene. While other miniworlds coexist in this room, for example the storm in a jar, small, inhabited houses in the bookcase, and a tiny plane landing on the ceiling, these, in contrast to the underfloor and chair, are looked at from the outside, not in a cross-section revelation.

The technique clearly resonates to the theme of imagination, of seeing through what is apparent and searching for a deeper reality. Although this complex philosophical viewpoint is presented in simplistic terms for the child-reader, "At last I had learned how to look. I had learned that hopes and dreams are not just inside your head, and that I could keep *Atlantis* and Grandfather in my heart forever," for the adult reader the notion of penetrating apparent reality is communicated at a more sophisticated level. The multiple modes of visioning are further dramatized by the variety of styles of presentation: the surrealism of the train that whooshes out of the fireplace and disappears through a brick tunnel in the bookcase in the next room—while the boy is in both rooms simultaneously; or the bathroom scene that combines the pretty colors of a romance or fairy tale with the surrealism of nonexistent steps reflected in a mirror, and adds aspects of a horror film—the giant cockroach emerging from behind the tile or the snaky tongue coming up through the bath drain.

Like the picture of Monet's famous Bridge at Giverny in this version of which we can see a somewhat impressionistically depicted cartoon frog sitting on the bridge and a large, clearly delineated fish swimming in the pool beneath, the juxtaposition of styles creates a somewhat deconstructive effect. It is the adult reader who will understand the intention and sophistication of this approach. The young child will simply enjoy it; the older child will question it. Although the level of understanding and interpretation will differ, and many of the allusions will be over the head of the child-reader, directed entirely to the adult who has perhaps been persuaded by the back cover to "Read to a Child! The most important 20 minutes of your day," the intricacies of Thompson's presentation can be shared with delight between adults and children and enable them to form a collaboration in decoding this picturebook, pointing out details and jokes to one another.

Thompson's is in some ways the simplest of the three dual-address picturebooks I have selected. Tord Nygren's *The Red Thread* (*Den röden tråden*), a picturebook almost totally devoid of words and filled with pictures of children and characters from children's literature, should be as clearly intended for children as Thompson's *Atlantis*. But it is not so very clear. Although the back cover of the American edition offers a brave description, "a group of children follow a red thread and discover strange and exotic worlds: a forest full of hidden trolls, a magical garden, a Pierrot tightrope-walking to the moon, and an artist's sketching table come alive," this description falsely claims a narrative that is not there. The descriptive paragraph that follows, ending in "*The Red Thread*'s wealth of curious details and dramas will inspire readers to create equally elaborate stories of their own" is more to the point, for the book's challenge is the tension between narrative expectation and disjunctive pictures.

Like Sendak's book, the work raises many questions about audience and intent. If it were not for the red thread, the book would be easier to comprehend, for each doublespread offers a fascinating situation and experience. Only one of these has a clear narrative component: the journey depicted near the center of the book where a little man dressed in green images his sweetheart and travels to find her. His various modes of trans-portation are fanciful and entertaining: He hitches a ride on a bee, para-chutes into a pond using his umbrella, sits on a lily until a dragonfly takes him for a flight, and then takes advantage of rides from a snail, a grass-hopper, and an owl. The final miniscene shows him and the woman of his dreams with their arms around each other, perched on a leaf.

But all of the other doublespreads offer a kaleidoscope of scenes: a carousel horse has broken free with its child rider and is becoming real; a child in Victorian costume watches her toy yacht go out to sea; a range of recognizable characters drawn primarily from a variety of art works and children's books watch a large egg that is about to hatch; on an artist's drawing board pen, pencil, and brush create musicians already playing, while a green witch brushes into a heap the notes from a sheet of music; Linnaeus lectures two children on botany amid a field of giant plants, with a distant view of van Gogh painting. And so it goes on: a scene in-volving trolls; another with puppets; a girl on a bicycle; a night scene in which a group of people watch a tightrope walker on a rope hitched to the moon; a boy reading in bed while children's book characters pour from his bookcase and run across the room.

The doublespreads offer a wide variety of styles: realism, caricature, fantasy, the grotesque, and the surreal, and the clothes suggest a variety of times, cultures, and perspectives. The pictures are all quite acceptable for children, many of the characters are recognizable to them, especially the ones from the children's books, and children feature in almost all, as ac-tors or as audience. In addition, many of the activities are very relevant to children's lives: the carousel ride, the toy boat, the magic show, the pup-pets, the bicycle ride, kite flying, and the storybook characters. Yet the adult reader is continually puzzled and challenged. Some of the charac-ters are not so easy to recognize; who are they? Why are such disparate groups brought together in one doublespread? Why are Linnaeus and van Gogh juxtaposed? Could it be that they view nature in different ways? Why do some characters reappear in various doublespreads and others don't? What is the connection, what is the narrative progress, and how does the symbolic red thread link all of these together?

At one level at least this is a metafictive picturebook, for it fore-grounds the creative process itself, making this the very subject of the book for any thinking adult, and for the children's literature critic an exer-cise in relating narratology to image. Is the red thread there to inspire the creative impulse to storytelling, or does it mock the adult reader's need to make sense of the book? Following the thread from beginning to end, as it passes over the right-hand margin to reappear in the connecting spot on the next left-hand margin, the reader finds it sometimes going straight across the page, sometimes meandering unsystematically, sometimes playing a part in the picture (as tightrope for example) and sometimes not, but (except in the journey already described where it teases us with its conventional progression in marking the progress) without apparent linear intent. Eventually it comes full circle and passes across the cover to begin again.

The title of the book and the behavior of the thread thus stimulate a significantly different reading experience for child and adult, but not one that is collaborative in the manner of Thompson's, where each offers aspects of their own perceptual experience for the other's enjoyment. It is not inconsequential that the child/adult relationship depicted in *Atlantis* is one of loving guidance that leads the child to discover his own resources, whereas the relationship in *The Red Thread* is very different. Adults control, entertain, instruct, and mesmerize children; they sometimes hide behind masks, or play conjuring tricks. But the gap between the children and the adults is clearly set and it is the adults who hold the knowledge and display their talents, while the children are generally observers, most often entranced by what the adults are doing, but sometimes turning away. One such example of the latter situation is the child who sits on the left of the night sky, tightrope picture. While the adults are caught up in gazing at this miraculous sight, the child looks directly and thoughtfully at the reader, uninterested in the adults' shenanigans.

While the child-reader can follow the thread from picture to picture, it is the older reader who is driven to struggle with finding meaning, logic, and progression that the thread provokes. The green witch on the final spread this time sweeps the last words from the page into a heap of single letters on the floor. The last word is that there is no word, and that these posturing adults may spend their lives searching for it to no avail. Although Nygren's adult audience will find more to interpret than the child, the underlying suggestion is that the child's view is straighter, simpler, less neurotic, and more serene.

Sendak's choice of the nursery rhyme as his declared text in *We Are All in the Dumps with Jack and Guy* makes a historic claim for his presentation of a speaking picture of the world's ills in social, political, and economic terms, for so-called nursery rhymes began as popular political and social commentary, like folktales moving from an adult context into literature supposedly fit for children and sustained within childhood culture long after the original meanings became hard to access and sometimes permanently lost. In this choice, Sendak implicitly anticipates those who will question the appropriateness of this book for children and draws attention to a traditional view of what has been judged fit material for them. Sendak alerts the reader to an unusual experience to come with a combination of signals: the reversed book jacket with a picture on the front and the title on the back; the coarse brown kraft paper serving as flyleaf; the text printed on the inside flap of the cover; and the picture of the near-naked toddler dressed only in a loincloth who howls on the frontispiece with the title directly above his naked head and below his bare feet.

Unlike earlier illustrations of others' works, for example those inspired by Grimms' *Dear Mili* (1980), the text of the first half of *Dumps*, featuring the first of the two nursery rhymes Sendak has selected and combined, is almost buried in words of his own, creating a complex subtext for the reader. This subtext completely invades the illustrations, and its coherence, hard to understand even on its own, is in continual conflict with the words that appear in all parts of the illustrations: as dialogue in balloons, as signposts, as lettering on discarded cartons, but most of all as newspaper headlines, articles, and advertisements that make sad, ironic, and bitingly satiric comments on the plight of the children, on the state of the community at large, and on the rapaciousness of some and poverty of others in an economically turbulent world. Interspersed among these complex and sophisticated messages, all well beyond the understanding of children, are personal messages and autobiographical notes from Sendak's own life.

As the book proceeds, the layering of text, illustration, and other dialogue, word messages and references contrives a collage of meaning that reflects and comments upon itself in a truly postmodern manner. The rats' bridge game takes place in the shadow of a real bridge; the children cry "Trumped" beneath the Trump Tower; a child wears a T-shirt with a Wild Thing on it; references to Sendak's doctor are hidden in the illustration. Yet this allusive word/image play is directed to an adult understanding, not that of a child; so is, for example, the visual reference to concentration campus. And the children's voices crying "Lost! Tricked Trumped Dumped!" as the rats take the baby are replaced by the newspaper text that continues the verbal commentary. Presented initially on the front cover by the headlines "Leaner Times, Meaner Times," "Homeless Shelters," and the more fanciful "Children Triumph," "Kid Elected President," the newspapers' print becomes increasingly legible as the children's voices fail, giving the effect of a rising volume of social commentary to replace their cries.

Although some of the allusions in Thompson's book are directed to the adult reader, in Sendak's *Dumps*, because of this intrusive subtext and the sophisticated allusions as well as the choice of subject, there is a ongoing sense that this is a picturebook addressing adults rather than a child audience. Yet the pictures themselves, and the story line unencumbered with words is understandable by children, as Lawrence Sipe's reader response experiment demonstrates.[7]

Though a limited study with just two children, a first-grade and a second-grade boy, Sipe's interview record clearly reveals that although the two had different reactions, both could follow the events with little problem. The older boy, who came from a less affluent background, empathized with the homeless, motherless children and was concerned with differentiating the realistic and fantasy aspects of the story before he was satisfied. The younger boy found the book amusing, and Sipe points out the degree of cartoon-like "humor some subtle, some slapstick"[8] that appealed to the child, where the adult response is to take the book very seriously. Both children followed the actions of the plot, recognized the moon/cat metamorphosis, the rescue of Jack and Guy, and perceived the ending as a happy one. Both children became very involved in the story, and neither paid any attention to the newspaper subtext that an adult reader finds hard to ignore.

Sendak has stated many times that surviving childhood is a real challenge, and his vision of what children need to support them is clearly not in accord with the more romanticized view of childhood that Nygren depicts and that Thompson supports. Sipe definitely asserts Sendak's view when he alleges that "we err greatly in rejecting certain themes as inappropriate or harmful to the tender sensibilities of the young." Sendak has always argued that "by . . . pandering to the need of adults to feel that their children are 'innocent'—in these ways we deprive them of the types of books that will befriend them and help them on their perilous journey to adulthood."[9]

Adults are very aware of the ways in which children's experiences today differ from the childhood they remember, and this sense of difference is further distorted by backward glances through the mists of reminiscence. It is unreasonable to suppose that, as the cultural context changes, children's literature should not also be in flux. Although it is just a few years since shocked librarians across the country employed white correction fluid to diaper Mickey's offensive genitals, exposed as he fell out of his clothes into the Night Kitchen, if we were to go back a couple of centuries or so we would find parents taking their children to public hangings for their entertainment value. Today technology brings video games, graphically explicit sex, shopping channels, and violence in the movies and in the news right into the home, while the ever-present

Walkman surrounds the individual in a personal and often cacophonous universe. In this context, a book that presents the plight of the homeless where rats play cards for human lives seems less shocking than simply contemporary.

Unlike the two other books discussed, the relationship between adult and child is highly problematic both within the context of the work, and in the dual audience relationship. There are no adults in *Dumps*—unless we consider the gangster rats and the nurturing moon/cat as adult substitutes. Although they live in a world created by adults, the children are on their own, and their survival derives from their sense of responsibility and support for one another. And, unlike Thompson's and Nygren's books, it appears that the children and the adults are, in part at least, reading different texts. Nygren's work appeals to different levels of interpretation with his audiences, and Thompson's book offers some adult-only allusions within his incredibly detailed illustrations, but Sendak uses an alternative voice that demands the adult readers' attention and offers a political/social commentary on the piece. A collaboration between child and adult readers is thus complicated in an almost perverse manner, for it sets child and adult against each other so that the reading experience becomes rather a separate than a joint one. While both Thompson and Sendak create a subtext of words within images, the political message of Sendak's subtext dominates the adult reader's interpretation; and Thompson's subtext enriches and amplifies his gentler message of observation and imagination.

NOTES

1. See particularly Maria Nikolajeva's *Children's Literature Comes of Age: Toward a New Aesthetic* (New York and London: Garland, 1996), esp. Chapter 3.

2. Erika Rothwell, "'You Catch it if you Try to do Otherwise': The Limitations of E. Nesbit's Cross-Written Vision of the Child," *Children's Literature* 25 (1997): 62, 68.

3. Julia Briggs, "E. Nesbit, the Bastables, and The Red House: A Response," *Children's Literature*, 25 (1997): 73.

4. Jacqueline Rose, *The Case of Peter Pan, or The Impossibility of Children's Fiction* (London: Macmillan, 1984), 69.

5. "How many of the following can you find: fish, doors, books, mice, birds, stairs and/or ladders, boats, trees?"

"Take five seconds to look at the next person who enters the room: what color are this person's eyes; . . . does the person's shirt have buttons?"

6. I found especially interesting Rose's account of the reviews of the first performances that suggested that the adult might like to take along a child to increase his enjoyment of the play.

7. Lawrence R. Sipe, "The Private and Public Worlds of *We Are All in the Dumps with Jack and Guy,*" *Children's Literature in Education* 27, no. 2 (1996): 87–107.

8. Ibid., 102.

9. Ibid., 88.

REFERENCES

Briggs, Julia. "E. Nesbit, the Bastables, and The Red House: A Response." *Children's Literature* 25 (1997): 71–85.

Knoepflmacher, U. C., "Kipling's 'Just-So' Partner: The Dead Child as Collaborator and Muse." *Children's Literature* 25 (1997): 24–49.

Kooistra, Lorraine Janzen. "Goblin Market as a Cross-Audienced Poem: Children's Fairy Tale, Adult Erotic Fantasy." *Children's Literature* 25 (1997): 181–204

Nikolajeva, Maria. *Children's Literature Comes of Age: Toward a New Aesthetic.* New York and London: Garland, 1996.

Nygren, Tord. *The Red Thread.* New York: R & S Books; Farrar Strauss and Giroux, 1988.

Rose, Jacqueline. *The Case of Peter Pan, or, The Impossibility of Children's Fiction.* London: Macmillan, 1984.

Rothwell, Erika. "'You Catch it if you Try to do Otherwise': The Limitations of E. Nesbit's Cross-Written Vision of the Child," *Children's Literature* 25 (1997): 60–70.

Sendak, Maurice. *We Are All in the Dumps with Jack and Guy.* New York: Harper Collins, 1993.

Sipe, Lawrence R. "The Private and Public Worlds of *We Are All in the Dumps with Jack and Guy,*" *Children's Literature in Education* 27, no. 2 (1996): 87–107.

Thompson, Colin. *Looking for Atlantis.* New York: Alfred A. Knopf, 1993.

CHAPTER 7

"Ages: All"

Readers, Texts, and Intertexts in *The Stinky Cheese Man and Other Fairly Stupid Tales*

RODERICK McGILLIS

"ceci n'est pas un essai"

Sitting in a gazebo on a hot summer afternoon somewhere in western Canada, four writers, one of whom is also an illustrator of prominence, find themselves engaged in a heated discussion concerning audience and the difference between allusion and intertextuality in literary texts. The four conversationalists are Harriet Childe-Pemberton, Evelyn Sharp, George Cruikshank, and Maurice Maeterlinck. Each of them has some knowledge of writing for both children and adults. As they converse, various children who are playing in the garden enter the gazebo, at times offering outbursts of playful wisdom. And at some point a man who is wearing swimming trunks, and who looks amazingly like Burt Lancaster, happens by; he says his name is Tex Avery. Let's listen in on the conversation.

Childe-Pemberton: Oh, dear, that's what I said about fifteen minutes ago. Don't you people ever listen? I'll try again: a book such as *The Stinky Cheese Man and Other Fairly Stupid Tales* is hardly an example of what the word *Intertextuality* means. On the other hand, Anthony Browne's recent book, *Willy's Dream*, is as good an example of Intertextuality as you could ask for. It connects directly with Browne's other work, especially but not solely with the "Willy" books. Browne deliberately creates a weave, interconnecting his own work which also connects with a great variety of other work from the surrealism of Magritte, Dali, and others to popular film (most obviously *King Kong*) to past children's books (fairy tales, the "Alice" books and so on). Anyone reading these books must know that other stories and texts intersect with the one he or she is reading. You see, Intertextuality is only possible when two conditions exist: The writer puts the reader in the know, so to speak, and the writer fashions a *text* rather than a *work* of literature. Allusion is for works of literature; Intertextuality is for texts. That's why the word "text" is in it. Or if you want to know more, read my fairy tales.

Cruikshank: Well Harriet, I'll resist the snide remark here, but I suggest my own refashioned Fairy Tales are superior examples of what we mean by intertextuality than what you speak of. Here we have stories that better their originals, if I may be so bold as to assert this. This fellow, what's his name, Bloom—I recall someone saying he's all Bloom and Doom—whatever you think of his wacky theories, says something sensible about the writer who clearly has in mind another work . . .

Childe-Pemberton: Work or text? Be precise, now, George.

Maeterlinck: And what about that Frauds on the Fairies business?

Cruikshank: I'm not getting into a debate with Harriet, and you Maurice will not distress me with that person whose name shall not pass my lips. You both well know what I mean—that thing we read that has a plot with a beginning, middle, and end. I say, an artist of whatever kind cannot but have a previous work or works in mind when he creates his own art.

Childe-Pemberton: He or she, George.

Cruikshank: I stand corrected, Harriet.

Sharp: George, you assume that Aristotle settled things about plot and that's that. But that's not that. What is an end? What is a beginning? And what if middles come at the beginning—*in medias res*, you remember? What about certain kinds of writing, life-writing, for example? What of oral forms, especially those culturally different from ours? But we're getting away from the subject before us: intertextuality. For me, we can talk until doomsday (or Bloomsday, if you prefer), and not really get to the important point. The important thing is . . .

Maeterlinck: I'm interrupting here Evelyn not to be rude, but to suggest that you, with your personal views, are going to be hard-pressed to assert what the important point is. When it comes to Intertextuality, we are speaking of a formal feature of a text or work or whatever. We can't go beyond this fact. There is nowhere beyond formalism. An intertextual flag asks the person reading or viewing the—let me call it "object," for now—reading or viewing the object to think about several formal properties:

1. how do the plots of the interconnected two or more objects compare?
2. how do the characters in the interconnected two or more objects compare?
3. how do the structures—and by structure I mean order of events, combination of metaphors or images, configurations of characters, binary aspects of place, and such like—of the interconnected two or more works compare?
4. how do the use of line or color or compositional features or predominent shapes in a visual field compare?

A convenient listing of the variety of intertextual activity, jumping off from how a "focus" text (the text we are reading at the moment) relates to other texts, is available in a very fine book by an Australian fellow, John Stephens. The book I refer to is *Language and Ideology in Children's Fiction* (1992, See pages 84–86).

And as far as I am concerned, we can use this rather nasty little book, *The Stinky Cheese Man*, as an example, although my own work offers ample, and I daresay more satisfyingly complex, examples of what I'm referring to. The thematic aspects of the formal features I mention are rich in my books, but *Stinky*, well, that's pretty slight, isn't it.

Cruikshank: I couldn't agree with you more—or at least with the gist of what you are saying. This book is for children, and therefore it ought to have something to teach them; instead it flaunts authority and makes ridiculous both itself and the stories it uses for its intertextual frivolity.

Childe-Pemberton: Yes, the book seems to make fun of authority—I agree—and to ridicule just about everything in a harmless way, but this is not entirely the case. Take, for example, its presentation of female characters: these are either disgustingly hoydenish (I think of the Little Red Hen and Little Red Running Shorts) or passive beyond belief (I think of the Princess with the Bowling Ball or even worse, Cinderumpelstiltskin). Finally, the patriarchal Giant is the most dominant character in the book. Here is a fairy tale book that outpatriarchs even the Brothers Grimm or Andersen.

Sharp: I think we are forgetting the wider implications . . .

Maeterlinck: The most obvious connection in this book is with classic fairy tales by the Brothers Grimm and Hans Christian Andersen, although a few of the intertextual connections are with folk material unrelated to specific writers. This is one reason why the creators of this book can get away with their parodic fun; they are playing with stories no longer protected by copyright. Here intertextuality takes the form of parody. And we all know children love parody. Parody is a form ready-made for both adults and children. It has a leveling force.

Cruikshank: Er, are we speaking here of Parody or Pastiche? And when does quotation or imitation become parody or pastiche?

Maeterlinck: To answer your second question first, I note quickly that parody "has a stronger bitextual determination than does simple quotation or even allusion: it partakes of both the code of a particular text parodied, and also of the parodic generic code in general."[1] So we can see the stories in *Stinky* depend on the code of the classic fairy tales, but they use these codes in a manner that is distinctly parodic or off-kilter, comic, even carnivalesque.

For my money the answer to your first question is: parody. But I know what you refer to and I am uneasy with this designation for *Stinky*. Since I called on Linda Hutcheon above, I might also note that she argues that "parody is not extramural in its aim" (43). I agree.

Cruikshank: You seem open to self-contradiction here, but I'll let this pass. You might say that *The Stinky Cheese Man* is a parodic text, but if you go on to assert that Parody is without an extraliterary aim—which I take it is what Hutcheon, and hence you who quote Hutcheon, mean—then you are not really talking about Parody, as far as I am concerned. Parody is entrance from the side, a sidling approach to something. From the point of view of Intertextuality, nothing could be more clearly asking readers or viewers to think of two or more texts at once than Parody. And as far as I am concerned, the only reason for Parody is to correct something that needs correcting, like all those so-called classic Fairy Tales that border on the Sybaritic. Yes, that's right, I said Sybaritic. To parody these tales is—or at least should be—to correct them.

Sharpe: Hem, did I hear that correctly?

Childe-Pemberton: If what you say is true, George, then Parody does not differ from Satire. Each attacks something the artist thinks needs chastening. Would you not agree?

Maeterlinck: But Parody is strictly related to art; it doesn't traffic in life. Satire directs itself at life's foibles. But in any case, we don't have to sort this out now because our subject is Intertextuality. And I agree with George

that Parody is supreme Intertextualty. This is probably why it is so preva-
lent in works for the young. What better way to introduce young readers to
the fact that literature and art are a great weave of interconnected stories,
tropes, character types, conventions, and so on? Intertextuality seems tai-
lor-made for children because it is so pedagogically useful.

Sharp: Isn't it Oscar Wilde who says Parody is praise in awkward dress?

Cruikshank: No.

Childe-Pemberton: Gentlemen, stop a minute. We are in danger of forgetting George's question regarding Pastiche. I know the context of his question. As he points out when he asserts that Parody is a corrective technique
or mode, this type of art is not hermetically sealed within art itself. It has a
purpose, as we used to say before the world became purposeless.

Sharp: I've heard it called a porpoise, and the world has yet to become
porpoiseless . . .

Childe-Pemberton: Pray, let me continue.

*But before Harriet can continue, a small female child wanders dreamily
into the gazebo and moves to the middle of the assembled adults, then begins slowly to depart. We can only just hear her reciting in a whisper: "I
wandered lonely as a cloud / That floats on high / And I'll return to do my
homework / Only when pigs fly."*

Cruikshank: Damned nuisance, these little blighters.

Childe-Pemberton: As I said, allow me to go on. George assuredly has
Frederic Jameson in mind when he raises the issue of Pastiche as opposed to Parody. Since Maurice has already done so, I'll also take the
Liberty of quoting. But first I must explain that Jameson's notion of Parody and Pastiche rests on his sense of culture in the late century entering
a phase of overload. Too much information, too many social codes and
conventions, too much fashion, too many ideolects have resulted in fragmentation. Any hope for a collective project seems abandoned in the pursuit of the hedonism that no longer is quite so new. Here's what he says:

> Pastiche is, like parody, the imitation of a peculiar or unique, idiosyn-
> cratic style, the wearing of a linguistic mask, speech in a dead lan-
> guage. But it is a neutral practice of such mimicry, without any of
> parody's ulterior motives, amputated of the satiric impulse, devoid of

laughter and of any conviction that alongside the abnormal tongue you have momentarily borrowed, some healthy linguistic normality still exists.[2]

The Stinky Cheese Man strikes me, as I have indicated before, as a particularly repulsive example of Pastiche, a book about nothing—like that American TV show, what-d'ye-call-it. The stories go nowhere. The best example of this is the Pastiche called "Little Red Running Shorts," a nonstory in which the characters refuse to take part in the plot thus ending the narrative before it begins. This is silliness not even Lewis Carroll can match.

At this precise moment, another child, this time a boy, dashes into the gazebo, twirls around three times, and chants: "Jack be Nimble, Jack be quick, / Jack stand still; you're making me sick." Then he runs out.

Maeterlinck: What is going on here?[3] Can't someone control those children?

Sharp: Maybe we should listen to them.

Maeterlinck: Maybe we should sort out where we are in our conversation. All in all, I agree with the drift of what we are saying. Intertextuality and parody have much in common; they are both formal features of textuality. And they are both "always after-the-event rewritings of other texts."[4] In parody, as the Frenchman Lecercle argues, the parodist's voice displaces the voice of the original author—one voice takes over from another. So we might say that Jon Scieszka's voice takes over from Hans Andersen's in the retelling of "The Ugly Duckling" in the story called, "The Really Ugly Duckling." But *The Stinky Cheese Man* is a collaboration between Scieszka and Lane Smith, the illustrator, and the two of them displace the voice not only of Andersen, but also of the Brothers Grimm, Charles Perrault, Joseph Jacobs, Richard Chase, and Anonymous. A story such as "Cinderumpelstiltskin" combines at least two previous texts, both of which exist in several versions. In other words, the Parody here is not restricted to one prior text, but rather it directs itself to several texts whose origins are not certain. Whose voice is being parodied here? Of course the answer to this question is difficult, if not impossible, for any of us to supply. For Lecercle, this is Parody *in extremis*. For him, a Parody is "monological" (173); but what we have here is a "parody of a parody" or what Lecercle terms "pastiche" (170). Here he obviously parts ways with Jameson, whether he has read him or not.

Childe-Pemberton: Yes, the range of targets for Parody in this book is vast. As much as I dislike the book, I can agree that the Parody here is not one-dimensional.

Cruikshank: Yes, yes. Just take one story, for example. "Giant Story" is short; I'll recite it for you:

THE END
of the evil Stepmother
said "I'll HUFF and SNUFF and
give you three wishes."
The beast changed into
SEVEN DWARVES
HAPPILY EVER AFTER
for a spell had been cast by a Wicked Witch
Once upon a time.

This brief antinarrative is the kind of thing we sometimes see in collective story-making in classrooms or computer games. In just thirty-nine words, we have direct allusions to "The Three Little Pigs," "The Beauty and the Beast," and "Snow White and the Seven Dwarves." Other familiar tags—three wishes, a spell cast by a witch, and of course once upon a time—could well derive from any number of fairy tales. The range of possibilities grows even wider when we consider "happily ever after" because this is a phrase that almost never appears in fairy tales, but which most readers think does appear in almost all tales. And finally, "the end" refers to all stories, but once again only in an illusory sense, since readers tend to think that all stories have an end, but as "Giant's Story" indicates, this is not necessarily the case. This story, then, is not a Parody; it is a Parody of a Parody and draws into it stories we might relate to Perrault, Madame d'Aulnoy, the Grimm Brothers, or just about all those whom we connect with the classic fairy tales.

I might add that the illustration accompanying this story is even more wide in its range of allusion. The picture is a collage constructed from a great many bits of other illustrations, some quite familiar and others less easy for me to identify. A quick glance shows bits from Heinrich Hoffmann's *Struwwelpeter*, Kurt Weisse's "The Story of Ping," Denslow's Tin Man from *The Wizard of Oz*. The entire effect is reminiscent of an image from Braque or Picasso. Several techniques are apparent: line drawing, pencil, watercolor, woodcut, silhouette, photograph. This picture made up of pictures is more multivocal than the story it illustrates—

or doesn't illustrate. The point in all this is reversal. In its several parts the story and illustration make clear sense, but put together they make *non*sense. Here Parody serves to cancel out Significance and Meaning.

Childe-Pemberton: Very impressive, George. But don't you think the significance in this story and illustration is a little more meaningful than you are willing to admit? I confess I don't like this offensive book—note the misogynist touches in that almost the only women either mentioned or shown are the evil stepmother, the wicked witch, and the crone. And then in the illustration, we have the female reduced to synecdoche: a golden slipper, a young girl's hat, and possibly two lips shown upside down (perhaps calling on our memory of Mr. Warhol's multiple display of Marilyn's Lips). And yet the point seems to be that creation partakes of *bricolage*, n'est-ce pas, Maurice? These two—Scieszka and Smith—are *bricoleurs*. They have no vision of their own; they can only piece together bits from previous children's stories and illustrations to fashion their own book. They seem to be saying that this is how writers and illustrators create all books. They seem to be pointing out the artificiality of bookmaking, its inherent arbitrariness except for the fact of the strong hold of convention on us. They challenge convention. In this, they are subversive, but to what purpose? Really these are anarchic twerps who in the end reinforce the very conventions they ostensibly set out to overturn.

Sharp: Careful now. The illustration we are talking about is "rendered in oil and vinegar."

Cruikshank: Ha ha. Oil and vinegar, eh. That's pretty good, Evelyn. The book is a tossed salad, eh. Not bad, not bad.

Sharp: Alas, I can't take credit for that joke.

Cruikshank: Oh. Whatever. Hey, we're finally getting somewhere. In terms of its Formal qualities—and that's all that matters anyway—this book is a Parody, or a Baroque Parody, what Lecercle calls Pastiche. And from the point of view of Intertextuality, we can see that the book sets out to make direct connections to other books and stories. A while ago, I mentioned Bloom, Harold rather than Leopold or Allan or Morely, and his wacky theories. But he is interested in Influence, and Influence is hardly the important thing here. What we can see is that once the writer or artist chooses a convention (a genre), he inevitably engages in conversation with those who came before him, and people in conversation do not inevitably desire to defeat those with whom they are conversing, or to "kill" them. The Father, in other words, is not always the object of the conversing writer or artist. Entering in the conversation at this point of *The Stinky Cheese Man* are fables, folktales, fairy tales, didactic works, fantasies, and so on. As Bakhtin and later Kristeva show, intertextuality means more than simply direct allusion or quotation. The point is clearly and accurately stated in a recent book by a critic of children's books—believe it or not. Maria Nikolajeva rightly points out that the "meaning of the text is revealed for the reader or researcher only against the background of previous texts, in a clash between them and the present text." Texts cannot avoid looking back at previous texts and also looking "forward towards new, yet unwritten texts." She sensibly notes that it is possible "to distinguish between *dialogics* where the relation to a previous text is conscious, and *intertextuality* where it can be both conscious and unconscious."[5] Whether conscious or unconscious, a writer or artist who enters a discourse, must perforce . . .

Cruikshank: . . . engage in conversation with everyone who has come before. Yes. Correct. I couldn't have put it better myself. Language traces, and we are helpless to kick them over; we cannot kick over the traces. We are more obviously kicking against the pricks, and we cannot help but be affected by those pricks. The desire to stand alone, to be original, to speak our own language is always frustrate. We can only enter a conversation, not initiate one.

As if fate decreed a proof of this, a new figure enters the scene. This is the person in swimming trunks, the Burt Lancaster look-alike. Flexing his impressive biceps, he makes himself at ease and offers an observation.

Avery: Hi, my name is Tex, Tex Avery, and I just happened to hear what this fellow was saying about being original. I also see this book on the table here, *The Stinky Cheese Man and Other Fairly Stupid Tales.* I've looked at this book; it's a rip-off, man. This book is cocky in its irreverence, but this kind of thing has been done before. It ain't new. In fact, evidence of my own work is clear in there. And you don't have to sit there with your jaws dropping to the floor. If you want proof take a look at the picture of the cow in the story of "The Stinky Cheese Man." The drawing is distinctly Merry Melodies stuff. Only we did it better in "Red Hot Riding Hood," "Little Rural Riding Hood," "Swing Shift Cinderella," and the like.

Maeterlinck: I believe, Sir, that you have hit George's point precisely. If you are alive at all in the world, then you cannot hope to avoid using the language you inherit.

Cruikshank: The Language you inhabit in the manner a fish inhabits water.

Sharp: Who said that?

Cruikshank: I did. Just now.

Avery: Okay, people. You're way ahead of me. I can see this. But my fairy tales, fractured before their time, were for the army as well as for kids. I'm referring to the series of films we made that we might call "the RED HOT RIDING HOOD group." We even had an army sergeant working with us on those films, and "when we finished cutting and dubbing the first RED HOT RIDING HOOD, we got it down to the projection room where we always ran the picture for the producer and the whole group. And the sergeant spotted the thing and he roared."[6] We had difficulty with the censor on that one, I can tell you. But our audiences—kids and combat troops alike—loved it. You might check out "Red Hot Riding Hood" (1943) in connection with "Little Red Running Shorts." Well, I gotta run, but before I do you might consider that fairy tales of the kind you are talking about aren't so much burlesques as they are "brilliantly curdled tales."[7]

And he was gone.

Maeterlinck: I say, what was that all about? Who was that rather bold and uncouth fellow?

Childe-Pemberton: I don't know, but I hope never to see him again.

Sharp: Oh, stop all this fussing and bluster. You people never listen to anyone but yourselves; it's time you stopped posturing and listened. Please, just sit back for a moment and hear what you've not been hearing. First, your notions of Intertextuality are frighteningly closed, text-bound. Don't be so myopic; don't be so pathetically self-serving.

Maeterlinck: Now, Evelyn, you mustn't grow hysterical.

Sharp: Shut up and listen. Formalism is all right, as far as it goes; the problem is that it doesn't go far enough. Even Kristeva, as John Mowitt points out, extends "the domain of the textual well beyond the literary field."[8] Let me shift ground to the sense of intertextuality put forth by Pierre Bourdieu; he offers a positive revision of the ideas you've been presenting and our book, *The Stinky Cheese Man*, offers a fine example of the kind of Intertextuality Bourdieu articulates. In his book, *The Field of Cultural Production* (1993), Bourdieu criticizes the Russian formalists because "they consider only the system of works, the network of relationships among texts, or In- tertextuality." Consequently, "they are compelled to find in the system of texts itself the basis of its dynamics."[9] But the basis of literary dynamic rests on cultural, economic, political, and, hence, historical ground. In other words, as I understand it, the notion of Intertextuality is arid unless we connect it to the field of cultural production, or to that which lies out- side literature. If we recall postmodernism's claim that text is everywhere, is everything, then we might accept that a text's referents might well be nonliterary texts. To give a simple example, many of the so-called chil- dren's books of the later nineteenth century are intertextually related to such extraliterary concerns as Evolution, the problem of the poor, the "Woman Question," child labor, even the maintenance or dismantling of the class system. Think of such books as *Granny's Wonderful Chair* or *The Water Babies* or *The Princess and the Goblin* or *Mopsa the Fairy*. Kingsley and Macdonald clearly take up the question of Darwin; Frances Browne and Jean Ingelow confront the "woman question" in subtle ways; and Browne clearly critiques the Victorian obsession with the nobility of work and the class system that a celebration of work rests upon.

But what I'm talking about has its sinister side. If you haven't read Marsha Kinder's *Playing with Power in Movies, Television, and Video Games* (1991), then do so. Ms. Kinder examines the market-driven as- pects of Intertextuality, showing just how complicit the network of inter- textual connections between books, movies, TV, video games, and toys is with the late capitalist emphasis on products consuming consumers. Ac- cording to Ms. Kinder, the impetus to Intertextuality in the various as- pects of children's cultural products relates to an "interactivity" intent on fashioning "precocious consumers."[10] Intertextuality in the service of the marketplace: this is what we've come to.

But the book we have been talking about could not be clearer on this matter of extratextual textuality. The dust jacket contains much that takes us into nonliterary territory. Where to begin? Well, look at the front cover; it has the appearance of a tabloid with its bold title occupying nearly the entire visual field. On the left are samples of pictures the reader will see in full inside. On the lower right is a partial list of the book's contents. All this serves as invitaton for the prospective reader/purchaser to enter the book, but to enter knowing the implications of the book go far beyond just its formal features. The allusion to tabloid newspapers should prepare us for the broad strokes within; like tabloid journalism, this book will shame- lessly play with (manipulate) the material it refashions. And also like the tabloids, this book will employ sensationalism in the service of the economic motive. The aim is to convince the reader to buy the book, and to do so the creators are going to surprise and even shock the reader. How audacious can this book be is the question the reader asks, and just watch us fly is the challenge the book's two creators give in reply.

The irony here is ambiguous. The front flap of the dustjacket continues to play with kinds of textuality. Here we see the rhetoric of advertisement: "ONLY $16.00!" the top of the flap proudly states. And for this you get "56 action-packed pages, 75% more than those old 32–page 'Brand-X' books." Even the narrator turns up here to promote the book: the figure of Jack appears at the bottom holding a medallion that informs us that these stories are "NEW! IMPROVED! FUNNY!", that they are "GOOD!", that the book is a smart purchase, and that we should "BUY! NOW!" Appearing to temper this emphasis on the economic good sense the reader will display if he or she buys the book, is the back cover. Here another of the book's characters, the strident Little Red Hen, points to the Bar Code which contains the ISBN number and hollers a diatribe against the ugliness of the book and its pointlessness.

Throughout the book, we have such playful attention brought to the conventions of book publishing, but here on the cover this playful attention focuses entirely on the book's function in the marketplace. Make no mistake, this book participates in the market system; it is complicit with the capitalist concern for product. On the other hand, the insistence of paratextual detail to draw attention to itself in this book emphasises the "transactional" nature of this text. Paratext, as Genette so gracefully clarifies, is "always the conveyor of a commentary that is authorial or more or less legitimated by the author" and it exerts an "influence on the public" that better prepares that public to read and understand the text.[11] Here the paratextual matter serves as something of an warning, much as the Surgeon General's warning on a packet of cigarettes warns the buyer to beware. (In fact, inside the book, on the page that contains the "Introduction," we find apparently stamped on the page, just such a Surgeon General's Warning.) We might conclude that this book is serious in its desire to promote iconoclasm. The "photographs" of the artist and illustrator on the back flap of the dustjacket might corroborate this subversive activity. According to these photographs, Jon Scieszka looks amazingly like George Washington and Lane Smith is the spitting image of Abraham Lincoln, two American presidents deeply associated with rebellion and emancipation.

If, as Jacqueline Rose asserts, the "writing that is currently being promoted for children is that form of writing which asks its reader to enter into the story and to take its world as real, without questioning how that world has been constituted, or where, or who, it comes from,"[12] then *The Stinky Cheese Man* is an aberration. It flaunts its unreality, and it openly discusses the manner in which narratives come into being, and it teasingly nudges the reader to think about authorship when it proffers pictures of Washington and Lincoln as likenesses of Scieszka and Smith. What is an author? And can authors write revolutionary scripts? (I might add as a passing aside that the pictures of two famous presidents reminds us that this is a quintessentially American book—as you, Harriet, appear to intuit.)

And finally, before I cease and desist, I must ask whether or not the revolution evident in this book, its emancipatory project, is not directed at the entire systematizing of reading, its incorporation into an institution that serves the best interests of the state. If there is something we may label "systemic reading," this book challenges that by drawing attention to it. Whether this drawing attention results in complicity with or subversion of the system remains for the reader to decide, and to show in his or her reading and the actions that may result from that reading.

And now that I have reached the subject of the reader, let me say that readers, like books, come in all sizes, shapes, colors, and ages. When we begin to speak of readers in transaction with texts, we begin to construct the kind of readers we have in mind. We all know books published and marketed for young readers that come with recommended ages: preschool, 5–7, 7–9, 9–12, and YA [Young Adult]. Such age groupings are convenient, but pretty meaningless. *The Stinky Cheese Man* draws attention to the artificiality of such categories; inside the front flap of the dustjacket, as the bottom, we read: "Ages: All." Under this are the words, "Reinforced Binding," signaling that this book is sturdy and a good choice for library collections. The strong binding is also an indication that the book can take a lot of rough handling of the type perhaps equated with young readers. In any case, the book announces that it, like all good books published and marketed for young readers since Newbery, appeals to young and not so young alike.

No, mayhap not alike, but nevertheless the book offers something for everyone. Take once again, the front cover with its bold title: *The Stinky Cheese Man and Other Fairly Stupid Tales*. "Stinky" and "Fairly Stupid" are complicit with the young person's desire to trangress. Both are impolite and therefore subversive of adult decorum. Adults, however, may find the rather weak pun—fairly stupid tales/fairy tales—amusing, and of course most of us have experienced the blueness of cheese. The word "stupid" itself will mean something different to an adult, especially an adult with a literary background, from what it will mean to a child. But a more intricate joke for the adult is visual: the depiction of the Stinky Cheese Man himself smack in the middle of the page. The drawing of the Stinky here reflects the drawing of the Gingerbread man in various illustrated retellings of that story, for example, the one by Anne Rockwell in *The Three Bears and 15 Other Stories* (1975). The rendering of Stinky announces the parodic intent of the book as much as the title does. Adults in the know will understand that this book will offer fairy tales with a difference, since the title story derives from a fairy tale that is unusual in that its protagonist is a meal. Gingerbread or cheese—it does not matter—each will end in the stomach of a predator. Predation is what this is all about, even the predations of the marketplace.

Is anyone still awake?

Cruikshank: (yawn) And so what does this have to do with Intertextuality, dare I ask?

Sharp: Intertextuality is a reflection of the human condition. We are, all of us, creatures of Intertextuality: child and adult inhabit Intertextuality. We are simultaneously master of and slaves to language. In our desire to take control of our lives, we speak and in speaking hope to clarify what it means to be a subject by taking up a position in language. But every position is occupied and we can only sit in someone else's lap. The palimpsest is the only true order of textuality. But understanding this, choosing a lap, entering into the conversation (if I may alter the metaphor), is the only way we have of gaining a perspective on what we read or see that allows us to understand the forces—both literary and nonliterary—at work vying for our subjectivity.

Maeterlinck: Shall we go outside and have a cigarette?

Childe-Pemberton: I've heard that one before.

As they leave the gazebo, a gaggle of young children race by singing: "Run, Run, / As fast as you may; / You'll not catch us, / Don't care what you say."

NOTES

1. Linda Hutcheon, *A Theory of Parody: The Teaching of Twentieth-Century Art Forms* (New York and London: Methuen, 1985), 42.

2. Frederic Jameson, *Postmodernism or, the Cultural Logic of Late Capitalism* (Durham, N.C.: Duke University Press, 1991), 17.

3. If I may intrude an author's voice, then I would say another way of putting this is: "Something is happening here / But you don't know what it is / Do you, Mr. Jones."

4. Jean-Jacques Lecercle, *Philosophy of Nonsense: The Intuitions of Victorian Nonsense Literature* (London and New York: Routledge, 1994), 169.

5. Maria Nikolajeva, *Children's Literature Comes of Age: Toward a New Aesthetic* (New York and London: Garland, 1996), 153, 154.

6. Joe Adamson, *Tex Avery: King of Cartoons* (New York: Da Capo Press, 1975), 182.

7. Raymond Durgnat, *The Crazy Mirror: Hollywood Comedy and the American Image* (New York: Delta, 1970), 185.

8. John Mowitt, *Text: The Genealogy of an Antidisciplinary Object* (Durham, N.C.: Duke University Press, 1992), 111.

9. Pierre Bourdieu, *The Field of Cultural Production,* ed. and introduced Randal Johnson (New York: Columbia University Press, 1993), 179–180.

10. Marsha Kinder, *Playing with Power in Movies, Television, and Video Games: From Muppet Babies to Teenage Mutant Ninja Turtles* (Berkeley, Los Angeles, and London: University of California Press, 1991), 38.

11. Gérard Genette, *Paratexts: Thresholds of Interpretation,* trans. Jane E. Lewin (Cambridge: Cambridge University Press, 1997), 2.

12. Jacqueline Rose, *The Case of Peter Pan, or The Impossibility of Children's Fiction* (London: Macmillan, 1984), 62.

REFERENCES

Adamson, Joe. *Tex Avery: King of Cartoons*. New York: Da Capo Press, 1975.

Bakhtin, M. M. *The Dialogic Imagination*. Trans. Caryl Emerson and Michael Hoquist. Austin: University of Texas Press, 1981,

Bloom, Harold. *Anxiety of Influence*. London, Oxford, and New York: Oxford University Press, 1973.

Bourdieu, Pierre. *The Field of Cultural Production*. Ed. and introduced by Randal Johnson. New York: Columbia University Press, 1993.

Browne, Anthony. *Willy's Dream*. Cambridge, Mass.: Candlewick Press, 1998.

Durgnat, Raymond. *The Crazy Mirror: Hollywood Comedy and the American Image*. New York: Delta, 1970.

Genette, Gerard. *Paratexts: Thresholds of Interpretation*. Trans. Jane E. Lewin. Cambridge: Cambridge University Press, 1997.

Hutcheon, Linda. *A Theory of Parody: The Teaching of Twentieth-Century Art Forms*. New York and London: Methuen, 1985.

Jameson, Frederic. *Postmodernism or, the Cultural Logic of Late Capitalism*. Durham, N.C.: Duke University Press, 1991.

Kinder, Marsha. *Playing with Power in Movies, Television, and Video Games: From Muppet Babies to Teenage Mutant Ninja Turtles*. Berkeley, Los Angeles, and London: University of California Press, 1991.

Kristeva, Julia. *Desire in Language: A Semiotic Approach to Literature and Art*. Trans. Thomas Gora, Alice Jardine, and Leon S. Roudiez. New York: Columbia University Press, 1980.

Lecercle, Jean-Jacques. *Philosophy of Nonsense: The Intuitions of Victorian Nonsense Literature*. London and New York: Routledge, 1994.

Mowitt, John. *Text: The Genealogy of an Antidisciplinary Object*. Durham, N.C.: Duke University Press, 1992.

Nikolajeva, Maria. *Children's Literature Comes of Age: Toward a New Aesthetic*. New York and London: Garland, 1996.

Rockwell, Anne. *The Three Bears & 15 Other Stories*. New York: Thomas Y. Crowell, 1975.

Rose, Jacqueline. *The Case of Peter Pan, or The Impossibility of Children's Fiction*. London: Macmillan, 1984.

Scieszka, Jon and Lane Smith. *The Stinky Cheese Man and Other Fairly Stupid Tales*. New York: Viking, 1992.

Stephens, John. *Language and Ideology in Children's Fiction*. London and New York: Longman, 1992.

PART III

Oppression, Repression, Subversion, Transgression: Crossover and Censorship

CHAPTER 8

Writing for a Dual Audience in the Former Soviet Union
The Aesopian Children's Literature of Kornei Chukovskii, Mikhail Zoshchenko, and Daniil Kharms

LARISSA KLEIN TUMANOV

It is not difficult to find quotations describing the historical disaster that was the Soviet Union. This one is from Eugène Ionesco: "Soon we will celebrate the fiftieth anniversary of the Russian Revolution. This revolution was intended to be the liberation of a better society. It was fifty years of catastrophes, wars, crimes, tyranny and tragedy. Never did a movement which wanted to disalienate humanity end up alienating it more."[1] It was in this sociopolitical context, and specifically under a regime of ideological censorship, that the Russian authors I am concerned with were active. These particular extraliterary circumstances were undoubtedly a most important factor influencing them to create "children's" works directed at an audience of both children and adults.

Using what came to be known in Russian as "Ezopov iazyk" (Aesopian language), a "language of hidden meanings and deceptive means [used] to criticize . . . national life, politics and society,"[2] the writers of what can be called "Aesopian children's literature" envisaged, first of all, an insightful adult reader. This reader was expected to "naturalize" the text in question, making sense of allusions, irony, parody, allegory, and so forth, specifically against the backdrop of Soviet reality, for example, the Stalinist terror. In other words, the work would be read in relation to what Jonathan Culler describes as the "socially given text, that which is taken as the 'real world,'" as well as in relation to "a general cultural text: shared knowledge which would be recognized by participants as part of culture."[3] Second, Aesopian children's literature implied a child reader who would naturalize any given work as (innocent) children's literature. And, third, there was another hypothetical adult reader: the censor, who, it was hoped, would read more like a child and not perceive (or even attempt to perceive) any subversive Aesopian subtext.

In what follows, I would like to consider the interplay of these possible readers in works by three authors: Kornei Chukovskii (1882–1969), Mikhail Zoshchenko (1895–1958), and Daniil Kharms (1905–1942), expanding on what has already been written concerning Aesopian language by looking at some examples and integrating certain pertinent material that others have excluded. Before I turn to the individual authors, however, it would be helpful to discuss further the nature of Aesopian language and its use specifically in children's literature.

SCREENS, MARKERS, AND AMBIVALENCE

In what is the only extended study of the poetics of Aesopian language—a phenomenon which incidentally existed under tsarist censorship as well—Lev Loseff discusses the function of "screens and markers" in the relations among author, censor, and reader, as well as the vital importance of ambivalence. Regarding screens and markers, Loseff explains that if a work is examined "with an eye to its Aesopian content . . . it separates, as it were, into two sets of literary devices, each with an opposite intent: the devices of one group are bent on concealing the Aesopian text, while the devices of the other draw attention to that same Aesopian text. The former are screens, the latter markers."[4] Loseff continues by saying that "while screens and markers may be realized in different elements of a literary work, it is frequently one element which is the realization of both screen and marker and which indicates . . . the invariably dual nature of an Aesopian utterance."[5] Thus, this anticensorship tactic relied heavily on ambivalence: that which could be taken by the enlightened (adult) reader as Aesopian could be read by others (that is, the child reader and the censor) as being non-Aesopian.

Not confined to fiction, Aesopian language thus meant, for example, that Bakhtin's *Tvorchestvo Fransua Rable i narodnaia kul'tura srednevekov'ia i renessansa* (The œuvre of François Rabelais and popular culture in the Middle Ages and Renaissance)[6] could be read as simply a literary/cultural study of the Middle Ages and the Renaissance. At the same time, however, the "screen" could become a marker: a title stressing that the work concerned the past was, in fact, frequently an invitation for the Aesopian-minded reader to consider how the text may be encoded to comment on the present. Indeed, written during the worst years of the Stalinist terror, Bakhtin's book, originally a doctoral dissertation, can be interpreted as "a submerged critique of Stalinism."[7] Bakhtin's inquiries into the double-voiced mode or "dialogism" of Rabelais and Dostoevsky can thus be taken as a marker indicating that multiplicity of meaning was to be sought in his own writing as well.[8]

At the same time, in the former Soviet Union scientific articles, journalistic writing, literary criticism, historical studies, translations, and, of course, original works of poetry and prose could all likewise become parables, allegories, and so forth, about Lenin, Stalin, and life under Communism in general. As Loseff sees it, the function of Aesopian works—whether in tsarist or Soviet times—was always to attack the "power of the State,"[9] giving the Aesopian reader (and I would say certainly the writer as well) the chance to experience a catharsis in the form of "a victory over repressive authority."[10] Thus, Bakhtin's carnivalesque "deflationary" devices, discussed at length in his study of Rabelais, were exactly what he and countless others employed in the form of Aesopian language.

The use of children's literature to conceal subversive content represents a particularly intriguing issue in the study of Aesopian language, and there were many practitioners of what Loseff calls the genre of "quasi-children's literature."[11] Undoubtedly a very important screen, aside from the mere fact of making a given work appear to be "just children's literature," was the author's creation of other children's works that were truly in no way Aesopian. In order not to arouse the suspicion of the censor, for all writers, of course, the Aesopian work had to be the exception and not the rule. Deming Brown explains, for example, concerning Evgenii Evtushenko, a very popular poet for adults: "Extremely prolific, he surrounds his politically provocative poetry with reams of verse that is 'safe.' "[12]

Another factor to keep in mind concerning the screen specifically in children's literature is that, even if a given work was Aesopian, peritextual features—particularly the illustrations—could camouflage this fact beyond what would be achieved by the ambivalence of the text itself. For example, one Aesopian children's poem discussed by Loseff is Daniil Kharms's "Million" (A million), a seemingly patriotic marching song that marks its Aesopian nature by amounting to nothing but an absurd exercise in counting children. This poem, however, was accompanied by a visual interpretation that stressed exclusively the non-Aesopian, "children's" level: that is, "the routine illustration of a troop of Young Pioneers toting drums and banners, [and for this reason] the poem does not at first glance distinguish itself from the great bulk of Pioneer songs and verse."[13]

Further screening of a work's Aesopian mode also could be achieved depending on where that work was located within a book or magazine.

"Editors," writes Elena Sokol, "have placed 'Million' at the beginning of the three recent collections of Kharms's work for children [published in 1962, 1967, and 1972], attempting to exploit what little ideological potential the poem might have."[14] In this way, the message (to be taken especially by the censor) was that the work genuinely represented an expression of patriotic fervor on the part of the author, intended, like other "good" children's literature in the Soviet era, to contribute to the all-important *vospitanie* or "character-education" of the child.[15] Whereas, as Loseff's analysis makes clear, a Soviet adult "reading between the lines" of "Million" would have seen otherwise and not been betrayed by either the ideologically filled illustrations or the text's prominent positioning.

I would like now to look at works by Chukovskii, Zoshchenko, and Kharms in order to consider two issues: first, what makes these texts Aesopian and, therefore, addressed to a select group of "thinking" adults; and second, what makes the same works appear to be children's literature intended to fool the censor, but also, I would argue, genuinely to appeal to a junior audience. Thus, in my opinion, Loseff's above term "quasi-children's literature" should read "quasi/genuine children's literature." Incidentally, a "thinking" parent (or other adult) would always have had the option of using Aesopian children's literature to introduce the child to the fine art of Aesopian writing/reading, thereby showing the youngster that what appeared to be truly for her or him actually concealed other, more complex planes. This would, however, certainly have had to be done with utmost caution in a society where it was not unheard of (and even encouraged) for children to denounce their own flesh and blood.

KORNEI CHUKOVSKII

Along with Samuil Marshak, Kornei Chukovskii holds a particularly prominent place in the history of twentieth-century Russian children's literature. This poet, journalist, memoirist, critic, scholar, and literary translator wanted not merely to write for children, of which he himself had four. Like Marshak, Chukovsii also sought to establish a new, playful body of works to replace the dull, often painfully didactic prerevolutionary "Lilliputian literature"[16] that failed to take into consideration the proclivities and preferences of real, live children. Thus, the same sort of development that had taken place in English children's literature in the nineteenth century and even before was initiated only in the twentieth century in Russia.

As in the case of Marshak, the impetus for Chukovskii's desire to transform the realm of children's poetry in particular came from a pro-

longed stay in England during which he discovered English nursery
rhymes, as well as the joys of such writers as Carroll, Lear, and Milne. In
addition to this discovery of the English tradition, which "represents an
acute understanding of children and an ability to communicate with them
on their own terms through fantasy and play,"[17] Chukovskii also con-
ducted his own extensive research into the language, thought, play, art,
and imagination of young children. The results of this research, published in *Ot dvukh do piati* (*From Two to Five*), served to further justify
his view that the old variety of Russian children's literature was completely inadequate. Central to Chukovskii's argument is that children
themselves both invent and want in their literature nonsense and also
rhymes of the sort that are found in folk sources and, particularly, in folk
rhymes. Thus, in addition to being influenced in his own writing by the
literature and folklore of England, Chukovskii also took Russian folklore
as an important source of inspiration and recommended that other children's poets do the same.

Elena Sokol (1984) as well as Andreas Bode (1989) analyze in detail
the folkloric and quintessentially childlike nature of Chukovskii's *skazki*
or "verse tales,"[18] demonstrating that this is very much children's literature. Aside from rhymes, rhythms, and nonsense that were carefully con-
cocted to charm the young reader and to hold his or her attention—and
which would simultaneously have made the censor see this as literature
for children—another way that Chukovskii sought to please his child audience was by often making anthropomorphized animals the focus of his
verse tales. On the one hand, in this way, a link was forged with innumerable such animal characters in children's books throughout the world, as
well as with the fables and beast tales that have always held a prominent
place in children's reading. On the other hand, Chukovskii's animals
were notably very innovative for his time, making his tales appear even
fresher against the backdrop of existing children's fare:

> Even the wild procession of animals that the poet unleashed—croco-
> diles, camels, elephants, apes, snakes, giraffes, and hippoptamuses—
> seemed provocative: up till then only bunny rabbits, squirrels, foxes,
> bears, and wolves along with household animals such as chickens, cats
> and mice had been allowed to romp through the pages of Russian chil-
> dren's books.[19]

Chukovskii also has a number of humanlike insects, including the lead
character in "Tarakanische" (The cockroach) and the heroine of "Mukha-
tsokotukha" (The chatterbox fly).

Chukovskii's own research and his works themselves thus provide ample evidence that this was a writer who was keenly interested in appealing to a child readership. And he succeeded so brilliantly that Maria Nikolajeva would not be alone in calling Chukovskii "the greatest innovator and pathfinder in Soviet children's literature."[20] At the same time, however, some of Chukovskii's very childlike works also clearly imply an enlightened adult reader.

In Chukovskii's case, something that could be taken as an extratextual marker of possible Aesopian language in his children's texts was his keen scholarly interest in the subject. The final chapter of *Masterstvo Nekrasova* (Nekrasov's Artistry), Chukovskii's well-known book on Nikolai Nekrasov (1821–1878), is namely on "Ezopova rech'" (Aesopian discourse). The clearest marker of Chukovskii's own Aesopian language, however, is the subject matter of some of his poems: a subject matter that simultaneously serves as a screen.

Take, for example, the above-mentioned verse tale "Tarakanische." It is, on the one hand, a simple children's tale about a happy community of playful animals who are first introduced to the reader as part of a typical Chukovskiian nonsense parade: bears riding a bike, an upside-down cat, mosquitoes on a balloon, lions in a car, a toad on a broom, and so forth, all of whom laugh while eating *prianiki* (Russian spice cakes). Suddenly, into this peaceful, pastoral realm comes an evil and mighty cockroach, the *tarakanische,* whom the child might recognize as the typical *glavnyi zlodei* (arch villain) of the fairy tale and also akin to the *idolishche* (idol monster) of Russian folklore.[21] The animals so fear this beast who threatens to swallow them and to have their children for dinner that they helplessly accept the cockroach's domination. One day, however, a kangaroo comes by and declares, much like the boy in Andersen's "The Emperor's New Clothes," that this is not a formidable giant but rather an ordinary cockroach. A sparrow who subsequently arrives out of the blue obviously agrees with the kangaroo: The evil bug promptly disappears through the avian beak. Harmony is thus restored, as is so commonly the case in works of children's literature, and the joyous dance to celebrate the disappearance of the evil insect constitutes more Chukovskiian nonsense that would delight the young reader at least as much as the opening "parade" section.

On the other hand, the enlightened adult reading the same work in the 1920s and beyond would perceive an additional semantic level. In the above-mentioned study of Nekrasov, Chukovskii himself stresses the importance of considering a work of literature in relationship to its sociopolitical context: He explains, for example, the meaning of certain passages from Nekrasov as they were created for and would have been interpreted by the liberal reader in the 1860s under conditions of oppressive tsarist censorship. Of chief importance to a sociopolitical reading of "Tarakanische," first published in 1923, is that the cockroach has a mustache, a feature that is highlighted numerous times in the poem.

For the adult reading according to Culler's category of "cultural vraisemblance,"[22] the cockroach and its mustache necessitate specifically an interpretation of the text that takes into account an important fact: among the coded appellations for Stalin were "the old boy with the mustache, the one with the whiskers, whiskers, [as well as notably] the cockroach."[23] Thus, to a Russian Aesopian reader, Chukovskii's simple children's poem about an anthropomorphized member of the *Blattidae* family became "an allegorical picture of the political situation in a nation brought to heel by the dictatorship of a trifling political faction, at once feared and loathed by the majority of its citizens."[24] As Chukovskii writes in the poem: "The animals resigned themselves to the mustached-one . . . may he croak!"[25] that was surely a sentiment shared by many of Chukovskii's fellow-citizens. But no savior/sparrow would come to rid them of their iron-fisted, mustachioed leader who was in power from 1922–1953.

The Aesopian nature of "Tarakanische" is emphasized further by the fact that in another of Chukovskii's poems that I have mentioned, "Mukha-tsokotukha" (The chatterbox fly, 1924), the plot is similar to that of the former work: An evil spider suddenly arrives at the house of the fly, captures her and all of the fly's friends, who have just been enjoying tea from the fly's new samovar flee, leaving the fly to have her blood sucked out. But at the last moment a little mosquito comes to save the screaming fly: The mosquito chops off the spider's head with his sabre and subsequently marries the thankful fly. Felicity Ann O'Dell notes that, like "Tarakanische," "Mukha-tsokotukha" is "generally accepted as having a deeper level of social and political comment. It tells of an ordinary fly who is attacked by a malicious old spider (commonly taken as Stalin). All the fly's comrades hide in dark corners as they are too afraid to help."[26] It is interesting to note in this context that, aside from daring to engage in Aesopian language, Chukovskii himself was generally quite fearless in facing the daunting Soviet power system:

> During and after the Stalinist terror, Chukovskii tried to help many people who were arrested or repressed, writing reams of letters to well-connected acquaintances, but he also kept himself out of trouble. His essential optimism, class background [i.e., his mother, Ekaterina

Korneichukova, was a peasant] and work habits suited the Soviet model; it did not hurt that Lenin himself had praised his early work on Nekrasov.[27]

Equally, if not more fearless than Chukovskii, was Mikhail Zoshchenko, to whom I will turn next.

MIKHAIL ZOSHCHENKO

Kornei Chukovskii as well as Maksim Gor'kii, Viktor Shklovskii, Osip Mandel'shtam, and Aleksei Voronskii were among the strongest supporters of Mikhail Zoshchenko,[28] a writer who, although exceedingly popular, continually risked his status in the eyes of the Party by writing satirical works that were often marked by ideological imprecision and Aesopian language. In comparison to Chukovskii, for whom writing for children came early in his career and supplanted his chance to ever become known as an author of (original) literature for adults, Zoshchenko turned to writing for a younger readership quite late in his active career.

To a large degree, Zoshchenko's children's production can be seen as an attempt to write specifically the sort of "serious, positive works"[29] that were being demanded in the 1930s, works that would perhaps vindicate him in the eyes of those critics who saw his previous (adult) output as frivolous and even subversive. Zoshchenko's children's œuvre includes *Liolia and Minka* (1938–1940), a "thinly-veiled autobiographical . . . series of first-person childhood reminiscences with clear moral teachings."[30] Another prominent cycle of children's stories by Zoshchenko, and the ones that are of particular interest to me here, are his tales about Lenin. They first appeared in 1939 and 1940, mostly in the journal *Zvezda* (*The star*) where Zoshchenko himself later served on the editorial board. The stories also came out a few times in book form during this same period under the title *Rasskazy o Lenine* (Stories about Lenin): in late 1939/early 1940 by Detgiz (50,000 copies); in 1941 by Biblioteka Ogoniok (50,000 copies), and again in 1941 by Uchpedgiz (25,000 copies).[31] These figures are important because the Soviet Union, with its centrally planned economy and absence of commercial accountability, was well-known for its huge print runs, particularly of children's books. This meant that if any Aesopian language did get past the censorship, then it had the chance of reaching possibly even millions of readers.

Especially with their serious illustrations, Zoshchenko's Lenin stories certainly would have appeared to be didactic literature directed at a

junior readership. As Linda Hart Scatton maintains, the apparent goal of
Zoshchenko's *Rasskazy o Lenine* was to present an elevated, hagiographic-
like image of the man who was first among equals. This was in line with an
established tradition of leaders' "hagiographies." In Zoshchenko's very
short Lenin stories, written in a simple way accessible to children, the
young Soviet reader would have learned, for example, that Lenin is: "truth-
ful ('The Carafe'), fearless ('Little Grey Goat'), brilliant, well-disciplined
in mind and body ('How Lenin Studied') . . . brave, considerate and solicitous of others ('An Attack on Lenin'), law-abiding and unpretentious
('Lenin and the Sentry'),"[32] and so forth. But once again, as in the case of
Chukovskii, Zoshchenko also gave certain texts a double meaning that
would most likely not have been within the grasp of the Soviet child reader
and that even the censor obviously did not fully perceive. In the words of
Keith Booker and Juraga Dubravka, the narratives about Vladimir Ilyich
"can be read as iconographic apotheoses of Lenin intended to instill good
socialist values in Soviet children. But it is also quite possible to read the
Lenin stories as a sly satirical assault on the Soviet 'cult of personality' that
tended to deify leaders like Lenin and Stalin."[33]

The enlightened Soviet adult reader probably would have known how
in Zoshchenko's works for adults ambivalence can leave the meaning of a
story open. For example, in the story "Bednost'" (Poverty, 1925) Lenin's
obsessive drive to give electrical power to the people is shown as both positive and negative: the narrator is pleased to have light that makes him
clean up his sordid room in a communal apartment; on the other hand, the
poor landlady hates the light and, having no money or the desire to fix up
her living space, cuts the wires so that the bedbugs will not be able to see
(and laugh at) her shabby furniture. The squalor lit up by the electric light
undermines the positive propagandistic connotations of discourse on
Lenin's electrification drive. Although in the relatively liberal 1920s it was
possible for Zoshchenko to imply in such an obvious way that the positive
was, in fact, perhaps negative and that life under the new regime left something to be desired, in 1939–1940, and particularly in children's stories
purporting to be propagandistic/hagiographic, Zoshchenko could hardly
have been so forthright. Yet a related questioning of positive versus negative in connection with the image of Lenin is nonetheless present.

For example, in "Serenk'kii kozlik" (Little Grey Goat) Lenin is indeed portrayed as "fearless."[34] The narrator says as much at the beginning: "When Lenin was little, he was hardly scared of anything. He would
bravely enter a dark room. He did not cry when he was told scary stories.
And in general he hardly ever cried."[35] In contrast, Lenin's younger

brother, Mitia, is said to often "cry his heart out." Particularly painful for Mitia is the well-known song about a little grey goat who decides one day to leave the grandma who loves him and go off for a walk in the woods. Mitia is said to bawl each time he gets to the tragic close of the song: "Grey wolves attacked the little goat; grandma was left with nothing but horns and hoofs."[36] Little Lenin insists that Mitia not be scared and not cry. Mitia agrees, and the song is sung once more by him and some other children. This time Mitia sings bravely, although the narrator informs us that Mitia cannot help but shed "just one little tear" at the final line concerning poor grandma who is left without the one whom she adored.

While, to the child reader and the censor, the story may have yielded a straightforward message about bravery in general and Lenin's bravery in particular, the implications of Mitia's crying, and especially the closing emphasis on his last little tear, stress the fact that he cries not so much out of fear but more out of compassion or sympathy. The enlightened adult reader would thus see this as a story that is fundamentally ambivalent: not crying is good but, if it means a lack of compassion, it is bad. The real Lenin is known to have issued such orders as the public hanging of one hundred *kulaks* (rich peasants) in the province of Penza "so that the peasants would take fright and submit," and, as part of his offensive against the Orthodox church, to have declared that "priests resisting seizures of church property were to be shot: the more the better."[37] An adult reader who had heard rumors or otherwise suspected that Lenin had this dark, intensely misanthropic, and even bloodthirsty side would have wished that, rather than being little Mitia's "teacher," he might have taken a lesson from his brother about the need to shed at least the odd "little tear."

At the same time, the Aesopian Soviet reader might have perceived no small amount of irony concerning Lenin's method of trying to make little Mitia stop crying: "He turned to Mitia, made a scary face and purposely sang in a frightful and loud voice: GREY WOLVES ATTACKED THE LIT-TLE GOAT."[38] Such mean, childish taunting certainly clashes with the expected (and official) image of Lenin as a "Communist Christfigure."[39] Thus, "Serenk'kii kozlik" can be seen to both inflate and deflate the image of the great Lenin. Additionally, the fact that this story, like Bakhtin's dissertation, was written at the height of the Terror—a time when countless grandmothers and others were having to face the disappearance of their loved ones at the hands of Stalin's "wolves"—makes it quite possible to interpret the song about the little goat who goes off never to return as an Aesopian allegory. This song is incidentally similar in this respect to a poem by Daniil Kharms that I will consider below. Furthermore, given these contemporary events, the young Lenin's lack of compassion could even be read as a veiled comment concerning Stalin's icy heart, too.

Another example of Zoshchenko's Aesopian deflation of Lenin is found in "Pokushenie na Lenina" (An attack—or assassination attempt—on Lenin). As Scatton explains, this tale does present Lenin as "brave, considerate and solicitous of others."[40] In order not to shock his wife and sister when he arrives home, seriously wounded by several bullets, Zoshchenko presents Lenin insisting on going up the stairs alone: "And everyone around him was amazed that at such a frightening time Lenin would be thinking not about himself but about other people. And so Lenin ascended the steep staircase to the third floor all by himself."[41] He is thus, according to this sentence, as amazing as Christ walking on water. Lenin's miraculous behavior, however, is undercut—at least partially—by the line that follows: "It's true that he was supported on both sides, but nevertheless he walked by himself."[42] One wonders, what would be the necessity of the last limiting statement if this were a truly straightforward hagiographic account. The Soviet adult reader would perhaps have been aware that the same sort of undercutting technique is found elsewhere in Zoshchenko. For example, in "Bania" (The bathhouse) the naïve "man-in-the-street" narrator, who has just praised American bathhouses to the sky, says: "Our bathhouses are not bad either. But worse. Although it is also possible to wash yourself."[43] This "objectivity" is particularly satiric in light of Zhdanov's words in his speech to the First All-Union Congress of Soviet Writers (1934), when he spoke of presenting life "not simply as objective reality . . . but rather as reality in its revolutionary development. The truthfulness and exactitude of the artistic image must be linked with the task of ideological transformation."[44]

What is perhaps most ironic about Zoshchenko's "aesopianization" of Lenin is that in his 1912 article, "Partiinaia organizatsiia i partiinaia literatura" (The Party Organization and Party Literature), Lenin himself declared Aesopian language to be a thing of the tsarist past and henceforth completely unnecessary: "Accursed days of Aesopian talk, literary bondage, slavish language, ideological serfdom! The proletariat has put an end to this corruption which choked everything alive and fresh in Russia."[45] Thus, Lenin, a man who claimed to be saving the muzzled Russian people, ended up as a leader featured in works, like Zoshenko's, that invited much reading between the lines.

DANIIL KHARMS

Daniil Kharms, born Daniil Iuvachiov, had some thirty pseudonyms, of
which Kharms eventually became the main one. Along with other members of his avant-garde literary group Oberiu (an acronym for the Association for Real Art), Kharms was invited to write for children and went on
to contribute abundantly to two magazines that were under editor-in-chief
Samuil Marshak. The magazine *Iozh* (The hedgehog) was for primary
school children and was published between 1928 and 1935. *Chizh* (The
siskin), for preschool children, appeared in the years 1930 and 1941. Cu-
riously, Kharms, who was childless, apparently had a certain aversion to
children. For example, one statement found in the Kharms archives in St.
Petersburg reads: "I don't like children, old men, old women and rational
old people." And further on the same page is the macabre remark: "Poi-
soning children is cruel. Yet you have to do something with them."[46] But
regardless of what may have been the author's own views, he turned out to
be a great children's author, which was a good thing, given that the modernist aesthetic and themes of his works for adults were completely out of
line with the official vision of Soviet literature.

At the same time, Kharms's literature for adults—like that of other
members of the Oberiu—often was characterized by a dadalike, child-
minded outlook, and general playfulness. It was specifically for this that
Marshak took a particular interest in the Oberiu writers—and particularly
Kharms—when Marshak was trying, along with Chukovskii, to establish
the above-mentioned new variety of literature for Russian children.
Kharms ended up creating numerous children's works—both poetry and
prose—that are highly imaginative and filled with much playfulness and
happy nonsense that Kharms learned, in part, from reading Carroll and
Lear. In short, Kharms, in ways reminiscent of Chukovskii, embraced the
child (or childlike) reader wholeheartedly.

For example, "as the title itself betrays, in 'Play' ('Igra,' 1930) verbal play is enhanced by thematic play. It is a playful poem about play."[47]
This poem has the classic fairy tale architectonic structure: three boys
pretend to be a car, a ship, and an airplane. The poem is, furthermore, full
of dynamic action, which is so characteristic of children's literature, and
it comes alive as each character tells the others in turn what vehicle he
has become and produces the appropriate sound: "Ga-ra-rar" "Du-du-
du" and "Zhu-zhu-zhu!" When a cow suddenly appears and blocks the
boys' way, thereby interrupting the game for a time, its animal sound creates a playful contrast with the mechanical sound imitations made by the
three children.

Another equally amusing and playful poem by Kharms, "Tsirk Print-inpram" (The Printinpram circus), presents the child reader with a most unique circus. In this circus Kharms notably makes the forces of nature (e.g., mosquitoes, swallows, the moon) perform right alongside more typical circus performers (a parrot, tigers, lions, a strongman). But the child (who likely knows the conventions of the circus) would be amazed by the fact that even the typical circus performers are hardly typical: Only Kharms could come up with a parrot whose act involves eating a "soaked radish" and a strongman who lifts an elephant with his teeth.[48]

Like Chukovskii and Zoshchenko, Kharms was thus clearly concerned with addressing a juvenile readership, and he did so admirably: as one critic put it, "the works of Daniil Kharms were for children that very holiday which, in the words of V. Belinskii, was what every little book addressed to the young should be."[49] Yet, once again, in certain children's works, Kharms also reserves an important place for the hypothetical adult reader. The particular Aesopian work by Kharms that I would like to focus on is "Iz doma vyshel chelovek" (A man left home), a small poem that had a huge effect on Kharms's career—and his life—because the censor happened to see through the screen.

To the Soviet child reader, the work in question would likely have appeared to be just a quaint narrative about a man who is related to other absent-minded characters such as the one in Marshak's 1930 work *Vot kakoi rasseiannyi* (That's how absent-minded he is).[50] Kharms's man leaves home one day, begins a long voyage by foot without ever stopping, goes into a wood once at dawn, and disappears:

> *A man left home to wander far*
> *without looking back*
> *and took along, and took along*
> *a long stick and a sack.*
>
> *He kept on walking straight ahead*
> *and sleeping not a wink.*
> *He ate no bread, he ate no bread,*
> *and nothing did he drink.*
>
> *One day in early morning light,*
> *he saw a wood so tall.*
> *He went right in, he went right in*
> *and vanished—sack and all.*

> But if somehow, somewhere, someone
> this stranger ever sees,
> then right away, then right away
> do come and tell us please.[51]

The young Soviet reader might have been left at the end of the poem contemplating the amusing fact that a character is lost, and everyone is being asked to look for him. But the Aesopian adult reader would have seen that against the backdrop of Stalinism in 1937, when the poem was written, "the plot—about how 'a man left home' and 'from that time vanished'—was no longer the stuff of fairy tales but the essence of reality."[52] Incidentally, although the 1937 adult reader could not have known this, we can now see that this plot is, in fact, echoed countless times throughout Kharms's adult œuvre. In this context, then, the final plea at the end of "Iz doma vyshel chelovek," that the reader try to find the missing man, can be seen not only as typical Kharmsian metafictional play, but also as a way of thematizing the irreversibility of Soviet atrocities: The implication is that tracking down a literary character would be as impossible as retrieving one of Stalin's countless victims.

THE DANGERS OF AESOPIAN CHILDREN'S LITERATURE

Unfortunately, the subtext of "Iz doma vyshel chelovek" was not concealed well enough, and what happened after the poem was published in the third number of *Chizh* in March 1937 is related in detail in Kharms's diary: He was abruptly cut off from his means of earning a living, and, starving during the following months, he often wished for God to grant him a quick death. Although Kharms did somehow survive this horrible period, it would not be long until he would "leave home and vanish" for good: he was arrested in 1941, likely in part for the "questionable" nature of his children's literature, and he died under uncertain circumstances early the following year. "Iz doma vyshel chelovek" has thus taken on a powerful and sadly prophetic meaning concerning its author.

While Kharms did not survive Stalin's purges during which "no fewer than 2500 writers were murdered or thrown into prisons and labor camps,"[53] Zoshchenko miraculously did. He was, however, eventually condemned to a literary death as one of the prime targets of an official crackdown on the arts in 1946. Although, as Rebecca Domar argues, what happened was truly a retroactive condemnation of the nature of his work in general,[54] it is interesting to note that what apparently set off this condemnation was Aesopian language in two of Zoshchenko's children's works.

Zoshchenko himself was inclined to believe that the Lenin story "Lenin i Chasovoi" (Lenin and the sentry) was directly to blame: when first published it included a character whom Stalin supposedly took to be himself, that is, the rude party official with a mustache. But the story that had an even greater role to play in Zoshchenko's fate is "Prikliucheniia obez'iany" (The adventures of a monkey). This is an odd tale, in which a boy ends up tending to the "character education" of a monkey and raises the animal in such a way that, according to the boy, it can teach children as well as adults a thing or two. Whereas to a Soviet child this might have appeared to be simply a happy narrative about a boy and his new pet, A. Zhdanov, Secretary of the Central Committee of the Communist Party, had another opinion: he describes "Prikliucheniia obez'iany" as "a vulgar lampoon on Soviet life and on Soviet people [in which] Zoshchenko's malicious, hooliganlike depiction of our way of life is accompanied by anti-Soviet attacks."[55]

Although Zoshchenko wrote a letter to Stalin, denying any Aesopian intentions in his works, he nonetheless was cast out of the Soviet Writers' Union, and his works were banned. Zoshchenko was finally readmitted to the Union of Soviet Writers in 1953, and during the de-Stalinization year 1956, he experienced a certain public vindication, when some of his stories again became available. But Zoshchenko never regained his previous popularity, and, having suffered from poor health and severe depression for a long time, the author died in 1958.

In the case of Chukovskii, on the other hand, it does not appear that his Aesopian language got him into any particular trouble. Rather, the fact that Chukovskii's children's literature was banned and only republished during the post-Stalinist "thaw" seems to be attributable more to his use of nonsense and other features of his works than to Aesopian factors. Attacks by the "leftist pedologists," who were opposed to such things as the "unreal gibberish of fairy tales," "anthropomorphism," and "verbal play," as well as the general push for the politicization and "real life" focus of literature in the Soviet Union forced Chukovskii himself to "publicly reject his works as old-fashioned and affirm the need to write new ones about the future."[56] In general, then, although his career and life were hardly ideal, Chukovskii, who died in 1969, had by far the best fate of the three authors under consideration.

Fortunately, the era of Aesopian literature, Aesopian children's literature, and everything Soviet is over, and by 1991 the censorship was buried.[57] Now, it is all just a very intriguing and terribly frightening chapter in the pages of Russian history.

NOTES

1. Eugène Ionesco, *Présent passé, passé présent* (Paris: Mercure de France, 1968), 134. All translations are my own unless otherwise indicated.

2. Ray J. Parrott Jr., "Aesopian Language," in *Modern Encyclopedia of Russian and Soviet Literature*, vol. 1 (Gulf Breeze, Fla.: Academic International Press, 1977), 39.

3. Jonathan Culler, *Structuralist Poetics* (London: Routledge, 1975), 140. Cf. Peter Rabinowitz *Before Reading: Narrative Conventions and the Politics of Interpretation* (Ithaca, N.Y.: Cornell University Press, 1987), 21, 72.

4. Lev Loseff, *On the Beneficence of Censorship: Aesopian Language in Modern Russian Literature* (Munich: Verlag Otto Sagner, 1984), 51.

5. Ibid., 52.

6. The 1984 English translation of Bakhtin's book by Helene Iswolsky bears the simplified title *Rabelais and his World* (Bloomington: Indiana University Press, 1984).

7. M. Keith Booker and Dubravka Juraga. *Bakhtin, Stalin, and Modern Russian Fiction.* (Westport, Conn.: Greenwood Press, 1995), 2.

8. Ibid., 11. Incidentally, in a paper related to my own, "Misreading the Cross-Writer: The Case of Wilhelm Hauff's *Dwarf Long Nose*," Maureen Thum specifically uses Bakhtin to describe how this nineteenth-century author got his subversive ideas past the censors. See *Children's Literature* 25 (1997): 1–23.

9. Loseff, *On the Beneficence of Censorship*, 221.

10. Ibid., 230.

11. Ibid., 86.

12. Deming Brown, *Soviet Russian Literature Since Stalin* (Cambridge: Cambridge University Press, 1978), 114.

13. Loseff, *On the Beneficence of Censorship*, 207.

14. Elena Sokol, *Russian Poetry for Children* (Knoxville: University of Tennessee Press, 1984), 139.

15. Felicity Ann O'Dell, *Socialisation Through Children's Literature: The Soviet Example* (Cambridge: Cambridge University Press, 1978), 5.

16. Iurii Tynianov, "Kornei Chukovskii," *Soviet Studies in Literature* 24, no. 2 (1988): 96.

17. Sokol, *Russian Poetry for Children*, xv.

18. Ibid., 6.

19. Andreas Bode, "Humor in the Lyrical Stories for Children of Samuel Marshak and Kornei Chukovskii," *The Lion and the Unicorn* 13, no. 2 (1989): 42. Cf. Sokol, *Russian Poetry for Children*, 89–90.

20. Maria Nikolajeva, *Children's Literature Comes of Age: Toward a New Aesthetic* (New York: Garland, 1996), 86.

21. E. M. Neiolov, "Perestupaia vozrastnye granitsy," in *Problemy detskoi literatury* (Petrozavodsk: Petrozavodskii gosudarstvennyi universitet 1976), 57.

22. Culler, *Structuralist Poetics*, 141.

23. Loseff, *On the Beneficence of Censorship*, 36. One wonders if the latter title has anything to do with the fact that Stalin's original surname was the Georgian Dzhugashvili, the first syllable of which recalls the Russian word *zhuk* (beetle).

24. Ibid, 199.

25. Kornei Chukovskii, *Skazki* (Moskva: Detskaia Literatura, 1993), 9.

26. O'Dell, *Socialisation Through Children's Literature*, 57.

27. Sibelan Forrester, "Kornei Ivanovich Chukovskii," in *Reference Guide to Russian Literature*, ed. Neil Cornwell (Chicago: Fitzroy Dearborn, 1998), 234.

28. Linda Hart Scatton, "Mikhail Mikhailovich Zoshchenko," in *Reference Guide to Russian Literature*, ed. Neil Cornwell, 930.

29. Ibid, 931.

30. Ibid.

31. Iu. V. Tomashevskii, ed. *Litso i maska Mikhaila Zoshchenko* (Moskva: Olimp, 1994), 357–358.

32. Linda Hart Scatton, *Mikhail Zoshchenko: Evolution of a Writer* (Cambridge: Cambridge University Press, 1993), 133.

33. Booker and Juraga, *Bakhtin, Stalin, and Modern Russian Fiction*, 86.

34. Scatton, *Mikhail Zoshchenko*, 133.

35. Mikhail Zoshchenko, *Twelve Stories*, selected and annotated by L. LaRocco and S. Paperno (Columbus, Ohio: Slavica, 1989), 9.

36. Ibid.

37. Richard Pipes, *The Unkown Lenin* (New Haven: Yale University Press, 1996), 10, 11.

38. Zoshchenko, *Twelve Stories*, 10.

39. O'Dell, *Socialisation Through Children's Literature*, 178.

40. Scatton, *Mikhail Zoshchenko*, 133.

41. Zoshchenko, *Twelve Stories*, 13.

42. Ibid.

43. Ibid, 40.

44. Quoted in O'Dell, *Socialisation Through Children's Literature*, 178. See Loseff, *On the Beneficence of Censorship*, 203–204 concerning Aesopian language in another of Zoshchenko's Lenin stories: "O tom, kak Leninu Podarili Rybu" (How Lenin was given a fish).

45. Quoted in Loseff, *On the Beneficence of Censorship*, 7.

46. Daniil Kharms, Druskin Fund, no. 219, sheet 50, Archive Department of the Saltykov-Shchedrin Library, St. Petersburg. For more on Kharms see my article

(with V. Tumanov) entitled "The Child and the Child-like in Daniil Charms," *Russian Literature* 34, no. 2 (1993): 241–269.

47. Sokol, *Russian Poetry for Children*, 135. The poem is found in Kharms, *Letiat po nebu shariki*, ed. A. A. Aleksandrov and N. M. Kavin (Krasnoiarsk: Krasnoiarskoe Knizhnoe Izdatel'stvo, 1990), 48–51.

48. Kharms, *Letiat po nebu shariki*, 68–70.

49. Anatolii Aleksin, "Daniil Kharms: stikhotvoreniia," *Detskaia literatura* 4 (1989): 73.

50. Marshak's *Vot kakoi rasseiannyi* was first published in 1930 (Moskva: Gosizdat), illustrated by V. Konashevich. This absentminded man does such things as putting on his pants as if they were a shirt and sitting for two days in a detached train car, wondering why each time he opens the door he is still in Leningrad.

51. Kharms, *Letiat po nebu shariki*, 68–70.

52. Vladimir Glotser, ed. "Daniil Kharms: 'Bozhe, kakaia uzhasnaia zhizn' i kakoe uzhasnoe u menia sostoianie.' Zapisnye knizhki. Pis'ma. Dnevniki." *Novyi Mir* 2 (1992): 222.

53. Maria Nikolajeva, "Russian Children's Literature Before and After Perestroika," *Children's Literature Association Quarterly* 20, no. 3 (1995): 108.

54. Rebecca Domar, "The Tragedy of a Soviet Satirist: The Case of Zoshchenko," in *Through the Glass of Soviet Literature*, ed. Ernest Simmons (New York: Columbia University Press, 1953), 207.

55. Quoted in Domar, "The Tragedy of a Soviet Satirist," 205.

56. Sokol, *Russian Poetry for Children*, 9, 10.

57. See A. Blium, "Kak bylo razrusheno 'ministerstvo pravdy': sovetskaia tsenzura epokhi glasnosti i perestroiki (1985–1991)," *Zvezda* 6 (1996): 212–221.

REFERENCES

Aleksin, Anatolii. Foreword. "Daniil Kharms: stikhotvoreniia." *Detskaia Literatura* 4 (1989): 73.

Bakhtin, Mikhail. *Rabelais and His World*. Trans. Helene Iswolsky. Bloomington: Indiana University Press, 1984.

Blium, Arlen. "Kak bylo razrusheno 'ministerstvo pravdy': sovetskaia tsenzura epokhi glasnosti i perestroiki (1985–1991)." *Zvezda* 6 (1996): 212–221.

Bode, Andreas. "Humor in the Lyrical Stories for Children of Samuel Marshak and Kornei Chukovskii." *The Lion and the Unicorn* 13, no. 2 (1989): 34–55.

Booker, M. Keith and Dubravka Juraga. *Bakhtin, Stalin, and Modern Russian Fiction*. Contributions to the Study of World Literature, no. 58. Westport, Conn.: Greenwood Press, 1995.

Brown, Deming. *Soviet Russian Literature Since Stalin.* Cambridge: Cambridge University Press, 1978.

Chukovskii, Kornei. *From Two to Five.* Rev. ed. Trans. and ed. Miriam Morton. Berkeley: University of California Press, 1968.

———. *Masterstvo Nekrasova.* Tom 4. *Sobranie sochinenii v shesti tomakh.* Moskva: Khudozhestvennaia Literatura, 1966.

———. *Ot dvukh do piati.* Tom 1. *Sobranie sochinenii v shesti tomakh.* Moskva: Khudozhestvennaia literatura, 1966. 333–725.

———. *Skazki.* Moskva: Detskaia Literatura, 1993.

Culler, Jonathan. *Structuralist Poetics.* London: Routledge, 1975.

Domar, Rebecca. "The Tragedy of a Soviet Satirist: The Case of Zoshchenko." In *Through the Glass of Soviet Literature*, ed. Ernest Simmons, 201–243. New York: Columbia University Press, 1953.

Forrester, Sibelan. "Kornei Ivanovich Chukovskii." In *Reference Guide to Russian Literature*, ed. Neil Cornwell, 232–234. Chicago: Fitzroy Dearborn, 1998.

Glotser, Vladimir, ed. "Daniil Kharms: 'Bozhe, kakaia uzhasnaia zhizn' i kakoe uzhasnoe u menia sostoianie.' Zapisnye knizhki.Pis'ma. Dnevniki." *Novyi Mir* 2 (1992): 192–224.

Ionesco, Eugène. *Présent passé, passé présent.* Paris: Mercure de France, 1968.

Kharms, Daniil. Druskin Fund. Archive Department of the Saltykov-Shchedrin Library, St. Petersburg.

———. *Letiat po Nebu Shariki.* Ed. A. A. Aleksandrov and N. M. Kavin. Krasnoiarsk: Krasnoiarskoe Knizhnoe Izdatel'stvo, 1990.

Loseff, Lev. *On the Beneficence of Censorship: Aesopian Language in Modern Russian Literature.* Trans. Jane Bobko. Munich: Verlag Otto Sagner, 1984.

Marshak, Samuil. *Vot kakoi rasseiannyi: Khudozhnik V. Konashevich delaet knigu.* Moskva: Sovetskii Khudozhnik, 1988.

Neiolov, E.M. "Perestupaia vozrastnye granitsy." In *Problemy detskoi literatury.* 53–72. Petrozavodsk: Petrozavodskii gosudarstvennyi universitet 1976.

Nikolajeva, Maria. *Children's Literature Comes of Age: Toward a New Aesthetic.* New York: Garland, 1996.

———. "Russian Children's Literature Before and After Perestroika." Children's Literature Association Quarterly. 20, no. 3 (1995): 105–111.

O'Dell, Felicity Ann. *Socialisation Through Children's Literature: The Soviet Example.* Cambridge: Cambridge University Press, 1978.

Parrott, Ray J., Jr. "Aesopian Language." In *Modern Encyclopedia of Russian and Soviet Literature.* Vol. 1., 39–45. Gulf Breeze, Fla: Academic International Press, 1977.

Rabinowitz, Peter. *Before Reading: Narrative Conventions and the Politics of Interpretation.* Ithaca, NY: Cornell University Press, 1987.

Scatton, Linda Hart. "Mikhail Mikhailovich Zoshchenko." In *Reference Guide to Russian Literature*, ed. Neil Cornwell, 929–931. Chicago: Fitzroy Dearborn, 1998.

―――. *Mikhail Zoshchenko: Evolution of a Writer.* Cambridge: Cambridge University Press, 1993.

Sokol, Elena. *Russian Poetry for Children.* Knoxville: University of Tennessee Press, 1984.

Thum, Maureen. "Misreading the Cross-Writer: The Case of Wilhelm Hauff's *Dwarf Long Nose.*" *Children's Literature* 25 (1997): 1–23.

Tomashevskii, Iu. V., ed. *Litso i Maska Mikhaila Zoshchenko.* Moskva: Olimp, 1994.

Tumanov, Larissa and Vladimir Tumanov. "The Child and the Child-like in Daniil Kharms." *Russian Literature* 34, no. 2 (1993): 241–269.

Tynianov, Iurii. "Kornei Chukovskii." *Soviet Studies in Literature* 24, no. 2 (1988): 95–100.

Zoshchenko, Mikhail. *Twelve Stories.* Selected and annotated by L. La Rocco and S. Paperno. Columbus, Ohio: Slavica, 1989.

CHAPTER 9

Crossing Borders from Africa to America

PAULA T. CONNOLLY

Tales about talking bears, rabbits, foxes, and turtles would seem to offer a wondrous world of anthropomorphized animals for child readers. And if one were to ask children to identify the story of a brazen rabbit who illicitly enters a garden, tries to evade a farmer, then enjoys eating his fill of someone else's vegetables before being found out, they would probably cite Beatrix Potter's *The Tale of Peter Rabbit*. Few would question that book being defined as "children's literature"; indeed, it is a story that was originally written for a specific child, young Noel, the son of Annie Moore, Potter's former tutor. Moreover, Potter's concerns about its publication were clearly with her child audience—the size of the books, for example, she felt must match their small hands.[1]

Yet the specific elements that determine *how* one comes to define a work as "children's" or "adult" literature are less certain than the often pronouncement-like designations of literature for specific-aged audiences. Is it author intentionality, reader response, marketing, cultural context, or other contributing factors that lend to such a designation?[2] Another story that shares much of the basic plot of *The Tale of Peter Rabbit* is a case in point. In this story, the main character, an irrepressible rabbit, longs for some of the vegetables in a man's garden. The rabbit decides that the man "[o]bviously didn't believe in sharing. Being worried about Mr. Man's soul, [the rabbit] decided he'd *make* Mr. Man share." This rabbit then talks Mr. Man's young daughter into letting him into the garden, where he eats his fill. When the rabbit is caught in a trap, the farmer vows: "I got you this time. . . . And when I get through with you, ain' gon' be nothing left. I'm gon' carry your foot in my pocket, put your meat in the pot, and wear your fur on my head." Unlike Mr. McGregor, who only yells "Stop thief!" as he tries unsuccessfully to catch young Peter, Mr. Man plots this rabbit's demise and dismemberment with a sense of passionate enjoyment. This rabbit, however, eludes such a fate by tricking a passing fox into exchanging places with him. Although we may guess what fate awaits the gullible fox, we are only told that "[t]he story don't say what happened to . . . Fox. . . . Rabbit took care of himself. Now it's up to . . . Fox to take care of himself. That's the name of that tune."[3]

This second story, "Brer Rabbit Goes Back to Mr. Man's Garden," is not as easily categorized as Potter's, yet the specific differences between the two tales themselves—in apparent plot and character—are not, on the surface, keenly dramatic ones. Whereas Brer Rabbit faces clear dangers if he is caught, Peter had been warned that when his father had entered the garden, he had "had an accident there; he was put in a pie by Mrs. McGregor." Neither world is a kind one for rabbits, and in both cases the garden is a place that promises plenty, yet threatens entrapment and death. The stories speak of the transgressions of characters who steal, yet whose rebelliousness is admired by the reader. Yet when each rabbit is found out by the respective gardeners, their responses differ. Peter Rabbit flees terrified, and cries in despair when his now-plump belly prevents him from sneaking under a door to safety. Brer Rabbit, too, "quiver[s]" in the trap, fearful of what the man will do to him, yet these animals interact quite differently in their worlds. Peter finally escapes when he frees himself from the clothes he wears, returns to his natural state as a rabbit, and slips underneath a gate, "safe at last in the wood outside the garden." Although Brer Rabbit, held in a small trap, is more keenly caught than Peter, he is a quintessential trickster figure; here, the rabbit can speak to humans and animals alike. When his pleas for release are ignored by Mr. Man, Brer Rabbit uses his wits to escape by exploiting another's vulnerability for his own freedom and gain. Brer Rabbit, too, has no mother that sends him off or waits to care for him in the evening, no sisters like Flopsy, Mopsy, and Cottontail who offer a domestic world. He is alone in this world, dependent only on himself, and it is not only his satirical voice that shows him functioning more as an adult than a child figure. Whereas Peter ends up ill from his gluttony and rebelliousness, Brer Rabbit has no such later ills or qualms.

Yet these differences alone can barely be enough to designate only the former as a child's story. Indeed, this and other Brer Rabbit tales *are* children's stories, of a sort. Storyteller Augusta Baker recalls how as a child she would race home after school and beg her Grandmother for more stories about Brer Rabbit: "We would get comfortable [she writes] and start down Brer Rabbit's road. Small, helpless Brer Rabbit always defeated his adversaries—the large animals—with his wit, humor, and wisdom. In my smallness I related to the clever little hare who could always get out of the most difficult situations through his sharp wit."[4]

Yet these stories are not the *exclusive* property of such a young audience. Indeed, these stories of animals, adventurers, and tricksters have a complex history that eschews their designation as either exclusively adult or children's stories. First published and popularized by Joel Chandler Harris, a Southern White journalist in the United States, these stories were collected from slaves and ex-slaves Harris met in the years before and after the Civil War. In 1880, his *Uncle Remus: His Songs and Sayings* came out to vast popular success, and was later followed by seven other volumes of collected tales. The "Uncle Remus" of that title is the most problematic figure in Harris's collection. Not originating in the stories of slaves, Uncle Remus is a creation of Harris himself, who used the character as a function of the narrative frame. Here, the character, an elderly ex-slave who tells his stories to the young White son of the plantation owner, supports an image reminiscent of pro-slavery plantation novels, which depicted pleasant relations between slaves and masters and denied the racial oppression inherent in slavery.[5]

It was, many critics argue, particularly this depiction of a kindly and nostalgic ex-slave that underpinned the success of Harris's collections. Although, as Julius Lester notes in the Introduction to his current retelling of the "Uncle Remus" stories, "Uncle Remus is the most remembered character from a literature that justified slavery by portraying blacks who found slavery a haven, and freedom a threat and imposition,"[6] it was particularly that depiction that many White audiences appreciated. Uncle Remus was, as critic Robert Hemenway points out: "a figure who could contribute to the country's reunification. Uncle Remus reassured Southern whites about their darkest fears: free black people would love, not demand retribution. At the same time he assured Northern whites that abandoning black people was not a failure of moral responsibility. Uncle Remus, immensely popular, witnessed that black people would turn the other cheek, would continue to love, despite all the broken promises of American history."[7] These stories of animal adventures were thus not merely read to entertain children, but also to appease the psyche of adult Whites, both in the northern and southern United States.

The tales of Uncle Remus seem, therefore, to be stories about racial cooperation, yet this narrative frame with its fictional white audience denies the import of the center tales. As Julius Lester points out: "[w]hile such a setting added to the appeal and accessibility of the tales for whites, it leaves the reader with no sense of the important roles the tales played in black life."[8] The irony about Harris's narrative frame is that the stories were neither originally for a White audience, nor particularly for children. In that regard, Harris creates more than a fictional character in Uncle Remus—he creates a fiction about the narratives embedded within the frame. In fact, the tales themselves *fight* the frame of happy Uncle Remus and the concurrent idyllic presentation of slavery. The supreme irony about these stories being removed—as Lester argues—from African American experience is that they *were* the stories of those enslaved people.[9]

The American enslavement of Africans was a destruction of and attempt to reconstruct boundaries, in geographical, political, cultural, social, familial, individual, and ethical terms. Taken from their countries, forced to cross the Atlantic Ocean, then brought to an unfamiliar place with unfamiliar customs and languages, it is estimated that between thirty and sixty million Africans were brought to the Americas, subjected to both physical and psychological enslavement.[10] Enslavers sought to destroy, then reconstruct the identities of these people, as white captors denied their humanity and slave traders shattered their familial connections. Yet many Africans and their children found ways to evade such enslavement, certainly ways to recreate boundaries of culture and community to maintain a sense of distinct identity. Through songs, folktales, and a recreation of the religion meant to inculcate their subservience, enslaved Africans and their descendants were able to create communities that allowed them psychological identities distinct from those provided by the white community. Indeed, in their resignification of terms, they were able to create a language and world that whites did not understand and from which they were excluded, even though it was practiced in their midst.

The embedded tales of Uncle Remus—the stories within the narrative frame that were collected from those who experienced and survived slavery in the United States—are more than playful tales of the adventures of various animals. These folktales contain often highly symbolic language, codes in which the signifieds were obfuscated, tales in which the plights and victories of anthropomorphized animals paralleled their own plights as enslaved people. As historian Lawrence Levine has pointed out, "The rabbit, like the slaves who wove tales about him, was forced to make do with what he had. His small tail, his natural portion of intellect—these would have to suffice and to make them do, he resorted to any means at his disposal—means which may have made him morally tainted but which allowed him to survive and even to conquer."[11]

Indeed, the world of these stories is a dangerous, cruel, and violent one, in which a mishap can mean death. These tales showed the talents needed for survival in such a predatory place. Furthermore, they offered psychological release to those enslaved and a means of reifying an identity distinct from that as "slave" imposed by White masters. These tales strengthened group solidarity and allowed a means of undermining apparent white hegemony, not only because they allowed a way to verbalize aggression, but also because while they spoke of the master's world, the tales excluded a white audience. They became part of the coded language slaves created—what Ann Kibbey terms "linguistic virtuosity."[12] Through an array of coded language, rich in metaphor, imagery, and double signification, slaves could sing songs of freedom and tell rebellious folktales in the very presence of their masters, yet escape punishment. Levine argues:

> . . . [t]he white master could believe that the rabbit stories his slaves told were mere figments of a childish imagination, that they were primarily humorous anecdotes depicting the "roaring comedy of animal life." Blacks knew better. The trickster's exploits, which overturned the neat hierarchy of the world in which he was forced to live, became their exploits; the justice he achieved, their justice; the strategies he employed, their strategies. From his adventures they obtained relief; from his triumphs they learned hope.[13]

It was precisely because the tales *seemed* childish that slaves were able to recount them in public without fear of retribution. Indeed, that categorization of adult men and women as "childlike" creatures who needed the protection of whites served as a rationalization for slavery itself. What underwrote this Sambo stereotype was "the American attitude toward . . . Africans. . . . Most antebellum whites firmly believed that Africans were . . . innately . . . imitative . . . childish . . . submissive."[14] Here, "childish" is defined as specifically inferior and facile and—in a political and social context—a justification for the enslavement of millions of Africans. Yet what many of those enslaved did was to rewrite that notion of "childishness," to recreate the "Sambo" as a rebellious figure and use stories that were perceived as foolishly "childlike" as a sophisticated means of subversion.

These tales were used not only for the entertainment and "psychic relief"[15] of adults, but also as stories with didactic underpinnings, as they sought to teach survival skills to young enslaved children. In "Mr. Jack

Sparrow Meets His End," for example, Jack Sparrow goes to tell Brer Fox something, Brer Fox complains about deafness and urges the bird to come closer, eventually onto his tooth. "Mr. Jack Sparrow hopped on Brer Fox's tooth, and Brer Fox opened his mouth real wide and—GULP! Tattletales never do come to a good end."[16]

It was not the confines of age, but race, that demarcated the audience of these tales. These were stories for both children and adults, but they were children and adults within the slave community; whites, especially adult whites, were the intended excluded audience. Creating tales that would be seen by adult whites as merely a minor form of "children's" stories thus became a sophisticated means of rebellion, survival, psychological empowerment, and didactic lessoning for the entire enslaved community, adult and child alike.

When Julius Lester rewrote the Uncle Remus tales a century later, he attempted to retain and replicate many elements of such storytelling. Although he kept the title "Uncle Remus," he did not use Harris's narrative frame but instead retold the center tales, revising Harris's use of dialect to a "modified contemporary southern black English."[17] Lester's purpose is "to make the tales accessible again, to be told in the living rooms of condominiums as well as on front porches in the South."[18] As much as regional and socioeconomic differences are not barriers to the stories, neither is the audience's age. Arguing the fact that "folktales are now considered primarily stories for children is an indication of our society's spiritual impoverishment,"[19] Lester includes "contemporary references [that] . . . reflect that the tales were originally adult stories" and acknowledges that "there are lines and references in my telling of these tales that are for the enjoyment of adults, references that children may not understand."[20] At the center of these stories, as well, is their earlier context; Lester tells his readers: "The suffering of those slaves who created the tales will be redeemed (to a degree at least) if you receive their offering and make it part of your life."[21]

Just as Julius Lester critiques the single definition of folktales as children's literature and rewrites the tales to include an adult audience, so, too, does another of his works show the dissolution of neat boundaries of such categorization. Lester's *To Be a Slave*, which among its many awards was cited as a 1969 Newbery Honor Book, has been described as "One of the most powerful documents to appear in children's literature."[22] Ironically, however, this book is a compilation of adult texts—songs, slave narratives, proslavery tracts, interviews of former slaves made as part of the Federal Writers' Project in the 1930s, and even a discussion of racial hierarchy by Thomas Jefferson.

Here, Lester seeks to tell the story of slavery—from the capture of Africans, through their forced journey across the ocean, to their enslavement and later emancipation in the United States as a *series* of stories— that is, as a weaving of varied viewpoints and experiences. The textual pattern is a sophisticated one; it has neither a neat linear nor circular pattern. Indeed, it disrupts expected narrative lines, as it seeks to disrupt complacent notions of slavery and history. Lester presents not only different voices, but also often contradictory ones; neither does he exclude disquieting voices, like that of the complicit slave who spies on and betrays his fellow slaves. Lester's premise—"To be a slave was to be a human being under conditions in which that humanity was denied. They were not slaves. They were people. Their condition was slavery"[23]—is a premise that immediately positions those who were enslaved in the center of the discussion of slavery. Here, they are not only the subject, but the speakers, those whose experience becomes the means of authority.[24] It is the telling of lived experience that figures centrally in this text. Lester connects these excerpts with his own brief explanations or transitions, but always the primary material is foregrounded.

The experiences of slaves encompass those who are tortured, murdered, commit suicide; those who rebel against their plight either physically or psychologically; and those who were complicit with their white slaveholders. Lester clarifies language, but is never patronizing or facile in his descriptions. He explains terms some may not know; he cites statistics, then allows the individuals to speak, so that this is not a history of cold numbers but of passionate and feeling people. Excerpts tell us, as well, of whites who supported slavery, those—such as Thomas Jefferson—who questioned whether Africans were as intelligent as whites. He tells, too, of the experiences of both adults and children.

By privileging the testimony of former slaves, Lester immediately denies the hegemony of white narrative perspective. He further attacks the concept of white hegemony with the focus on the ways slaves created separate communities with value systems exclusive of the white slaveholders. Value systems redefined acceptable behavior, so that stealing within the slave community was condemned, but stealing from the slaveholder was not. But if this text confronts and denies notions of white cultural hegemony of the nineteenth century, it also confronts and denies hegemonic notions of the definition of "children's" and "adult" literature. In *To Be a Slave*, Lester does not edit out difficult recountings of sexual exploitation, violence, and murder that might be deemed inappropriate for a young audience. He does not attempt to make these texts palatable for adolescents by sanitizing history or the testimony of these people. Indeed, the passion with which he directs the reader through passages, and the passion of the entries themselves, denies the possibility of a dry retelling of facts. Lester's selections are unflinching—both in language and in the scenes they describe. An excerpt from former slave Sallie Crane recounts: "We hardly knowed our names. We was cussed for so many bitches and sons of bitches and bloody bitches and blood of bitches. We never heard our names scarcely at all. First young man I went with wanted to know my initials! What did I know 'bout initials?" (29–30).

The separation of "children's" literature suggests a cultural construction of children, a time of increased vulnerability and protection afforded the young. It is particularly appropriate that Lester's *To Be a Slave* denies the often neat separation of literatures by age and uses defined "adult" literatures to create his text, for he is describing a time that offered little protection to enslaved children. Excerpts in Lester's book include recountings of families separated and children sold from parents who love them but are unable to save them from the auction block. Although not exclusively focusing on children, Lester nonetheless shows how children enjoyed no protection through any segment of the journeys of slaves. Of the middle passage, the sea journey from Africa to the Americas, Lester includes an excerpt from a narrative that describes how the white slavetraders who "fastened the irons on these mothers took the children out of their hands and threw them over the side of the ship into the water. When this was done, two of the women leaped overboard after the children" (25). In a time when children could be murdered by slavetraders without compunction, there are recorded incidents of mothers who killed their own children rather than have them endure slavery: "My mother told me . . . [about] a women who was the mother of seven children and when her babies would get about a year or two of age, he'd sell them and it would break her heart. . . . When her fourth baby was born and was about two months old, . . . she said, 'I just decided I'm not going to let ol' master sell this baby; he just ain't going to do it.' She got up and give it something out of a bottle and pretty soon it was dead" (40).

In one particularly horrific example of the vulnerability of children and the inability of their parents to protect them, Lester quotes Ida Hutchinson who recalls how the slave women would take their children into the fields because the master did not want "them to lose time walking backward and forward nursing. They built a long trough like a great long old cradle and put all these babies in it every morning when the mother come out to the field. . . . [A]ll at once . . . the rain came down in great sheets. And when it got so they could go to the other end of the field, that trough was filled with water and every baby in it was floating round in the water, drowned" (38).

To Be a Slave offers no gentle or indifferent view of slavery; neither does it offer a promise of happiness or resolution. Indeed, the ending of *To Be a Slave* is a patently uncomfortable one that denies any ready resolution to racial conflict. This is particularly apparent in its final entry, an excerpt from an interview in the 1930s during which Thomas Hall responds:

> Lincoln got the praise for freeing us, but did he do it? He give us freedom without giving us any chance to live to ourselves and we still had to depend on the southern white man for work, food, and clothing. . . . You are going to get a story of slavery conditions and the persecutions of Negroes before the Civil War and the economic conditions concerning them since that war. You should have known before this late day all about that. . . . Harriet Beecher Stowe wrote *Uncle Tom's Cabin.* I didn't like her book and I hate her. . . . the white folks have been and are now and always will be against the Negro. (156)

Hall's rejection of white hegemony is multitiered. He castigates white icons of emancipation—Stowe, Lincoln, and the Yankee soldiers; he redefines the heroes of abolition and the Civil War as emblems of white hypocrisy; he denies the narrative perspective which largely places the Civil War in the foreground and slavery as a background setting device for white heroes; and he ultimately denies accepted categorizations of history. Race becomes the means of definition and categorization—in experience and ideology—for him.

The thirteen illustrations in *To Be a Slave* reflect such conflicts, for the black and white drawings by Tom Feelings often use those tones in symbolic and racial terms. In the first image facing the title page, a black man, clothed in white pants, his wrists held with white chains, stands facing a world of whiteness, deep blackness covering only a thin space behind him. Connected to that world he is forced to leave behind, the means and pervasiveness of oppression are defined by the whiteness about him. White as a symbol of oppression is clear, too, in other illustrations, as in the vastness of space above a man "on the auction block" (41), the fields of cotton surrounding slaves who work in the fields (67), and the hoods and burning cross of the Klu Klux Klan (149). The illustrations reflect the excerpts of *To Be a Slave*, and in that way they, too, reflect the problems with clear boundaries between "children's" and "adult" literatures.

The problem with definition of genre by audience age is apparent, too, in Tom Feelings's later work, *The Middle Passage: White Ships/ Black Cargo*. This book tells the story of the forced journey of Africans to the Americas. It has been estimated that only as many as one-third of those people may have survived an ocean journey marked by beatings, rapes, starvation, diseases, overcrowded quarters, murder, and suicide.[25] This is a story, like Lester's, that tells of the horrors of slavery with passion and honesty, yet except for a brief introduction by historian John Henrik Clarke and foreword by artist Tom Feelings, this is a story told entirely in pictures. Tom Feelings explains why:

> I started reading everything I could find on slavery and specifically the Middle Passage. . . . But some of the writers' overbearing opinions, even religious rationalizations and arguments . . . made me feel, the more words I read, that I should try to tell this story with as few words as possible, if any. Callous indifference or outright brutal characterizations of Africans are embedded in the language of the Western World. It is a language so infused with direct and indirect racism that it would be difficult, if not impossible, using this language in my book, to project anything black as positive. This gave me the final reason for attempting to tell the story through art alone. I believed strongly that with a picture book any African in this world could pick up and see and feel what happened to us on those ships.[26]

What Feelings does in *The Middle Passage* is show us the horrors of this forced crossing. In shades of black and white, from the initial drawing—a full two-page spread of sweeping lines and softened tones in which the faces of two Africans imposed upon the picture show their relationship to the scene, and a bird is flying above as an image of freedom—the scene soon changes; the drawings fracture from such a full spread to panel drawings often surrounded by white margins. Here it is whiteness that marks unspeakable cruelties, not only as the blank white margins confine the images of these people, but in the scenes themselves, as ghostly White men beat and kill Black men and rape Black women. It is, too, a white ship that drives Africans who scream in pain, across the ocean. Describing his creative process in the foreword, Feelings writes: "muted images flashed across my mind. Pale white sailing ships like huge white birds of prey, plunging forward into mountainous rising

white foaming waves of cold water, surrounding and engulfing everything." As in *To Be a Slave*, Feelings's use of white and black is representational of the racial oppression inherent in the African slave trade. The
bird of freedom shown in the initial scene of Africa has become this ship
bird-of-prey and nature turns predatory. In a later two-page paneled set
of drawings, the white boat sits like a representational medallion in the
top center, cutting a wake through white waters as it continues to the
Americas, yet looking closely one sees black figures left behind in its
wake, other bodies falling from the sides of the boat. The top panel that
this drawing interrupts allows a view of what is happening on that boat—
as white figures take the bodies of innumerable Africans lying haphaz-
ardly in grotesque piles, and toss them overboard. In the bottom panel,
white sharks swim about the body of a black man, ready to devour him.
Tormentors both aboard the ship and in the ocean, the white sharks mirror the white slave traders in the top panel, just as the two panels on either side of the ship mirror each other. To attempt to describe these
drawings in words is to diminish their power. That is another reason for
the picture book format; without the limitations of words, Feelings was
able to create "images [with] . . . a definite point of view and the *passion*
in them that reflected clearly the experience of the people who endured
this agony."

The Middle Passage has been categorized, alternately, as an adult
and children's book. The explicit scenes of violence and rape would
seem to suggest an adult audience, but the use of what is categorized as a
"children's genre"—the picture book—problematizes that. To Feelings,
"picture books" are more than a form for the child. He follows the origins of the genre to African storytelling. To create this book, he believed,
he would "use everything [he] had ever learned about the power of picture books." He continues:

> Storytelling is an ancient African oral tradition through which the val-
> ues and history of a people are passed on to the young. And essentially
> I am a storyteller. Illustrated books are a natural extension of this
> African oral tradition. Telling stories through art is both an ancient and
> modern functional art form that enables an artist to communicate on a
> large scale to people young and old. I could use the form of historical
> narrative pictures telling a complete story to adults.

The importance of storytelling in his work is clear in the way Feelings invited people into his studio to look at sketches while they were

still in progress. These drawings became, in some way, a *series* of stories, as was Lester's *To Be a Slave*. Feelings not only tells the story of millions of enslaved Africans, but he also notes: "I listened [to those black people who came into my studio] as they voluntarily opened up and told me about the joyful and the sorrowful things in their lives. And I began to soak up all this information. All those stories, all those things that as one person I could never experience in a single lifetime. Then when I was alone I let it seep slowly into all of my art." As Feelings recalls, he would also hear the voice of his deceased maternal grandmother telling him to continue the work "because you are not doing this just for yourself." The people he invited into his studio were defined by commonly shared cultural pasts, not by age, for he invited "all kinds of people, young and old."

Indeed, at various literary conferences, Feelings also has noted the importance of this story for the young. Critics have responded similarly. *The Middle Passage* has received the Coretta Scott King Award, which acknowledges outstanding African American children's authors and illustrators, and reviewers have noted the book's potential dual audience, as did Betsy Hearne, who wrote that it "will provoke discussion among junior-high and high school students (not to mention adults)."[27]

Like *To Be a Slave* and, a century earlier, the tales of Brer Rabbit, *The Middle Passage* in not a book confined by the limitations of audience age. That issue is a keenly intriguing one in these cases, for these texts allow examinations of traditional boundaries of form and audience. Julius Lester uses adult narratives to create a book for adolescents; Tom Feelings uses a children's form to create a book for adults. Each permeates limiting notions of "children's" or "adult" literatures by using narrative forms typically designated for the "other" audience. Lester and Feelings seek to tell stories of how slavery attempted to destroy cultural boundaries and reestablish other, oppressive ones, in which people were viewed and treated as chattel. Their crossing borders of genre and audience draws not only upon traditions of storytelling from American slaves and earlier African folktales, but it also serves as a keen statement on the politics of using classification as a means of marginalization and, hence, oppression. *To Be a Slave* is not only a book *for* adolescents any more than *The Middle Passage* is exclusively *for* adults. By permeating the boundaries of narrative form, Lester and Feelings define themselves as "storytellers," as those whose works are a *series* of stories, representing many others, both young and old, and giving voice to those whom history might silence.

Lester's description of the Uncle Remus tales fits as well his and Feelings's work in *To Be a Slave* and *The Middle Passage*: ". . . storytelling is a human event, an act of creating relationship. In a traditional setting, storytelling creates and re-creates community, making a bond between the living and the living, the young and the old, the living and the dead. . . . The storyteller resides at the vortex of the mystery, resolving it by means that do not rob us of mystery."[28] Drawing upon traditions within and before the enslavement of Africans in the Americas, Lester and Feelings bring "storytelling" to current generations of both children and adults in their separate texts and as they do so, they also elude the marginalization of categories—in terms of history, aesthetics, and audience.

NOTES

1. Beatrix Potter, *The Tale of Peter Rabbit* (1902. London: Frederick Warne, 1987). For background on the story and its publication, see Leslie Linder, *A History of the Writings of Beatrix Potter* (London: Frederick Warne, 1971), 4, 95.

2. See Peter Hunt, *Criticism, Theory, and Children's Literature* (Oxford: Basil Blackwell, 1991), especially chapters 1–3, for a discussion on the debate about defining "children's" literature.

3. Julius Lester, "Brer Rabbit Goes Back to Mr. Man's Garden," in *The Tales of Uncle Remus: The Adventures of Brer Rabbit*, illus. by Jerry Pinkney (New York: Dial Books, 1987), 81–86.

4. Augusta Baker, introduction to *The Tales of Uncle Remus: The Adventures of Brer Rabbit*, by Julius Lester, vii.

5. For various discussions of the Uncle Remus character, see R. Bruce Bickley, Jr., ed, *Critical Essays on Joel Chandler Harris* (Boston: G. K. Hall, 1981). For an example of a proslavery plantation novel, see John Pendleton Kennedy, *Swallow Barn, or A Sojourn in the Old Dominion*, ed. Jay B. Hubbel (1832. New York: Harcourt Brace, 1929). The problematic presentation of "Uncle Remus" is the primary reason the Disney film *Song of the South* (1946), a retelling of Brer Rabbit stories with an Uncle Remus character, has not been rereleased in recent years.

6. Julius Lester, foreword to *The Tales of Uncle Remus: The Adventures of Brer Rabbit*, xv.

7. Robert Hemenway, "Introduction: Author, Teller, and Hero," in *Uncle Remus: His Songs and His Sayings* (New York and London: Penguin Books, 1982), 20.

8. Lester, foreword to *The Tales of Uncle Remus*, xv.

9. In his foreword to *The Tales of Uncle Remus*, Lester points out that these tales "represent the largest single collection of Afro-American folktales ever collected and published" (xiii).

10. See John Henrik Clarke, introduction to *The Middle Passage: White Ships/Black Cargo* (New York: Dial Books, 1995) n. p., for a précis of the middle passage.

11. Lawrence W. Levine, *Black Culture and Black Consciousness: Afro-American Folk Thought from Slavery to Freedom* (Oxford and New York: Oxford University Press, 1977), 112.

12. Ann Kibbey, "Language in Slavery: Frederick Douglass's *Narrative*," in *Prospectus: The Annual of American Cultural Studies* 8 (1983): 163–182.

13. Levine, *Black Culture and Black Consciousness*, 114. For further discussions of coded languages and slave folktales, see Levine, esp. 81–135. See John W. Blassingame, *The Slave Community: Plantation Life in the Antebellum South* (New York and Oxford: Oxford University Press, 1979) for a discussion of the ways folktales served as "important psychological devices" for surviving slavery (129). See John W. Roberts, *From Trickster to Badman: The Black Folk Hero in Slavery and Freedom* (Philadelphia: University of Pennsylvania Press, 1989) for a discussion of the connections between African and African American folktales.

14. Blassingame, *The Slave Community*, 227. Also see Blassingame for a discussion of other stereotypes used to rationalize slavery, esp. 223–248.

15. Levine, *Black Culture and Black Consciousness*, 115.

16. Julius Lester, "Mr. Jack Sparrow Meets His End," in *The Tales of Uncle Remus*, 37. For further discussion about the didactic purposes of these tales, particularly for children, see Levine, *Black Culture and Black Consciousness*, 125, and Blassingame, *The Slave Community*, 127.

17. Lester, foreword to *The Tales of Uncle Remus*, xviii. Lester discusses the Uncle Remus character in that foreword, esp. xiv–xvi and in *The Last Tales of Uncle Remus* (New York: Dial Books, 1994), x–xii. Lester has also published two other collections of Uncle Remus tales: *More Tales of Uncle Remus: Further Adventures of Brer Rabbit, His Friends, Enemies and Others* (New York: Dial Books, 1988) and *Further Tales of Uncle Remus: The Misadventures of Brer Rabbit, Brer Fox, Brer Wolf, the Doodang, and Other Creatures* (New York: Dial Books, 1990).

18. Lester, foreword to *The Tales of Uncle Remus*, xvi.

19. Ibid., xv.

20. Ibid., xx.

21. Ibid., xxi.

22. Margaret A. Dorsey, review of *To Be a Slave*, *Library Journal* 93 (15 December 1968): 4,733.

23. Julius Lester, *To Be a Slave*, illus. Tom Feelings (New York: Scholastic, 1968), 28.

24. See William L. Andrews, introduction to *Six Women's Slave Narratives*, ed. Henry Louis Gates, Jr. (New York: Oxford University Press, 1988), xxix–xli, for a discussion of the slave as object ("eye") and subject ("I") of his or her own story. Harriet Jacobs and other former slaves would demand authority through their "testimony"; as Jacobs writes "Only by experience can any one realize how deep, and dark, and foul is that pit of abominations [slavery]." See Jacobs, *Incidents in the Life of a Slave Girl, Written by Herself*, ed. L. M. Child, 1861. Reprint, ed. Jean Fagan Yellin (Cambridge: Harvard University Press, 1987), 2.

25. Clarke, introduction to *The Middle Passage*, n. p.

26. Tom Feelings, foreword to *The Middle Passage*, n. p. All following references from Tom Feelings are from this foreword.

27. Betsy Hearne, review of *The Middle Passage, Bulletin of the Center for Children's Books* 49 (December 1995): 125.

28. Lester, introduction to *The Last Tales of Uncle Remus*, x.

REFERENCES

Andrews, William L. Introduction to *Six Women's Slave Narratives*, ed. Henry Louis Gates, Jr., xxix–xli. New York: Oxford University Press, 1988.

Bickley, Jr. and R. Bruce, ed. *Critical Essays on Joel Chandler Harris*. Boston: G. K. Hall, 1981.

Blassingame, John W. *The Slave Community; Plantation Life in the Antebellum South*. New York and Oxford: Oxford University Press, 1979.

Clarke, John Henrik. Introduction to *The Middle Passage: White Ships/Black Cargo*. New York: Dial Books, 1995.

Dorsey, Margaret A. Review of *To Be a Slave*. *Library Journal* 93 (15 December 1968): 4733.

Feelings, Tom. *The Middle Passage: White Ships/Black Cargo*. Introduction by John Henrik Clarke. New York: Dial Books, 1995.

Harris, Joel Chandler. *Uncle Remus: His Songs and His Sayings,* ed. Robert Hemenway. New York and London: Penguin Books, 1982 [1880].

Hearne, Betsy. Review of *The Middle Passage. Bulletin of the Center for Children's Books* 49 (December 1995): 125.

Hemenway, Robert. "Introduction: Author, Teller, and Hero." In *Uncle Remus: His Songs and His Sayings*. New York and London: Penguin Books, 1982.

Hunt, Peter. *Criticism, Theory, and Children's Literature*. Oxford: Basil Blackwell, 1991.

Jacobs, Harriet. *Incidents in the Life of a Slave Girl, Written by Herself*. Ed. L. M. Child, 1861. Reprint, ed. Jean Fagan Yellin. Cambridge: Harvard University Press, 1987.

Kennedy, John Pendleton. *Swallow Barn, or A Sojourn in the Old Dominion.* Ed.
     Jay B. Hubbel. 1832. New York: Harcourt Brace, 1929.
Kibbey, Ann. "Language in Slavery: Frederick Douglass's *Narrative.*" *Prospectus: The Annual of American Cultural Studies* 8 (1983): 163–182.
Lester, Julius. *To Be a Slave.* Illus. Tom Feelings. New York: Scholastic, 1968.
———. *The Tales of Uncle Remus: The Adventures of Brer Rabbit.* New York:
     Dial Books, 1987.
———. *More Tales of Uncle Remus: Further Adventures of Brer Rabbit, His
     Friends, Enemies and Others.* New York: Dial Books, 1988.
———. *Further Tales of Uncle Remus: The Misadventures of Brer Rabbit, Brer
     Fox, Brer Wolf, the Doodang, and Other Creatures.* Illus. Jerry Pinkney.
     New York: Dial Books, 1990.
———. *The Last Tales of Uncle Remus.* New York: Dial Books, 1994.
Levine, Lawrence W. B*lack Culture and Black Consciousness: Afro-American
     Folk Thought from Slavery to Freedom.* Oxford and New York: Oxford University Press, 1977.
Linder, Leslie. *A History of the Writings of Beatrix Potter.* London: Frederick
     Warne, 1971.
Potter, Beatrix. *The Tale of Peter Rabbit.* 1902. London: Frederick Warne, 1987.
Roberts, John W. *From Trickster to Badman: The Black Folk Hero in Slavery and
     Freedom.* Philadelphia: University of Pennsylvania Press, 1989.

PART IV

Distinctions, Demarcations, and Double Address

CHAPTER 10

"What happened?"
The Holocaust Memoirs of Isabella Leitner

ADRIENNE KERTZER

In *Saving the Fragments: From Auschwitz to New York*, the second of four Holocaust memoirs written by Isabella Leitner, the narrator questions her obsessive need to return to "that terrible terrain again and again." Recognizing that her physical liberation has not produced an equivalent liberation of memory, she recognizes also the psychological burden of her memories of Dr. Mengele and her impossible desire to be free of those memories: "I want you dead not only in reality, but in memory, too" (*S*, 49).[1] The narrator's frustration turns her to the complexities and challenges that confront the survivor who wishes to tell children about the Holocaust:

> Will we have the heart to tell them what we know? We will have to, because history cannot be trusted. It distorts. Will anyone believe the unbelievable? (*S*, 49)

I begin with this quotation, for in its five brief sentences, it raises narrative and ethical issues central to the way the telling of the Holocaust functions as a border between adult and children's texts. Questions about what we should and can tell children about the Holocaust, the purpose behind our telling, and our understanding of what exactly children will find "unbelievable," are relevant in light of the very different narrative choices Leitner makes in each of her four texts, and particularly resonant

Note: Excerpts from *The Big Lie: A True Story* by Isabella Leitner are used by permission of Scholastic Inc. Copyright © 1992 by Scholastic Inc.

in light of the memoir Leitner published immediately after *Saving the Fragments*. For unlike the three other memoirs directed at adults and young adults (*Fragments of Isabella: A Memoir of Auschwitz* [1978], *Saving the Fragments: From Auschwitz to New York* [1985], and *Isabella: From Auschwitz to Freedom* [1994]), *The Big Lie: A True Story*, published by Scholastic in 1992, is clearly intended for young children. Not only do so many memoirs complicate the narrator's insistence on a simple opposition between the distortions of history and the truthfulness of the survivor's witness ("history cannot be trusted. It distorts"), the narrative choices of the children's book confirm that Leitner herself is unable or unwilling to tell children everything she knows. For in *The Big Lie*, Leitner chooses to tell children a very different story from the one she tells adults.

Complicating what Leitner "knows" is her subject position as both daughter and mother. Although the maternal inspiration behind all her work is undeniable, that inspiration works in two contradictory ways. Writing as the survivor/daughter, Leitner in her adult texts incessantly mourns the murder of her mother, Teresa Katz; writing as the teacher/ mother, she suppresses the pain of that ongoing mourning even as she attempts to write the future-looking text that her own mother might have written. For paradoxically the act of writing maternally for children necessitates a muting, not only of the dead mother's voice, but of the mother's symbolic role in saving her daughter's life. It is as though the only way Leitner can honor her mother and the values her mother represents is by constructing a maternal narrative voice that is appropriate for young children[2] at the cost of suppressing her complex memories of her own mother, the one she still mourns.

The result of this narrative decision is not just a children's book radically different from the three adult memoirs, but a final adult memoir itself influenced by the muting of the mother's positive role in the children's book. One sign of this is the deletion in the fourth memoir of a crucial line in the first memoir linking the narrator's acts of resistance to her listening "to my inner voices, to the infallible truth my mother had taught me" (*F*, 54). In contrast, although the fourth memoir, *Isabella: From Auschwitz to Freedom*, includes new material that speaks forcefully to the unresolved trauma of her mother's murder (and therefore refutes easy clichés about the healing effects of time), it omits this particular maternal tribute. Given that the omission comes in a book that merges the first two memoirs and deletes little else, a book published only two years after Leitner published *The Big Lie*, I can only question whether the minimizing of the mother's role in the children's book has in turn affected the adult work. Regardless whether this particular deletion was initiated by an editor, Irving A. Leitner (Leitner's spouse and co-author), or by Leitner herself, what is significant is that the deletion only becomes possible after Leitner publishes the children's book.

For if the dead mother's legacy is faith in the human potential for goodness, dignity, and humanity, to recall the mother's words is to risk recalling the Leitner children's failure to listen to their mother's painfully accurate prediction, "Hitler will lose the war, but he'll win against the Jews" (*F*, 6). More disturbing, to recall the dead mother's voice is to remember witnessing the destruction of that maternal faith in the future. That trauma is recounted in *Fragments of Isabella,* when the six children watch in immobilized horror as a sixteen-year-old SS officer beats their mother, and the children know that if they move to defend her, they will only see her murdered before them (*F*, 7). That this moment is traumatic is confirmed by the persistence of paralytic language in the adult memoirs, for example, the reenactment of Leitner's traumatic paralysis in 1975 when she recognizes in the faces of German tourists, the possible murderers of her mother, and begs her husband and children: "Help me. I can't walk" (*F*, 110). In a new fragment added to *Isabella: From Auschwitz to Freedom*, the narrator similarly explains her inability to visit Kisvárda[3] thirty-four years after her expulsion: "I was paralyzed by my emotions" (*I*, 205).

Unwilling to burden children with the memories that provoke this sense of paralysis, Leitner omits such episodes and such quotations in *The Big Lie*, yet this narrative strategy is itself compromised as Leitner attempts to write a story for young children and is hard-pressed to come up with the lesson such books require. Without the memory of the mother's voice, there is no lesson; survival makes no sense. Attempting to simplify her Holocaust narrative for young children, Leitner presents a catalogue of "facts," but such facts on their own provide no lesson unless we conclude that the narrative's numb tone is itself a lesson, that the daughter who dares not let children know what she still feels about the murder of her mother does not know what else there is to say. The result is a book with a radical disjuncture, similar to that found in Puritan children's poetry, in which the moral about the vanity of chasing the butterfly seems totally separate from the pleasure of the poem that precedes it. In the same way, Leitner's "Afterword" to *The Big Lie* functions to provide the lesson and to explain the book's title, a lesson and explanation that are not at all evident in the narrative proper.

When Leitner calls her children's text *The Big Lie*, the "Afterword" explains that the title is a reference to the big lie repeatedly propagated by

Hitler that Jews were responsible for German unemployment. The connection between this abbreviated history lesson (six years of war summed up in six pages) and Leitner's account of her Hungarian family's deportation, imprisonment, and liberation is puzzling; an "Afterword" that spoke about the historical deportation of Hungary's Jews in the spring and summer of 1944 might make sense, but Hungary is not even mentioned in the "Afterword," and the reluctance of the United States government to grant visas to European Jews, a reluctance that made it impossible for Leitner's father to free his family, is similarly omitted.

In view of all that Leitner omits in *The Big Lie*, the book's title inadvertently hints at a more complicated lying, the lying a mother/writer/survivor must engage in when the very act of remembering her own mother inhibits her from endorsing fully her dead mother's faith in the future. That Elie Wiesel is quoted on the dust jacket of *The Big Lie*, "I believe in survivors' testimonies more than in any other writings on the Holocaust . . . ," seems to suggest that survivors speak a truth that is unavailable elsewhere, but the "truth" of *The Big Lie* is radically different from the "truth" Leitner expresses in her other texts. And the "truth" of the "Afterword" is itself framed by a self-consciousness about language, a questioning that also appears elsewhere in Leitner, for example, in "*Lager* Language," a chapter added to *Fragments of Isabella* in the Laurel/Dell 1983 paperback and also included in *Isabella: From Auschwitz to Freedom* (although Leitner claims to have written it in Hungarian in 1945), where she records "the one language even God cannot understand" (*I*, 227). The self-consciousness of both the first sentence of *The Big Lie*'s "Afterword," "History calls the years 1939 to 1945 the time of World War II" (*BL*, 74) and its last sentence, "Nazi Germany's war against the Jews has come to be known as the Holocaust" (*BL*, 79), alerts us to the difficulty of finding the right words for the events Leitner is describing. If history cannot be trusted, one reason is the inadequacy of its language.

What the labels, "World War II" and "the Holocaust," elide is the specific personal experience of a woman who loses two sisters and a mother. At any time finding the right words for telling children about the death of mothers is a challenge, but how do we tell children about the maternal deaths occasioned by Nazi policy? If we have to tell children "what we know" (*S*, 49), are we more or less responsible if we choose not to tell them everything? Leitner implies that she is fulfilling a survivor's painful moral duty; we "have to" tell children "what we know" but the fact that she structures this duty as a question indicates a profound hesitation about this duty. Children should not forget what we tell them (the exhortation "Never forget" is so familiar—what we should not forget is not always so clear). For if we tell our children what we know, do we not run the risk of burdening them too, making them inheritors of our nightmares? Are there some things that it is necessary to forget, not to tell children? The ambiguous example of Leitner's own mother is useful here, for it is not at all clear whether the inspiring final words Leitner attributes to her mother in the adult memoirs were even spoken by the mother on the train to Auschwitz, or rather imagined by the daughter who read in her mother's silence the words she needed to hear. Similarly, the mother never says to Leitner that she knows that she is going to her own death: "She keeps smiling, and it is driving me mad, because deep inside I know she knows" (*F*, 6). Would Leitner really have preferred that her mother speak the truth that they both suspect? Or is it part of the mother's heroism that she remains silent? Leitner's own silence in *The Big Lie* regarding her response to her mother's death may then be read as a tribute to her mother's behavior.

Central to these questions is the question of belief. For how can Leitner convey her personal knowledge of "the unbelievable" to anyone, let alone to children? In a new introduction written in 1993 for her fourth memoir, Leitner alludes to the difficulty she faced in 1945 of needing to speak about her experiences but not knowing who her audience was: Her sisters already "knew everything" and those who were not there "were unable to understand anything" (*I*, 15). That Leitner initially writes her fragments in Hungarian hints that her ideal readers can only be her mother and the other dead. For the rest of us, "Auschwitz was—and is—unfathomable" (*I*, 15). The language that refers to Holocaust events as both "unfathomable" and "unbelievable" is common in survivor memoirs directed at adults, a narrative strategy by which survivors express both their impossible communicative task and their moral resistance to events that they know are all too real. But to call these events "unfathomable" and "unbelievable" is to indulge in a language of mystery and incomprehension that children's books about the Holocaust do not permit. Why tell children about the Holocaust unless we think that such events can be understood, understood and then avoided? Yet excluding the "unbelievable," which is what Leitner does when she writes for children, has radical implications for the lesson that Leitner thinks is necessary to market *The Big Lie* as a children's book, and suggests that there is an unresolvable contradiction between her own understanding of her life and what she thinks children will and should believe.

In all of the books, although Isabella Leitner is listed as the primary author, her husband, Irving A. Leitner, also is named on the title page as either editor or coauthor. Named as general editor and author of the epilogue, "This Time in Paris," in *Fragments of Isabella*, he is listed as coauthor in the other three texts. Leitner dedicates *Fragments of Isabella* to her husband: "My husband tiptoed around me with deep, delicate concern. This book belongs to him." The same dedication appears in *Isabella: From Auschwitz to Freedom*, supplemented by a dedication to the United States Holocaust Memorial Museum. The extent of the husband's role in three of the books is uncertain; the smaller font size of "with Irving A. Leitner" that appears on the title page of *The Big Lie* may imply a lesser role, but the dustjacket description of authority as well as the acknowledgment of his assistance, "Without the help of my husband . . . this book would not have been possible," implies something greater. On the dustjacket, Isabella Leitner is described as the writer of two previous books, a board member of the Juvenile Diabetes Foundation, and wife of "author Irving A. Leitner." Such complexities of authorship prohibit any simple conclusions that assume that the different narrative choices of the adult and children's texts are Isabella Leitner's alone. But these choices may be reflective of North American cultural attitudes about what is appropriate in children's reading about the Holocaust, and in the way a woman survivor speaks about her Holocaust experience, whether to children or to adults.[4] For although I agree with Judith Miller's ironic conclusion, "the Holocaust does not 'teach,' "[5] there may well be (as there is in the material that Miller examines) a "lesson" in Leitner's multiple tellings. It is a lesson about the challenges of Holocaust representation, about the difficulty of telling children "what we know," and the complications that ensue when the daughter who mourns and the mother who teaches are one and the same, but our generic divisions and psychological suppositions demand that we treat them separately.

There are numerous differences between the children's version and the adult versions—for example, the shift from fragments and present tense in the adult memoirs to chapters and past tense in the children's book—but the most striking is the erasure of the anger, fury, and grief of the daughter-survivor who cannot forget the murder of her mother in the gas chambers of Auschwitz, and how this erasure in turn affects the very possibility and nature of a lesson. This anger and grief compels the adult texts where the memory of the mother's voice, eyes, and smile is a never-ending torment, and the narrative tone is consequently bitter, ironic, and confused as it attempts "to comprehend what cannot be comprehended"

(*F*, 3). Despite the uplifting title of the most recent memoir, *Isabella: From Auschwitz to Freedom*, and the more coherent organization present- ing a chronological narrative that seemingly celebrates the move from Auschwitz, to Liberation, to America, the additional fragments, in partic- ular the three new fragments at the end, reinforce the adult memoirs' focus on the traumatic loss of the mother. Indeed, the clarity achieved by the chronological reorganization of the material covered in *Fragments of Isabella* and *Saving the Fragments* does not fit the accompanying compli- cated textual apparatus that remains as fragmentary and contradictory as the multiple memoirs themselves. Preceding the three "books" of the memoir proper is a new poem, "May 31, 1944," and a new introduction; following it is both the epilogue of the first memoir and the introduction, now renamed an "Afterword," to the second.

Such narrative confusion is notably absent in the children's version. *The Big Lie* begins with the autobiographical voice: "My name is Isabella, and I was born in a small town called Kisvarda" (*BL*, 12), a voice that carefully controls reference to the mother. In Chapter 2, "Mama sewed yellow stars on our clothes," and prompts her six adolescent children to clean their space in the ghetto by telling them: " 'We don't know how long we'll be here, so we must be clean. We mustn't get sick' " (*BL*, 21, 26). The narrator does not pass judgment on the wisdom of her mother's ad- vice; she simply reports. Similarly, in Chapter 3, describing the train ride to Auschwitz, the narrator allows herself only one brief reference to her mother: "Mama held Potyo close to her body" (*BL*, 34). A doublespread map of the train journey from Kisvarda to Auschwitz separates Chapters 3 and 4. It is a highly stylized map in which there are, with the exception of Budapest and Odessa, no towns except for those towns that the train passes through. No other towns matter.

The unnamed mother (she is identified as Teresa Katz only in the adult texts) and Potyo, the youngest sister to whom Leitner dedicates *The Big Lie*, are gassed upon arrival in Auschwitz. This memory obviously torments Isabella Leitner, for every text she writes repeats the dates she cannot forget: 28 May 1944, her own and her mother's birthday; 29 May 1944, departure to the ghetto; 31 May 1944, arrival in Auschwitz. In *Fragments of Isabella*, the late fragment, "May," acknowledges that since 1944, the scent of May is "the smell of burning flesh. The burning flesh was your mother." The narrator states bluntly that time does not heal: "For more than twenty years I have walked zombie-like toward the end of May, deeply depressed, losing jobs, losing lovers, uncomprehending." If she now has moments in May when she doesn't smell burning flesh, "That is not happiness, only relief." The book that she wishes to write but cannot is the one that would address the dead mother unambiguously: "I want to tell my mother that I kept her faith, that I lived because she wanted me to" (*F*, 94–95). She wants to, but the daughter's anger and grief keep getting in the way. It is always one of her siblings whom Leitner praises for behavior that reflects the mother's values; for Leitner herself, the tension between her mother's values and the countervalues of her own memories problematize any simple endorsement. The answers that mothers teach are unbalanced by the questions daughters learn in Auschwitz.

On the train to Auschwitz, Leitner imagines the mother instructing her children to see beyond the world of Auschwitz, to look forward and have faith: "You can nourish your children's souls and minds, and teach them that man is capable of infinite glory" (*F*, 16–17), yet the tone in the adult texts coarse, bitter, and ironic. The first night in Auschwitz, Philip (Leitner's brother) says: "Eat. If they give you shit, eat shit. Because we must survive. We have to pay them back" (*F*, 27). When Leitner and two of her sisters escape during a forced march to Bergen-Belsen, the harshness of Philip's language returns: "All that grease and fat without bread is murder on our stomachs, but the cycle of eating and shitting does not stop" (*F*, 82). Even the American visas that Leitner's father obtains too late are understood this way: "They could be framed . . . or used for toilet paper" (*F*, 9).

But in Chapter 4 of *The Big Lie*, it is not just Philip's excremental language that is softened and modified: "Eat whatever they give you, because we must survive. . . . one day we will be free. And we will pay them back" (*BL*, 44). What is lost is the inscribing of the mother's words and the mother's faith as essential to how Leitner understands and remembers her survival. For example, Leitner gives two versions of a message that Philip sends his four sisters in Auschwitz. In *The Big Lie*, the message says: "You must live. You simply must. I love you" (*BL*, 53). In *Fragments of Isabella*, the narrator generalizes that Philip's message is always the same:

> You must survive. You must live. You simply must. We not only have to
> pay them back. That is not reason enough. We must build a future free
> of bloodshedding. (*F*, 29)

Leitner repeats Philip's final sentence in her first memoir's concluding sentence when she vows to her dead mother that she will teach her children "to love life, to respect man, and to hate only one thing—war" (*F*, 98). Yet despite this vow and the way Leitner implies that its content links her to the teaching of a mother whose "intelligence and enlightenment were legendary" (*F*, 11), Leitner elects not to pass this maternal tribute on to the child readers of *The Big Lie*, and then deletes the sentence containing the vow to the mother in *Isabella: From Auschwitz to Freedom*. Similarly, Leitner mentions in both *The Big Lie* and *Fragments of Isabella* that in the workcamp, Birnbaumel, as a form of resistance she would stop digging as soon as the guards turned away. But it is only in the first adult memoir that she links this resistance and her survival to the words of her dead mother: "My mother had told me not to aid my enemy. In that forest in Birnbaumel in December, I remembered her. I honored her and kept myself alive" (*F*, 53). Significantly, *Isabella: From Auschwitz to Freedom* qualifies Leitner's certainty that it is the daughter's obedience to the mother's words that keeps her alive. The conviction and simplicity of "I honored her and kept myself alive" is replaced by the more tentative and uncertain, "I honored her and tried to keep myself alive" (*I*, 62). Such omissions and revisions indicate more than the different choices Leitner makes when writing for children in *The Big Lie*; they indicate how the need to suppress traumatic memories about the mother in the children's text affects in turn the presentation of the mother in the final adult text. In the final text, Leitner still honors her mother, but the positive connection between that honoring and her own survival seems less evident even as the trauma remains.

What is certain is that the horror of losing the mother cannot be explored in *The Big Lie*, as though its suppression marks the border between the coherent children's version and the traumatized adult texts. In *The Big Lie*, the mother's words are minimally reported: the futile shout to her children upon arrival in Auschwitz: "'Stay with me! Stay together!'" and then, after Mengele sends the mother and younger sister, Potyo, to the left, a final maternal statement, "'Be strong. . . . I love you.'" (*BL*, 41, 42). In Chapter 5, where the narrative voice must calmly explain to the child reader what Auschwitz was, the mother's death is reported only in the context of, and as illustration of, the method of the general killing: "Those sent to the left by Dr. Mengele, like Mama and Potyo, were led directly to their deaths" (*BL*, 46).

The extent of the erasure, the deliberate omission of Leitner's personal grief and anger through a controlled maternal voice that teaches children the facts that they need to know, is starkly apparent when one reads the adult memoirs, and sees how even in the fourth memoir, "in the waning years of my life," putting her two earlier adult memoirs together can give Leitner at most only "a measure of peace" (*I*, 16). This erasure of the personal voice may be necessary to achieve the placidity of the calm voice that explains to children what Auschwitz was, yet such placidity can only be achieved by excluding the tormented self-definition of the adult memoirs: "We were born of mothers the smell of whose burning flesh permeates the air" (*F*, 49). This tormented self-definition also explains "what Auschwitz was," but it is an explanation that terrifies.

Most would agree that such exclusions are necessary to the way Holocaust literature is presented to young children. Thus, Hazel Rochman praises Leitner's discretion in *The Big Lie*, her emphasis on "Only the facts."[6] In her 1993 *Booklist* review, Rochman praises Leitner's narrative decisions:

> There's no rhetoric, no tears, no hand-wringing about "atrocity" and "horror." The book is short, the type spacious. Just facts. The telling has the elemental power of the best children's literature, in which the simplicity is poetic and speaks volumes.[7]

The casual reference to poetic simplicity and speaking volumes indicates how easily we accept the minimizing of the impact of the mother's death as a necessary feature of the best children's literature. How does this silence speak? Do we really believe that children can hear in silence what we imagine would traumatize them if written down? The surprising implication that it is adults who need more than facts, whereas for children facts alone are sufficient, fails to recognize that unresolved grief and anger over the death of one's mother could itself be considered a "fact." It also ignores another cultural "fact," that adults, too, are uncomfortable when women mourn their mothers too long (and that maybe they learned this fact from the children's books that they read).

Further evidence that adult readers prefer not to notice an adult woman's obsession with her mother's death is evident in the introduction by Howard Fast to the second adult memoir, *Saving the Fragments*. Although the title of *Saving the Fragments* implies a resolution to the story begun in *Fragments of Isabella*, that shaping and chronology are false to Leitner's incessant return to what she regards as the central event of her life, the loss of her mother. *Saving the Fragments* begins with an epigraph about 31 May 1944, the day when "the natural order of the universe" is altered because "the heart of my mother was floating in the smoke-filled sky of Auschwitz." The narrator still lives with that vision: "I have tried to rub the smoke out of my vision for forty years now, but my eyes are still burning, Mother." This epigraph appears in an even

more forceful manner in the fourth memoir, in that "forty years" is now
too brief and the word "decades" (*I*, 11) must take its place.

But even in an adult text, such a relentless vision is troubling, and
very remote from the vision of the female author constructed by Howard
Fast's introduction, an introduction that complicates any simple opposi-
tional relationship between what can be said in children's and adult texts
about the Holocaust. What can be said by a woman also is at issue, for
Fast's introduction is remarkable in its deliberate refusal to acknowledge
the extent of Leitner's anger and grief. Fast calls Leitner "an innocent. . . .
A young girl [she was twenty when deported]" (*S*, x), whose "very existence is an affirmation of life, a song of hope, [and tactlessly] a clear
bright flame that defies the murderers of mankind" (*S*, x). But where are
the hope and innocence in the narrative voice who rejoices at the chaos at
the end of the war: "Still, it is good to know that there is shit on their pi-
anos" (*S*, 22)? Insisting on reading her story as one of love and redemp-
tion, Fast infantilizes and feminizes Leitner's account, discounting the
possibility that her stylistic choice of fragments is deliberate and offers its
own analysis of her experience: "Isabella Leitner does not attempt to analyze, to explain, to create historical patterns. She cannot; she was a young
girl, beloved and innocent, and all she sees and remembers is recalled
through the eyes of a young girl" (*S*, xi). Given such authorial innocence
and youth, Fast concludes that it is up to him to draw the lesson and direct
the reader to the purpose of Leitner's book, a pointing that inadvertently
and ironically shows that such a lesson is not apparent, that Leitner's
memoir is not so easily reduced to the hopeful lessons many North American readers wish to take from Holocaust writing. Fast must tell us the lesson in case we miss it, and falsely think that young girls or older women
have a right to their anger:

> Even as it took her from the horrors of the crematorium into freedom, it
> will take you, the reader, into a new place of compassion. These frag-
> ments are a preachment, a sermon on the wonder and goodness and
> value of life. All is possible if men and women deal in trust and love.
> With hatred and suspicion, all will perish. This is the essence and
> teaching of Isabella's fragments of memory. (*S*, 12)

How can Fast derive this lesson from a book that begins with the torment of the narrator's smoke-filled eyes, that continually refers to her
pain and anger, that calls into doubt the very possibility of healing? "The
images in our heads are so powerful, they probably will not respond to

the healing of time; they probably will be our companions until we die" (*S*, 41). Simple faith in "wonder and goodness and value of life" is not conveyed by statements such as: "Our mourning is awash in complexities we cannot untangle" (*S*, 98). And to find a sermon when the adult memoirs deliberately avoid any simple explanations for the narrator's survival (was it the support of her sisters? Her prayer to her mother? Chance? The unnamed attaché?) is a further demonstration of Fast's determination to make Leitner's memoir say only what he thinks it should. That Fast's reading of *Saving the Fragments* is now reprinted as part of the textual apparatus of *Isabella: From Auschwitz to Freedom* is further evidence of the cultural need to direct the reader away from Leitner's unresolved trauma, for simply repeating the titles of the additional three concluding chapters, "I went home . . . I did not," "Scents and Images," and "Fear" indicates how this final memoir ends with a woman who can never be free, but always trapped in two times, the present and 1944: "The Nazis are burning my mother." In the final chapter, she defines the age of the youthful German musicians by counting their births "decades after their elders melted down my mother" (*I*, 207, 210).

And Fast is not alone in his insistent and obtuse cheerfulness. A *School Library Journal* review of *Saving the Fragments* is clearly relieved that Leitner's "upbeat style . . . assures readers of her desire to put the past behind her and get on with her life."[8] Another more astute reviewer in *Kirkus Reviews* recognizes that Leitner has not been able to put the past behind her and therefore pans the book for its subjectivity and failure to give North American readers the kind of moral and affirmative ending that they look for in Holocaust stories:

> Basically it falls flat at the end. As such, it adds disappointment to apathy. Leitner went through hell and lived to tell about it, and nobody doubts the nobility and goodness of her instincts. But it takes more than good instincts to make a vital book.[9]

There is nothing "upbeat" about Leitner's concluding reference to the silences that accompany the surviving daughters' reunion with the father who had escaped to the United States in 1939 but was unable to obtain visas for his wife and children: "We have no answers to his questions. We are frightened, bewildered. What can we say to him?" (*S*, 107).

In contrast, the Epilogue to *Fragments of Isabella*, "This Time in Paris," written by Irving A. Leitner, refuses to find a hopeful lesson and insists upon Leitner's continuing torment. As Leitner moves toward the

end of her first memoir, the fragments become increasingly brief and in-
conclusive, as though she is struggling and failing to find the closure that
American Holocaust memoirs require. Arriving in the United States on
8 May 1945, the very day the war ends in Europe, she speaks of the
giant and invisible Sorrow that accompanies her, her vision of the dead
that a year later keeps her from seeing her own face in the mirror: "But
all I can see is smoke" (*F*, 92). "May" becomes an annual reminder not
of her birthday, but of the time "[t]he world ended" (*F*, 94); "Peter" is the
son whose birth she announces to her dead mother; "Richard" is the second son who is "the sound of [the mother's] soul" (*F*, 98). But not even
the birth of the two children gives closure, for Leitner still begs the
mother to help her: "Help me, Mama. Help me to see only life" (*F*, 97).

The Epilogue that follows, with its account of two vacations (1960
and 1975) in Europe, confirms that for Irving A. Leitner the only lesson
in *Fragments of Isabella* is the one that refuses closure, that acknowledges the survivor's continuing anger, fury, and paralyzing grief. The last
night of the Leitner family's second trip to Paris, in the Café Cristal (another Kristallnacht?), Isabella Leitner is overcome by a group of German-speaking tourists who, looking for *lebensraum*, surround her table.
The sound of the German they speak, their appearance and age, paralyze
her: "He could be the one who killed my mother" (*F*, 110).

The function of this Epilogue in which the spouse and his son, Peter,
come to the aid of the still traumatized survivor is very different from the
"Afterword" that replaces it in *The Big Lie*. Like the striking difference
conveyed by the two titles, the one speaks to the shattering of the self, the
other strives to give the child reader an explanation for the Holocaust. It is
fitting that in the Epilogue it is the adolescent son, Peter, who wants to
help his mother by doing "something . . .We just can't leave it like this. It's
too frustrating" (*F*, 111). Peter's solution is to write the words, Auschwitz, Bergen-Belsen, Dachau, on a note that the father delivers to the German tourists. Whether the tourists are indeed affected by the accusation of
these words is left unsaid.

What the "Afterword" and Epilogue do share is a structural similarity, one in which the "lesson" is detached and separate from the survivor's narrative, a separation that problematizes the very idea of a lesson
and the ability of the survivor/memoirist to write that lesson. And the difference between the two endings indicates that it is not enough to say pi-
ously that we must tell children about the Holocaust. What we tell them
and how we tell them (let alone what they hear, when we tell them) is far
more complicated. When children's books demand a narrative voice

whose primary function is to explain events, the writer whose adult texts dispute the possibility of such coherence, clarity, and explanation is faced with difficult narrative decisions, decisions that may necessitate excising the very daughterly grief that motivates her writing.

Hence, when David L. Russell concludes "Reading the Shards and Fragments: Holocaust Literature for Young Readers" by rhetorically asking: "What is appropriate for young readers? [and then answers] The truth, the truth, the truth,"[10] I find the rhetorical force of his wishful thinking beside the point. For what is "the truth" in Leitner's multiple tellings? The dustjacket's claim that *The Big Lie* will enable "children to come to terms with the brutality of the past while giving them hope for a future that promises *never again*," is hardly descriptive of a book whose only reference to the future is the concluding sentence, "We were ready to start life anew in America" (*BL*, 72), and whose factual narrative gives the young reader no advice on how to achieve that desired future. Similarly, Russell's well-intentioned exhortation elides the difficulty of reconciling the "truth" we tell children and the vision of the dead mother. For the truths that Leitner cannot tell children are multiple and maternal. They include the painful, far from hopeful, truth of *Saving the Fragments*: "But my pain and anger keep intruding, however hard I try to fix my gaze on the road that is supposed to deliver me into the future" (*S*, 41). But they also include the "unbelievable" possibility that Leitner escapes the bullet of the *Oberscharführer* on 23 January 1945 because her dead mother intercedes. Having appealed to an indifferent God, the terrified daughter prays to her mother:

> Where is my mother? She will protect us. Mama! Where are you? Somebody is trying to kill your children. The *Oberscharführer* is coming to kill us. He is coming closer. . . closer. He is right here.
>
>   He is gone.
>   What happened? (*F*, 71)

In the world of "the unbelievable" that constitutes the Holocaust universe, this question, with its obvious suggestion that Teresa Katz did save her daughters' lives, can only be written in an adult text. Adults may question whether the mother did intercede, but such questions are themselves further evidence of an adult text. When we insist that children's texts must explain the Holocaust, we are quite able to tell them that six million died (that horrific fact is believable) but questions about survival that find their answer in a place for the dead mother remain in the realm of "the unbelievable," part of the daughter's story that Isabella Leitner must omit as she struggles to tell children what she knows and to keep faith with her dead mother's promise:

> I cannot leave you with what you see here. I must leave you with what I see. . . . And wherever I'll be, in some mysterious way, my love will overcome my death and will keep you alive. (*F*, 17)

NOTES

1. Quotations from Isabella Leitner's works are cited in the text with the abbreviations listed below.

F: Isabella Leitner, *Fragments of Isabella: A Memoir of Auschwitz*, ed. and with an epilogue by Irving A. Leitner (New York: Thomas Y. Crowell, 1978).

S: Isabella Leitner with Irving A. Leitner, *Saving the Fragments: From Auschwitz to New York*, introduction by Howard Fast (New York: New American Library, 1985).

BL: Isabella Leitner with Irving A. Leitner, *The Big Lie: A True Story*, illustrated by Judy Pedersen (New York: Scholastic, 1992).

I: Isabella Leitner and Irving A. Leitner, *Isabella: From Auschwitz to Freedom* (New York: Anchor Books/Doubleday, 1994)

2. One of the complexities that necessitates speaking about children without precise age references in Leitner's work is that her memoirs never directly say how old she is when she goes to Auschwitz, an omission that is striking given her emphasis on the ironic significance of her birthday. The single reference to age, "I have lived barely two decades" (*F*, 71), appears just prior to the narrator's appeal to the dead mother to protect her from the threat of death. At the very moment when death seems imminent, perhaps because death does seem imminent, she refers to herself as a child. Leitner clearly thinks of her twenty-year-old self as a child in 1944 and wants the reader to think of her as a child (see also, "Inside, deep in my being, I am just a child" [*F*, 58]). Even if both *Fragments of Isabella* and *Saving the Fragments* have been reviewed as both young adult books and adult books, given Leitner's construction of herself as a child during the Holocaust, I do not think that her writing constructs the young adult reader as a category separate from the adult reader.

3. Leitner's birthplace, Kisvárda, appears with the accent in the adult memoirs; in *The Big Lie: A True Story*, Kisvarda has no accent.

4. Editorial choices and publishers' views on how to market the Holocaust are a further complication.

5. Judith Miller, *One, by One, by One: Facing the Holocaust* (New York: Touchstone, 1991), 279.

6. Hazel Rochman, review of *The Big Lie* by Isabella Leitner *Booklist* 89, no. 11 (1 February 1993): 982.

7. Ibid., 982.

8. Pam Spencer. Review of *Saving the Fragments* by Isabella Leitner. *School Library Journal* (August 1986): 114.

9. Review of *Saving the Fragments* by Isabella Leitner. *Kirkus Reviews* 53, no.14 (15 July 1985): 702.

10. David L. Russell, "Reading the Shards and Fragments: Holocaust Literature for Young Readers," *The Lion and the Unicorn* 21.2 (1997): 279.

REFERENCES

Leitner, Isabella. *Fragments of Isabella: A Memoir of Auschwitz*. Ed. and with an epilogue by Irving A. Leitner. New York: Thomas Y. Crowell, 1978.

———. "*Lager* Language," in *Fragments of Isabella: A Memoir of Auschwitz*, ed. and with an epilogue by Irving A. Leitner, 122–128. New York: Laurel/Dell, 1983.

Leitner, Isabella with Irving A. Leitner. *The Big Lie: A True Story*. Illus. Judy Pedersen. New York: Scholastic, 1992.

———. *Isabella: From Auschwitz to Freedom*. New York: Anchor Books/Doubleday, 1994.

———. *Saving the Fragments: From Auschwitz to New York*. Introduction by Howard Fast. New York: New American Library, 1985.

Review of *Saving the Fragments* by Isabella Leitner. *Kirkus Reviews* 53, no. 14 (15 July 1985): 702.

Miller, Judith. *One, by One, by One: Facing the Holocaust*. New York: Touchstone, 1991.

Rochman, Hazel. Review of *The Big Lie* by Isabella Leitner. *Booklist* 89, no. 11 (1 February 1993): 982.

Russell, David L. "Reading the Shards and Fragments: Holocaust Literature for Young Readers." *The Lion and the Unicorn* 21, no. 2 (1997): 267–280.

Spencer, Pam. Review of *Saving the Fragments* by Isabella Leitner. *School Library Journal* (August 1986): 114.

CHAPTER 11

Maintaining Distinctions
Realism, Voice, and Subject Position in
Australian Young Adult Fiction

JOHN STEPHENS

It has become something of a truism in the discourses surrounding children's literature that the boundary between children's and adults' literature is disappearing and a significant crossover literature is emerging. To examine a body of works produced within a particular culture, such as Australian young adult literature of the 1990s, is to discover an opposite tendency: that most authors from across the spectrum of fictive genres and cultural formations demonstrate a clear sense of addressing a preadult audience and of constructing a particular range of subject positions as cultural *desiderata* offered to that audience.

An informative place to begin such an enquiry is the work of Tim Winton, who has won wide acclaim as a writer both for adults and children, but maintains a firm distinction between his two audiences. His three books for older "children," the *Lockie Leonard* trilogy, are narrated in language that is a version of early teen demotic, tell stories about characters no older than fourteen, and have a target audience between the ages of ten and fourteen. They pick up young adult readers at the lower end of that age category, but do not have any appeal for adult readers. In a perceptive comparison of *Lockie Leonard, Human Torpedo* (1990), Winton's first novel for children, and *Cloudstreet* (1991), the adult novel that established Winton's international reputation, Richard Rossiter observes that the same ideological system informs both texts: Winton's belief in "order, pattern, stability"[1] affects the structure and outcomes of his narratives and is conveyed thematically in their concern with identity and the importance of belonging, their endorsement of hard (honest) work and family unity, and their affirmation of spirituality, faith, or religion.

What clearly distinguishes the books is a difference in degrees of explicitness, with the children's book presenting a view of the world that is more sharply polarized between positive and negative representations.

Winton may in some ways appear to be an extreme example, and other books, now with an implied audience only in the thirteen-plus age group, have articulated the moral relativism and emotional desolation that in commonsense classification will tend to push a book toward an adult readership. Books often cited as examples include John Marsden's *Dear Miffy* (1997), most of Sonya Hartnett's work since *Wilful Blue* (1994), and Margo Lanagan's *Touching Earth Lightly* (1996). The "problem" with *Wilful Blue* and *Touching Earth Lightly* is that they incorporate a range of the possible values available within a pluralistic and diverse culture and, unlike Winton's novels, do not overtly privilege one group of values over another. The response of adults as literary gatekeepers is to worry that youthful readers will lack the intellectual and emotional maturity and the skills of literary and moral discrimination and judgment necessary to assess the options presented, and hence to argue that such books fall into the adult domain. The cultural and ethical dialogue incorporated into such books reflects, on a wider scale, a debate about the origin and basis of *meaning*. As elsewhere in the Western world, young Australian people are sceptical about the traditional sources of meaning—religion, nation, community, family, career—and, not surprisingly, the nature of meaning has become the central focus of the fiction produced for them.

In his discussion of Winton, Rossiter concluded that the distinction between the books for adults and children lay not in any specific aspect, but a bundle of narrative elements: content, structure, handling of narrative voice, characterization (specifically in the way in which notions of childhood are constructed through characterization), and the fluid boundary between realistic and visionary elements in the adult novels. Content, structure and voice are, simply, more complex in *Cloudstreet* than in *Lockie Leonard, Human Torpedo*. Such distinctions have strong explanatory force where the audiences are as clearly discriminated as by Winton's novels; a replication of Rossiter's analysis with a more recent pair, *The Riders* (1994) and *Lockie Leonard, Legend* (1997), would yield the same conclusion. If the key discriminators are applied in analysis of novels for older young adult readers, however, they most often turn out to be more like *Cloudstreet* than like the *Lockie Leonard* books, but seem different in two crucial, interrelated ways implicit in Rossiter's argument. First, the orientation of cultural and ethical metanarratives, especially in terms of notions of the real, is grounded in (neo)humanistic attitudes to culture and relationships rather than postmodernist, moral, and cultural relativist attitudes. Second, the effects of narrative voice in producing reader subject positions proffer reading positions aligned with the implicit social ideologies of texts. What is often quite overt in the narrative strategies of books for younger readers is still present, but now more tacit.

Arguments about appropriate audiences mainly focus on contemporary realism. The boundary in some fantasy subgenres is endemically more blurred, but the one remove from contemporary reality suggests that, culturally, there is less at issue. The same can be said of historical fiction, even if it were much read by today's young readers. Hartnett's oeuvre includes the uncharacteristic *Black Foxes* (1996), a semiparodic, "costume" Gothic romance set in the first half of the nineteenth century, in which the boundary between adult and young adult audiences has disappeared. This novel makes at least as much space for relativism, alienation, and cynicism (alongside elements of fidelity and altruism) as in her contemporary realist texts, but has not been found particularly controversial. Underlying the unease with some young adult fiction is a perception that it deviates from the metanarratives deemed appropriate for the age group.

Fictions of early to middle adolescence typically assume and valorize concepts of individual agency, that is, the capacity to act independently of constraints imposed by society, but in doing so assume versions of subjectivity that conform to a humanist conception of the self. Contemporary young adult realism, on the other hand, often shows an awareness that such representations are idealistic, and that the depiction of characters within social relationships in fiction may not correspond with lived experience. To replace it with a mechanistic view of individuals constructed within and determined by social institutions offers young readers a fairly negative worldview, however, and is in fact very rare. One is hard-pressed to think of more than five or six Australian examples. A further possibility, to depict empowered individuals capable of acting independently and of making choices about their lives, but to ground motivation in a cultural relativist ideology, also is problematic, because of its potential to become confused with "personalized" values that, as Eckersley argues, elevate individuals above all other considerations, and become "another means by which the individual, inadvertently, becomes estranged from others, cocooned in personal opinions that need no external validation or justification."[2] The question for authors, then, is how to negotiate these ideologies so that realist fictions can offer their readers empowering critiques of social processes.

A perennial problem, for authors, readers, and critics alike, is a pervasive misunderstanding of the nature of literary realism. When considered from the perspective of certain commonplace assumptions concerning referentiality and subjectivity in much literary, critical, and cultural theory in the second half of the twentieth century, the persistence of realism in children's fiction might be taken as a sign of its naivety—in fact, its difference from adult literature. Debates in Australia over the representation of the putatively real in young adult fiction perpetuate this vulnerability, because arguments have been situated within the assumption that *realism* is to be evaluated on the basis of a focused text's capacity to mirror *reality*. In a notable instance in 1997 it took this direction because it was a media debate, with the oversimplifying and sensationalizing that is a prerequisite before children's or youth literature can be of public interest, but practitioners (both writers and mediators of that writing) engaged in discussion within the frame of a naive concept of mimesis. Conceptually, the formulation of *realism* in the catalyst newspaper article was hopelessly unsound, and the various "authorities" cited in the article were subsequently subjected to this formulation (whether or not they knew any better):

> Young adult literature is carving up the literary nature strip and hanging wheelies on the hard-baked bitumen of realism. . . . Recent debate has focused not on morality or ideology but *vérité* and a particular bleak (honest?) strain of social realism for young adults, who belong to a generation exhibiting unprecedented levels of pessimism and uncertainty about the future.[3]

Realism is here assumed to be something already present and knowable, implicitly defined by materiality of things and actions ("hanging wheelies on the hard-baked bitumen"), by the entirely false opposition to morality and ideology, by the slick (and misleading) slipping along the semantic chain of "realism . . . *vérité*[4] . . . social realism," and finally by conflating textuality and an imagined, overgeneralized audience. The article also subscribes to the common misconception that only misery, deprivation, suffering, and violence are real. Such a confusion of ideas offers no basis for rational discussion.

A subsequent article in *Viewpoint*, a magazine dedicated to reviewing young adult literature, posed the question "How Real is 'Too Real'?" and again proceeded as if the real were a self-evident category, defining it tautologically, and vacuously, as "real language, real characters, real plot, real theme, real ideas, real style, real structure."[5] There is an inchoate recognition here that realism might be a product of discourse, but in practice the argument relies on the rough, empirical position within which this debate over realism took place—that is, an assumption that perceived objects and events have an existence and nature independent of the perceiver's knowledge or act of perception. Another way to put this, more pertinent for fiction writing, is to say that for the empirical realist things exist as something independent of epistemology and discourse. From a commonsensical standpoint, and for practical reasons, such a view of reality can be conceded (setting aside the relativist argument that the existence of something depends on the perceiver's ability to conceptualize it, and then on the particular language that expresses it), but it becomes immediately irrelevant once the object enters discourse. Therefore, although *that* perception can't occur unless the object of perception has existence and a particular nature, as soon as that object of perception is *represented*, incorporated into a specific discourse always already framed by the writer's version of a contemporary epistemology, a plethora of moral and social judgments are predicated about that object. As Rimmon-Kenan argues, "All that a narrative can do is create an illusion, an effect, a semblance of mimesis, but it does so through diegesis."[6] It follows, then, that to claim for a fiction the naive defence that "I tell it as it is," to assume an unproblematic relationship between reading a text and knowing reality, or to challenge a reality represented because it is not *everyone's* consensus reality, are inane positions. An ironical paradox here is that much (most?) contemporary young adult realism in its quest for the empirically "real" eschews the self-reflexivity—*de rigeur* in contemporary adult literature— that might foreground and perhaps authenticate the ethical judgments always at least implicit in the process of representation. That so much of Australian young adult realism runs counter to the more general predominance of diegesis over mimesis in contemporary (adult, international) fiction is itself apt to constitute a discernible boundary marker.

The argument I set aside earlier, that the existence of something depends on the perceiver's ability to conceptualize it, and then on the particular language that expresses it, exposes the vulnerability of realism as a mode. Jacqueline Rose's provocative declaration of children's fiction as an "impossibility" in *The Case of Peter Pan* (1984) was grounded largely in standard expressions of certain poststructuralist assumptions concerning referentiality and subjectivity that especially challenge realist modes of writing. Critical theories about referentiality and subjectivity have, of course, moved a long way since the publication of *The Case of Peter Pan*, and children's fiction itself, especially young adult fiction, has developed some new forms and emphases since then (for example, an increase in the number of novels with multiple narrators and/or poly-focalization; a belated engagement with modernism; some exploration of postmodernist forms; the emergence of gay and lesbian subjectivities; a general textual acknowledgment that children only ever have limited agency). Rose's strictures against realistic fiction written for young readers, and her claim that it remains wedded to a nineteenth-century aesthetic, are matters still in need of discussion, however. When she writes that the "ethos of representation" that constitutes fictions written for young readers is "characterized by its basic demand for identity in language, that is, for language as a means to identity and self-recognition," she points to something about how texts speak to and about children that remains almost self-evidently true.[7] It underpins Sheahan-Bright's notion of realism, for example. Language as textual strategy seeks to call its audience into particular kinds of subject position that affirm ideas about individual identity and about its ethical and political relationships with the social world. If, however, those ideas about identity and its relationships are deemed suspect—if, for example, the subjectivities so constituted assume a social formation sustained by certain power configurations—a critic might well look for ways to interrogate those textual strategies. For example, that might be the function of the character Lynx in Margaret Clark's *Care Factor Zero* (1997), who simply disappears from the novel after Chapter 7, in which Larceny, the main character, visits his wealthy parents' home and expresses her approval of his desire to attain an agential selfhood by defining himself against the socially specific milieu of his professional-class parents, and their affluence and high culture interests. The effect of the reverse-classism may be to oppose what Rose defines as a tendency for children's literature to use narrative to valorize an overspecified version of subjectivity by "secur[ing] the identification of the child [reader] with something to which it does not necessarily belong."[8] But since *any* version of subjectivity constructed in fiction will be overspecified, critics really can only avoid arguing from their own narrowly defined social judgments by interrogating the processes of representation ("narrative") rather than the represented existents of character and setting.

One way, then, to challenge the social authority of narrative is to describe how narrativization in the realist mode interpellates readers. Thus the illusion that the relationship between text and world is actual and transparent is seen to be developed by erasing those narrative forms that would disclose the presence of a (quasi-)author mediating between what is represented textually and the text's audience. Sociocultural or moral perspectives are no longer enunciated by an identifiable narrative voice, but such perspectives are embodied by the text's events and existents (that is, characters and settings) and by strategies for aligning character subject positions and reading subject positions. For example, we can point to the preponderance of first person narration in the second half of this century, with an especially strong form in the fad for doubled first person narrations of the late 1980s and early 1990s—this latter type overtly suggests that events are perceived and resolutions reached through a dialogic and negotiative process, thus affirming a confluence of perspective and, hence, validity of outcome. A similar effect derives from the marked increase, since the 1960s, say, in the employment of intense character focalization, especially when framed by a narrating voice scarcely differentiated from the character-focalizer's in register, idiom, or syntax. It is on the basis of such narrative forms that Rose defines realism in children's fiction as:

> that form of writing which attempts to reduce to an absolute minimum our awareness of the language in which a story is written in order that we will take it for real (the very meaning of "identification"). . . . [realism is based in the conviction that] the best form of expression is that which most innocently ("no dishonesty," "no distortion") reflects the objects of the real world.[9]

A book that uses a young person as focalizer presents events from a perspective that can seem relatively naive, a strategy that may have two important effects: first, an implied reader occupies a position of knowingness or informational power, though in discovering the point of view implied in the text readers are likely to be discovering the text's moral message. Second, this strategy can be reinforced by a focalizing character's own growth in awareness, which in adolescent fiction is usually a discovery and internalization of that same moral message. The following passage, from *Lockie Leonard, Human Torpedo*, illustrates both perspectives:

> He reached across and touched the wetsuit over her breast. It was cold to the touch. His hand moved up the zip and drew the zip down to her belly. She had a bikini on under the suit and she shivered in the sudden cold rush of air. Inside, her skin was hot and smooth. He slipped his hand inside her top and felt her nipple harden from the cold. Maybe it

wasn't talk and love and ideas after all; maybe it was just this he
wanted.

Vicki's head was back and her eyes were closed. Her neck was
white and graceful. He kissed her there and felt sad, sad like he'd never
been before.[10]

In describing something Lockie experiences, this passage moves backward and forward between narration and character focalization, though
that shift is only overt at the end of each paragraph where a thought is expressed in the character's idiom. Otherwise it is marked by allusions to
perception and feeling. The control of the scene by a narrator's language
here at times at a distance from the teen demotic which is its usual staple
in this novel implies that the experience is generalizable. The passage
builds toward a point of climax: it is, of course, implying a build toward a
sex act—the undressing, the caressing, and so on, but presents instead an
anticlimax by simply diverting into an unexpected emotion. That the moment culminates in a feeling of sadness is no accident, because here is
the moral point. To put it bluntly: Sadness and loss are the consequence
of socially deviant behavior, although Winton leaves his readers space to
deduce the message for themselves by connecting the two uses of *felt*
("felt her nipple harden"; "felt sad") and the two points where character
language emerges. In short, the premature entry into an "adult" experience is a form of alienation and loss.

In contrast, then, young adult fiction would arguably approach most
closely to adult fiction when it employs third person narration and,
within that, uses language and focalization in a way that will from time
to time foreground textuality. Hartnett's *Wilful Blue*, for instance, reads
like an adult novel not only because its characters are all over twenty, nor
because it is narrated as three distinct temporal voices, nor because
events are polyfocalized, but also because its language refuses mere
transparency. For example, the following passage represents Grere's
mind-stream while maintaining a self-conscious narratorial voice:

It had been an accident, this dying of Guy's, as unexpected and stunning as a nightmare to a peaceful mind. Guy, who had never spent a
day in hospital, never been stitched up, never broken a bone. Guy, who
conserved his energy as if it was something precious and rare, whose
step upon the earth had been light: he should have lived forever, he
could have outlived them all! An *accident*: it was so unlike him it was
almost laughable, ludicrous.[11]

The novel's large-scale narrative irony is that Guy actually died by suicide, and the complex narrative structure will unfold this story even as Jesse and Walt reiterate, for Grere's benefit, the fiction about the accident. The double perspective already enters the text at moments such as the above through its stylistic devices: the syntactic patterning, hesitancies, and inversions; the series of doublets ("unexpected and stunning; never stitched up, never broken a bone; precious and rare; laughable, ludicrous"); the intrusive analogies ("as a nightmare to a peaceful mind"); and the suggestions of poetic, even archaic, formulations ("whose step upon the earth had been light"). This is language that calls attention to itself.

It can be further argued about narrativization that it produces an inconsistency between the randomness that would characterize events if they were mapped from the real world and the strong commitment to teleology in children's realist fiction. In other words, the patterning or structuring of events and existents, so that the meaning of the parts is shown to inhere in the outcome toward which they move, asserts the existence of design or purpose in society, the cosmos, or whatever. The works of Catherine Jinks are very interesting here, especially since she turned her hand to adult novels. So far, like Winton, she has not attempted a boundary-crossing work, but in a historical/realistic tetralogy set in the European Middle Ages, commencing with *Pagan's Crusade* (1992), she has used realist forms in combination with a sophisticated grasp of indeterminacy and self-reflexive strategies of fabulation in order to produce represented selfhoods of a less teleology-affirming, more contingent kind than Winton's, and that presage an adult treatment of adult themes. The principal recurrent theme of Jinks's fiction is contact between people of different cultures, whether experienced as a meeting of socioeconomic groups that are virtually mutually incomprehensible, as in her first novel, *This Way Out* (1991), or the "first contact" stories of her sci-fi novels *The Future Trap* (1993) and *Eye to Eye* (1997). Characters who are alienated, outsiders, experience self-growth through entrance into intersubjectivity. *Little White Secrets* (1997), her second adult novel, pursues this theme through the experiences of a Sydney school teacher who goes on a year's exchange to a small Canadian fishing village. The language of *Little White Secrets* is more transparent than the language of *Wilful Blue*, and the teacher, David French, is himself a young adult, but this seems clearly an adult novel for several reasons: because of the age and interests of the rest of the characters; because of the deceptively simple depiction of the petty jealousies and intrigues of those characters; because the focalization is split between David and

Alice, his fifty-six-year-old Canadian neighbor; and because of the novel's self-conscious structure and almost cavalier accumulation of un-resolved loose ends, and a tension at the close between story closure and thematic open-endedness that serves to refuse the kind of teleological outcome expected in a children's or young adult novel. The Jinks novel that has most in common with *Little White Secrets* is the slightly later young adult sci-fi novel *Eye to Eye*, but here intercultural contact is ex-plored *via* two first person narrators (a "primitive" desert child and the highly developed artificial intelligence of the computer of a space ship) and the process of mutual education leads to a positive and constructive outcome in story and theme.

There is an a priori condition for selecting between random and tele-ological processes in realist fiction that is notionally invalidated by those poststructuralist commonplaces (or, better, now clichés) about referen-tiality and subjectivity deployed by Rose. Early in *The Case of Peter Pan* she yokes together two key poststructuralist propositions:

> We use language to identify ourselves and objects in the world. But *the pronoun 'I,' which apparently gives us that identity, only has as its meaning whoever happens to be using it at the time; and it is no simple term of unity and cohesion,* as the processes of the dream, our ability to lie, or merely to deceive ourselves, all too clearly demonstrate. Objects are defined in language, but *the relation between the linguistic term and its referent is arbitrary . . . ; and the meaning of one word can only be fixed with reference to another,* in a process which finally has us going round in circles (the chase through the dictionary from one entry to the next to find out what a word *really* means).[12]

The attempt by any writer of fiction to use "language as a means to iden-tity and self-recognition" would thus founder for two reasons: the gap between verbal sign and referent has always already canceled the possi-bility of using language to produce such a determinate outcome; and "identity and self-recognition" are humanistic fictions, whereas the human ego actually lacks coherence or unity. It would be possible to dis-miss this double cancellation of the efficacy of fiction as a temporary the-ory whose vogue has been in steady decline over the past decade, and the formulations deployed here are themselves strategic fictions of a gross kind and would be easy to demolish, though to do that only in part re-futes the informing position: thus "the pronoun *I*" is the most simplistic conceptualisation of subjectivity (and the least adequate allusion to the doctrine of "the death of the subject");[13] and the equation of "meaning" with dictionary entries (by means of a tiny allegorical narrative) willfully ignores both the constitution of significances within syntagmatic structures and the practical employment of "the visual, the objectal and the behavioural" as interpretants of verbal signs.[14] Rose might thus be said to be formulating a couple of poststructuralist commonplaces in a way that presumes their "truth" and maximizes their rhetorical effect. Although the argument itself is unconvincing, the underlying propositions about referentiality and subjectivity are still significant because they have leaked into culture more generally and have an impact on how fiction is written and, at least in "educated communities," read.

Acknowledging that the relationships between sign and referent are unstable has important implications for realism. It enhances our ability to descry the workings of ideology in representation; it can remind us that debates about realism are always actually debates about how we understand language to operate, and how the world is (re)constructed textually; and it potentially challenges the naive "I tell it as it is" versions of realism propounded by some contemporary authors and their more vocal critics (whether supporters or detractors). It is more productive, however, to regard sign/referent instabilities as corollaries of a dialectical interplay between our understanding of the world ("the visual, the objectal and the behavioural") and the range of objects or situations to which words refer.[15] In other words, relationships between signs and referents produce coherences as well as the disruptions and deferrals prominent in the more simplistic formulations of poststructuralist dogma. These coherences are possible for a couple of reasons. First, phenomena are not constructed by language, and language is not determined by phenomena: rather, they produce one another dialectically, and one is privileged over the other principally for ideological purposes. Second, meaning does not inhere in individual words within individual idiolects, but in larger units of discourse—sentences, and beyond.

A key strategy in the pattern of coherences that is fiction is the often tightly woven interdependence of character focalization, subject positions (both of characters and readers), and ideologies of the self. It is a reasonable generalization that the great majority of Australian young adult novels, deeply concerned as they are with questions of identity and subjectivity, presuppose some version of a self that is unique and essential, existing prior to and independent of social structures and cultural background. The few realist fictions posited on the opposed concept of subjectivity as fully interpellated within social formations would include

Marsden's *Dear Miffy*, Burne's *Fishnets*, and probably Hartnett's *Sleeping Dogs*. But even Larceny, the self-determined solipsist of *Care Factor Zero*, exhibits an interiorized belief in essential selfhood: summing up Lynx, she concludes that, "He was culturally confused in his own head. He was really an individual: his own person. But he had to find that out for himself."[16] Such perceptions in contemporary realist novels are still informed by the principle that language functions as a means to identity and self-recognition, and this is emphasized when, as in fiction such as Clark's, there is little distinction between the voices of narrator and focalizer. Nevertheless, to attribute to them a conception of selfhood coincident with that commonly attributed to the nineteenth-century realist *Bildungsroman* is anachronistic. Rather, constructions of the self in such fictions now have more in common with recent neohumanist accounts of subjectivity as something contingent and heterogeneous—that is, reformulations of ideas about "the subject" developed in opposition to the fragmented, dispersed, or annihilated subject of modernity. Agnes Heller expresses such a position clearly in her claim that the "centre of the self" is "the thing, the person, the cause we are involved in, beyond and above everything else," and to choose "the foci on which our personality begins to develop" is an act of self-choosing that is an enabling movement toward a sense of identity. A question Heller poses is, how is self-understanding constituted in a world that no longer has recourse to the metanarratives of religion, traditional social formations, and essential selfhood that once furnished its meaning?[17] The question is very pertinent for young adult novels such as *Care Factor Zero* and, say, Wendy Orr's *Peeling the Onion* (1996). The first overtly evokes a world from which those metanarratives have effectively disappeared, and in which Larceny's suicide at the close of the novel seems an inevitable outcome because of her society's failure to enable constructive choices for her. In contrast, *Peeling the Onion* is about the formation of subjectivity through a self-conscious quest for selfhood. The narrator, seventeen-year-old Anna, disabled by spinal and head injuries suffered in a car accident, must reconstitute her selfhood under these new conditions.

Young adult novels that are structured as a quest for the self usually center on characters who are represented as solipsistic, fragmented, or displaced and their stories articulate a quest for a sense of identity that is stable, coherent, unique, and whole—an essential self. The quest narrative articulates three interrelated concerns. First, it is a quest for a sense of one's place and purpose in both the physical and social world. Anna, the first-person narrator, stresses her sense of dismemberment—physically, socially, and emotionally—after she has been disabled. Her narrative articulates her struggle to find a new place for herself and a new way of being. The quest for selfhood narrative also typically entails two processes: the transition from solipsism to intersubjectivity; and a parallel quest for the selfhood of an other.[18] These two features are crucial for development of plot and character in *Peeling the Onion*. Anna's past life, and her descent into the world of her physical pain, are utterly solipsistic: her narrative centers much of the time on what she thinks other people think of her and she categorizes, stereotypes, and dismisses many of the other people around her. As the novel progresses she is represented as becoming more aware of the otherness of other people. The quest for selfhood is effectively a quest for intersubjectivity. This move out of solipsism is expressed in part by a romantic paradigm—as is very often the case—as Anna falls into reciprocated love.

The commonplace notion of "finding one's self" that underlies the quest narrative has clear ideological implications. It is posited on the existence of a self that is unique and essential and that exists prior to and independent of social structures and cultural background. Selfhood is not equated here with power in or over the world, though many, possibly still most, children's novels certainly do make that equation. The young characters in these novels are instead pushed about by social, institutional, and historical forces, and have a limited capacity to influence what shapes their lives. Instead, they develop what Heller describes as the capacity to choose "the foci on which . . . personality begins to develop." She characterizes the condition of selfhood in modernity as a cluster of open possibilities:

> Modern men and women are contingent; they are also aware of their contingency. Mere possibilities are empty, yet they can be filled with a great, even infinite variety of contents. Mere possibility is the potential of personal autonomy; it is also the potential of a total loss thereof. Modern men and women are unstable and fragile, yet they seek a certain degree of firmness. They easily stumble into chaos, therefore they need at least a fragment of "cosmos" to make sense of their own lives and, possibly, render meaning to it.[19]

Young adult novels usually incorporate that fragment of "cosmos," simultaneously foregrounding and affirming it through the strategy of aligning reader subject position with the subject position of focalizing characters who glimpse meaning in some condition larger than mere selfhood.

Young adult novels draw on characteristic strategies by which realistic fictions render actuality, shape it, and make it meaningful, but these strategies now acknowledge the fragility, but not indeterminacy, of signification. Thematically, this gives them much in common with adult fiction. So, too, does the characteristic alignment of narrative with characters who are not themselves the source of meaning, knowledge, or action, and who tend to be puzzled by the operations of power informing the social formations they inhabit. But a distinction is maintained by the thematic domination of identity issues and the deployment of focalization in order to realize particular subject positions. Jinks's novels are symptomatic in finding significance in the intersubjective states realized from dialogue between selves and others; *Care Factor Zero* and, in most cases, the so-called nihilist fictions also in effect affirm this by presenting its denial as destructive of both the individual and social fabric. In other words, where literature for preteen readers imposed significance on actual or verisimilitudinous events and existents by organizing them teleologically, young adult novels rather imply that social apparatuses are radically meaningless, and significance is grounded rather in the everydayness of interpersonal relationships. This, it seems to me, places them in a middle ground between literature for children and literature for adults.[20]

NOTES

1. Richard Rossiter, "Speaking to Adults, Speaking to Children: Tim Winton's *Cloudstreet* and *Lockie Leonard, Human Torpedo,*" *Southerly* 53 no. 5 (1993): 96.

2. Richard Eckersley, "The Culture of Meaning, the Meaning of Culture," *Magpies Magazine* 12, no. 2 (1997): 7.

3. Kate Legge, "Life Sucks, Timmy," *The Australian Magazine* (8–9 March 1997): 10.

4. Presumably the switch into French is not just to imply that the writer assumes that "theory" derives from French thought, but makes an allusion to *cinema vérité*. That, of course, simply compounds the theoretical confusion.

5. Robyn Sheahan-Bright, "How Real is 'Too Real'?," *Viewpoint* 5, no. 3 (1997): 6.

6. Shlomith Rimmon-Kenan, *Narrative Fiction: Contemporary Poetics* (London and New York: Routledge, 1983), 108.

7. Jacqueline Rose, *The Case of Peter Pan, or The Impossibility of Children's Fiction* (London: Macmillan, 1984), 139. Rose continues to be cited as a source of the idea that the identity politics shaping children's books "colonize" children (see Roderick McGillis, *The Nimble Reader: Literary Theory and Children's Literature*

(New York: Twayne Publishers, 1996), 18–19, 119; Perry Nodelman, *The Pleasures of Children's Literature*, 2nd ed. (New York: Longman, 1996), 166), an idea that does seem to have a strong explanatory force. Nevertheless, the premise on which the proposition is grounded is a conjunction of three speculative hypotheses rather than an existential fact: the poststructuralist theory of indeterminacy; the theory of fragmented subjectivity; and the Freudian theory of the unconscious. There are equally plausible alternative theories for each, though they are often muted by the late twentieth-century habit of confusing "theory" with poststructuralism.

8. Rose, *The Case of Peter Pan*, p. 63.

9. Ibid., p. 65.

10. Tim Winton, *Lockie Leonard, Human Torpedo* (Ringwood, Vic.: McPhee Gribble, 1990), 84.

11. Sonya Hartnett, *Wilful Blue* (Ringwood, Vic.: Viking, 1994), 9.

12. Rose, *The Case of Peter Pan*, p. 17; my italics.

13. Rose returns to "the pronoun *I*" in her concluding chapter, but there in a more Althusserian reading: all subjects *necessarily* have to take up a position of identity in language, but children's fiction seeks to eliminate agency and impose a position (141).

14. See Robert Scholes, *Textual Power* (New Haven and London: Yale University Press, 1985), 109.

15. See Hilary Putnam, quoted in Harry E. Shaw, "With Reference to Austin" *Diacritics* 20, no. 2 (1990): 88.

16. Margaret Clark, *Care Factor Zero* (Sydney: Random House, 1997), 127.

17. Agnes Heller, "Death of the Subject?," in *Constructions of the Self*, ed. George Levine (New Brunswick, N.J.: Rutgers University Press, 1992), 282.

18. Robyn McCallum, *Ideologies of Identity in Adolescent Fiction* (New York: Garland Publishing, 1999), passim.

19. Heller, "Death of the Subject?," p. 282.

20. An earlier version of part of this paper was presented at the "Making It Real" Conference, Deakin University, 22 March 1997.

REFERENCES

Burne, Philippa. *Fishnets*. St. Leonards, N.S.W.: Allen & Unwin, 1997.

Clark, Margaret. *Care Factor Zero*. Sydney: Random House, 1997.

Eckersley, Richard. "The Culture of Meaning, the Meaning of Culture." *Magpies Magazine* 12, no. 2 (1997): 6–8.

Hartnett, Sonya. *Wilful Blue*. Ringwood, Vic.: Viking, 1994.

———. *Sleeping Dogs*. Ringwood, Vic.: Viking, 1995.

———. *Black Foxes*. Ringwood, Vic.: Viking, 1996.

Heller, Agnes. "Death of the Subject?," in *Constructions of the Self*, ed. George
   Levine, 269–284. New Brunswick, N. J.: Rutgers University Press, 1992.

Jinks, Catherine. *This Way Out*. Norwood: Omnibus Books, 1991.

———. *Pagan's Crusade*. Melbourne: Oxford University Press, 1992.

———. *The Future Trap*. Norwood: Omnibus Books, 1993.

———. *Pagan's Scribe*. Norwood: Omnibus Books, 1996.

———. *Eye to Eye*. Ringwood, Vic.: Puffin Books, 1997.

———. *Little White Secrets*. Ringwood, Vic.: Penguin Books, 1997.

Lanagan, Margo. *Touching Earth Lightly*. St. Leonards, N.S.W.: Allen & Unwin,
   1996.

Legge, Kate. "Life Sucks, Timmy." *The Australian Magazine* (8–9 March 1997):
   10–18.

Marsden, John. *Dear Miffy*. Sydney: Macmillan, 1997.

McCallum, Robyn. *Ideologies of Identity in Adolescent Fiction*. New York: Garland Publishing, 1999.

McGillis, Roderick. *The Nimble Reader: Literary Theory and Children's Literature*. New York: Twayne Publishers, 1996.

Nodelman, Perry. *The Pleasures of Children's Literature*. 2nd ed. New York:
   Longman, 1996.

Orr, Wendy. *Peeling the Onion*. St. Leonards, N.S.W.: Allen & Unwin, 1996.

Rimmon-Kenan, Shlomith. *Narrative Fiction: Contemporary Poetics*. London
   and New York: Routledge, 1983.

Robinson, Nicola. "Illiteracy, Misery, and Moral Decay: the Sins of Young Adult
   Fiction." *Australian Book Review* (December 1995/January 1996): 36–41.

Rose, Jacqueline. *The Case of Peter Pan, or The Impossibility of Children's Fiction*. London: Macmillan, 1984.

Rossiter, Richard. "Speaking to Adults, Speaking to Children: Tim Winton's
   Cloudstreet and *Lockie Leonard, Human Torpedo*." *Southerly* 53, no. 5
   (1993): 92–99.

Scholes, Robert. *Textual Power*. New Haven and London: Yale University Press,
   1985.

Shaw, Harry E. "With Reference to Austin." *Diacritics* 20, no. 2 (1990): 75–92.

Sheahan-Bright, Robyn. "How Real is 'Too Real'?," *Viewpoint* 5, no. 3 (1997):
   5–6.

Winton, Tim. *Lockie Leonard, Human Torpedo*. Ringwood, Vic.: McPhee Gribble, 1990.

———. *Cloudstreet*. Ringwood, Vic.: Penguin Books, 1991.

———. *The Riders*. Sydney: Macmillan, 1994.

———. *Lockie Leonard, Legend*. Sydney: Macmillan, 1997.

PART V

Tradition and Innovation: Modernism, Postmodernism, and Beyond

CHAPTER 12

Crossing Borders
Calvino in the Footprints of Collodi

ALIDA POETI

What—some may ask—do Carlo Lorenzini, better known as Collodi (1826–1890), and Italo Calvino (1923–1985) have in common?

Born a century earlier than Calvino, Collodi was a moderately educated, conservative, Catholic, Florentine journeyman, part-time journalist, soldier, and gambler, who began writing romance novels, second-rate comedies, and a series of elementary school textbooks on commission only to keep up with his gambling debts, yet he produced the first and most influential Italian literary work for children. Calvino, on the other hand, was a true man of letters, a freethinking, Ligurian, disillusioned Marxist intellectual, who started his career as a politically committed neorealist writer, then became a prestigious editor, reviewer, translator, and author of some of Italy's best and most controversial experimental narratives this century.

Well, they have at least three things in common: first, they both crossed the presumed boundaries between children's and adult literature, and some of their best-known works transcend both categories and address a dual readership of adults and children. Second, they both translated, rewrote, and came to appreciate fables and folktales, the genre that originally was intended for adults, but is today enjoyed by children and studied by adults. In 1875 Collodi, who had a good command of the French language, was commissioned by his friends, the publishers Alessandro and Felice Paggi, to translate the fairy tales of Charles Perrault, Madame d'Aulnoy, and Madame Leprince de Beaumont. The result was a "tuscanised," more homely version of the famous fairytales called *I racconti delle fate* (Fairy tales).[1] Similarly in 1954, Einaudi assigned to their associate,

Calvino, the task of collating, editing, and rewriting Italy's rich heritage of oral folktales. He was asked to compile a national selection of Italian folktales that could be read and enjoyed by all Italians[2] and would be comparable to the one produced in Germany by the brothers Grimm. The creative fantasy and "magic realism" with which Calvino had begun to spin his own tales in the early 1950s made him an ideal candidate for this onerous task. From among the two hundred folktales rewritten by Calvino, Einaudi later published, in their series Libri per Ragazzi, two selections with illustrations specifically for children: *L'Uccel belverde e altre fiabe italiane* (The fine greenbird and other Italian fables, 1972) and *Il Principe granchio e altre fiabe italiane* (The Crab Prince and other Italian fables, 1974).[3]

A third point of connection between Collodi and Calvino is that their works interested the same illustrator, Sergio Tofano, who was, among other things, himself a writer of children's books.[4] He had a fairly unique and very distinctive style both of narrating and drawing for youngsters. It has been said that Sergio Tofano's illustrations allow one "to escape through the window of fantasy and take a breath of surrealist air [and to] marry the natural with the wondrous."[5] The imaginatively digressive nature of his drawings makes the mundane seem miraculous, and the prodigious, the fablelike seem ordinary; Tofano could make the absurd assume an air of familiarity.[6] Likewise, in both Collodi's classic and Calvino's many works, the boundaries between fiction and truth spill over in both directions. Furthermore, the subtle irony constantly used by the two authors matches the irony found in Tofano's best-known children's classic, *Romanzo delle mie delusioni*. In this parody of a *Bildungsroman*, which nevertheless explores the process of socialization of its young hero, he does not advocate escapism to the world of fairy tales, but rather asks the reader to believe in "the logic of fables," to have an open mind and be receptive to certain unusual types of events as well as to their opposite. Calvino shares this notion. In his introduction to the *Fiabe italiane* he states: "Folklore could teach us no better lesson poetic or moral [than] to fashion a dream without resorting to escapism."[7] On another occasion, when giving his definition of what constitutes *la littérature fantastique*, he suggests that an appreciation of this genre demands "the acceptance of a different logic based on objects and connections other than those of everyday life or dominant literary conventions." And he adds that "the pleasure of fantasy lies in the unraveling of a logic with rules or points of departure or solutions that keep some surprises up their sleeves."[8]

This is precisely what Collodi intuitively knew when he created *Le avventure di Pinocchio* in 1881;[9] he knew how to surprise the reader and make recognizable everyday reality exist side by side with the enchanted, the magical, and the surreal. Starting with personal memories,[10] he achieved a "visionary transfiguration" of reality through "the inexhaustible wealth of the imagination."[11] Collodi told the story of a puppet that comes to life and is a *ragazzo di strada*, a street kid, who incidentally also admonishes children to take care and encourages them to stay at school. But he does so without moralizing. Any lesson that may be learned from the text is inherent to the plot and thus perfectly acceptable.

For his characters and situations Collodi draws freely from traditional Italian forms of storytelling: from folklore, fables, and legends to the puppet theater and the *commedia dell'arte*. Realism and fantasy are so tightly interwoven in this story that real life country folk, carpenters, innkeepers, fishermen, policemen, schoolchildren inhabit the same space as talking cats and foxes, sententious crickets, wise old owls, grave gorilla judges, and fairies with blue hair. *Pinocchio* is a comedy in which there is suffering, written in sympathy with those who know best what it is to mean well, to have good intentions yet poor resolve in the face of temptation. Its honest naturalism and realism about children and the world they must survive do not detract from the sense of marvel and adventure. The rapid narrative pace is compelling; the style is simple and precise and has a lightness of touch that keeps the moral dramatic and playful. The language is rich, transparent, and it reflects the spoken Tuscan idiom that Manzoni, Italy's most influential novelist, considered the ideal medium of communication with a national readership that in the nineteenth century could hardly call Italian their mother tongue. Collodi, mindful of the literary needs of a newly unified Italy still struggling for a national identity, contributed to the affirmation of the national language and his children's classic assumed determinant status in Italian culture.[12]

Evidence of how deeply entrenched *Pinocchio* is in the Italian imagination is given by Italo Calvino in an interview with Maria Corti. In this rare interview, he acknowledges that among the readings that had contributed to his formation, at the top of the list he would have to place Collodi's children's classic, a book he regarded as an exemplary model of narration.[13] Calvino appreciated its incisive, ironic, joyous, hyperbolic style; its fast rhythmic flow; its balanced economical composition; its strong visual appeal; its varied use of language; and its creatively transgressive originality. It is therefore not surprising that these same qualities are found in Calvino's own literary production. What he prized most in writing can be summed up as clarity, precision, agility, accessibility, and inventiveness.[14]

Calvino opted to write in the same national standard linguistic medium elaborated, among notable others, precisely by Collodi. His *Marcovaldo ovvero le stagioni in città* (Marcovaldo or seasons in the city)[15] can in fact be viewed as a collection of stories fashioned in the mold of *Pinocchio*, as Angela Jeannet[16] shows in her reading of the text. She focuses on linguistic choices, narrative strategies, thematic and metanarrative elements to reveal the degree of intertextuality that exists between the two texts. She highlights, for example, the many instances in which the lexicon privileges certain colloquial verbs like *acchiappare, acciuffare, badare, cascare pigliare, spiccicare,* frequently used by Collodi. She points out the numerous obvious Tuscanisms used by Calvino to set the familiar tone of his text (*allampanato, arzillo, babbo, bestiola, in fretta e furia, pizzicorino, uggia,* and so forth). She illustrates the abundance of expressions and constructions found in the *Marcovaldo* stories that specifically recall Collodi's storytelling devices, many of which are borrowed from folktales (questions that foster suspense and engage the audience in the narrative process, vague temporal markers, particular connectives that mark transitions, colloquial inversions of the subject for emphasis, ironic use of hyperbole).

The *Marcovaldo* stories were written at different times in two sets of ten;[17] the second set reinforced the lexical and narrative choices of the first, but, unlike the first, it intentionally addressed a proposed audience of young readers. In this second set, Jeannet observes that "the number of Tuscanisms and Collodianisms increases dramatically."[18] This is an interesting point for, as far as I could ascertain, it was the only occasion in which Calvino wrote specifically for youngsters. Normally the texts that are proposed for younger readers by Calvino's publishers are the same ones originally intended for a general public.

What is it then that makes Calvino metaphorically a follower in the footprints of Collodi? What turns a number of his writings intended for adults into texts that are appealing and accessible to readers of different age groups? The answer probably lies in the sources of Calvino's inspiration and the experimental, highly interactive nature of his narrative style, evident already in his earliest writings.

Calvino's first novel, *Il sentiero dei nidi di ragno* (The path to the spiders' nest), written in 1946, and most of the early short stories, especially those in *Ultimo viene il corvo* (Last comes the crow),[19] "told of picaresque adventures in an Italy of wartime and postwar upheaval."[20] These were realistic narratives that depicted the problems of Italian society and addressed questions of social justice. Yet, although by all accounts they were politically committed neorealist texts, they contained elements of fantasy, romance, and chivalry that gave them lyric and poetic overtones.

In these early Calvino stories, fantasy was not the cheery fantasy of children's literature, but a conscious vehicle for dealing with the deepest human concerns. At the age of twenty-eight, however, after having attempted to write *I giovanni del Po* (Young people of the Po),[21] another so-called *engagé* novel, Calvino admitted to himself that writing in a neorealist manner was not what he felt he wanted to do. "Thus [he writes] I began doing what came most naturally to me—that is following the memory of the things I had loved best since childhood. Instead of making myself write the book I ought to write, the novel that was expected of me, I conjured up the book I myself would have liked to read."[22] Therefore, as a *divertissement*, almost for fun, in a few months he wrote *Il visconte dimezzato*[23] (*The Cloven Viscount*), the first novel of the trilogy of *I nostri antenati*[24] (*Our Ancestors*).

This bizarre book is a happy blend of history and extreme fantasy for it has as protagonist a man cut in half by a cannonball who continues to live as two separate halves,[25] one good, the other bad. Despite the mixture of grotesque and humorous elements in the story, it contains serious philosophical and social reflections that express "a positive belief in conceptual freedom, in the power to image changes and to create and control new worlds."[26] Much in the same spirit and style, Calvino started writing the *Marcovaldo* stories. They were all texts that privileged the imagination and provided accounts of adventure, in which, if one were to find social or pedagogical normative messages, they would be witty and presented in the same dramatic, pithy, entertaining way as in *Pinocchio*.

Of the three *Ancestor* novels, the one most often directed at children and young adults is *Il barone rampante* (*The Baron in the Trees*). Originally published in 1957, it later appeared both as an illustrated edition (1959) and an annotated school edition (1965). *The Baron in the Trees* is a particularly self-reflective text, with many intertextual references, which the younger reader can hardly be expected to recognize or appreciate fully. Nevertheless, as it is the story of a twelve-year-old boy who in a moment of rebellion takes to the trees where he lives for the next fifty years, it can be read on many levels and be appealing to adventure-loving youngsters. Set against the historical background of the late eighteenth and early nineteenth century, it gives an oddly detached, bird's-eye view of history as Cosimo, the young rampant baron, sees it. Having distanced himself from society, yet participating from above in events of great historical significance, enables him to discuss history as "a survivor of mythical thought,"[27] that is to say, as one who can see through the myths that society constructs for itself. The book discusses man's attempt to discover the true nature of the past and the meaning of history. It shows how "histories" are recorded and how they reflect only specific points of view,[28] which do not always present the whole picture.

The story is constructed in such a way that the reader's sympathies always lie with Cosimo, although his older, more conservative, and passive brother Biagio is the narrator of his sibling's adventures, adventures that always tend to offer alternatives to orthodox living. The book is as much an historical adventure as an adventure in reading, of moving through the universe of the printed page and discovering the relationships that exist between different texts and between diverse accounts of the same events. It plays narrative games with the reader and engages the more imaginative ones in the art of combinations until the demarcation between truth and fiction is totally blurred. In the text the reader discovers Cosimo's *smania di raccontare*, his urge to narrate and embellish and hold his listener captive, so much so that "tale and truth seem linked by a tenuous thread on which the story teller performs acrobatic feats."[29] The same feats, one can say, that are performed in fables.

Among the sources of inspiration for this trilogy, Calvino mentions Robert Louis Stevenson, the *conte philosophique,* especially Voltaire's *Candide,* as well as the tales of Hoffmann and other German Romantics, but it is Stevenson whom he speaks of most. He believes that for Stevenson "writing meant translating an invisible text containing the quintessential fascination of all adventures, all mysteries, all conflicts of the will and passions scattered throughout the books of hundreds of writers. It meant translating them into his own precise and almost impalpable prose, into his own rhythm which was like that of dance-steps at once impetuous and controlled."[30] The same can be said of Calvino's relationship with texts, problems, ideologies, and social structures of his own time. He always deals with them with "lightness," a sense of adventure, and an open, inquisitive, questioning mind.[31]

Another font from which Calvino acknowledged having drawn inspiration—quite different from that of either the epic fantasies of Italy's literary tradition, its folktales, and oral tradition, or the influential writings of major European authors—is the comic strip. His appreciation of comics started even before he could read, when as a child he had a passion for the *Corriere dei Piccoli,* the then most widely circulated weekly for children. In the 1920s and 1930s, it used to publish the best-known American comic strips alongside some homespun ones that often were illustrated by Sergio Tofano.[32] Calvino, in *Six Memos for the Next Millennium*, explains how the comics had a decisive influence on the development of his style:

> I would spend hours following the cartoons of each series from one issue to another, while in my mind I told myself the stories, interpreting the scenes in different ways—I produced variants, put together the single episodes into a story of broader scope . . . then connected the recurring elements in each series, mixing up one series with another, and inventing new series in which the secondary characters became protagonists. . . . I preferred to ignore the written lines and to continue with my favorite occupation of daydreaming *within* the pictures and their sequence.
>
> This habit undeniably caused a delay in my ability to concentrate on the written word . . . But reading the pictures without the words was certainly a schooling in fable-making, in stylization, in composition of the image.[33]

Comics, or at least a certain type of comic strip, taught Calvino to appreciate what in the *Lezioni americane* (*Six Memos . . .*) he calls *visibilità*. He explains it as "visual imagination" or "the power to bring visions into focus with our eyes shut, of bringing forth forms and colors from the lines of black letters on a page."[34] A writer who has this visual imagination can tap into a repertoire "of what is potential, of what is hypothetical, of what does not exist and has never existed, and perhaps will never exist but might have existed"[35] and make anything visible to his readers. Comic strips also force one to use imagination to fill in the missing links and make the leaps of fantasy required to go from frame to frame. Undoubtedly comics contributed to his preference for *leggerezza* (lightness), *esattezza* (exactitude, precision), and *rapidità* (pace). Perhaps they also inspired the fifth desirable quality literature should have according to Calvino, which is *molteplicità* (multiplicity) or the ability to give many possible readings to the same reality, the same string of words or images.

There is an obvious link between the character Marcovaldo and Il Signor Bonaventura, Tofano's popular comic strip hero. In the introduction he wrote for the 1966 school edition of *Marcovaldo*, Calvino draws his young readers' attention to this link:

> A funny and melancholic figure is Marcovaldo, the protagonist of a series of modern fables, which . . . remain faithful to a classic narrative pattern: that of the story told in comic strips in children's magazines.[36]

The structure of the adventures, which normally end up badly for Marcovaldo, is not dissimilar to that of the misfortunes that, on the contrary, end well for Mr. Bonaventura. According to the esteemed Calvino critic, Ulla Musarra Schroeder,[37] however, Marcovaldo has more traits in common with the husband or father in the American "family strips" of the 1920s and 1930s, who was likewise a stereotypical character on whom every possible misfortune fell. But Marcovaldo is also a Chaplin-like figure, who, like the little tramp, manages never to lose his dignity, unlike his American comic strip counterparts. He does, however, have a brash, rather bossy wife, five children, and a suffocating life in the inner city of some anonymous industrial town. Each story is set against the same background, each follows the same narrative scheme, and each has the same predictable ending,[38] much like all fairy tales. As Eco points out, with serials "one believes one is enjoying the novelty of the story (which is always the same), while in fact one is enjoying it because of the recurrence of a narrative scheme that remains constant."[39]

Maria Corti speaks of *elementi ludico-fantastici* in the Marcovaldo stories, alluding to the fantasy games that the poor alienated, sensitive, naïve Marcovaldo progressively plays, after he discovers that the imagination is the only way out of the concrete jungle to the jungles where tigers roam freely. As the stories become more fantastical, there is a marked increase in the stylistic similarities with comics, where, from one frame to the next, one may have to pass from the supposedly real to the impossible or the imagined.[40]

Even in more recent years, when Calvino's writings became more experimental, more metaphysical, and his fantasies were based on scientific thought and mathematical models, he continued to play mental games with the reader and to involve his interlocutor in the creative process. A good example that illustrates this trend is found in the short story, "The Origin of the Birds,"[41] often anthologized in school texts. In it Calvino ingeniously exploits the comic strip with all its conventions to allow the reader to make up the story where the narrator's memory seems to falter. Qfwfq, the narrator, who is like matter and has been around from time immemorial and cannot be destroyed, constantly exhorts you, the reader, not to read too closely, or take things too literally. He tells you to fill in the details for yourself or even to make up intervening adventures or alternate lines of action if you do not like the one he suggests.

A typical Calvino text is thus one with which the reader must interact; one that engages you in a game and in the adventure of reading and creating meaning. Part of the pleasure of immersing oneself in a Calvino text is that it requires this more active type of reading and does not crush you with the weight of its authorial authority. This interactive quality is, I believe, what makes even some of Calvino's more abstract texts enjoyable to both older and the younger readers who, in today's multimedia society, have come to enjoy, and indeed expect, a certain degree of interactivity.

In conclusion, the intellectual avant-garde writer Calvino, whose career was a seemingly endless invention, expands the possibilities of fiction. His belief that fairy tales contain explanations of life, the human condition, and the potential destiny of men and women, allows him to treat his own serious subjects with droll social witticism and unbridled imagination. Calvino's art demonstrates freedom of the mind and action; the action necessary to transport the reader beyond the alienation of the many filters and mediations imposed on the reader by institutionalized education. The ebullience, the youthful life-affirming joyfulness of Calvino's texts sends our minds in unusual directions and helps us come to grips with the diversity and open-endedness of all knowledge.

A century ago, at the dawn of a new social, political, and economic era, Collodi, while instilling a love of freedom and adventure, inspired children to go to school and stay in school until they had an education that would pave their way in society. Half a century later, while proposing the same love of freedom and adventure, Calvino inspired children to question, to think for themselves and not to stand in awe of the theories, ideologies, and the canned ideas of mass culture. Calvino never intentionally set out to write for children or to be pedagogically controversial. Both publishers and educational authorities, however, considered some of his texts valuable alternatives to the contemporary abundance of children's literature, which seems to be dominated by consolatory and edifying themes, woven together with artificial models of behavior and political correctness.

NOTES

1. Available in the 1976 Adelphi edition.

2. The collection of 200 folktales, selected from all the regions where a dialect of Italian is spoken, were retold by Calvino in standard Italian and published in 1956 as *Fiabe Italiane* (Turin: Einaudi), with an introduction by the author.

3. These fairy tales are not necessarily only the ones originally intended for children. Calvino states that, although "folktales especially intended for children exist . . . as a separate genre [with] the following characteristics: a theme of fear

and cruelty, scatological or obscene details, lines of verse interpolated into the prose and slipping into nonsense rhymes, . . . [their] coarseness and cruelty . . . would be considered wholly unsuitable in children's books today" ("Introduction," in *Italian Folktales*, trans. G. Martin (Harmondsworth: Penguin, 1982), xxx).

4. See *Romanzo delle mie delusioni* (The story of my disappointments) (Turin: Einaudi, 1977 and 1981), first serialized in the *Corriere dei Piccoli* in 1917 then published as a volume in 1925, and *Sette favole coi fiocchi* (last reprint by Marzocco). This volume contains a selection of stories taken from his earlier anthologies, *Storie di cantastorie* (1919–1920) and *Cavoli a merenda* (1920).

5. Cf. *"Tofano illustra i suoi testi mostrando la capacità di evadere dalla finestra della fantasia verso una boccata d'aria surrealista [e] di sposare il naturale con il meraviglioso"* (my translation), quoted in P. Boero and C. De Luca, *La letteratura per l'infanzia* (Rome-Bari: Edizioni Laterza, 1995), 161.

6. Renato Simoni noticed the *"natura immaginosamente divagante* of Tofano's drawings and his ability to represent a world where *non già l'umano diventa meraviglioso, ma il fiabesco diventa umano e l'assurdo prende un'aria borghese e familiare"* (in Boero and De Luca, *La letteratura per l'infanzia*, 161).

7. Calvino, "Introduction," in *Italian Folktales*, xxxii.

8. Italo Calvino, *The Literature Machine: Essays*, trans. P. Creagh (London: Secker & Warburg, 1987), 72.

9. It was first serialized as *La storia di un burattino* between July 1881 and January 1883 in the children's magazine *Giornale per i bambini* and published as a volume in 1883 with its present title. There still are numerous editions available, but the standard critical edition is taken to be the one ed. Ornella Castellani Pollidori, 1983.

10. Goldthwaite defines *Pinocchio* as a "folk epic, cautionary fable, parable on original sin," "a story about *la dolce vita* and the wages of sin, told by no civic-minded do-gooder but by a man who had dealt away his own life in smoke-filled rooms" (J. Goldthwaite, *The Natural History of Make-believe* [New York: Oxford University Press, 1996], 183). Goldthwaite thus sees the adventures of the puppet Collodi creates for his readers' amusement as a travesty of the author's own life as a gambler.

11. Calvino, *The Literature Machine*, 73.

12. Before the introduction of compulsory education for children after unification (1871), Italy's many dialects and regional variants hindered the development of a widely spoken national language. *Pinocchio*'s wide appeal to both children and adults, however, did more to spread the use of the language than the many school textbooks Collodi wrote on commission; nevertheless his classic was considered by a ministerial commission to be unfit for educational purposes in spite of its merits. See Boero and De Luca, *La letteratura per l'infanzia*, 22.

13. "*Ogni elenco credo deva cominciare da* Pinocchio *che ho sempre considerato un modello di narrazione, dove ogni motivo si presenta e ritorna con ritmo e nettezza esemplari, ogni episodio ha una funzione e una necessità nel disegno generale della peripezia, ogni personaggio ha un'evidenza visiva e un'inconfondibilità di linguaggio*" (Maria Corti, "Intervista a Italo Calvino" in *Autografo* 2, no. 6 [October 1985]: 48).

14. See *Una pietra sopra* (Turin, Einaudi 1980) and *Six Memos for the Next Millennium* (Cambridge, Mass.: Harvard University Press, 1988).

15. The twenty stories that comprise *Marcovaldo ovvero le stagioni in città* were published in 1963 with illustrations by Sergio Tofano and reprinted by Einaudi in a school edition in 1966 with an introduction and notes by the author. Ten of the stories, written between 1952–1957, had previously been published as a separate section, entitled "Gli idilli difficili," of Calvino's *I Racconti* (Turin: Einaudi, 1958).

16. A. Jeannet, "Collodi's Grandchildren: Reading *Marcovaldo*," *Italica* 71, no. 1 (1994): 56–77.

17. Maria Corti, "Testi o macrotesto? I racconti di Marcovaldo di I. Calvino," in *Il viaggio testuale: Le ideologie e le strutture semiotiche* (Turin: Einaudi, 1978), 182–197.

18. A. Jeannet, "Collodi's Grandchildren": 59.

19. Turin, Einaudi, 1949. Most of these stories are also in *I Racconti*.

20. Italo Calvino, *Our Ancestors*, trans A. Colquhoun (London: Picador-Pan Books, 1980): vii.

21. Appeared only in instalments in *Officina* nos. 9–12 (1957–1958).

22. "Introduction," in *Our Ancestors*: vii.

23. Turin: Einaudi, 1952.

24. Turin: Einaudi, 1960. This is the title given to the collected trilogy of *Il visconte dimezzato*, *Il barone rampante*, *Il cavaliere inesistente*, with a preface, later withdrawn by the author, because he preferred his texts to be read and commented according to the reader's own parameters without the limitations of authorial intent. See A. H. Carter, *Italo Calvino: Metamorphoses of Fantasy* (Ann Arbor: UMI Research Press, 1987), 157, note 4.

25. This is a fairly common *topos* in world literature, but also directly reminiscent of the Venetian folktale, "Il dimezzato" (The Cloven Youth). See Calvino, *Italian Folktales*, 99–102.

26. Carter, *Italo Calvino: Metamorphoses of Fantasy*, 32

27. Ibid., 37

28. In this text Calvino plays with the notion of point of view largely through Biagio, the principle narrator, who reveals how stories are compiled from personal observation but much of the time the author has to rely on second-

hand information, hearsay, and speculation (see *The Baron in the Trees*, in *Our Ancestors*, 89).

29. J. M. Carlton, "The genesis of *Il barone rampante,*" *Italica* 61, no. 3 (1984): 201.

30. Calvino, "Introduction," in *Our Ancestors*, viii.

31. Cf. *"Un'opera narrativa [deve essere] fruibile* (enjoyable) *e significante su molti piani che si intersecano"* (Calvino, "Nove domande sul romanzo," *Nuovi Argomenti* 38–39 [1959]: 8).

32. Among the American cartoons Calvino singles out The Katzenjammer Kids, Felix the Cat, Maggie and Jiggs (Bringing up Father) (see *Six Memos*, 93). One of the more popular comic strips illustrated by Tofano to which Calvino refers is *Le sventure del Signor Bonaventura*.

33. *Six Memos*, 93–94.

34. Ibid., 90.

35. Ibid., 91.

36. Marcovaldo ovvero le stagioni in città, 3; translation mine.

37. "La funzione del fumetto nella narrativa di Italo calvino," *Civiltà Italiana* 29, no. 1 (1995): 184.

38. See Corti, "Testi o macrotesto?": 182–197. She illustrates that there are two cycles or sets of Marcovaldo short stories, which have two slightly different narrative schemes and thus two possible endings: total disillusionment (the first set) or escape into a fantasy world through the window of the mind (the second set), but they are still recurring elements of a single macrotext.

39. Umberto Eco, "Interpreting Serials," *Limits of Interpretation* (Bloomington: Indiana University Press, 1990), 86.

40. A good example can be found in "La città smarrita nella neve" (*Marcovaldo*, 32–37). Marcovaldo is patiently shoveling away mountains of snow when a violent sneeze causes such a displacement of air that a vortex sucks up all the snow and hurls it into the sky.

41. In *T con zero* (Turin: Einaudi, 1967). This series of short stories that illustrates the paradoxes of space and time and has been translated into English, in the Harcourt Brace edition (New York, 1969), as *t zero*, and in the Abacus edition (Reading, 1983), as *Time and the Hunter*.

REFERENCES

Boero, P. and C. De Luca. *La letteratura per l'infanzia*. Rome-Bari: Edizioni Laterza, 1995.

Calvino, Italo. "Nove domande sul romanzo." *Nuovi Argomenti* 38–39 (1959): 7–12.

_____. *Marcovaldo ovvero le stagioni in città*. Turin: Einaudi, 1966.

_____. *Our Ancestors*. Trans. A. Colquhoun. London: Picador-Pan Books, 1980.

_____. *Una pietra sopra*. Turin: Einaudi, 1980.

_____. *Italian Folktales*. Trans. G. Martin. Harmondsworth: Penguin, 1982.

_____. *Time and the Hunter*. Trans. W. Weaver. Reading: Abacus-Sphere Books, 1983.

_____. *The Literature Machine: Essays*. Trans. P. Creagh. London: Secker & Warburg, 1987.

_____. *Six Memos for the next Millennium*. Trans. P. Creagh. Cambridge, Mass.: Harvard University Press, 1988.

Carlton, J. M. "The genesis of *Il barone rampante*." *Italica* 61, no. 3 (1984): 195–206.

Carter, A. H. *Italo Calvino: Metamorphoses of Fantasy*. Ann Arbor: UMI Research Press, 1987.

Collodi, Carlo. *I racconti delle Fiabe*. Milan: Adelphi, 1976.

_____. *Le avventure di Pinocchio*. Ed. Ornella Castellani Pollidori. Pescia: Fondazione Nazionale Carlo Collodi, 1983.

Corti, Maria. "Testi o macrotesto? I racconti di Marcovaldo di I. Calvino," in Il viaggio testuale. Le ideologie e le strutture semiotiche, 182–197 Turin: Einaudi, 1978.

_____. "Intervista a Italo Calvino." *Autografo* 2, no. 6 (October 1985): 47–53.

Eco, Umberto. "Interpreting Serials." In *Limits of Interpretation*. Bloomington: Indiana University Press, 1990.

Goldthwaite, J. *The Natural History of Make-believe*. New York: Oxford University Press, 1996.

Jeannet, A. "Colloidi's Grandchildren: Reading *Marcovaldo*" *Italica* 71, no. 1 (Spring 1994): 56–77.

Schroeder, Ulla M. "La funzione del fumetto nella narrativa di Italo calvino." *Civiltà Italiana*, 29, no. 1 (1995): 179–192.

CHAPTER 13

Two Crosswriting Authors
Carl Sandburg and Lennart Hellsing

LENA KÅRELAND

This chapter deals with the American author Carl Sandburg and his influence on the Swedish poet Lennart Hellsing, who like Sandburg has written for both children and adults. In many respects Carl Sandburg can be seen as a forerunner to Hellsing, both in theory and practice. This study will consider the relationship between Sandburg's and Hellsing's productions for adults and for children, as well as the special art of crosswriting child and adult in general. In Sweden very little research has been devoted to Carl Sandburg. His connection to Lennart Hellsing has not been discussed at all, except by the Swedish critic Eva von Zweigbergk who, in her 1965 survey of the history of Swedish children's literature, sees a similarity in the way the two authors deal with nonsense and imagination, as well as verbal acrobatics.[1]

Writing for both children and adults is not a new phenomenon. In Swedish literature, Selma Lagerlöf is a good example of a well-known author for adults who was asked (by the Swedish Association of Teachers) to write a book for children, in this case for all Swedish children. That was the origin of *Nils Holgerssons underbara resa genom Sverige* (*The Wonderful Adventures of Nils*), published in 1906–1907, a children's book that has contributed more than most to making Sweden known all around the world.

Note: Excerpts and quotations from *Daniel Doppsko* (Helsinki: Holger Schildts förlags AB, 1959), and from *The Pirate Book,* trans. William Jay Smith (London: Ernest Benn Ltd., 1972; published in Sweden as *Sjörövarbok;* by Rabén and Sjögren, Stockholm, 1965), are used by permission of the author, Lennart Hellsing.

Along with Astrid Lindgren, Lennart Hellsing is one of the most prominent authors of children's books in Sweden. He belongs to the group of authors who pioneered the renewal of children's literature at the end of World War II. In quite a remarkable way Hellsing has given Swedish children's literature both a new linguistic form and a new content. Even though he has been translated into about ten other languages, however, he is not as well known abroad as in Sweden. It is not easy to find expression for his verbal linguistics, playful nonsense, and poetic imagery. Lennart Hellsing made his debut in 1945 with the publication of a book for children, *Katten blåser i silverhorn* (The cat blows the silver horn) and a volume of poetry for adults, *Akvarium* (*Aquarium*). The same year he also introduced to the Swedish public a translation of poetry by A. A. Milne, *När vi var mycket små* (When we were very young).[2]

THE SPECIFICITY OF CHILDREN'S LITERATURE

Crosswriting has become the common term for authors who address both children and adults in the same texts. This term also is used to refer to an author whose oeuvre contains both works for children and works for adults.[3] Sandburg and Hellsing are crosswriting authors in both senses of the word. A study of the many parallels and resemblances between these two authors provides an opportunity to reflect generally on the theme of border crossings and narratives for a dual audience of children and adults. In recent years children's literature research has given a great deal of attention to the issue of the specificity of children's literature as well as to the borderline between the two literatures. The discussion has centered particularly on a comparison of children's texts and texts for adults. This broader approach, which not only compares children's texts with each other but also considers them in relation to mainstream texts for adults, has been of great importance. In many respects, studies of this kind can lead to an expansion of the theoretical and methodological framework of children's literature.[4]

Many studies have examined the ways in which authors for adults have been influenced by children's literature. This is particularly the case for avant-garde movements such as dadaism and surrealism. Representatives of dadaism underscored the authenticity of the child and appreciated children's language for its anarchical liberty. The future was to be found in children with their strong imagination. The child had managed to preserve the original and the natural as the source of pure energy. The surrealist movement also emphasized the child's imaginative life, and in the first surrealist manifesto in 1924, André Breton talked about the magic and enchantment of childhood. The child was free from all constraint: "Chaque matin, des enfants partent sans inquiétude. Tout est près, les pires conditions matérielles sont excellentes. Les bois sont blancs ou noirs, on ne dormira jamais."[5]

In her pioneering book *Alice to the Lighthouse* (1987), the British researcher Juliet Dusinberre has shown the influence of Lewis Carroll's *Alice in Wonderland* on Virginia Woolf's modernism.[6] One of her theses is that many modernist authors found inspiration in their childhood reading. The child became a symbol of freedom, a freedom that also meant the author's freedom from traditional realist writing and from repressive Victorian education and culture.[7] In *The Land of Lost Content,* Rosemary Lloyd, professor at Bloomington University, discusses how French modernist authors like Baudelaire, Mallarmé, and Rimbaud return to the child's way of experiencing the world.[8] My own study *Modernismen i barnkammaren: Barnlitteraturens 40-tal* (Modernism in the nursery: Swedish children's literature in the 1940s), also deals with authors for adults who have found inspiration in the child and in children's literature. The main theme of my investigation is the modernist movement in Sweden and its relationship to the development of children's literature during the 1940s. At the end of the decade modernism made its breakthrough in literature for adults in Sweden; it was no longer considered avant-garde, but had become part of the literary establishment. The criteria used to evaluate texts were based essentially on a set of modernist values. In children's literature modernist features also were appearing. New trends in child psychology and new educational theories influenced the conception of the child, and together with modern aesthetical theories they created a favorable ground for a radical renewal of Swedish children's books. One of the leading representatives of this new tendency in children's literature was Lennart Hellsing.

Many opinions about the differences between children's literature and literature for adults have been presented. To a great extent, earlier children's literature research neglected literary aspects in favor of pedagogical considerations. As literature for children was, from the beginning, more related to the pedagogical field than to the aesthetical, it is easy to understand why the borderline between the two literatures was pronounced and difficult to cross. During the last ten to fifteen years, children's literature has been seen in a broader perspective. Furthermore, much contemporary children's and youth literature has become more like adult literature, that is, more complex in style, form, and content. The right of children's literature to be literature seems to have been accepted.[9]

The specific features of children's books have been discussed by many researchers. Peter Nodelman uses the word "sameness," when he compares children's literature with literature for adults. This expression means that children's literature is not "unique" but a literature that follows specific patterns.[10] Another way of looking at children's literature is to examine how it addresses readers. In this regard, Barbara Wall talks about three forms of addressees: the double addressee, the single addressee, and the dual addressee.[11] Zohar Shavit, who has studied children's culture in general from a semiotic point of view, maintains that children's literature in itself has a double attribution.[12]

When one considers the authors of children's books themselves and how they understand their authorship, it is worth noting how often they confess that they are not writing for children. Even if some of them admit that they write for the child within themselves, it is evident that many authors of children's literature almost seem to deny the occupation that they nevertheless make a living on. This phenomenon is the result of what we could call the Cinderella complex of children's literature, that is to say, an inferiority complex resulting from its low status in relationship to literature for adults. Children's literature and children's authors must defend themselves. The authors are speaking from a weak position; they are very much aware of the indifference of well-established authors of literature for adults.[13]

TWO POPULAR POETS

Both Sandburg and Hellsing transgressed borders in their writing. These two authors and their work allow us to approach the issue of crosswriting not only from an aesthetical point of view but also from a more sociological one, considering the role of the market, the publisher, the critic, the reader, and the literary tradition. Before starting the analysis of Sandburg's and Hellsing's literary texts, however, I would like to give a brief survey of their careers. Both Sandburg, who was of Swedish extraction, and Hellsing started their career by publishing articles and poetry in newspapers. Sandburg first came to the American scene as a journalist and obtained a solid reputation in this field. As a reporter, he agitated for socialism, and he published pacifist poems in *The Chicago Daily News* at the beginning of the twentieth century. At the end of World War I he spent some time in Stockholm as a war correspondent.[14]

Sandburg's other fields were poetry, history, biography, and fiction. In a biography about Sandburg, Penelope Niven emphasizes the unique crosspollination of his work. His journalism fed his poetry, which colored his biographical work, and his work as a biographer-historian influenced his work as a folk musician, collector, and performer.[15] After Sandburg's death in July 1967 the *New York Times* described him as "the American bard." After the publication of his important biography of Abraham Lincoln, Sandburg was regarded as a symbolic "voice of America." The Lincoln biography consists of six volumes, on which Sandburg had worked for thirty years. The last part of the biography, *The War Years* (1939), was awarded the Pulitzer Prize in 1940. The critics were full of enthusiasm and the biography sold extremely well.[16]

Both Sandburg and Hellsing are popular poets, much appreciated by the general public. Sandburg, for example, was baptized "the Poet of the People" in 1922. As in the case of Sandburg's poetry, Hellsing's verses are still sung by schoolchildren all around Sweden. Sandburg collected old folksongs, which he published in 1927 in the well-known volume *The American Songbag*, a scholarly collection of 280 folksongs from all regions of America. He also made records for children, as did Hellsing. Hellsing also is a very all-round author, who has been active as a translator, critic, researcher, and book collector. He worked for a long time as a critic of children's books in a daily newspaper, where he also could express his general view of children's literature. He always has taken a great interest in the development of children's literature and has written several theoretical articles about children's books. At an early stage he actively promoted research in the field of children's literature, and he worked energetically for the creation of the Swedish Institute for Children's Books in Stockholm, established in 1965.

Sandburg also was an entertainer who often appeared on television reciting his poetry. In his biography, *Carl Sandburg* (1961), Harry Golden describes how the author read one of his poems while Gene Kelly was dancing in 1959. The poem presented lent itself very well to rhythm and visual interpretation:

> *Tell your feet the alphabet.*
> *Tell your feet the multiplication table.*
> *Tell your feet where to go, and watch 'em go*
> *and come back.*

To Sandburg, TV was a suitable medium for reaching an audience. There rhythm and words could be combined and the concrete visualized.

> *Can you dance a question mark?*
> *Can you dance an exclamation point?*

> *Can you dance a couple of commas?*
> *And bring it to a finish with a period?*[17]

Sandburg and Hellsing were both travelers and vagabonds. Sandburg rather soon outgrew the boundaries of his hometown, Galesburg, Illinois. He was the eternal Hobo and the constant metaphor of both his life and his work is the traveled road. Once he wrote about what he found most tremendous about life, namely that we never arrive anywhere but always are on the move.[18] The young Hellsing also went abroad and made long journeys, for instance to Africa. Travelling, adventures in different parts of the world, and eternal change also are typical ingredients in Hellsing's poetical world, where the setting is constantly changing. This feature of Hellsing's production can be related to the mania for travelling, so typical of modernism, and to the boundlessness of modernity.

In studying the theoretical literature on Hellsing and Sandburg, one notes that, whereas Sandburg is regarded mainly as an author for adults, Hellsing is regarded mainly as author for children. Hellsing has received awards for his children's books many times, but never for his poetry for adults. The reviews of his children's books have been much more positive than has the criticism of his poetry for adults. Nevertheless, at the beginning of his career, Hellsing was closer to writers for adults than to authors for children. He met with a large number of young modernist poets, artists, and musicians who belonged to the field of adult culture. During the 1940s he published as many books for children as for adults. Later, during the 1950s and the 1960s, his production of children's books was more important than his poetry for adults. Was Hellsing's ambition perhaps to pursue a career as an author for a dual readership? How important were the expectations of the market in the beginning? How conscious or unconscious was, in fact, his choice of audience? Did he choose the field of children's literature because the competition was not as stiff?

In this context, I want to stress the importance of the extremely good and friendly relationship that Hellsing established with the publisher of his children's books. The best known and most prestigious publisher in Sweden, Bonniers, had rejected his first children's book. On the other hand, it was Bonniers who published his first two volumes of poetry for adults. But they had refused the first manuscript of poems for adults that Hellsing had sent them in 1944. In order to get his children's book printed, Hellsing contacted a small and rather new, more avant-garde publishing house, willing to take risks and more interested in symbolic than in economic capital. This publisher also intended to promote modern children's literature in particular. The relationship between publisher and author was much less formal and strict at this small publishing house than with the big, well-known publisher, Bonniers.

Hellsing's contacts with these two different publishing houses clearly illustrate the fact that children's literature and literature for adults were judged separately and by different criteria. In this context, we should bear in mind that, particularly in the 1940s, writing for children had a relatively low status. Already at the beginning of the 1950s, however, Hellsing had attained a strong position in the field of children's literature. On the other hand, his position in the field of adult literature was more peripheral. At present Hellsing is regarded exclusively as an author for children, and researchers have not paid much attention to his poems for adults. In handbooks of the history of literature for adults, he is not mentioned at all.

While Hellsing withdrew more and more from the field of adult literature, Sandburg's literary career took a different direction. Sandburg is an example of a mainstream author who decided to cross over to children's literature. It was in the middle of his career that his children's books appeared, but all the time he also was writing for adults. Even if scholars often mention his books for children in their studies, many of the major critics of Sandburg's work don't seem to have read them. Normally they consider his children's book production as incidental.[19] Today Sandburg's two books about Rootabaga, *Rootabaga Stories* and *Rootabaga Pigeons*, are almost forgotten. Early in the 1990s, however, some previously unpublished Rootabaga stories were found. They were printed in 1993 under the title *More Rootabagas*.[20] Thus far, my analysis of the two authors has looked mainly at the marketing of their books, and in particular the importance of the publisher's role. It also is worth considering to what extent the conventions of the genre govern the writing and the narrative. What kinds of strategies are used to appeal to adults or to children?

A UNIVERSAL FORM OF ART

Both Sandburg and Hellsing wanted to produce a kind of universal work of art. Music, image, and movement are important constituents of their poetry. Sandburg "wrote for both the ear and the eye," states Gay Wilson Allen.[21] Hellsing collaborated with musicians who set his verses to music. Sandburg, who sang and played the guitar himself, did interviews with jazz musicians as a reporter, and as a poet collected and seriously studied songs and music, in particular from the labour movement. He was very interested in Negro music. In *Smoke and Steel* (1920), there is a poem titled "Jazz Fantasia" that describes how a small band builds up its music.

> *Drum on your drums, batter on your banjoes,*
>
> *sob on the long cool winding saxophones.*
> *Go to it, O jazzmen.*
>
> *Sling your knuckles on the bottoms of the happy*
> *tin pans, let your trombones ooze, and go husha-*
> *husha-hush with the slippery sand-paper.*[22]*

Sandburg's compassion for poor people, the oppressed, and the exploited, always found expression in his writing. He called himself a seeker, a singer, a traveler, and he became the passionate champion of people who did not have the words or power to speak for themselves. In many aspects he was a literary outsider. During the 1920s he was considered too radical and propagandistic, and he was attacked for his romanticism and form-lessness. In the 1950s he also was criticized, and the poetic quality of his poems was called into question. The representatives of new criticism were not especially charmed by his poetic style. On the other hand, the Beat poets of the 1960s admired him. Many have praised Sandburg for his "barbaric strength" and his "mystic realism."[23]

Both Sandburg and Hellsing were engaged in an intensive interplay with tradition, and both found inspiration in old poetry, folklore, and in the oral tradition. Hellsing was particularly interested in old nursery rhymes. On the other hand, both authors represent modernity and innovation. Moreover, both Sandburg and Hellsing were influenced by Chinese poets like Li Po. The intensively visual nature of Li Po's work can be seen as a characteristic feature of their poetry. Sandburg also found inspiration in the Japanese haiku, and Hellsing manifested an interest in Chinese calligraphy in his poetry for adults. Furthermore, Sandburg's and Hellsing's ideas about the role of art have much in common. They both thought that art should be a civilizing force and a humanizing power. Consequently, they

---

* Excerpt from "Jazz Fantasia" in *Smoke and Steel* by Carl Sandburg, copyright 1920 by Harcourt, Brace & Company and renewed 1948 by Carl Sandburg, reprinted by permission of the publisher.

believed that art has the power to touch and transform the quality of daily life. They both supported the aesthetic theory that states that art addresses primarily our senses and our perception of the world. The basic role of art is to revive our joy of life. Hellsing has constantly assumed the child's perspective. He has been a spokesman of the type of children's literature that emanates from the needs of modern children and has its setting in contemporary and everyday life. It is nonetheless true that the exotic and adventures in foreign parts of the world also have a place in his work.

Hellsing's interest in dance, movement, and playfulness in a wide sense was typical of the new conception of play that developed during the 1940s. During this decade the general aesthetic discussion in Sweden frequently treated the old question concerning the interaction between different forms of art. Music and painting gave inspiration to authors of both children's books and books for adults. Many modernist poets also drew attention to childhood and gave considerable prominence to the child in their poetry. According to Hellsing, children understand better than adults that images, words, music, and dance are magical things with the capacity to transform everyday life into a perpetual feast. Sources of inspiration in this respect were the British critic and poet Herbert Read and his important work *Education through Art* (1943), and the Dutch cultural historian Johan Huizinga and his study *Homo ludens* (1938). These authors, with their new awareness of the significance of play, had an impact on both children's and adult literature. In the field of Swedish children's literature, Hellsing is a pioneer and forerunner in his ambition to combine different forms of art into a unified whole.

Sandburg was introduced in Sweden in 1935 with a collection of poetry. His poetry was an example of free verse, which at that time was regarded as something rather new in Sweden. The critics found that Sandburg's poems showed in quite an extraordinary way what free, unrhymed verse could give. In the United States the first recognition of Sandburg as an author occurred much earlier, in 1916, when the *Chicago Poems* were published. These poems deal with ordinary people, men and women from the laboring classes, and with situations from everyday life. They express the roughness and brutality of industrial society: skyscrapers, steel, exploitation, and mobility. They capture the constantly changing America, in particular the Midwest. Above all, Sandburg's poems created the Chicago myth, the myth of the big city, "City of the Big Shoulders," lacking culture and beauty but full of youth, vitality, and joy.[24] *Chicago Poems*, which had opened up "unpoetic" areas of life as material for poetry, marked an important break with conventions. Sandburg defended the poet's right to cultivate any style suitable for his own purpose. For Sandburg language should know no bounds.[25]

Sandburg's first book published for children, *Rootabaga Stories* (1922), was written for his youngest daughter. These stories, translated into Swedish in 1950, lie close to the popular and the primitive. In 1930 Sandburg published a collection of poems, *Early Moon,* for young readers. Most of the poems were taken from Sandburg's collections of poetry for adults. The volume begins with a very interesting preface, "Short talk on poetry," in which Sandburg tries to explain what poetry is about, and how it has developed. Sandburg protests against those who claim that free verse is something new, a characteristic of modern poetry. Instead, he maintains that poems of ancient Chinese writers, such as Li Po and Tu Fu, already show how strange and marvellous moments of life can be captured and compressed into the style that we call free verse.

The poetic methods used by Sandburg and Hellsing have much in common. What links them is their preference for the concrete and for everyday objects. Both often use the concrete to visualize inner feelings, and both have a tendency to animate objects. For example, one of Sandburg's poems in *Early Moon* describes how "the iron rails run into the sun." And in "Even Numbers" the houses are personified:

> *Two houses leaning against each other like drunken*
> *brothers at a funeral,*
> *Two houses facing each other like two blind wrestlers*
> *hunting a hold on each other,*
> *These four scrawny houses I saw on a dead level*
> *cinder patch in Scranton, Pennsylvania.*

Even the words are animated in the following poem in *Early Moon*, called "Primer lesson":

> *Look out how you use proud words.*
> *When you let proud words go, it is not easy to call them back.*
> *They wear long boots, hard boots; they walk off proud;*
> *they can't hear you calling—*
> *Look out how you use proud words.*[26]*

---

* "Primer Lesson" in *Slabs of the Sunburnt West* by Carl Sandburg, copyright 1922 by Harcourt Brace & Company and renewed 1950 by Carl Sandburg, reprinted by permission of the publisher.

In his poetry for adults Sandburg also uses personification often, as in the well-known poem "Skyscraper":

> *By day the skyscraper looms in the smoke and sun and has a soul.*
> *Prairie and valley, streets of the city, pour people into it and they mingle*
> *among its twenty floors and are poured out again back to streets*
> *prairies and valleys.*
> *It is the men and women, boys and girls so poured in and out all day*
> *that give the building a soul of dreams and thoughts and memories.*[27]*

In her study, Penelope Niven states that Sandburg discovered his own poetic style and subjects in the raw material of his vibrant daily life.[28] The same could be said about Hellsing. The feeling for rhythm and the use of onomatopoeic expressions also are common to Hellsing and Sandburg. Both share a fascination for the meanings and mysteries of language. Both wrote a sort of poetic prose, and their stories normally do not have any plot in the traditional sense. Absurdism and nonsense are common elements in the world of play, dance, song, music, and movement that is found in *Rootabaga Stories* or in many of Hellsing's poems.

It is evident that Sandburg's intention was to address not only children but also adults with his Rootabaga stories, which are therefore a good example of crosswriting. In a letter written in 1922 to Anne Carroll Moore, he states:

> Some of the Rootabaga Stories were not written at all with the idea of reading to children or telling. They were attempts to catch fantasy, accents, pulses, eye flashes, inconceivably rapid and perfect gestures, sudden pantomimic moments, drawls and drolleries, gazings and musings—authoritative poetic instants—knowing that if the whirl of them were caught quickly and simply enough in words the result would be a child lore interesting to child and grownup.[29]

To his publisher, Alfred Harcourt, he wrote that "the book is 'For People from 5 to 105 Years of Age.' "[30] And in a letter to his friend Helen Keller, Sandburg wrote that by young people he meant "those who are children and those grownups who keep something of the child heart."[31] At the same time Sandburg was aware of children's special perception, and he states in another letter to Alice Corbin Henderson: "They [the children]

---

* Excerpt from "Skyscraper" in *Chicago Poems* by Carl Sandburg, copyright 1916 by Holt, Rinehart and Winston and renewed 1944 by Carl Sandburg, reprinted by permission of Harcourt Brace & Company.

are the anarchs [*sic*] of language and speech and we'll have a lot of fun whether it's a real book or not." [32] He viewed his stories about Rootabaga as a refuge from the imbecility of a frightened world.[33] This didn't prevent him, however, from taking his writing for children very seriously. "They [the Rootabaga stories] have got my best blood and heartbeats and breath."[34] The commercial and critical success of *Rootabaga Stories* was considerable. The book's sales far exceeded the editor's expectations.[35] It was advertised as "Fanciful Stories for Children." "The children asked questions, and I answered them," Sandburg said when describing how he wrote his Rootabaga stories.[36] Critics labeled them minor classics, and characterized them as "cadenzas upon the child's pleasure in names, in the sounds of words, in the setting loose of fantasy in a village as wide as the sight in a child's eye."[37]

WRITING AGAINST TRADITION

Both Sandburg and Hellsing wrote against tradition. Challenging the rules of classical children's literature, they created, in a sort of protest against tradition, new worlds and new characters. Thus we do not find any kings, princes, or princesses in their works. Sandburg had read the fairy tales of Hans Christian Andersen but he had found anything of that kind in his own country and he declared: "I was tired of princes and princesses and I sought the American equivalent of elves and gnomes. I knew that American children would respond, so I wrote some nonsense tales with American fooling in them."[38] With his stories about Rootabaga, Sandburg was considered to have developed a new field in American fairy tales (according to a *New York Times* reviewer), and he had shown great respect for the child's imagination. "Children are the only people I never lie to," he confessed once.[39] Sandburg's view of children corresponds to Hellsing's. The latter once said that it is with the children you must start, as grown-up people are already wasted.[40]

In the following presentation and analysis of Sandburg's *Rootabaga Stories,* it is my intention to study its connection with Hellsing's writing for children. In the collection of Hellsing's children's books donated to the Swedish Institute for children's books in Stockholm, there is a copy of the Swedish translation of the Rootabaga stories, published in 1950. It is thus evident that Hellsing was aware of Sandburg's work.

Much of the fun in the Rootabaga stories lies in the way that Sandburg creates names and places. He plays with absurd sounds and comic imagery in the same manner that Hellsing did later in his verses for children. The theme of naming is introduced already in the first story of the book. Gimme the Ax, who lives in a house "where everything is the same as it always was," decides to let his children name themselves:

> "The first words they speak as soon as they learn to make words shall be their names," he said. . . . When the first boy came to the house of Gimme the Ax, he was named Please Gimme. When the first girl came she was named Ax Me No Questions. . . . And then because no more boys came and no more girls came, Gimme the Ax said to himself, "My first boy is my last and my last girl is my first and they picked their names themselves."[41]

Among the figures in the Rootabaga stories we find a lot of odd characters such as Pigs with Bibs On, The Potato Face Blind Man, Poker Face the Baboon, Hot Dog the Tiger, Blixie Bimber, Henry Hagglyhoagly, Hatrack the Horse, the two Christmas Babies Goggler and Gaggler, and Dippy the Wisp and Slip Me Liz. It is evident that the names are chosen because they are funny to pronounce, especially for children. They have a nice taste in the mouth. They are comic and absurd, and they go along with the tradition of nonsense, built on different kinds of alliteration, sound, and euphony. As we can see, the characters in the Rootabaga stories are hardly any ordinary people but a lot of animated animals and objects such as the Dollar Watch, six umbrellas taking off their straw hats to show respect to one big umbrella, and deep red roses going back and forth between the clock and the looking glass. In Rootabaga country there are also two royal figures, the Queen of the Cracked Heads and the King of the Paper Sacks, who can be seen as contrasts to the king and queen of the traditional fairy tale.

The way Hellsing names his characters reminds us of Sandburg. One of the pincipal characters in Hellsing's children's books is Krakel Spektakel, and his friend is named Opsis Kalopsis; both are nonsense words in which the sounds and repetitive elements are important. Other names of the same kind are Pant Pantalong and Ellen Dellen du von Essen. Certain names are chosen to illustrate the behavior of the characters: Miss Now One Way Now Another and Uncle Try Not with Me.

In the Rootabaga stories, Sandburg creates a special world with its own geography and its own way of living. When Gimme the Ax is on his way to Rootabaga, he passes the Over and Under country and arrives in the country of the balloon pickers, where the sky is thick with balloons. The next station is the country of the circus clowns. In the country of Rootabaga the railroad tracks change from straight to zigzag and all the pigs have bibs on. In Rootabaga one finds the big city, the Village of Liver-and-Onions; another city called the Village of Cream Puffs, situated on the upland corn prairie; and a skyscraper to the Moon.

Traveling is a dominant theme in *Rootabaga Stories*, as we have seen. Gimme the Ax and his family's decision to leave their house appears as a sort of protest against an unchanging life. They find that "it is too much to be anywhere too long." At the railway station they buy a ticket "to ride where the railroad tracks run off into the sky and never come back" (9). Their neighbors say to each other: "They are going to Kansas, to Kokomo, to Canada, to Kankakee, to Kalamazoo, to Kamchatka, to Chattahooochee" (6). A special geography is also created in Hellsing's books for children, where the names of countries, cities, rivers, and lakes illustrate the author's tendency to play with words. Thus we find Everyman's country, the cities of By No Means and Otherwise, and the lake of In This Manner.

In his composition of the Rootabaga stories, Sandburg follows the pattern of the folktale in many ways. The books about Rootabaga consist of several short episodes whose titles are close to the grotesque with its combination of high and low, and quite opposite elements. The composition of the stories also resembles fables, riddles, and Rudyard Kipling's *Just So Stories*. A rapid look at the different titles of the stories illustrates this influence: "How the Animals Lost Their Tails and Got Them Back Travelling from Philadephia to Medicine Hat," "What Six Girls with Balloons Told the Gray Man on Horseback," or "Slipfoot and How Nearly Always Never Gets What He Goes After." The composition, characterized by short, rapid sequences, evokes films. During the 1920s, Sandburg was very interested in motion pictures and saw at least six movies a week.[42]

In many respects Sandburg's stories are closer to poetry than to prose. He sometimes presents and describes his characters in a rather poetic and romantic way. Thus, Wing Tip the Spick's eyes are "clear light blue" and their color is "the same as cornflowers with blue raindrops shining on the silver leaves in a summer sun shower" (30). The ternary principle of the fairy tale is used in a poetically romantic way in the story "The White Horse Girl and the Blue Wind Boy." White Horse Girl "rode one horse white as snow, another horse white as new washed sheep wool, and another white as silver" (160), while Blue Wind Boy likes listening to the winds. There was a blue wind of day time and there was a night wind "with blue of summer stars in summer and blue of winter stars in winter." And there was a third blue wind of the times between night and day, "a blue dawn and evening wind" (161). Hellsing, too, often follows the ternary principle when he composes his stories. Sandburg's use of poetic tools, such as alliteration, repetition, onomatopoeic expressions, and cataloguing in the manner developed by Walt Whitman, also can be seen in his poetry for adults. For instance, the poem "Potato Blossom Songs and Jigs" starts in the following manner, which also make us think of A. A. Milne's *Winnie-the-Pooh*:

> *Rum tiddy um,*
> *tiddy um,*
> *tiddy um tum tum.*
> *My knees are looselike, my feet want to sling their sleeves.*
> *I feel like tickling you under the chin—honey—and a-asking: Why Does a*
> *   Chicken Cross the Road?*[43]*

MODERN TECHNOLOGY AND MODERNITY

Sandburg was fascinated by modern technology. According to Joanne Lynn, he loved zest, action, and growth.[44] In the Rootabaga stories, one notices an interest in modernity and in the process of the modernization of society. For instance, new means of transport are mentioned. Likewise Hellsing, who was trained as an engineer, was interested in technology. He writes, for example, about electricity, electrical works, waterworks, and often about elevators. Many different means of transport are found in his books: airplanes, trains, and boats. Speed and rapidity are stressed in the works of both authors, who thus illustrate the principles of futurism, which felt that these concepts should be expressed in literature. Sandburg's *Complete Poems* contains a poem titled "Portrait of a motorcar," in which the car is described as "a long-legged dog of a car . . . a gray-ghost eagle car," which "runs in the blood" of its driver (106). The Rootabaga stories start with the train journey that Gimme the Ax and his children enjoy together. "Not even the Kings of Egypt with all their climbing camels, and all their speedy, spotted, lucky lizards, ever had a ride like this," he said to his children (11).

It is not my intention to suggest that Hellsing was directly influenced by and imitated Sandburg's literary style. What is interesting is an

---

* Excerpt from "Potato Blossom Songs and Jigs" in *Cornhuskers* by Carl Sandburg, copyright 1918 by Holt, Rinehart and Winston and renewed 1946 by Carl Sandburg, reprinted by permission of the publisher.

illustrative comparison, which shows that Sandburg and Hellsing wrote in the same tradition. Their ideas concerning the child and the child's relationship to poetry have much in common. On reading Sandburg's books, Hellsing certainly received a kind of affirmation of his own poetic methods. What is most essential in Hellsing's poetic vision is to give voice and body to the text. Poetry is recreated within and by the reader's, that is to say, the child's body. Both Sandburg's and Hellsing's poetry are extremely oral, in the sense that it is important how the words sound.

In addressing children, both Sandburg and Hellsing often use themes taken from their poetry for adults and transformed. It is interesting, however, to note that there is a considerable difference between Hellsing's poetry for adults and his writing for children. His poems for adults are strikingly traditional compared with his children's books. On the other hand, Sandburg's writing for adults and for children does not diverge very much. The way in which both Sandburg and Hellsing include the reader when they write for adults as well as for children is very similar to verbal storytelling. Both utilize elements from the oral tradition. Their common tendency to exaggerate also can be mentioned. Hellsing's writing for children reveals clearly his conception of art as game and play. Convinced that stories for children must contain action, both authors have created a literature that gives the reader a sense of adventure. In Hellsing's metafictional texts, the role of the artist is transformed and the artist becomes a playing being among others.

Sandburg found beauty in motifs and objects not earlier described in poetry, such as a farm silo or a series of tall coal chutes "rising as silhouettes on a moonlight night."[45] This can be seen in his books for adults as well as in his books for children. He has a functional perception of beauty, and consequently he is no friend of unnecessary decorations. In the preface of *Early Moon* he states: "The most beautiful room is the one which best serves those who live in it. . . . Nearly always, what serves, what is appropriate to human use, is beautiful enough."[46] The combination of the concrete and the visual on one hand, and a narration full of absurdity, playfulness, and nonsense on the other, links the two poets. Everyday life is thus very present in Rootabaga, where Blixie Bimber, when she is flipping out of the kitchen, does not forget to say goodby to the dishpan, the dishcloth, or the towel for drying the dishes. Hellsing describes everyday things, such as supermarkets and vacuum cleaners. Both Sandburg and Hellsing often start with something familiar. Then they elucidate it in a new and unexpected fashion that evokes the literary methods of the Russian avant-garde, formalism, and dadaism. Sandburg and Hellsing transgressed various kinds of borders. Those transgressions contributed to artistic innovation. Influenced by the aesthetics of modernism Hellsing is often daring and provocative in his writing for children.

Some of Hellsing's books for children even caused controversy and gave rise to lively discussions among the critics. He himself has said that his ambition was to break with the tradition of Elsa Beskow, the most well-known Swedish author and illustrator during the first half of the twentieth century. In the title of his classic study, Harold Bloom coined the expression "Anxiety of influence," which accurately describes Hellsing's ambition as an author for children. He wanted to break with conventions and tradition, in particular he wanted to create something new and different from the work of Elsa Beskow, the Swedish artist and author who had had a considerable influence on Swedish children's literature since the beginning of the twentieth century. Helling's ambition was to be a sort of provocateur. And he succeeded in this ambition: The story about the wild life of the pirates in *Sjörövarbok* (*The pirate book,* 1965), was too provocative in many respects. When the second edition of the book was published, the illustrator, Poul Ströyer, had to put a dress on the nude woman dancer in one episode.

Boken om Bagar Bengtsson (*The book about Baker Bengtsson*), 1966), inspired by a character from a popular Swedish song, deals with death. Here too, Hellsing's funny and absurd way of treating such a serious theme as death was too provocative for readers at that time. Sandburg's use of slang in his poetry also was regarded as provocative. According to Sandburg himself, "slang is language that takes off its coat, spits on its hands, and goes to work." In Hellsing's children's books, the themes are often peculiar and untraditional. He does not always find his subjects in the child's environment, and in his literature for small children he does not always follow Lucy Sprague Mitchell's advice about the "Here and Now." On the contrary, his musicality and his equilibristic play with the sounds and meanings of words are in line with the theories presented in Mitchell's preface to her *Here and Now Story Book* (1921). Mitchell's book was introduced in Sweden in 1939 by the same publisher that had put out Hellsing's first children's book. It also is known that Hellsing, together with some colleagues, discussed Mitchell's theories in the 1940s.

Hellsing's verses appeal to all of a child's senses: hearing, sight, feeling, smell, and taste. To him the most important thing is not the rational meaning of the words but the play aspect and the function of the words as play material. Mitchell also underscored how children play with words in a natural and spontaneous way, while most adults have forgotten "how to play with anything, most of all with words."[47] Such a polarization between adults and children is evident in Hellsing's work. He emphasizes the spontaneity and openmindedness of the child in contrast to the rationality of the adult. Hellsing often builds his poems around the different meanings and the ambiguity of words. For instance, in *Sjörö-varbok,* a whole poem is composed around different senses of the verb "strike." In the verses about the adventures of the pirates, Hellsing also plays with the stereotypes of pirates using repetition and onomatopoeic expressions. The following provides an excellent example:

> *Pirate Plummer*
> *becomes a plumber.*
> *Pirate Mason*
> *becomes a mason.*
> *Pirate Proctor*
> *becomes a doctor.*
> *Black-eyed Smith becomes a blacksmith.*
> *Lolloping lobster!*
> *Lollipop!*
> *Jolly Roger*
> *to the top!*[48]

NO FAMILIES BUT A LOT OF DANCING

Like Sandburg, Hellsing animates objects, especially food of various kinds. He writes about vegetables such as parsnips and chives, beetroots and pumpkins. They are all in perpetual movement: Mister Cucumber is dancing both the waltz and the mazurka, and in a skirt with embroidery Selma Celery is dancing by. In Hellsing's work dancing has a poetic power, to which the poet has recourse. A whole book, full of philosophy and wisdom, is devoted to the life of bananas, *Bananbok* (The banana book, 1975). Another book, *Ägget* (The Egg, 1978), tells the story of an egg, the beginning of everything. To a great extent Hellsing's art is universal, and according to Barbara Wall's theories they have a dual addressee. A book such as *Oberons gästabud* (Oberon's banquet), with its subtitle "A Shakespeariad for ungrown-ups," offers a good example of his attitude toward classical heritage. Hellsing's poems about the boy Hamlet who does not want to go to school, Lady Macbeth and her mania for purity, and the girl Julia on her balcony are all written in blank verse. Hellsing's disrespectful use of classical literature parallels Sandburg's approach to the classics. A fine example is his poem "Grieg Being Dead":

> *Grieg being dead we may speak of him and his art.*
> *Grieg being dead we can talk about whether he was any good or not.*
> *Grieg being with Ibsen, Björnson, Leif Ericson and the rest,*
> *Grieg being dead does not care a hell's hoot what we say.*
>
> *Morning, Spring, Anitra's Dance,*
> *He dreams them at the doors of new stars.*[49]

In Sandburg's Rootabaga stories there is hardly any traditional family life. Instead there is a story about two skyscrapers who have decided to have a child. In the night they lean toward each other whispering. They come to the conclusion that their child must be a free child not standing still all its life in a street corner. When the child arrives, it is a railroad train, the fastest long-distance train in Rootabaga (137). Nor do Hellsing's books deal with ordinary families. As his characters are always on the move, it is not easy for them to raise a family. In Hellsing's poetical world home is disowned, in a conscious protest against traditional children's books with their idyllic descriptions of family life. In *Musikbussen* (The music bus, 1948), however, there is a more normal family, but the description of this family is contrary to all requirements for realism. The father and mother with their twenty children, consisting of ten sets of twins, live in the biggest and reddest bus in the world. The bus travels all around the country playing music. It is true that the nursery is the setting of some of Hellsing's stories, but only as a sort of decor. Other relationships are created in Hellsing's books. For instance, eight sewing needles seek contact with a thimble. Even more surrealistic is the meeting between a tea strainer and an Englishman. In one of his Rootabaga stories, Sandburg, for his part, describes the wedding procession of the Rag Doll and the Broom Handle, a union that is also quite out of the ordinary (101).

The combination of sound, music, and movement is a frequently occurring theme in Hellsing's writing. One poem is about a man playing his mouth-organ so that everything in the kitchen dances away with him. The activity of the playing man has parallels with Dionysian and chaos-producing forces in life. The playing man makes a clean sweep of everything that is old and traditional. The magic forces of art and music

---

are illustrated in many other poems by Hellsing. A boy playing the harp also succeeds in creating activity in a kitchen, where a kitten is dancing with a herring and a corkscrew with two corks. In *Daniel Doppsko* (Daniel Ferrule, 1959), a story about a boy's journey at sea, the composition and content have many similarities with Sandburg's Rootabaga stories. There is a lot of singing in the book, and the boy is playing the flute. As we have seen, music also is important in Sandburg's Rootabaga stories. Here Potato Face Blind Man often plays his accordion for the pleasure of the ears of the passers-by (45). Henry Hagglyhoagly has bought a Spannish Spinnish Splishy guitar, and in the cold winter night he walks to Susan Slackentwist's to serenade her (175).

This chapter has examined a number of parallels between two cross-writing authors, Carl Sandburg and Lennart Hellsing. We have see that, although the two authors belong to different countries and generations, they have much in common: a childlike approach to life, a special appreciation of wonder and adventure, musicality, and a strong verbal imagination. In challenging the tradition, they both transgressed borders and contributed to renewal. The principal aim of Hellsing's poetry is to initiate the child's feeling for life. The last word is given to Sandburg, through his character the Potato Face Blind Man, who softly sings: "Be Happy in the Morning When the Birds Bring the Beans" (59).

NOTES

1. Eva von Zweigbergk, *Barnboken i Sverige 1750–1950* (Stockholm: Rabén & Sjögren, 1965), 381.

2. A. A. Milne, *När vi var mycket små*, trans. Lennart Hellsing and Claes Hoogland (Stockholm: Kooperativa Förbundets förlag, 1945).

3. See *Children's Literature* 25 (1997): vii.

4. Boel Westin, "Vad är barnlitteraturforskning?", in *Litteraturvetenskap— en inledning*, ed. Staffan Bergsten (Lund: Studentlitteratur, 1998), 126.

5. André Breton, *Oeuvres complètes*, vol. 1 (Paris: Gallimard, 1988), 340.

6. Juliet Dusinberre, *Alice to the Lighthouse: Children's Books and Radical Experiment in Art* (Basingstoke: Macmillan, 1987), 1–34.

7. Juliet Dusinberre, "Dreams of Freedom: E. M. Forster, Virginia Woolf and Children's Literature," in *Modernity, Modernism and Children's Literature*, ed. Ulf Boëthius (Stockholm: Centrum för Barnkulturforskning, 1998), 75–95.

8. Rosemary Lloyd, *The Land of Lost Content: Children and Childhood in Nineteenth-Century French Literature* (Oxford: Clarendon, 1992).

9. Maria Nikolajeva, *Children's Literature Comes of Age: Toward a New Aesthetic* (New York and London: Garland Publishing, Inc., 1996), 5–6.

10. Peter Nodelman, "Interpretation and the Apparent Sameness of Children's Novels," *Studies in the Literary Imagination: Narrative Theory and Children's Literature* 18, no. 2 (1985): 5–20.

11. Barbara Wall, *The Narrator's Voice: The Dilemma of Children's Fiction* (Basingstoke: Macmillan, 1991).

12. Zohar Shavit, *Poetics of Children's Literature* (Athens, Ga.: University of Georgia Press, 1986).

13. Sonja Svensson, "Barnböcker finns dom?", in *Böcker ska blänka som solar*, ed. Boel Westin (Stockholm: Rabén & Sjögren, 1988), 30.

14. Björn Fontander, *Carl Sandburg: Den evige luffaren* (Stockholm: Carlson Bokförlag, 1995), 21.

15. Penelope Niven, *Carl Sandburg: A Biography* (New York: Charles Scribner's Sons, 1991), 446.

16. Gay Wilson Allen, *Carl Sandburg* (Minneapolis: University of Minnesota Press, 1972), 32.

17. Harry Golden, *Carl Sandburg* (Cleveland and New York: The World Publishing Company, 1961), 25, 26.

18. Fontander, *Carl Sandburg*, 132.

19. Joanne L. Lynn, "Hyacinths and biscuits in the Village of Liver and Onions: Sandburg's Rootabaga Stories," *Children's Literature* 8 (1980): 120.

20. Fontander, *Carl Sandburg*, 83.

21. Wilson Allen, *Carl Sandburg*, 36.

22. Carl Sandburg, *Complete Poems* (New York: Harcourt, Brace and Company, 1950), 179.

23. Lynn, "Hyacinths and Biscuits," 118.

24. Wilson Allen, *Carl Sandburg*, 17.

25. Richard Crowder, *Carl Sandburg* (New York: Twayne Publishers, 1964), 57 and 60.

26. Sandburg, *Complete Poems*, 38, 59.

27. Ibid., 31.

28. Niven, *Carl Sandburg*, 225.

29. Herbert Mitgang, *The Letters of Carl Sandburg* (New York: Harcourt, 1968), 220.

30. Ibid., 212.

31. North Callahan, *Carl Sandburg: His Life and Works* (University Park and London: The Pennsylvania State University Press, 1987),109.

32. Ibid., 187.

33. Niven, *Carl Sandburg*, 363.

34. Ibid., 388.

35. Ibid., 406.

36. Golden, *Carl Sandburg*, 221.

37. Callahan, *Carl Sandburg*, 105. The cited characterization derives from Daniel Hoffman, consultant in Poetry at the Library of Congress.

38. Ibid., 105. See also Golden, *Carl Sandburg*, 389.

39. Golden, *Carl Sandburg*, 394.

40. Elly Jannes, "Krakel Spektakel i Äppelviken," interview with Lennert Hellsing, *VI-tidningen* (1956): 50–51.

41. Carl Sandburg, *Rootabaga Stories* (New York: Harcourt, Brace and Company, 1922), 3, 4.

42. Niven, *Carl Sandburg*, 389.

43. Sandburg, *Complete Poems*, 95.

44. Lynn, "Hyacinths and biscuits," 127.

45. Carl Sandburg, *Early Moon* (New York: Harcourt, Brace and Company, 1948), 18.

46. Ibid., 18.

47. Lucy Sprague Mitchell, *Here and Now Story Book* (New York: E. P. Dutton and Company, 1921), 61.

48. Lennart Hellsing. *The Pirate Book,* freely adapted from the Swedish by William Jay Smith (London: Ernest Benn Limited, 1972).

49. Sandburg, *Complete Poems*, 227.

REFERENCES

Beckett, Sandra L. *Modernismen i barnkammaren: Barnlitteraturens 40-tal.* Stockholm: Rabén & Sjögren, forthcoming.

Breton, André. *Oeuvres complètes.* Vol. 1. Paris: Gallimard, 1988.

Callahan, North. *Carl Sandburg: His Life and Works.* University Park and London: The Pennsylvania State University Press, 1987.

Crowder, Richard. *Carl Sandburg.* New York: Twayne Publishers, Inc. 1964.

Dusinberre, Juliet. *Alice to the Lighthouse: Children's Books and Radical Experiment in Art.* Basingstoke: Macmillan, 1987.

———. "Dreams of Freedom: E. M. Forster, Virginia Woolf and Children's Literature." In *Modernity, Modernism and Children's Literature,* ed. Ulf Boëthius, 75–95. Stockholm: Centrum för barnkulturforskning, 1998.

Fontander, Björn. *Carl Sandburg: Den evige luffaren.* Stockholm: Carlson bokförlag, 1995.

Golden, Harry. *Carl Sandburg.* Cleveland and New York: The World Publishing Company, 1961.

Hellsing, Lennart. *The Pirate Book.* Trans. William Jay Smith. London: Ernest Benn Limited, 1972.

Jannes, Elly. "Krakel Spektakel i Äppelviken." Interview with Lennert Hellsing. *VI-tidningen* (1956): 50–51.

Kåreland, Lena, *Modernismen i barnkammaren: Barnlitteraturens 40-tal.* Stockholm: Rabén & Sjögren, 1999.

Knoepflmacher, U. C. and Mitzi Myers, ed. "Cross-Writing Child and Adult," special issue of *Children's Literature* 25 (1997): vii–289.

———. *Daniel Doppsko.* Helsingfors: Holger Schildts förlags AB, 1959.

Lloyd, Rosemary. *The Land of Lost Content: Children and Childhood in Nineteenth-Century French Literature.* Oxford: Clarendon, 1992.

Lynn, Joanne L. "Hyachinths and biscuits in the Village of Liver and Onions: Sandburg's Rootabaga Stories." *Children's Literature* 8 (1980): 118–132.

Milne, A. A. *När vi var mycket små.* Trans. Lennart Hellsing and Claes Hoogland. Stockholm: Kooperativa Förbundets förlag, 1945.

Mitchell, Lucy Sprague. *Here and Now Story Book.* New York: E. P. Dutton and Company, 1921.

Mitgang, Herbert. *The Letters of Carl Sandburg.* New York: Harcourt, 1968.

Nikolajeva, Maria. *Children's Literature Comes of Age: Toward a New Aesthetic.* New York and London: Garland, 1996.

Niven, Penelope. *Carl Sandburg: A Biography.* New York: Charles Scribner's Sons, 1991.

Nodelman, Perry. "Interpretation and the Apparent Sameness of Children's Novels," *Studies in the Literary Imagination: Narrative Theory and Children's Literature* 18, no. 2 (1985): 5–20.

Sandburg, Carl. *Complete Poems.* New York: Harcourt, Brace and Company, 1950.

———. *Rootabaga Stories.* New York: Harcourt, Brace and Company, 1922.

———. *Early Moon.* New York: Harcourt, Brace and Company, 1948.

Shavit, Zohar. *Poetics of Children's Literature.* Athens, Ga.: University of Georgia Press, 1986.

Svensson, Sonja. "Barnböcker finns dom?", in *Böcker ska blänka som solar,* ed. Boel Westin. Stockholm: Rabén & Sjögren, 1988.

von Zweigbergk, Eva. *Barnboken i Sverige 1750–1950.* Stockholm: Rabén & Sjögren, 1965.

Wall, Barbara. *The Narrator's Voice: The Dilemma of Children's Fiction.* Basingstoke: Macmillan, 1991.

Westin, Boel. "Vad är barnlitteraturforskning?", In *Litteraturvetenskap—en inledning,* ed. Staffan Bergsten. Lund: Studentlitteratur, 1998.

Wilson Allen, Gay. *Carl Sandburg.* Minneapolis: University of Minnesota Press, 1972.

CHAPTER 14

Postmodernism Is Over. Something Else Is Here. What?

LISSA PAUL

I don't know yet. The name of a new movement will emerge in time, from one of its defining characteristics, some of which are already present but not yet in high enough concentrations to be clearly visible. Now, in the late 1990s, the clutter of postformations (postmodern, postcolonial) reflect our *fin de siècle* concerns, magnified as end of millennial concerns. Focus on the new thing won't really begin in earnest until after the year 2000. The signs are here, but when I first tried to name them in a scholarly way—defining characteristic features and explaining their significance— I couldn't get the essay to work. So instead, I've decided to write this piece as an unfolding narrative, a journal of discovery, tracing the route of my tentative map making.

The mapping of a new arts movements doesn't have the cachet of sailing across uncharted oceans in wooden boats in search of gold and spice, but I've taken some of my writing lessons from those exploration narratives. Adventure stories about the journeys of exploration endure— but explanations by explorers speculating on the value of their finds (precious metals or a quick route to China) are subject to mockery. I've decided to heed the historical lesson and stick to the process of charting.

My specific reason for first attending to the description of a new movement has an explicit start date. In 1996, I was asked by Nancy Chambers, editor of the British children's literature journal, *Signal*, to be one of two judges (the other was Canadian author and storyteller Bob Barton) for the annual *Signal* poetry award. Bob and I were the first non-British judges, incidentally, since the inception of the award in 1979. For *Signal* poetry award judges, naming the winning book is a very small part of the job. The bigger and more difficult task involves writing the essay (published annually in the May volume of *Signal*) to explain not just the winning entry, but to provide a context for the body of work submitted that year. Essays written by previous *Signal* poetry award judges (including Anthea Bell, Aidan Chambers, Peter Hunt, Jan Mark, Margaret Meek, Brian Morse, Neil Philip, Alan Tucker, and John Wain) have produced what is probably the best historical record of the development of poetry published for children in this last quarter of the twentieth century. As the boxes of poetry books published in 1997 arrived, Bob and I recognized that our contribution would be included in this historical record, and we consciously tried to tune ourselves to the current cultural climate and to categorize the patterns of our reading.

In the end, we agreed, happily, to give the award to *Bad, Bad Cats* by Roger McGough, a funny, intelligent book, exhibiting a range of poetic styles and diction—and liked by the real children with whom we shared it. Bob and I liked the gentle mocking of poetic tradition in it, from Eliot's *Old Possum's Book of Practical Cats* to the nature poems of Wordsworth and Ted Hughes. As poetry accessible to young children tends to lose in the awards sweepstakes, we appreciated the opportunity to celebrate a book that could redress the balance. We are still both comfortable with our choice of *Bad, Bad Cats* as the winner. It is right for this particular historical moment, and fits with *Signal*'s mandate to privilege single poet collections over anthologies for the award. But I found myself increasingly drawn to a book that didn't win, one that wasn't even on Faber's list of books published for children in 1997, *The School Bag*, an anthology edited by Ted Hughes and Seamus Heaney. It will be seen, retrospectively I think, as a prescient book, capturing the spirit of the age— before that age has been clearly defined. That, says Hughes elsewhere, is what imaginative writers are supposed to do:

> In any social group, the imaginative writers are the most visible indicators of the level and energy and type of the imagination and other vital mental activities in the whole group. What everybody in the group shares in a hidden way, or needs to share, comes to expression in the writer. It is as if works of imaginative literature were a set of dials on the front of society, where we can read off the concealed energies. What happens in the imagination of those individuals chosen by the unconscious part of society to be its writers is closely indicative of what is happening to the hidden energies of society as a whole.[1]

Ultimately, I think, *The School Bag* will be seen to contain a blueprint for a new arts movement, one that attends to cultural clashes in the historical record (instead of the collage or bricolage of the modernist/postmodernist era), schooling rather than age as a defining characteristic, and valuing of memory over information. But I'm ahead of myself. That is the end of the story, and I'm still at the beginning.

I had requested *The School Bag* because its predecessor, *The Rattle Bag,* had won the *Signal* poetry award for the best book of poetry published for children in 1982. There was no real competition from single poet collections that year. And, over time, *The Rattle Bag* has proven its worth. It has been a constant companion, one of my favorite anthologies, the book I turn to in times of crisis, or when I need comfort—or when I unexpectedly need something special for a class. It offered poems when the Gulf War broke out in 1991 and when Diana, Princess of Wales, died in September 1997. On both occasions, it would have been wrong to go ahead with what had been planned for class and not acknowledge the events of the day.

The Rattle Bag was published when Hughes and Heaney were both ascending to the apexes of their careers. Although both were well-established, famous poets in 1982, *The Rattle Bag* appeared before Hughes was appointed Poet Laureate, and before Heaney was named a Noble Laureate, before they bore the weight of contemporary poetic tradition on their shoulders. While I was writing this essay, Ted Hughes died. That changed things. *The School Bag* now takes a place among Hughes's last books, something I didn't know when I began thinking about this essay, and wasn't on my agenda when I spoke about it at the Conference of the International Society for the Study of European Ideas (ISSEI) in Haifa in August 1998. Although I had already singled out *The School Bag* as a marker for the literature of a new movement, I hadn't contemplated Hughes not being here to usher in the new millennium.

The irony of the fact that Faber didn't think *The School Bag* suitable for their children's lists (despite the success of its predecessor, *The Rattle Bag,* on both children's and adult's lists) was not lost on Hughes and Heaney, I imagine. But in the omission of *The School Bag* from the children's lists, I think Faber missed what Hughes and Heaney understood precisely: "child" and "adult" are no longer defining categories. Schooling is. Age will become less important as a defining category for making distinctions and value judgments. Knowledge, particularly historical knowledge, will become increasingly important.

Despite the title, *The School Bag* doesn't look anything like a school anthology. Of the 270 poems in *The School Bag*, only three, by my count anyway, were deliberately written with children in mind: Lewis Carroll's "Jabberwocky," Walter de la Mare's "The Listeners," and Edward Lear's "The Owl and the Pussycat." The anthology also contains a lot of very long poems, and a lot of very long excerpts from very long poems. Anthologies for schoolchildren generally favor short poems: on the (faulty) grounds that children have short attention spans and poetry lessons (if there are any) tend to be cut to a forty-five minute class period, or, in England, to the new "literacy hour" with its carefully timed-to-the-minute slots for reading, writing, and talk. *The School Bag,* like its predecessor, is antithetical to the compartmentalization characteristic of contemporary educational policies, politics, and institutions.

In *The School Bag,* as in *The Rattle Bag,* Hughes and Heaney also eschew another staple of the school anthology: themed subheads. Poems are not identified neatly as being about winter or families or Christmas. The absence of prescribed subjects would likely put off all but the most literate teachers—so Faber's reluctance to even promote *The School Bag* for schools is understandable. Hughes and Heaney, however, not obliged to conform to government restrictions confining literature to the literacy hour, were free to engage in a more eloquent kind of schooling. As Heaney says in the introduction, the anthology is "gathered together on traditional bardic lines, a memory bank, a compendium of examples."[2]

The structure of *The School Bag* takes on a call and response antiphonal relationship. One poem speaks to another, each revealing something about its neighbors—by virtue of its fixed place in the anthology. The only extratextual interpretive clue is in a date, set next to each poem, though there is no hint of a chronological order. Hughes and Heaney used a similar trick, albeit not quite so upfront, to give the appearance of order to *The Rattle Bag.* There the poems are arranged alphabetically by title, providing a semblance of formal structure. But it is a false front. They are really playing the same kind of bardic game, in which secrets are revealed in the arrangement of the poems. *The Rattle Bag* begins, for example, with "Adieu, farewell earth's bliss," by Thomas Nashe, and ends with my favorite pregnant riddle poem, "You're" by Sylvia Plath. As in *The Rattle Bag,* there are secrets in the ending and beginning of *The School Bag.*

In the introduction to *The School Bag,* Seamus Heaney invokes Yeats's definition of poetry as a " 'singing school' . . . made up in the end of all of us who value poetry and want to remember it and make sense of it in our lives" (xvii). The first poem in *The School Bag,* fittingly, is Yeats' "Long-legged Fly." It sounds a warning, especially in its opening plea "that civilization may not sink" (3). The publication date, 1939, printed in the left margin, quietly reminds us to read the poem in the context of the beginning of World War II. The anthology ends with Thomas Hardy's "Afterwards," Emily Dickinson's "Because I could not stop for Death," and finally, an excerpt from John Dryden's *The Secular Masque*, dated 1700. The last quoted lines are, "tis well an old age is out, / And time to begin a new," and a stage instruction for a "dance of huntsmen, nymphs, warriors, and lovers" (561). Dryden, fittingly, was the first poet laureate. Another secret.

Originally, when I gave a version of this paper in Haifa, I read the last poems redemptively, about the death of the old millennium and the birth of the new. In the light of Hughes's death at the end of October 1998, I know there was more. Hughes had apparently known about his cancer for some time. So while the poems still work as birth-of-the-new poems, it is hard not to read a more private story in them. As I read Hardy's lines, I now know that Hughes must have meant them as his own epitaph too. "Afterwards" ends:

> And will any say when my bell of quittance is heard in the gloom,
> And a crossing breeze cuts a pause in its outrollings,
> Till they rise again, as they were a new bell's boom,
> 'He hears it not now, but used to notice such things'? (559)

Hardy's poem opens onto Emily Dickinson, the penultimate poem in the anthology:

> Because I could not stop for Death—
> He kindly stopped for me—
> The Carriage held by just Ourselves—
> And Immortality. (560)

The last poems in *The School Bag* now seem balanced precisely on the brink: between remembering things past—and looking, without flinching, to things future. It is the injunction to remember, which seems significant, as memorable things are endangered in the world of information technology. And so to one of the markers for the age after postmodernism. My guess is that in addition to the idea that schooling is a determining category, there will be a renewed emphasis on the value of memory.

The ability to know poetry by heart has long been out of fashion, but in a technological age, with so much information snowing us under with forgettable words and look-upable facts, there appears to be rising an atavistic desire for something sustaining, something to test all that incoming information against, something worth revisiting. In sensing that desire, I think

Hughes identifies one of the felt but unspoken *fin-de-siècle* anxieties: the tension between access to instant plentiful information (which in the end is empty) and a longing for something memorable. *The School Bag* ends, fittingly, with an essay by Ted Hughes on memorization techniques, the same essay he published in his book of 101 poems to memorize, also published in 1997: *By Heart.*

Hughes's focus on memory appears initially to be against the current grain of contemporary educational theory—with its privileging of information over knowledge. So it looks, overtly, as if it might be hard to argue that *The School Bag* is a cutting-edge book. It also looks like it should be difficult to argue that *The School Bag* could be about a new arts movement—because there aren't any new poems in it. In fact, one of the secrets of the book is that all the poets in the anthology were born before the editors. Hughes was born in 1930, Heaney in 1939, and the youngest poets represented (James K. Baxter, Allen Ginsberg, and Frank O'Hare) were all born in 1926. Heaney alludes to the fact that these are all old poems when he characterizes the anthology as "a homage to poets" who had schooled the editors. Again, I think that it is in the explicit attention to historical tradition that Hughes and Heaney demonstrate their prescience.

Despite the fact that all the poems are old, something in the arrangement prefigures a new poetic sensibility, a new poetic order: partly held in the relations between adults and children, partly held in a revisioning of the medieval landscape. The best demonstration is, I think, in a three-poem sequence with Lewis Carroll's "Jabberwocky" in the middle. "Jabberwocky" is preceded by the burial scene in *Beowulf* and followed by the deadly payback encounter between Gawain and the Green Knight in the terrifying outdoor chapel scene of the Green Knight.

In conventional anthologies for children, "Jabberwocky" makes frequent appearances, but always as a nonsense poem. In the history of children's literature it is a marker for sending up the serious didacticism characteristic of eighteenth-century poetry for children. Hughes and Heaney read it differently. They place "Jabberwocky" in the context of medieval heroic verse. Suddenly the meanings ricochet against one another: high tragedy against low comedy, elegiac diction against nonsense syllables, the rarefied exclusive world of medieval literature against the child's play of Carroll's Alice stories.

In Kevin Crossley-Holland's verse translation, Beowulf is "the kindest, the most gentle, / the most just to his people, the most eager for fame" (484). Although as an undergraduate I believed (as I was told to) that being "eager for fame" was a good thing in the medieval period, I couldn't quite rid myself of the sense that it rang untrue in my ears. Hughes and Heaney acknowledge the dislocation, by setting the serious ballad of Beowulf's epic fame and heroism against the comic ballad, "Jabberwocky." The clash between the two poems is startling.

When I read *The School Bag* for the first time, and began reading "Jabberwocky" fresh from the reading of *Beowulf*, I found myself suddenly awake to the head-cutting scene. As I read the familiar lines:

> *One, two! One, two! And thought and through*
> *The vorpal blade went snicker-snack!*
> *He left it dead, and with its head*
> *He went galumphing back. (484)*

Beowulf took on the appearance of a "beamish boy" carrying the head of Grendl—which looked, in my mind's eye, like the Jabberwock in the Monty Python movie.

Immediately after "Jabberwocky," Hughes and Heaney offer another off-with-his-head medieval text, the debt-collecting scene from the end of *Gawain and the Green Knight*, rendered in Hughes's translation, sharp and darkly lit as a story by Heinrich von Kleist. After the first feint—at which Gawain flinches, and the second, when he doesn't—the Green Knight brings down the axe for a third time:

> *Lightly he lifted the weapon, then let it down deftly*
> *With the barb of the bit by the bare neck,*
> *And though he swung full strength he hardly hurt him,*
> *But snicked him on that side, so the sheer edge*
> *Sliced through skin and fine white fat to the muscle,*
> *Then over his shoulders the bright blood shot to the earth. (490–1)*

It was the "snick" ("snyrt" in the vernacular, from Old Norse) of the sword that got me. Although I know both *Gawain* and "Jabberwocky" intimately, I never connected them. And I'd never connected the sharp, light cut of Carroll's "snicker-snack[ing] sword with the "snick" of the Green Knight's axe—until Hughes made the connection audible.

Both Hughes and Heaney acknowledge their deep affinities with medieval English and Irish verse forms and structures. Heaney's new verse translation of *Beowulf* is forthcoming. Hughes named one of his early collections, *Wodwo*, after an elusive creature who briefly haunts Gawain's dark forest. The affinity both poets have with medieval verse is not secret. In "Englands of the Mind," Heaney writes that Hughes's diction, like that of the Gawain poet, " is consonantal, and it snicks ["Jabberwocky" again]

through the air like an efficient blade, marking and carving out fast definite shapes." Later, in the same essay, Heaney links Hughes's poetry to
the "beautiful alliterating and illuminated form" of *Gawain and the Green
Knight*, and to "the cleaving simplicity of the Border ballad."[3]

Both the ballad tradition and medieval verse are well represented in
The School Bag, forming a backbone for the collection that enables the
editors to emphasize the significance of a favored form without breaking
one of their self-imposed structural rules: that there be only one poem
per poet. Anonymous provides the loophole. Of the 270 poems in the
collection, twenty-four are of Old English, Irish, and Welsh origin, a substantial chunk of the extant canon, and a lot of those are ballads of a kind.

The *Beowulf*, "Jabberwocky," *Gawain* extracts in the sequence from
The School Bag are linked by the ballad tradition of medieval verse. It is
by following the historical trace from medieval verse, through Hughes
and Heaney, that a poetics for an age after postmodernism begins to
emerge, but the critical question remains: how can *The School Bag* mark
something new when all the poems in it are old? The answer is that the
book sets the frames of reference for the new. New poets and new books
consolidate the patterns marked in *The School Bag,* especially in the link
between the medieval ballad form and contemporary verse.

One of the books Bob and I considered for the *Signal* poetry award
provides an especially good example of the shape of the new. *Say That
Again*, an anthology of Welsh poems published in 1997, edited by Mairwen Jones and John Spink, offers exactly the kind of conscious connection
between Welsh ballads and contemporary poetry, as Hughes and Heaney
do in their "bardic" arrangement of the poems in *The School Bag*.

Nigel Jenkins, one of the poets in *Say That Again*, writes in his introduction, that when he first learned Welsh, at twenty-seven, he did so
partly in order to engage in the Welsh poetic tradition: "a tradition in
which the poet is not some isolated crank on the margins of society, but a
'carpenter of song' with an important role to play in the lives of his or her
people."[4] As Hughes and Heaney tune medieval verse to modern ears, so
does Nigel Jenkins in his translation of "The Lady of Lynn y Fan Fach," a
traditional Welsh ballad of love and loss. He tells the story of the fairy
lady of the lake won by a mortal man—on condition that he not strike
her. The third 'strike' in their otherwise happy marriage ends in tragedy:

> Then one day at a funeral
> With laughter she did flute.
> To silence her he brushed her shin
> With his iron fettled boot.

> "Such mirth when all is woe," said he,
> "I cannot comprehend."
> "I laugh," said she, "for when folk die
> Their woes are at an end."
>
> "But your woes have just begun,
> From you I must depart:
> Our marriage contract by this blow
> Is torn, o love, apart." (15)

Jenkins sets this traditional ballad against a modern one, "The Ballad of Cwm Tryweryn," about the building of a dam and the flooding of a village as a pragmatic way of providing water for England. Like the traditional ballad that precedes it, it is a story of loss:

> Not a wall, not a tree did they leave in place,
> Lest memories should linger;
> They even evicted the dead from their graves
> That no bone should point a finger.
>
> As the river rose and flooded the cwm
> Despair swamped the living departed,
> And many a bungalowed, jobless refugee
> Died early, broken hearted. (20–1)

The poignancy and immediacy of the loss is there in the political use Jenkins makes of the ballad form. I was reminded of the way Hughes tracks the ballad tradition through the "revolutionary radicalism" of the Romantic poetry of Coleridge and Wordsworth:

> On the one hand, it is the indigenous form of narrative song, emerging from pure melody as no other poetic form does, and tending, in the most intense and admired specimens, to archetypal themes opening backwards into religious myth. On the other hand, it is the indigenous popular humdrum form of poetic narration, simply a way of telling ordinary though striking tales. Common to both extremes is a uniquely tempered style of plain and direct language. [5]

The "revolutionary radicalism" of "ordinary though striking tales" occurs frequently in *Say that Again*. It was one of the best books Bob and I reviewed for the *Signal* poetry award—though neither of us had heard of any of the poets before (this is probably a consequence of living in Canada and so having limited access to poetry not distributed in our country). There are five Welsh poets in the anthology (Nigel Jenkins, Jenny Sullivan, Iwan Llwyd, John Idres Jones, and Sheenagh Pugh), all apparently writing for children and adults. Each poet noted their Welsh heritage and cited cultural clashes with the English as one of the motivations for their poetry.

With *The School Bag* and *Say That Again* in mind, I found myself thinking about other poets changing the shape of English poetry—and turned at once to the Caribbean British poets I most admire: John Agard, James Berry, David Dabydeen, and Grace Nichols. All are far too young for inclusion in *The School Bag*, but all work out of a tradition to which Hughes and Heaney have been teaching me to attend. Here is poetry historically located in a moment of cultural conflict, and, with its mix of Creole and standard English, akin to medieval diction. David Dabydeen makes the connection clear when he writes about his discovery of medieval verse during his years at Cambridge, his love for the "sheer naked energy and brutality of the language, its 'thew & sinew,'" reminding him of the Creole of his childhood.[6] His words brought to mind Heaney speaking about Hughes's language: "His consonants are the Norsemen, the Normans, the Roundheads in the world of his vocables, hacking and hedging and hammering down the abundance and luxury and possible lasciviousness of the vowels." The example Heaney gives, is from "The Thought Fox," a very early famous poem by Ted Hughes: "I iMagine this MidnighT MoMent's foresT," a graphic rendering of the battle between the vowels and the consonants (154). Dabydeen notes the same mix of "lyrical and barbaric" in Creole (5). He says that "it's hard to put two words together in Creole without swearing. Words are spat out from the mouth like live squibs. . . . " (3). But the real link comes as Dabydeen outlines the Creole/standard English conflict as being analogous to the situation in medieval England:

> I began to see, albeit naively, the ancient divide between north and south in Britain, the Gawain poet standing in opposition to Chaucer in terms of a native idiom versus an educated, relaxed poetic line tending towards the form of the iambic pentameter. The north/south divide is of course evocative of the divide between the so-called Caribbean periphery and the metropolitan center of London. London is supposed to provide the models of standard English, and we in the Caribbean our dialect versions. (4)

Here is language characterized in a way not at all like the early modernist abstraction of Gertrude Stein or the postmodernist poetry of Canadian bill bisset's evocations of native chants. Modernist poets and artists were looking for something below the level where differences appear, for something natural and elemental, universal, something inspired by their perceptions of primitives (as the term was used in modernist tradition) and children.

A body of literature about the use of the primitive in the modernist period already exists, though the focus is on art rather than poetry. I had read some of it through the late 1980s and early 1990s and found myself returning often to *The Predicament of Culture* by James Clifford, *Primitive Art in Civilized Places* by Sally Price, *Gone Primitive* by Marianna Torgovnick, and *Imperial Eyes* by Mary Louise Pratt. But the relationship between the modernist artist and children's art has not been so well documented. Jonathan Fineberg's *The Innocent Eye,* is the only dedicated account I read. But the point made in all of the critical books is remarkably consistent: the 'primitive' and the child were not individualized, they were valued for representing something universal, for being sources of inspiration. Modernist artists and poets preferred abstraction (as in primitive masks and children's drawings) and repetition (as in ritual chants and children's games). Great European artists of the period were named and rewarded, in money and fame for their originality—though not always in their own time. Primitive artists and children were left out of the record, except as generic sources of inspiration. The traces of this aesthetic are present, or course, and so familiar they are unnoticeable: a child's drawing taped to a refrigerator is of little value, a Kandinsky painting in a museum (utilizing elements of child art) is worth a lot of money. Child art and primitive art were regarded as belonging to a timeless, ahistorical space, valuable because they were free from the taint of Western, European civilization. Picasso, Kandinsky, and others owned collections of primitive art and art by children.

What's changed in this age after postmodernism is that the primitive and the child are writing and talking back. The shift is visible if I set a modernist poet like Gertrude Stein—who wrote for adults and children—against a contemporary Caribbean-British poet, Grace Nichols, who also writes for both adults and children. I've traced the shift from "play" to "plai":

Stein uses timelessness, a progression through variation to render play:

> Some play every day, play all day, play every day and all day, play all day every day. Some play and play and play and play all day and play every day.

> Some play and remember what they play and ask to play that again
> the next day and they play it again the next day and play it all day and
> play and play.
> Some play every day. Some play all day. Some play to-day. Some
> play and play. Some play and play and play. Some play every day and
> all day. Some play away. Some play and play and play.[7]

The preference for abstraction, for modulating repetitions, was characteristic of modernism in the 1920s and 1930s. Stein, as American, lesbian,
an outsider, broke out of inscribed narrative order—and into something
not dependent on linearity, something akin to a playground chant. I was
reminded of the description of singing games (of the kind played especially by girls) given by Iona and Peter Opie: "games that are rhythmic
and repetitive, formal and enigmatic. . . . the stranger the words are the
greater the liberation into fantasy."[8]

Stein, like her famous friend Picasso, was interested in tapping into
something elemental, something below cultural difference. It is as if their
desire for child's play, a circling of an idea would serve to buttress them
against the violence of war around them. Stein talks about children and
poetry, as she produced it during the dark days of World War II:

> Somehow or other in war time the only thing that is spontaneously po-
> etic is children. Children themselves are poetry. The poetry of adults in
> wartime is too intentional. It is too much mixed up with everything
> else. My poetry was children's poetry, and most of it is very good, and
> some of it is as good as anything I have ever done.[9]

Stein's use of children is typical. These are abstract, universal children,
without voices of their own. The new movement, not caught in global war
has a different response: one that looks to an acknowledgement of the historical conditions that produced it. Children—and people who used to be
called, generically, primitives talk back. Here is "The Fastest Belt in
Town" from *Come On Into My Tropical Garden* by Grace Nichols*:

> *Ma Bella was the fastest belt in town*
> *Ma Bella was the fastest belt*
> *for miles and miles around*

---

* Reproduced with permission of Curtis Brown Ltd., London, on behalf of Grace
Nichols. Copyright Grace Nichols 1988.

In fact Ma Bella was the fastest belt
both in the East and in the West
nobody dared to put Ma Bella to the test

plai-plai
her belt would fly
who don't hear must cry

Milk on the floor
and ma Bella reaching for—de belt

Slamming the door
and Ma Bella reaching for—de belt

Scribbling on the wall
and Ma Bella reaching for—de belt

Too much back-chat
and yes, Ma Bella reaching for—de belt

. . . .

Until one day
Ma Bella swished
missed
and lashed her own leg

That was the day Ma Bella got such a welt
That was the day Ma Bella knew exactly how it felt
That was the day ma Bella decided to hang up her belt.[10]

"Plai-plai" is Creole, defined by *The Dictionary of Caribbean English* as an "echoic" term, "representing the sharpness of a lash or a slap."[11] Stein's repetitions of "play" resonate with an idea of childhood as an endless drifting of time. For Nichols, "plai-plai" is a sharp slap, a wake-up call. And she uses it to turn the tables on the previously unexamined rights of adults to punish children.

"The Fastest Belt in Town" marks a shift from the kind of poetry for children, which, all too often at the end of the twentieth century, still tends to be didactic, elegiac, or cute—despite Lewis Carroll's nineteenth-century subversions. Moral lessons about obedience and good behavior are still present in spades. Even though "The Fastest Belt in Town" still probably belongs to the genre of moral poetry for children in the style of, say, *Struwwelpeter*, the message has changed. It is a talking back poem—to paraphrase *The Empire Writes Back,* the title of a book on postcolonial discourse (which takes its cue from a line by Salman Rushdie). Creole is a talking back language, especially when used to reinvent standard English. Nichols explains the process:

> I like working in both standard English and Creole. I tend to want to fuse the two tongues because I come from a background where the two worlds, Creole and standard English, were constantly interacting, though Creole was regarded, obviously, as the inferior by the colonial powers when I was growing up and still has a social stigma attached to it in the Caribbean.
>
> I think this is one of the main reasons why so many Caribbean poets, including myself, are now reclaiming our language heritage and exploring it. It is an act of spiritual survival on our part, the need (whether conscious or unconscious) to preserve something that is important to us. It is a language that our foremothers and forefathers struggled to create and we are saying that it is a valid, vibrant language. We are no longer going to treat it with contempt or allow it to be misplaced.[12]

Creole defies the modernist notion of a search for the elemental, the primitive, the universal, and values instead history, the mix of colloquial and formal, values the source as well as the artistic rendering.

With Grace Nichols, I've bumped onto the shore of the new world. The journey is over. I'm here, but only beginning to understand what I've found. My initial, crude, evaluation of the features of this new landscape look like this. It is historically located in a cultural clash—as evidenced by clash between standard English and Creole, and backward, through the clash between the northern and southern English of the medieval period. That shifts the new movement from the collage or bricolage of the modernist/postmodernist period into something that acknowledges the power imbalances implicit in those histories. Related to that is the reconfiguration of the place of the primitive and the child. In the modernist/postmodernist phase it was something to do with being elemental, outside of the loop of the destructive influences of civilization. But that rendered the primitive and the child voiceless, as simply raw materials for use by artists. In the new movement, we see what Mary Louise Pratt calls "trans-culturation," the primitive and the child talk back. That's why Grace Nichols offers such a compelling voice, one right for our time.

   In the work of Ted Hughes, the reconfiguration of the primitive and the child is different. It is manifest in the easy slip in Hughes's work be-tween the pieces intended for children and those for adults. It is in the joke that *The School Bag* is not for children. It is in the shift in emphasis from "child" as a defining category to "schooling." The shift is toward a mem-ory schooled enough to remember dislocation rather than ignore it. And I think that in the contemporary idiom, there is a preference for the narra-tive. This is not a time for fragments or abstractions but for ballads, for memorable forms of verse, something to stand against the age of forget-fulness, of information overload. Maybe this is the age of remembering.

NOTES

1. Ted Hughes, "Foreword" to *Children as Writers 2* (London: Heinemann, 1975): iii.
2. Seamus Heaney and Ted Hughes, *The School Bag* (London: Faber, 1997): xvii.
3. Seamus Heaney, "England of the Mind," in *Preoccupations: Selected Prose 1968–78* (London: Faber, 1980), 153, 156.
4. Nigel Jenkins, *Say That Again* (Wales: Poet, 1997), 5.
5. Ted Hughes, "Myths and Metres," in *Winter Pollen: Occasional Prose*, ed. William Scammell (London: Faber, 1994), 322.
6. David Dabydeen, "On Not Being Milton: Nigger Talk in England Today," in *The State of the Language*, ed. Christopher Ricks and Leonard Michaels (Lon-don: Faber, 1990), 4.
7. Gertrude Stein, "Play," in *Portraits and Prayers* (New York: Random House, 1934). Quoted in "Gertrude Stein (1874–1946)," introduced and ed. Mar-ianne DeKoven, in *The Gender of Modernism*, ed. Bonnie Kime Scott (Bloom-ington: Indiana University Press, 1990), 525.
8. Iona Opie and Peter Opie, *The Singing Game* (Oxford: Oxford University Press, 1988), 26.
9. Scott, *The Gender of Modernism*, 508.
10. Grace Nichols, *Come On Into My Tropical Garden* (London: Young Lions, 1993), 28–29.
11. *Dictionary of Caribbean English*, s.v. "plai-plai."
12. Grace Nichols, "The Battle With Language," in *Caribbean Women Writ-ers: Essays From the First International Conference*, ed. C. J. Cudjoe (Wellesley: Calaloux, 1990), 284.

REFERENCES

Clifford, James. *The Predicament of Culture: Twentieth Century Ethnography, Literature and Art.* Cambridge, Mass.: Harvard University Press, 1988.

Dabydeen, David. "On Not Being Milton: Nigger Talk in England Today." *In The State of the Language,* ed. Christopher Ricks and Leonard Michaels, 3–14. London: Faber, 1990.

Fineberg, Jonathan. *The Innocent Eye: Children's Art and the Modern Artist.* Princeton: Princeton University Press, 1997.

Harvey, David. *The Condition of Postmodernity: An Inquiry into the Origins of Cultural Change.* Oxford: Blackwell, 1990.

Heaney, Seamus. "Englands of the Mind." In *Preoccupations: Selected Prose 1968–78,* 150–69. London: Faber, 1980.

Heaney, Seamus and Ted Hughes, eds. *The Rattle Bag.* London: Faber, 1982.

———. *The School Bag.* London: Faber, 1997.

Hughes, Ted. *Winter Pollen: Occasional Prose.* Ed. William Scammell. London: Faber, 1994.

———. "Foreword" to *Children as Writers* 2. London: Heinemann, 1975.

Hulme, Peter. *Colonial Encounters: Europe and the Native Caribbean 1492–1797.* London: Methuen, 1986.

Jones, Mairwen and Spink, John, eds. *Say That Again.* Illus. Suzanne Carpenter. Llandysul: Pont, 1997.

McGough, Roger. *Bad, Bad Cats.* Illus. Lydia Monks. London: Puffin, 1997.

Nichols, Grace. *Come on into My Tropical Garden.* London: Young Lions, 1993. Original edition, London: A & C Black, 1988.

———. "The Battle With Language." In *Caribbean Women Writers: Essays from the First International Conference,* ed. C. J. Cudjoe, 283–289. Wellesley: Calaloux, 1990.

Opie, Iona and Opie, Peter. *The Singing Game.* Oxford: Oxford University Press, 1988.

Pratt, Mary Louise. *Imperial Eyes: Travel Writing and Transculturation.* London: Routledge, 1992.

Stein, Gertrude. "Play." *In Portraits and Prayers.* New York: Random House, 1934. Quoted in "Gertrude Stein (1874–1946)," introduced and ed. Marianne DeKoven, in *The Gender of Modernism: A Critical Anthology,* ed. Bonnie Kime Scott. Bloomington: Indiana University Press, 1990.

Torgovnick, Marianna. *Gone Primitive: Savage Intellects, Modern Lives.* Chicago: University of Chicago Press, 1990.

Selected Bibliography

PRIMARY SOURCES

Aymé, Marcel. *Les Contes du chat perché*. Paris: Gallimard, 1939.

———. *Les bottes de sept lieues et autres nouvelles*. Folio Junior. Paris: Gallimard, 1988.

Berna, Paul. *Le cheval sans tête*. Paris: Éditions G. P. 1955.

Bosco, Henri. *L'Âne Culotte*. Paris: Gallimard, 1937.

———. *L'Âne Culotte*. Paris: Club des Jeunes Amis du Livre, 1956.

———. *L'Âne Culotte*. Folio Junior. Paris: Gallimard, 1983.

———. *L'enfant et la rivière*. Illus. E. Jalabert-Edon. Algiers and Paris: Charlot, 1945.

———. *The Boy and the River*. Trans. Gerard Hopkins. New York: Pantheon Books, 1956.

———. *The Fox in the Island*. 1956. Trans. Gerard Hopkins. London: Oxford University Press, 1958.

———. *Bargabot* [followed by] *Pascalet*. Paris: Gallimard, 1958.

———. *Barboche*. 1957. London: Oxford University Press, 1959.

Browne, Anthony. *Willy's Dream*. Cambridge, Mass.: Candlewick Press, 1998.

Bürger, Gottfried August: *Wunderbare Reisen zu Wasser und Lande, Feldzüge und lustige Abentheuer des Freyherrn von Münchhausen*. Göttingen: Dieterich, 1786.

Burne, Philippa. *Fishnets*. St. Leonards, N.S.W.: Allen & Unwin, 1997.

Calvino, Italo. *Il barone rampante*. Turin: Einaudi 1957.

———. "Nove domande sul romanzo." *Nuovi Argomenti* 38–39 (1959): 7–12.

———. *Marcovaldo ovvero le stagioni in città*. Turin: Einaudi, 1966.

_____. *Our Ancestors*. Trans. A. Colquhoun. London: Picador-Pan Books, 1980.

_____. *Una pietra sopra*. Turin: Einaudi, 1980.

_____. *Italian Folktales*. Trans. G. Martin. Harmondsworth: Penguin, 1982.

_____. *Time and the Hunter*. Trans. W. Weaver. Reading: Abacus-Sphere Books, 1983.

_____. *The Literature Machine: Essays*. Trans. P. Creagh. London: Secker & Warburg, 1987.

_____. *Six Memos for the next Millennium*. Trans. P. Creagh. Cambridge: Harvard University Press, 1988.

Carroll, Lewis. *Alice's Adventures in Wonderland*. New York: MacMillan, 1968 [1865].

_____. *Alice's Adventures Underground*. New York: Dover, 1965 [1886].

_____. *The Nursery Alice*. New York: Dover, 1966 [1890].

Cervantes Saavedra, Miguel de. *El ingenioso hidalgo Don Quixote de la Mancha*. Madrid: Lumen, 1986.

Chukovskii, Kornei. *Masterstvo Nekrasova*. Tom 4. *Sobranie sochinenii v shesti tomakh*. Moskva: Khudozhestvennaia literatura, 1966.

_____. *Ot dvukh do piati*. Tom 1. *Sobranie sochinenii v shesti tomakh*. Moskva: Khudozhestvennaia literatura, 1966. 333–725.

_____. *Skazki*. Moskva: Detskaia Literatura, 1993.

Clark, Margaret. *Care Factor Zero*. Sydney: Random House, 1997.

Collodi, Carlo. *I racconti delle Fiabe*. Milan: Adelphi, 1976.

_____. *Le avventure di Pinocchio*. Ed. Ornella Castellani Pollidori. Pescia: Fondazione Nazionale Carlo Collodi, 1983.

Feelings, Tom. *The Middle Passage: White Ships/Black Cargo*. Introduction by John Henrik Clarke. New York: Dial Books, 1995.

Dantz, Carl. *Peter Stoll: Ein Kinderleben*. Berlin: Verlag J.H.W. Dietz, 1925.

De la Mare, Walter: *The Three Mullah-mulgars*. London: Duckworth 1910.

_____. *Peacock Pie*. London: Constable 1913.

Dominik, Hans. *John Workman, der Zeitungsboy*. Leipzig: Koehler & Amelang, 1909.

Durian, Wolf. *Kai aus der Kiste*. Berlin: Franz Schneider, 1927.

Gaarder. Jostein. *Sophie's World: A Novel About the History of Philosophy*. New York: Farrar, Straus, & Giroux, 1994.

Giono, Jean. *Le petit garçon qui avait envie d'espace*. In *Les jolis contes N.P.C.K.* Vol. 6. Vevey (Switzerland): Société des Produits Nestlé S.A., 1949.

_____. *Le petit garçon qui avait envie d'espace*. Illus. Gilbert Raffin. Enfantimages. Paris: Gallimard, 1978.

_____. *L'Homme qui plantait des arbres*. Paris: Gallimard, 1983.

Harris, Joel Chandler. *Uncle Remus: His Songs and His Sayings*. 1880. Ed. Robert Hemenway. New York and London: Penguin Books, 1982.

Hartnett, Sonya. *Wilful Blue*. Ringwood, Vic.: Viking, 1994.

———. *Sleeping Dogs*. Ringwood, Vic.: Viking, 1995.

———. *Black Foxes*. Ringwood, Vic.: Viking, 1996.

Haugen, Tormod. *Skriket fra jungelen*. Oslo: Gyldendal, 1989.

Heaney, Seamus. "Englands of the Mind." In *Preoccupations: Selected Prose 1968–78*, 150–69. London: Faber, 1980.

Heaney, Seamus and Ted Hughes, eds. *The Rattle Bag*. London: Faber, 1982.

———. *The School Bag*. London: Faber, 1997.

Hellsing, Lennart. *The Pirate Book*. Trans. William Jay Smith. London: Ernest Benn Limited, 1972.

———. *Daniel Doppsko*. Helsingfors: Holger Schildts förlags AB, 1959.

Høeg, Peter. *Miss Smilla's Feeling for Snow*. Trans. F. David. New York: Farrar, Straus & Giroux, 1993.

Hughes, Ted. *Winter Pollen: Occasional Prose*. Ed. William Scammell. London: Faber, 1994.

———. "Foreword" to *Children as Writers 2*. London: Heinemann, 1975.

Jacobs, Harriet. *Incidents in the Life of a Slave Girl, Written by Herself*. Ed. L. M. Child, 1861. Reprint ed. Jean Fagan Yellin. Cambridge, Mass.: Harvard University Press, 1987.

Jannes, Elly. "Krakel Spektakel i Äppelviken." Interview with Lennert Hellsing. *VI-tidningen* (1956): 50–51.

Jinks, Catherine. *This Way Out*. Norwood: Omnibus Books, 1991.

———. *Pagan's Crusade*. Melbourne: Oxford University Press, 1992.

———. *The Future Trap*. Norwood: Omnibus Books, 1993.

———. *Pagan's Scribe*. Norwood: Omnibus Books, 1996.

———. *Eye to Eye*. Ringwood, Vic.: Puffin Books, 1997.

———. *Little White Secrets*. Ringwood, Vic.: Penguin Books, 1997.

Jones, Mairwen and Spink, John, eds. *Say That Again*. Illus. Suzanne Carpenter. Llandysul: Pont, 1997.

Kästner, Erich. *Pünktchen und Anton*. Berlin: Williams & Co., 1931.

———. *Das fliegende Klassenzimmer*. Stuttgart: Perthes 1933.

———. *Der 35. Mai oder Konrad reitet in die Südsee*. Berlin: Williams & Co., 1933.

———. *Emil and the Detectives*. Trans. Eileen Hall. London: Jonathan Cape, 1959.

———. *Fabian: Geschichte eines Moralisten*. In *Erich Kästner: Gesammelte Schriften*. vol. 2. Köln: Kiepenheuer & Witsch, 1959.

———. "Jugend, Literatur und Jugendliteratur." In *Erich Kästner: Gesammelte Schriften*. vol. 7. 216–223. Köln: Kiepenheuer & Witsch, 1959.

———. *Emil und die Detektive*. Hamburg: Dressler, 1970.

Kennedy, John Pendleton. *Swallow Barn, or A Sojourn in the Old Dominion*. Ed. Jay B. Hubbel. 1832. New York: Harcourt Brace, 1929.

Keulen, Mensje van. *Bleekers zomer*. Amsterdam: Thomas Rap, 1972.

———. *Overspel*. Amsterdam: De Arbeiderspers, 1982.

———. *Tommie Station*. Amsterdam: Querido, 1986.

———. *De rode strik*. Amsterdam: Atlas, 1994.

———. *Pas op voor Bez*. Amsterdam: Querido, 1996.

———. *Olifanten op een web*. Amsterdam: Atlas, 1997.

Kharms, Daniil. Druskin Fund. Archive Department of the Saltykov-Shchedrin Library, St. Petersburg.

———. *Letiat po Nebu Shariki*. Ed. A. A. Aleksandrov and N. M. Kavin. Krasnoiarsk: Krasnoiarskoe Knizhnoe Izdatel'stvo, 1990.

Lanagan, Margo. *Touching Earth Lightly*. St. Leonards, N.S.W.: Allen & Unwin, 1996.

Langer, Frantisek: *Bileho Klice*. Prague: Artia 1934.

Le Clézio, J. M. G. *Le Procès-verbal*. Paris: Gallimard, 1963.

———. *Mondo et autres histoires*. Paris: Gallimard, 1978.

———. *Désert*. Paris: Gallimard, 1980.

———. *Lullaby*. Folio Junior. Paris: Gallimard, 1980.

———. *Balaabilou*. Paris: Gallimard, 1985.

———. *Celui qui n'avait jamais vu la mer*. Folio Junior. Paris: Gallimard, 1988.

———. *La grande vie* [followed by] *Peuple du ciel*. Folio Junior. Paris: Gallimard, 1990.

———. *Villa Aurore*. Folio Junior. Paris: Gallimard, 1990.

———. *Voyage au pays des arbres*. Folio Cadet Rouge. Paris: Gallimard, 1990.

———. *Peuple du ciel*. Paris: Gallimard, 1991.

———. *Pawana*. Paris: Gallimard, 1992.

———. *Pawana*. Lecture Junior. Paris: Gallimard, 1995.

Leitner, Isabella. *Fragments of Isabella: A Memoir of Auschwitz*. Ed. and with an epilogue by Irving A. Leitner. New York: Thomas Y. Crowell, 1978.

———. "*Lager* Language," in *Fragments of Isabella: A Memoir of Auschwitz*, ed. and with an epilogue by Irving A. Leitner, 122–128. New York: Laurel/Dell, 1983.

Leitner, Isabella with Irving A. Leitner. *The Big Lie: A True Story*. Illus. Judy Pedersen. New York: Scholastic, 1992.

———. *Isabella: From Auschwitz to Freedom*. New York: Anchor Books/Doubleday, 1994.

———. *Saving the Fragments: From Auschwitz to New York*. Introduction by Howard Fast. New York: New American Library, 1985.

Lester, Julius. *To Be a Slave*. Illus. Tom Feelings. New York: Scholastic, 1968.

———. *The Tales of Uncle Remus: The Adventures of Brer Rabbit.* New York: Dial Books, 1987.

———. *More Tales of Uncle Remus: Further Adventures of Brer Rabbit, His Friends, Enemies and Others.* New York: Dial Books, 1988.

———. *Further Tales of Uncle Remus: The Misadventures of Brer Rabbit, Brer Fox, Brer Wolf, the Doodang, and Other Creatures.* Illus. Jerry Pinkney. New York: Dial Books, 1990.

———. *The Last Tales of Uncle Remus.* New York: Dial Books, 1994.

Lindgren, Astrid. *Mästerdetektiven Blomkvist.* Stockholm: Rabén & Sjögren, 1946.

Marsden, John. *Dear Miffy.* Sydney: Macmillan, 1997.

Marshak, Samuil. *Vot kakoi rasseiannyi: Khudozhnik V. Konashevich delaet knigu.* Moskva: Sovetskii Khudozhnik, 1988.

Matthiessen, Wilhelm. *Das Rote U.* Köln: Hermann Schaffstein Verlag, 1932.

McGough, Roger. *Bad, Bad Cats.* Illus. Lydia Monks. London: Puffin, 1997.

Milne, A. A. *När vi var mycket små.* Trans. Lennart Hellsing and Claes Hoogland. Stockholm: Kooperativa Förbundets förlag, 1945.

Mitchell, Lucy Sprague. *Here and Now Story Book.* New York: E.P. Dutton and Company, 1921.

Nichols, Grace. *Come on into My Tropical Garden.* London: Young Lions, 1993. Original edition, London: A & C Black, 1988.

Nygren, Tord. *The Red Thread.* New York: R & S Books; Farrar Strauss and Giroux, 1988.

Opie, Iona and Opie, Peter. *The Singing Game.* Oxford: Oxford University Press, 1988.

Orr, Wendy. *Peeling the Onion.* St. Leonards, N.S.W.: Allen & Unwin, 1996.

Pohl, Peter. *Janne, min vän.* Stockholm: AWG, 1985.

Prévert, Jacques. *Contes pour enfants pas sages.* Paris: Gallimard, 1977.

———. *Words for All Seasons.* Trans. Teo Savory. Greensboro, N.C.: Unicorn Press, 1980.

Potter, Beatrix. *The Tale of Peter Rabbit.* 1902. London: Frederick Warne, 1987.

Pullman, Philip. *Northern Lights.* London: Scholastic, 1995 (published in the United States as *The Golden Compass*).

———. *The Subtle Knife.* London: Scholastic, 1997.

Řezač, Václav. *Kluci, hurá za nim!* Prague:Artia 1964.

Rockwell, Anne. *The Three Bears & 15 Other Stories.* New York: Thomas Y. Crowell, 1975.

Saint-Exupéry, Antoine de. *The Little Prince.* San Diego: Harcourt Brace Jovanovich, 1971.

Sandburg, Carl. *Complete Poems.* New York: Harcourt, Brace and Company, 1950.

————. *Rootabaga Stories*. New York: Harcourt, Brace and Company, 1922.

————. *Early Moon*. New York: Harcourt, Brace and Company, 1948.

Scieszka, Jon and Lane Smith. *The Stinky Cheese Man and Other Fairly Stupid Tales*. New York: Viking, 1992.

Sendak, Maurice. *Higglety Pigglety Pop!*. New York: Harper & Row, 1967.

————. *We Are All in the Dumps with Jack and Guy*. Harper Collins: New York, 1993.

Silverstein, Shel. *The Giving Tree*. New York: Harper & Row, 1964.

Stein, Gertrude. "Play." In *Portraits and Prayers*. New York: Random House, 1934. Quoted in "Gertrude Stein (1874–1946)," introduced and ed. Marianne DeKoven, in *The Gender of Modernism: A Critical Anthology*, ed. Bonnie Kime Scott. Bloomington: Indiana University Press, 1990.

Streatfeild, Noel. *Ballet Shoes*. London: Dent, 1936.

Thompson, Colin. *Looking for Atlantis*. New York: Alfred A. Knopf, 1993.

Tournier, Michel. *Vendredi ou les limbes du Pacifique*. Paris: Gallimard, 1967.

————. *Friday*. Trans. Norman Denny. Garden City, N.Y.: Doubleday, 1969.

————. *Friday and Robinson: Life on Speranza Island*. Trans. Ralph Manheim. New York: Alfred A. Knopf, 1971.

————. *Vendredi ou la vie sauvage*. Paris: Gallimard, 1977.

————. *Le vent Paraclet*. Paris, Gallimard: 1977.

————. *Le coq de bruyère*. Paris: Gallimard, 1978.

————. *La fugue du Petit Poucet*. Paris: Éditions G. P., 1979.

————. *Gaspard, Melchior et Balthazar*. Paris: Gallimard, 1980.

————. *Barbedor*. Enfantimages. Paris: Gallimard, 1980.

————. *Les Rois Mages*. Folio Junior. Paris: Gallimard, 1983.

————. *Sept contes*. Folio Junior. Paris: Gallimard, 1984.

————. "Pierrot, or The Secrets of the Night." Trans. Margaret Higonnet. *Children's Literature* 13 (1985): 169–172.

————. *The Golden Droplet*. Trans. Barbara Wright. New York: Doubleday, 1987.

————. *Angus*. Paris: Signe de Piste Éditions, 1988.

————. *The Wind Spirit: An Autobiography*. Trans. Arthur Goldhammer. Boston: Beacon Press, 1988.

————. *Les contes du médianoche*. Folio Junior. Paris: Gallimard, 1989.

————. *The Midnight Love Feast*. Trans. Barbara Wright. 1989. London: Collins, 1991.

————. *La couleuvrine*. Lecture Junior. Paris: Gallimard, 1994.

————. *Le miroir à deux faces*. Paris: Seuil Jeunesse, 1994.

————. *Éléazar ou la source et le buisson*. Paris: Gallimard, 1996.

Vegter, Anne. *Verse Bekken!* (Fresh faces!). Amsterdam: Querido, 1991.

Weidenmann, Alfred. *Gepäckschein 666.* Bayreuth: Loewes, 1959.

White, T(erence) H(anbury). *The Once and Future King.* New York: Putnam, 1958.

————. *The Sword in the Stone.* New York: Putnam, 1963.

Winton, Tim. *Lockie Leonard, Human Torpedo.* Ringwood, Vic.: McPhee Gribble, 1990.

————. *Cloudstreet.* Ringwood, Vic.: Penguin Books, 1991.

————. *The Riders.* Sydney: Macmillan, 1994.

————. *Lockie Leonard, Legend.* Sydney: Macmillan, 1997.

Yourcenar, Marguerite. *Notre-Dame des Hirondelles.* Illus. Georges Lemoine. Enfantimages. Paris: Gallimard, 1963.

————. *Comment Wang-Fô fut sauvé.* Illus. Georges Lemoine. Folio Cadet Rouge. Paris: Gallimard, 1990.

Zoshchenko, Mikhail. *Twelve Stories.* Selected and annotated by L. La Rocco and S. Paperno. Columbus, Ohio: Slavica, 1989.

SECONDARY SOURCES

Abrams, Meyer Howard. *The Mirror and the Lamp: Romantic Theory and the Critical Tradition.* 1953. London: Oxford University Press, 1979.

Adamson, Joe. *Tex Avery: King of Cartoons.* New York: Da Capo Press, 1975.

Aleksin, Anatolii. Foreword. "Daniil Kharms: stikhotvoreniia." *Detskaia Literatura* 4 (1989): 73. Allsobrook, Marian. "Major Authors' Work for Children." In *International Companion Encyclopedia of Children's Literature,* ed. Peter Hunt and Sheila Ray, 691–709. London: Routledge, 1996.

Andrews, William L. Introduction to *Six Women's Slave Narratives,* ed. Henry Louis Gates, Jr., xxix–xli. New York: Oxford University Press, 1988.

Apseloff, Marilyn Faine. "Children's Books by Famous Writers for Adults," *Children's Literature* 2 (1973): 130.

————. *They Wrote for Children Too: An Annotated Bibliography of Children's Literature by Famous Writers for Adults.* Westport, Conn.: Greenwood Press, 1989.

Ariès, Philippe. *Centuries of Childhood.* London: Jonathan Cape, 1962.

Aubarède, Gabriel d'. "Écrire pour les enfants." *Les Nouvelles littéraires* 22 March 1956: 4.

Bakhtin, Mikhail. *The Dialogic Imagination.* Trans. Caryl Emerson and Michael Hoquist. Austin: University of Texas Press, 1981.

————. *Rabelais and His World.* Trans. Helene Iswolsky. Bloomington: Indiana University Press, 1984.

————. *Problems of Dostoyevsky's Poetics.* Minneapolis: University of Minnesota Press, 1984.

Beckett, Sandra. Unpublished interview with Michel Tournier, 7 July 1995.

——. "From the Art of Rewriting to the Art of Crosswriting Child and Adult: the Secret of Michel Tournier's Dual Readership." In *Voices from Far Away: Current Trends in International Children's Literature Research* 24, ed. Maria Nikolajeva, 9–34. Stockholm: Centrum för barnkulturforskning, 1995.

——. "Entretien avec Michel Tournier." *Dalhousie French Studies* 35 (Summer 1996): 66–78.

——. "The Meeting of Two Worlds: Michel Tournier's *Friday and Robinson: Life on Speranza Island*." In vol. 2 of *Other Worlds, Other Lives: Children's Literature Experiences*, ed. Myrna Machet, Sandra Olën, and Thomas van der Walt, 110–127. Pretoria: Unisa Press, 1996.

——. "Crosswriting Child and Adult: Henri Bosco's *L'Enfant et la rivière*." *Children's Literature Association Quarterly* 21, no. 4 (Winter 1996–97): 189–198.

——. *De grands romanciers écrivent pour les enfants*. Montréal: PUM; Grenoble: ELLUG, 1997.

——. "Adresato dvejinimas dabartineje prancuzi literaturoje" (Contemporary French children's books). *Rubinaitis* (Vilnius) 2, no. 7 (1997): 13–18.

——. "Amandine through the Looking Glass: Michel Tournier's 'Initiatory Tale' for Children," *Bookbird* 35, no. 2 (Summer 1997): 12–15.

——. "La Réécriture pour enfants de *Comment Wang-Fô fut sauvé*." In *Lectures transversales de Marguerite Yourcenar*, ed. Rémy Poignault and Blanca Arancibia, 173–185. Tours: Société Internationale d'Études Yourcenariennes, 1997.

——. "Crossing the Borders: The 'Children's Books' of Michel Tournier and Jean-Marie Gustave Le Clézio." *The Lion and the Unicorn* 22, no. 1 (January 1998): 44–69.

——, ed. *Reflections of Change: Children's Literature Since 1945*. Westport, Conn.: Greenwood, 1997.

——. *Modernismen i barnkammaren: Barnlitteraturens 40-tal*. Stockholm: Rabén & Sjögren, forthcoming.

Bekkering, Harry. "Oktober 1955. De Gouden Griffel voor de eerste maal uitgereikt—De emancipatie van de kinder-en jeugdliteratuur." (October 1955: The Golden Slate Pencil Awarded for the First Time—The Emancipation of Children's Literature). In *Nederlandse Literatuur een Geschiedenis* (Dutch literature, a history), ed. M. A. Schenkeveld-Van der Dussen et al., 743–751. Groningen: Martinus Nijhoff, 1993.

"Bibliothèque blanche." *Bulletin de la NRF* 75 (November 1953): 16.

"La Bibliothèque blanche." *Bulletin de la NRF* [1966].

Bickley, Jr. and R. Bruce, ed. *Critical Essays on Joel Chandler Harris*. Boston: G. K. Hall, 1981.

Blium, Arlen. "Kak bylo razrusheno 'ministerstvo pravdy': sovetskaia tsenzura epokhi glasnosti i perestroiki (1985–1991)." *Zvezda* 6 (1996): 212–221.

Blassingame, John W. *The Slave Community; Plantation Life in the Antebellum South.* New York and Oxford: Oxford University Press, 1979.

Bloom, Harold. *Anxiety of Influence.* London, Oxford, and New York: Oxford University Press, 1973.

Bode, Andreas. "Humor in the Lyrical Stories for Children of Samuel Marshak and Kornei Chukovskii." *The Lion and the Unicorn* 13, no. 2 (1989): 34–55.

Boero, P. and C. De Luca. *La letteratura per l'infanzia.* Rome-Bari: Edizioni Laterza, 1995.

Booker, M. Keith and Dubravka Juraga. *Bakhtin, Stalin, and Modern Russian Fiction.* Contributions to the Study of World Literature, no. 58. Westport, Conn.: Greenwood Press, 1995.

Boonstra, Bregje. "Er was eens een waseens"(Once upon a time there was a once-upon-a-time). In *Het Literaire Klimaat 1986–1992* (The literary climate, 1986–1992), ed. Nicolaas Matsier et al., 125–154. Amsterdam: De Bezige Bij, 1992.

Bosco, Henri. Letter to Armand Guibert, 11 July 1945.

———. "Les enfants m'ont dicté les livres que j'ai écrits pour eux." *Les Nouvelles littéraires* 4 December 1958: 4.

———. Letter to Henri Ehret, 27 July 1963, in "Henri Bosco voyageur. Le séjour en Grèce (juin–juillet 1963)." Critical edition by Claude Girault, *Cahiers Henri Bosco* 21 (1981): 28–29.

Bourdieu, Pierre. *The Field of Cultural Production.* Edited and introduced by Randal Johnson. New York: Columbia University Press, 1993.

Breen, Else. *Slik skrev de. Verdi og virkelighet i barneböker 1968–1983.* Oslo: Aschehoug, 1988.

Briggs, Julia. "E. Nesbit, the Bastables, and The Red House: A Response." *Children's Literature* 25 (1997): 71–85.

Brown, Deming. *Soviet Russian Literature Since Stalin.* Cambridge: Cambridge University Press, 1978.

Caradec, François. *Histoire de la littérature enfantine en France.* Paris: Albin Michel, 1977.

Carlton, J. M. "The genesis of *Il barone rampante.*" *Italica* 61, no. 3 (1984): 195–206.

Carpenter, Humphrey. *Secret Gardens: The Golden Age of Children's Literature.* London: Unwin Hyman, 1985.

Carter, A. H. *Italo Calvino: Metamorphoses of Fantasy.* Ann Arbor: UMI Research Press, 1987.

Catalogue lectures cadet. Paris: Gallimard Jeunesse, n.d.

Cawelty, John G. *Adventure, Mystery and Romance: Formula Stories as Art and Popular Culture*. Chicago: University of Chicago Press, 1976.

Chukovskii, Kornei. *From Two to Five*. Rev. ed. trans. and ed. Miriam Morton. Berkeley: University of California Press, 1968.

Clarke, John Henrik. Introduction to *The Middle Passage: White Ships/Black Cargo*. New York: Dial Books, 1995.

Clifford, James. *The Predicament of Culture: Twentieth Century Ethnography, Literature and Art*. Cambridge, Mass.: Harvard University Press, 1988.

Corti, Maria. "Testi o macrotesto? I racconti di Marcovaldo di I. Calvino," in Il viaggio testuale. Le ideologie e le strutture semiotiche., 182–197. Turin: Einaudi, 1978.

_____. "Intervista a Italo Calvino." *Autografo* 2, no. 6 (October 1985): 47–53.

Culler, Jonathan. *Structuralist Poetics*. London: Routledge, 1975.

Dabydeen, David. "On Not Being Milton: Nigger Talk in England Today." In *The State of the Language,* ed. Christopher Ricks and Leonard Michaels, 3–14. London: Faber, 1990.

Doderer, Klaus. "Erich Kästners 'Emil und die Detektive'—Gesellschaftskritik in einem Kinderroman." In *Erich Kästner. Leben—Werk—Wirkung*, ed. Rudolf Wolff, 104–117. Bonn: Bouvier, 1983.

Domar, Rebecca. "The Tragedy of a Soviet Satirist: The Case of Zoshchenko." In *Through the Glass of Soviet Literature*, ed. Ernest Simmons, 201–243. New York: Columbia University Press, 1953.

Dorsey, Margaret A. Review of *To Be a Slave*. *Library Journal* 93 (15 December 1968): 4,733.

Drabble, Margaret, ed. *The Oxford Companion to English Literature*. Oxford: Oxford University Press, 1985.

Drouve, Andreas. *Erich Kästner—Moralist mit doppeltem Boden*. Marburg: Tectum, 1993.

Durgnat, Raymond. *The Crazy Mirror: Hollywood Comedy and the American Image*. New York: Delta, 1970.

Dusinberre, Juliet. *Alice to the Lighthouse: Children's Books and Radical Experiment in Art*. Basingstoke: Macmillan, 1987.

————. "Dreams of Freedom: E. M. Forster, Virginia Woolf and Children's Literature." In *Modernity, Modernism and Children's Literature*, ed. Ulf Boëthius, 75–95.

Eckersley, Richard. "The Culture of Meaning, the Meaning of Culture." *Magpies Magazine* 12, no. 2 (1997): 6–8.

Eco, Umberto. "Interpreting Serials." In *Limits of Interpretation*. Bloomington: Indiana University Press, 1990.

Egoff, Sheila, G. T. Stubbs, and F. Ashley. *Only Connect*. New York: Oxford University Press, 1969.

Ewers, Hans-Heino. "Grenzverwischungen und Grenzüberschreitungen," *Julit* 1 (1976): 4–19.

———. "Das doppelsinnige Kinderbuch: Erwachsene als Leser und als Mitleser von Kinderliteratur." *Fundevogel* 14, no. 42 (1987): 8–12.

———. "Das doppelsinnige Kinderbuch—Erwachsene als Mitleser und Leser von Kinderliteratur." In *Kinderliteratur—Literatur auch für Erwachsene?*, ed. Dagmar Grenz, 15–24. München: Fink, 1990.

———. "Kinderliteratur, Literaturerwerb und literarische Bildung." In *Kinderliteratur, literarische Sozialisation und Schule*, ed. Bernhard Rank and Cornelia Rosebrock, 55–74. Heidelberg: Deutscher Studien Verlag, 1997.

Fineberg, Jonathan. *The Innocent Eye: Children's Art and the Modern Artist*. Princeton: Princeton University Press, 1997.

Forrester, Sibelan. "Kornei Ivanovich Chukovskii." In *Reference Guide to Russian Literature*, ed. Neil Cornwell, 232–234. Chicago: Fitzroy Dearborn, 1998.

Galef, David. "Crossing Over: Authors Who Write Both Children's and Adults' Fiction." *Children's Literature Association Quarterly* 20, no. 1 (1995): 29–35.

Garcin, Jérôme. "Interview avec Michel Tournier." *L'Événement du jeudi* 9–15 January 1986.

Gardam, Jane. "On Writing for Children: Some Wasps in the Marmalade." Part 1. *Horn Book Magazine* 60 (1978): 489–496.

Gardner, Martin, ed. *The Annotated Alice*. London: Penguin, 1977.

Genette, Gérard. *Narrative Discourse: An Essay in Method*. Ithaca, N.Y.: Cornell University Press, 1980.

Genette, Gérard. *Palimpsests: Literature in the Second Degree*. Trans. Channa Newman and Claude Doubinsky. Lincoln: The University of Nebraska Press, 1997.

———. *Paratexts: Thresholds of Interpretation*. Trans. Jane E. Lewin. Cambridge: Cambridge University Press, 1997.

Gillie, Christine, ed. *Longman Companion to English Literature*. London: Longman, 1977.

Glotser, Vladimir. Afterword to " 'Bozhe, kakaia uzhasnaia zhizn' i kakoe uzhasnoe u menia sostoianie': zapisnye knizhki, pis'ma, dnevniki." Novyi Mir 2 (1992): 192–224.

Goldthwaite, J. *The Natural History of Make-believe*. New York: Oxford University Press, 1996.

Grenz, Dagmar. "Erich Kästners Kinderbücher in ihrem Verhältnis zu seiner Literatur für Erwachsene." In *Literatur für Kinder*. ed. Maria Lypp, 155–169. Göttingen: Vandenhoeck & Ruprecht, 1977.

Harvey, David. *The Condition of Postmodernity: An Inquiry into the Origins of Cultural Change*. Oxford: Blackwell, 1990.

Hearne, Betsy. Review of *The Middle Passage. Bulletin of the Center for Children's Books* 49 (December 1995): 125.

Heller, Agnes. "Death of the Subject?", in *Constructions of the Self*, ed. George Levine, 269–84. New Brunswick, N.J.: Rutgers University Press, 1992.

Hemenway, Robert. "Introduction: Author, Teller, and Hero." In *Uncle Remus: His Songs and His Sayings*. New York and London: Penguin Books, 1982.

Heydebrand, Renate von. Ed. *Kanon—Macht—Kultur*. Stuttgart: Metzler, 1998.

Histoire du livre de jeunesse d'hier à aujourd'hui, en France et dans le monde. Paris: Gallimard Jeunesse, 1993.

Hoven, Peter van den. *Grenzverkeer*. The Hague: NBLC, 1994.

Hulme, Peter. *Colonial Encounters: Europe and the Native Caribbean 1492–1797*. London: Methuen, 1986.

Hunt, Peter. *Criticism, Theory, and Children's Literature*. Oxford: Basil Blackwell, 1991.

Hunt, Peter, ed. *International Companion Encyclopedia of Children's Literature*. Routledge: London and New York, 1996.

Hutcheon, Linda. *A Theory of Parody: The Teaching of Twentieth-Century Art Forms*. New York and London: Methuen, 1985.

———. *A Poetics of Postmodernism: History, Theory, Fiction*. New York: Routledge, 1988.

Ionesco, Eugène. *Présent passé, passé présent*. Paris: Mercure de France, 1968.

Jameson, Frederic. *Postmodernism or, the Cultural Logic of Late Capitalism*. Durham, NC: Duke University Press, 1991.

Jeannet, A. "Colloidi's Grandchildren: Reading *Marcovaldo*" *Italica* 71, no. 1 (Spring 1994): 56–77.

Josselin, Jean-François. "Les enfants dans la bibliothèque" [Interview with Michel Tournier]. *Le Nouvel Observateur* 6 December 1971: 56–57.

Kanfer, Stefan. "A Lovely, Profitable World of Kid Lit" [Interview with Maurice Sendak]. *Time* 29 December 1980: 38–41.

Kåreland, Lena. *Modernism i barnkammaren: Barnlitteraturens 40-tal*. Stockholm: Rabén & Sjögren, 1999.

Karrenbrock, Helga. *Märchenkinder—Zeitgenossen: Untersuchungen zur Kinder- und Jugendliteratur der Weimarer Republik*. Stuttgart: M & P, Verlag für Wissenschaft, 1995.

Kibbey, Ann. "Language in Slavery: Frederick Douglass's *Narrative*." *Prospectus: The Annual of American Cultural Studies* 8 (1983): 163–182.

Kiesel, Helmut. *Erich Kästner*. München: C.H. Beck, 1981.

Kinder, Marsha. *Playing With Power in Movies, Television, and Video Games: From Muppet Babies to Teenage Mutant Ninja Turtles*. Berkeley, Los Angeles, London: University of California Press, 1991.

Knoepflmacher, U. C., "Kipling's 'Just-So' Partner: The Dead Child as Collaborator and Muse." *Children's Literature* 25 (1997): 24–49.

Knoepflmacher, U. C., and Mitzi Myers, eds. *Cross-Writing Child and Adult*, special issue of *Children's Literature* 25 (1997): vii–289.

Knoepflmacher, U.C., and Myers, Mitzi. " 'Cross-Writing' and the Reconceptualizing of Children's Literary Studies," *Children's Literature* 25 (1997): vii–xvii.

Kooistra, Lorraine Janzen. "Goblin Market as a Cross-Audienced Poem: Children's Fairy Tale, Adult Erotic Fantasy." *Children's Literature* 25 (1997): 181–204.

Koster, Serge. *Michel Tournier*. Paris: Henri Veyrier, 1986.

Kristeva, Julia. *Desire in Language: A Semiotic Approach to Literature and Art*. Trans. Thomas Gora, Alice Jardine, and Leon S. Roudiez. New York: Columbia University Press, 1980.

Kümmerling-Meibauer, Bettina. "Comparing Children's Literature." *Compar-(a)ison* II, special issue: *Current Trends in Comparative Children's Literature Research*, ed. Bettina Kümmerling-Meibauer (1995): 5–18.

———. "Annäherungen von Jugend- und Erwachsenenliteratur. Die schwedische Jugendliteratur der 80er und frühen 90er Jahre," *Der Deutschunterricht* 46 (1996): 29–45.

———. *Klassiker der Kinder- und Jugendliteratur. Ein internationales Lexikon*. 2 vols. Stuttgart: Metzler, 1999.

———. "Metalinguistic Awareness and the Child's Developing Sense of Irony: the Relationship between Pictures and Text in Ironic Picture Books," *The Lion and the Unicorn* 23, no. 2 (April 1999): 157–183.

Ladenthin, Volker. "Erich Kästners Bemerkungen über den Realismus in der Prosa. Ein Beitrag zum poetologischen Denken Erich Kästners und zur Theorie der Neuen Sachlichkeit," *Wirkendes Wort* 2 (1988): 62–77.

Lapouge, Gilles. "Michel Tournier s'explique." *Lire* 64 (December 1980): 28–46.

Lecercle, Jean-Jacques. *Philosophy of Nonsense: The Intuitions of Victorian Nonsense Literature*. London and New York: Routledge, 1994.

Legge, Kate. "Life Sucks, Timmy." *The Australian Magazine* (8–9 March 1997): 10–18.

Lemarchand, Jacques. "Livres pour enfants." *Bulletin de la NRF* 144 (December 1950): 13b-14a.

Levine, Lawrence W. *Black Culture and Black Consciousness: Afro-American Folk Thought from Slavery to Freedom*. Oxford and New York: Oxford University Press, 1977.

Lewis, C. S. "On Three Ways of Writing for Children." In *Only Connect*, ed. Sheila Egoff, G. T. Stubbs, and F. Ashley, 207–220. New York: Oxford University Press, 1969 [1952].

———. "On Stories." In *Essays Presented to Charles Williams*. London: Oxford, 1947.

Lhoste, Pierre. *Conversations avec J.M.G. Le Clézio*. Paris: Mercure de France, 1971.

Linder, Leslie. *A History of the Writings of Beatrix Potter*. London: Frederick Warne, 1971.

Lindgren, Astrid. "A Small Chat with a Future Children's Book Author." *Bookbird* 16 (1978): 9–12.

Lloyd, Rosemary. *The Land of Lost Content: Children and Childhood in Nineteenth-Century French Literature*. Oxford: Clarendon, 1992.

Loseff, Lev. *On the Beneficence of Censorship: Aesopian Language in Modern Russian Literature*. Trans. Jane Bobko. Munich: Verlag Otto Sagner, 1984.

Lukens, Rebecca. "The Child, the Critic and a Good Book." *Language Arts* 55 (1978): 452–454, 546.

Lynn, Joanne L. "Hyachinths and biscuits in the Village of Liver and Onions: Sandburg's Rootabaga Stories." *Children's Literature* 8 (1980): 118–132.

Lurie, Alison. *Don't Tell the Grownups: Subversive Children's Literature*. Boston: Little, Brown, 1990.

Magnan, Jean-Marie. "Écrire pour les enfants" [Interview with Michel Tournier]. *La Quinzaine littéraire* 16–31 December 1971: 11–13.

Matsier, Nicolaas et al., eds. *Het Literaire Klimaat 1986–1992* (The literary climate 1986–1992). Amsterdam: De Bezige Bij, 1992.

———. "Een kind is voor literatuur in de wieg gelegd." *Vrij Nederland*, Literary supplement (May 1996): 5.

McCallum, Robyn. *Ideologies of Identity in Adolescent Fiction*. New York: Garland Publishing, 1999.

McGillis, Roderick. *The Nimble Reader: Literary Theory and Children's Literature*. New York: Twayne Publishers, 1996.

McMahon, Joseph H. "Michel Tournier's Texts for Children." *Children's Literature* 13 (1985): 154–168.

Metcalf, Eva-Maria. "The Invisible Child in the Works of Tormod Haugen." *Barnboken* 1 (1992): 15–23.

Mieles, Miriam. "Zivilisationsraum Großstadt—Kinderliterarische Großstadtprosa in der Weimarer Republik," In *Naturkind, Stadtkind, Landkind: literarische Bilderwelten kindlicher Umwelt*, ed. Ulrich Nassen, 85–106. München: Fink, 1995.

Miller, Judith. *One, by One, by One: Facing the Holocaust.* New York: Touchstone, 1991.

Mowitt, John. *Text: The Genealogy of an Antidisciplinary Object.* Durham, N.C.: Duke University Press, 1992.

Neiolov, E.M. "Perestupaia vozrastnye granitsy." In *Problemy detskoi literatury,* 53–72. Petrozavodsk: Petrozavodskii gosudarstvennyi universitet, 1976.

Nichols, Grace. "The Battle With Language." In *Caribbean Women Writers: Essays from the First International Conference,* ed. C. J. Cudjoe, 283–289. Wellesley: Calaloux, 1990.

Nikolajeva, Maria. "Russian Children's Literature Before and After Perestroika." *Children's Literature Association Quarterly* 20, no. 3 (1995): 105–111.

———. *Children's Literature Comes of Age: Toward a New Aesthetic.* New York and London: Garland, 1996.

———. "Reflections of Change in Children's Book Titles." In *Reflections of Change: Children's Literature Since 1945,* ed. Sandra L. Beckett, 85–90. Westport, Conn.: Greenwood, 1997.

Nodelman, Perry. "Interpretation and the Apparent Sameness of Children's Novels," *Studies in the Literary Imagination: Narrative Theory and Children's Literature* 18, no. 2 (1985): 5–20.

———. *The Pleasures of Children's Literature.* New York: Longman, 1992.

Nodelman, Perry, ed. *Touchstones. Reflections on the Best in Children's Literature.* 3 vols. West Lafayette: Children's Literature Association, 1985–1989.

O'Dell, Felicity Ann. *Socialisation Through Children's Literature: The Soviet Example.* Cambridge: Cambridge University Press, 1978.

Ousby, James, ed. *The Cambridge Guide to Literature in English.* Cambridge: Cambridge University Press, 1993.

Parrott, Ray J., Jr. "Aesopian Language." In *Modern Encyclopedia of Russian and Soviet Literature.* Vol. 1., 39–45. Gulf Breeze, Fla.: Academic International Press, 1977.

Payot, Marianne. "Entretien: Michel Tournier." *Lire* (October 1996): 32–40.

Petit, Susan. "An Interview with Michel Tournier: 'I Write Because I Have Something to Say.'" In *Michel Tournier's Metaphysical Fictions,* 173–193. Amsterdam and Philadelphia: John Benjamins Publishing Co., 1991.

Postman, Neil. *The Disappearance of Childhood.* New York: Delacorte Press, 1982.

Pratt, Mary Louise. *Imperial Eyes: Travel Writing and Transculturation.* London: Routledge, 1992.

Rabinowitz, Peter. *Before Reading: Narrative Conventions and the Politics of Interpretation.* Ithaca, N.Y.: Cornell University Press, 1987.

Riesz, Janosz. "Komparatistische Kanonbildung. Möglichkeiten der Konstitution eines Weltliteratur-Kanons aus heutiger Sicht," *Jahrbuch Deutsch als Fremdsprache* 13 (1987): 200–213.

Rimmon-Kenan, Shlomith. *Narrative Fiction: Contemporary Poetics.* London and New York: Routledge, 1983.

Roberts, John W. *From Trickster to Badman: The Black Folk Hero in Slavery and Freedom.* Philadelphia: University of Pennsylvania Press, 1989.

Robinson, Nicola. "Illiteracy, Misery, and Moral Decay: the Sins of Young Adult Fiction." *Australian Book Review* (December 1995/January 1996): 36–41.

Rochman, Hazel. Review of *The Big Lie* by Isabella Leitner. *Booklist* 89, no.11 (1 February 1993): 982.

Ros, Bea and Margot Krikhaar. *Een spannend boek. Warm aanbevolen! Een onderzoek naar twintig jaar jeugdliteraire kritiek (1965–1984) (A thrilling book. Warmly recommended! A study of twenty years of children's literature reviews (1965–1984)).* Doctoral thesis, Nijmegen University, 1986.

Rose, Jacqueline. *The Case of Peter Pan, or The Impossibility of Children's Fiction.* London: Macmillan, 1984.

Rossiter, Richard. "Speaking to Adults, Speaking to Children: Tim Winton's *Cloudstreet* and *Lockie Leonard, Human Torpedo.*" *Southerly* 53, no. 5 (1993): 92–99.

Rothwell, Erika. " 'You Catch It If You Try to Do Otherwise': The Limitations of E. Nesbit's Cross-Written Vision of the Child," *Children's Literature* 25 (1997): 60–70.

Rousseau, Jean-Jacques. *Émile ou de l'éducation.* Paris: Gallimard, 1977.

Russell, David L. "Reading the Shards and Fragments: Holocaust Literature for Young Readers." *The Lion and the Unicorn* 21, no. 2 (1997): 267–280.

Scatton, Linda Hart. "Mikhail Mikhailovich Zoshchenko." In *Reference Guide to Russian Literature*, ed. Neil Cornwell, 929–931. Chicago: Fitzroy Dearborn, 1998.

———. *Mikhail Zoshchenko: Evolution of a Writer.* Cambridge: Cambridge University Press, 1993.

Scharrelmann, Heinrich. Ein kleiner Junge. *Was er sah und hörte, als er noch nicht zur Schule ging.* Hamburg: A. Jansson 1908.

Schenkeveld-Van der Dussen, M. A. *Nederlandse Literatuur, een Geschiedenis* (Dutch literature, a history). Groningen: Martinus Nijhoff, 1993.

Schikorsky, Isa. "Literarische Erziehung zwischen Realismus und Utopie—Erich Kästners Kinderroman 'Emil und die Detektive.' " In *Klassiker der Kinder- und Jugendliteratur*, ed. Bettina Hurrelmann, 216–233. Frankfurt: Fischer, 1995.

Scholes, Robert. *Textual Power.* New Haven and London: Yale University Press, 1985.

Schroeder, Ulla M. "La funzione del fumetto nella narrativa di Italo Calvino." *Civiltà Italiana*, 29, no. 1 (1995): 179–192.

Shavit, Zohar. *Poetics of Children's Literature*. Athens, Ga.: University of Georgia Press, 1986.

Shaw, Harry E. "With Reference to Austin." *Diacritics* 20, no. 2 (1990): 75–92.

Sheahan-Bright, Robyn. "How Real is 'Too Real'?," *Viewpoint* 5, no. 3 (1997): 5–6.

Singer, Isaac, Bashevis. "Isaac Bashevis-Singer on Writing for Children." *Children's Literature* 6 (1977): 9–16.

Sipe, Lawrence R. "The Private and Public Worlds of *We Are All in the Dumps with Jack and Guy*," *Children's Literature in Education* 27, no. 2 1(996): 87–107.

Sokol, Elena. *Russian Poetry for Children*. Knoxville: University of Tennessee Press, 1984.

Springman, Luke. *Comrades, Friends, and Companions*. New York: Peter Lang, 1989.

Stahl, John D. "Moral Despair and the Child as Symbol of Hope in Pre-World War II in Berlin," *Children's Literature* 14 (1986): 83–104.

———. "Canon Formation: A Historical and Psychological Perspective." In *Teaching Children's Literature. Issues, Pedagogy, Resources*, ed. Glenn E. Sadler, 12–21. New York: The Modern Language Association of America, 1992.

Stephens, John. *Language and Ideology in Children's Fiction*. London and New York: Longman, 1992.

Strausfeld, Michi. "Las Tres Edades: de ocho a ochenta y ocho años." *CLIJ* 50 (May 1993): 44–46.

Svensson, Sonja. "Barnböcker finns dom?", in *Böcker ska blänka som solar*, ed. Boel Westin. Stockholm: Rabén & Sjögren, 1988.

Thum, Maureen. "Misreading the Cross-Writer: The Case of Wilhelm Hauff's *Dwarf Long Nose*." *Children's Literature* 25 (1997): 1–23.

Toijer-Nilsson, Ying. "Tormod Haugen." In *De skriver för barn och ungdom*, 169–178. Lund: Bibliotekstjänst, 1991.

Tomashevskii, Iu. V., ed. *Litso i Maska Mikhaila Zoshchenko*. Moskva: Olimp, 1994.

Torgovnick, Marianna. *Gone Primitive: Savage Intellects, Modern Lives*. University of Chicago Press, 1990.

Tournier, Michel. "Quand Michel Tournier récrit ses livres pour les enfants." *Le Monde* 24 December 1971: 7.

———. "Michel Tournier: comment écrire pour les enfants." *Le Monde* 24 December 1979: 19.

———. "Écrire pour les enfants." In *Pierrot ou les secrets de la nuit*. Enfant-images. Paris: Gallimard, 1979.

————. "Michel Tournier: avant tout, plaire aux enfants." In *Barbedor*. Enfant-images. Paris: Gallimard, 1980.

————. "Writing for Children is No Child's Play." *UNESCO Courier* (June 1982): 33–34.

————. "Michel Tournier face aux lycéens." *Le Magazine littéraire* 226 (January 1986): 20–25.

Townsend, John Rowe. *A Sense of Story*. London: Longman, 1971.

————. *Written for Children*. London: Penguin, 1977.

Travers, Pamela. "On Not Writing for Children." *Children's Literature* 5 (1975): 15–22.

Tumanov, Larissa and Vladimir Tumanov. "The Child and the Child-like in Daniil Kharms." *Russian Literature* 34, no. 2 (1993): 241–269.

Tynianov, Iurii. "Kornei Chukovskii." *Soviet Studies in Literature* 24, no. 2 (1988): 95–100.

von Zweigbergk, Eva. *Barnboken i Sverige 1750–1950*. Stockholm: Rabén & Sjögren, 1965.

Wall, Barbara. *The Narrator's Voice: The Dilemma of Children's Fiction*. New York: St. Martin's Press, 1991.

Walsh, Jill Paton. "The Writer's Responsibility." *Children's Literature in Education* 4 (1973): 30–36.

Walter, Dirk. *Zeitkritik und Idyllensehnsucht: Erich Kästners Frühwerk 1928–1933*. Heidelberg: Winter, 1977.

Westin, Boel. "Vad är barnlitteraturforskning?", In *Litteraturvetenskap—en inledning*, ed. Staffan Bergsten. Lund: Studentlitteratur, 1998.

Worton, Michael. "Michel Tournier and the Masterful Art of Rewriting." *PN Review* 11, no.3 (1984): 24–25.

Zonnefeld, Jürgen. *Erich Kästner als Rezensent 1923–1933*. Frankfurt: Peter Lang, 1991.

Index

About the Editor and Contributors

Sandra L. Beckett is Professor of French at Brock University, where she teaches children's literature, women's writing, and twentieth-century French fiction. She is the author of three books on Henri Bosco and one on French children's literature, titled *De grands romanciers écrivent pour les enfants* (PUM, 1997). She has edited several volumes, including *Reflections of Change: Children's Literature since 1945* (Greenwood,1997). Her articles on children's literature have appeared in journals such as *ChLA Quarterly*, *The Lion and the Unicorn*, *Bookbird*, and *Canadian Children's Literature*. Her recent research has focused on intertextuality in children's literature and she is currently writing a book on retellings of *Little Red Riding Hood*. She is the 1999 Chair of the MLA Division on Children's Literature.

Paula T. Connolly is an Associate Professor of English at the University of North Carolina at Charlotte (USA), where she teaches courses in American and Children's Literature. She is the author of *Winnie-the-Pooh and The House at Pooh Corner: Recovering Arcadia*, published by Twayne-Macmillan in 1995. Her recent publications have focused on how the history of American slavery has been retold to current generations of children.

Lena Kåreland is Associate Professor at the University of Uppsala (Sweden). Previously she worked at the Swedish Institute for Children's Books in Stockholm. She has published several books and articles in the field of children's literature, in particular on postmodernism, picture

283

books, and Tove Jansson. She is currently working on a book about modernism and children's literature.

Adrienne Kertzer is Associate Professor of English at the University of Calgary, where she teaches children's literature and fiction. She currently is writing a series of essays on children's literature and Holocaust representation.

Bettina Kümmerling-Meibauer is *Lehrbeauftragte* (Lecturer) in German Literature at the Department for German Philology (Deutsches Seminar) at the University of Tübingen, where she teaches children's literature. She edited a special issue of *Compara(i)son* (1995) on "Current Trends in Comparative Children's Literature Research" and has published numerous articles on German and Scandinavian children's literature. She is the author of *Klassiker der Kinder- und Jugendliteratur: Ein internationales Lexikon* (Classics of children's literature: An international encyclopedia) (Metzler, 1999), a two-volume encyclopedia dealing with 530 children's classics from sixty-five countries.

Helma van Lierop-Debrauwer is Professor of Children's Literature at Leiden University in the Netherlands and Assistant Professor in Children's Literature at Tilburg University. She is on the editorial board of *Literatuur zonder Leeftijd* (Literature without age), a journal devoted to children's literature. She has published on literary socialization of young children, genres in children's literature, and dual-readership authors.

Roderick McGillis is Professor of English at the University of Calgary. He is editor of the literary theory column in *The Children's Literature Association Quarterly* and author of *The Nimble Reader* (1996). Forthcoming from Garland is a volume of essays he has edited: *Voices of the Other: Colonialism, Postcolonialism, and Neocolonialism in Children's Literature*.

Maria Nikolajeva is Associate Professor at the Departments of Comparative Literature, Stockholm University (Sweden) and Åbo Akademi University (Finland), where she teaches children's literature and literary theory. She is the author and editor of several books on children's literature, including *Children's Literature Comes of Age: Toward a New Aesthetic* (Garland, 1996), a ChLA Honor book. She also has published a large number of articles in international journals and essay collections.

Her academic honors include a Fulbright Grant at the University of Massachusetts, Amherst; a research fellowship at the International Youth Library, Munich; Donner Visiting Chair at Åbo Akademi University; and Nordic Scholar Award from the University of Edinburgh, Scotland. She was the President of the International Research Society for Children's Literature from 1993-97. At present she leads an interdisciplinary research project on children's literature at Åbo Akademi.

Lissa Paul is Professor in the Faculty of Education at the University of New Brunswick, where she teaches children's literature and literary theory. Her new book, *Reading Otherways* (1998), is published by The Thimble Press. She cowrote the *Signal* Poetry Award essay with Bob Barton in 1998, and, with Sandra Beckett, Lissa guest-edited a recent issue of *Signal* devoted to papers presented at the forum "The State of Children's Books in This Millennium and the Next," held at the 1997 Convention of the Modern Language Association.

Alida Poeti lives and works in Johannesburg where she lectures on nineteenth- and twentieth-century prose and poetry in the Department of Modern Languages and Literatures at the University of the Witwatersrand. Her research interests mainly concern marginal authors and have included a study of the alternative political theatre of Dario Fo and feminist productions of Franca Rame and Dacia Maraini, as well as Italophone writings by the first wave African immigrants who have claimed a voice in Italian literature. She first became interested in canonical authors writing children's literature while doing research on Elsa Morante. She has published numerous articles on Morante and is a regular contributor to *Italian Studies in Southern Africa*.

Carole Scott is Dean of Undergraduate Studies and a member of the English and Comparative Literature Department at San Diego State University. She has published articles in *Children's Literature*, *Children's Literature Association Quarterly*, and *The Lion and the Unicorn*, in Australia's *Papers* and *Orana*, and in collections of essays published in South Africa, Sweden, the United Kingdom, and the United States. She is currently coauthoring a work on picturebooks with Maria Nikolajeva.

Zohar Shavit is Full Professor of Semiotics and Culture Research at Tel Aviv University, where she is Head of the Program in Child's Culture and Education. For the past few years she has been conducting, together with the Institut für Jugendbuchforschung at Frankfurt University, a research project supported by the GIF on Books for Jewish Children in German-Speaking Countries, as well as a research project supported by the DFG on Children's Literature in Modernization process. She has published extensively in the fields of the semiotics of children's literature and children's culture, and the history of Hebrew and Jewish literatures and cultures. In 1996 she published *Just Childhood: Introduction to Poetics of Children's Literature*, a revised and expanded version of *Poetics of Children's Literature* written in association with Basmat Even-Zohar.

John Stephens is Associate Professor in English at Macquarie University (Australia), where his main teaching commitment is children's literature, but he also teaches and supervises postgraduate research in medieval studies, postcolonial literature, and discourse analysis. He is the author of *Language and Ideology in Children's Fiction*; *Retelling Stories, Framing Culture: Traditional Story and Metanarratives in Children's Literature* (with Robyn McCallum); two books about discourse analysis; and around sixty articles about children's (and other) literature. His primary research focus is on the relationships of texts produced for children (especially literature and film) with cultural formations and practices.

Larissa Klein Tumanov is completing her Ph.D. in Comparative Literature at the University of Alberta. Her dissertation concerns twentieth-century authors who have written for both children and adults. She presently resides in London, Ontario.